HORI-san and
MIYamura-kun

HORIMIYA 09

HERO × DAISUKE HAGIWARA

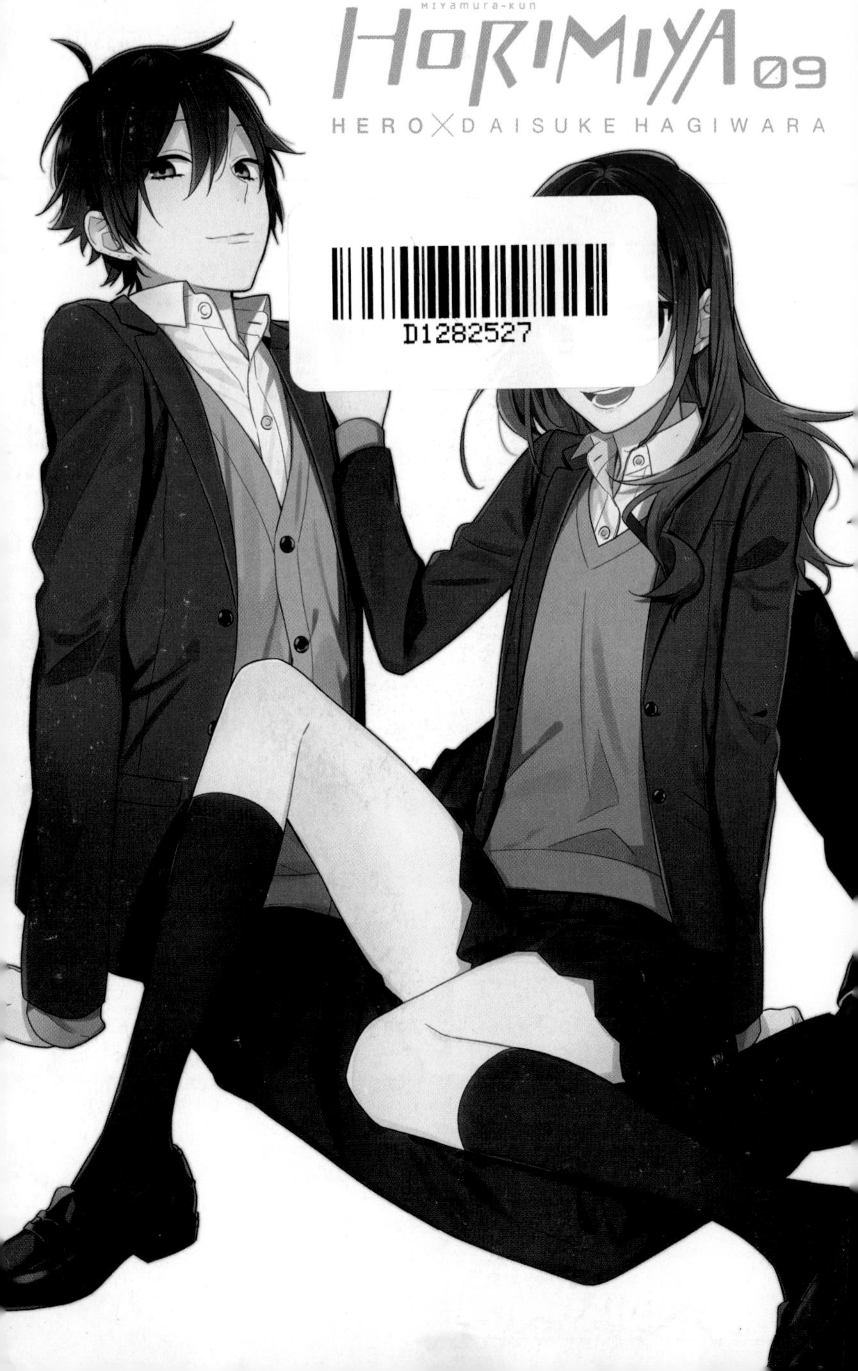

HORI-san and
MIYamura-kun

HORIMIYA

09

CONTENTS ★

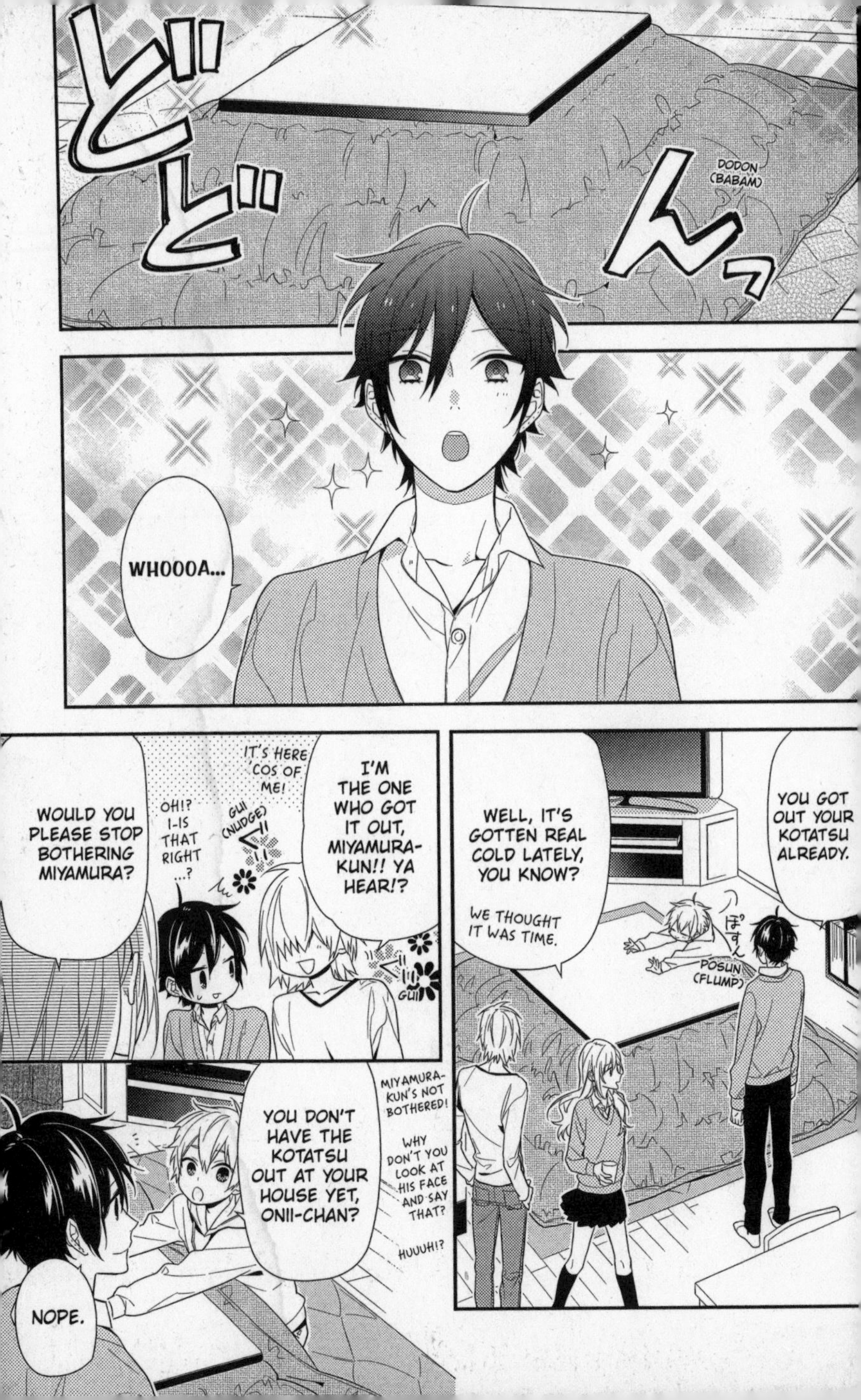
どどんっ
DODON (BABAM)
WHOOOA...
YOU GOT OUT YOUR KOTATSU ALREADY.
ぽすん
POSUN (FLUMP)
WELL, IT'S GOTTEN REAL COLD LATELY, YOU KNOW?
WE THOUGHT IT WAS TIME.
I'M THE ONE WHO GOT IT OUT, MIYAMURA-KUN!! YA HEAR!?
IT'S HERE COS OF ME!
GUI (NUDGE)
OH!? I-IS THAT RIGHT ...?
WOULD YOU PLEASE STOP BOTHERING MIYAMURA?
GUI
MIYAMURA-KUN'S NOT BOTHERED!
WHY DON'T YOU LOOK AT HIS FACE AND SAY THAT?
HUUUH!?
YOU DON'T HAVE THE KOTATSU OUT AT YOUR HOUSE YET, ONII-CHAN?
NOPE.

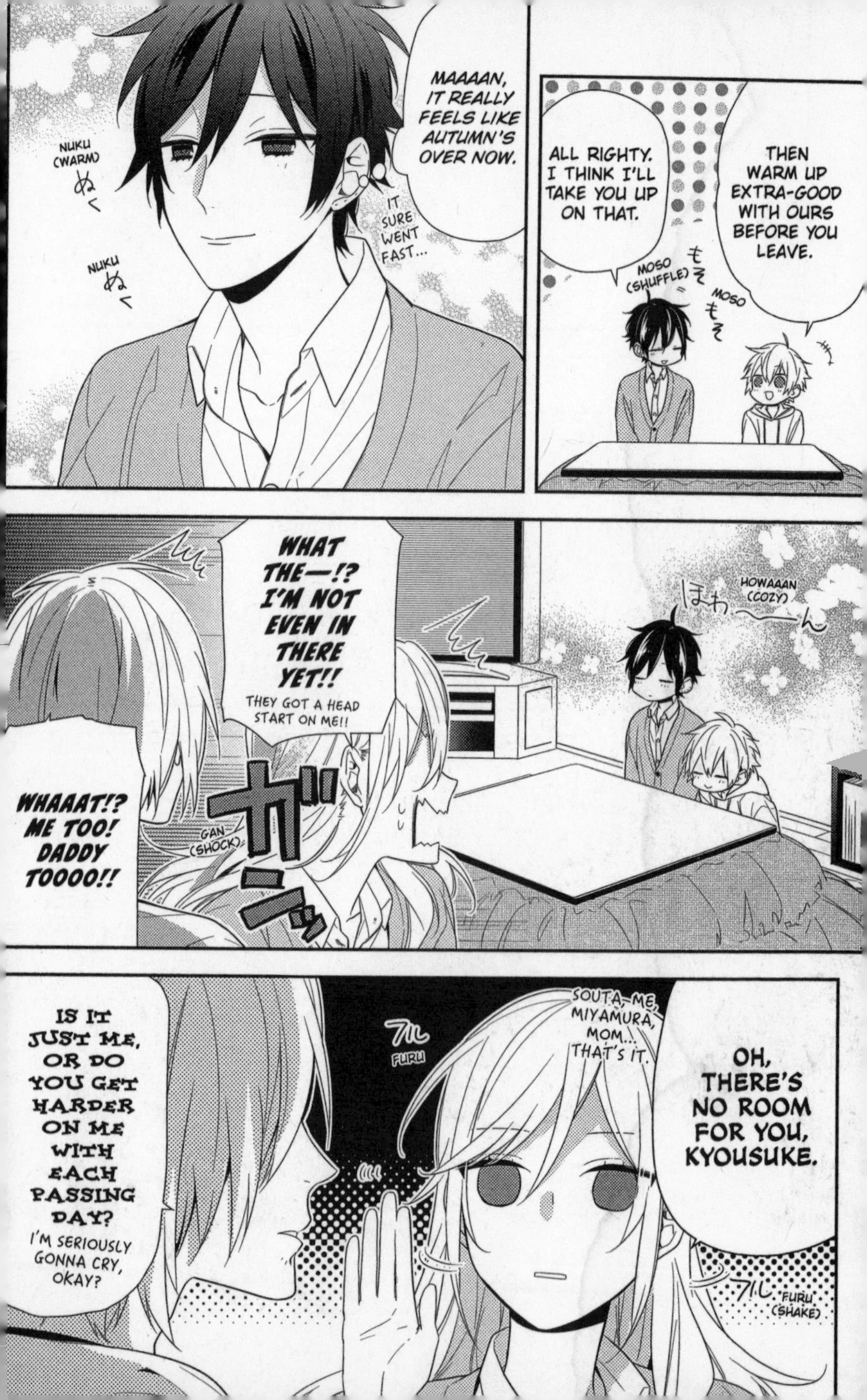
THEN WARM UP EXTRA-GOOD WITH OURS BEFORE YOU LEAVE.
ALL RIGHTY. I THINK I'LL TAKE YOU UP ON THAT.
MOSO (SHUFFLE) もそ
MOSO もそ
MAAAAN, IT REALLY FEELS LIKE AUTUMN'S OVER NOW.
IT SURE WENT FAST...
NUKU (WARM) ぬく
NUKU ぬく
HOWAAAN (COZY) ほわ～～ん
WHAT THE—!? I'M NOT EVEN IN THERE YET!!
THEY GOT A HEAD START ON ME!!
GAN (SHOCK)
WHAAAT!? ME TOO! DADDY TOOOO!!
OH, THERE'S NO ROOM FOR YOU, KYOUSUKE.
SOUTA, ME, MIYAMURA, MOM... THAT'S IT.
フル FURU (SHAKE)
フル FURU
IS IT JUST ME, OR DO YOU GET HARDER ON ME WITH EACH PASSING DAY?
I'M SERIOUSLY GONNA CRY, OKAY?

Page・57

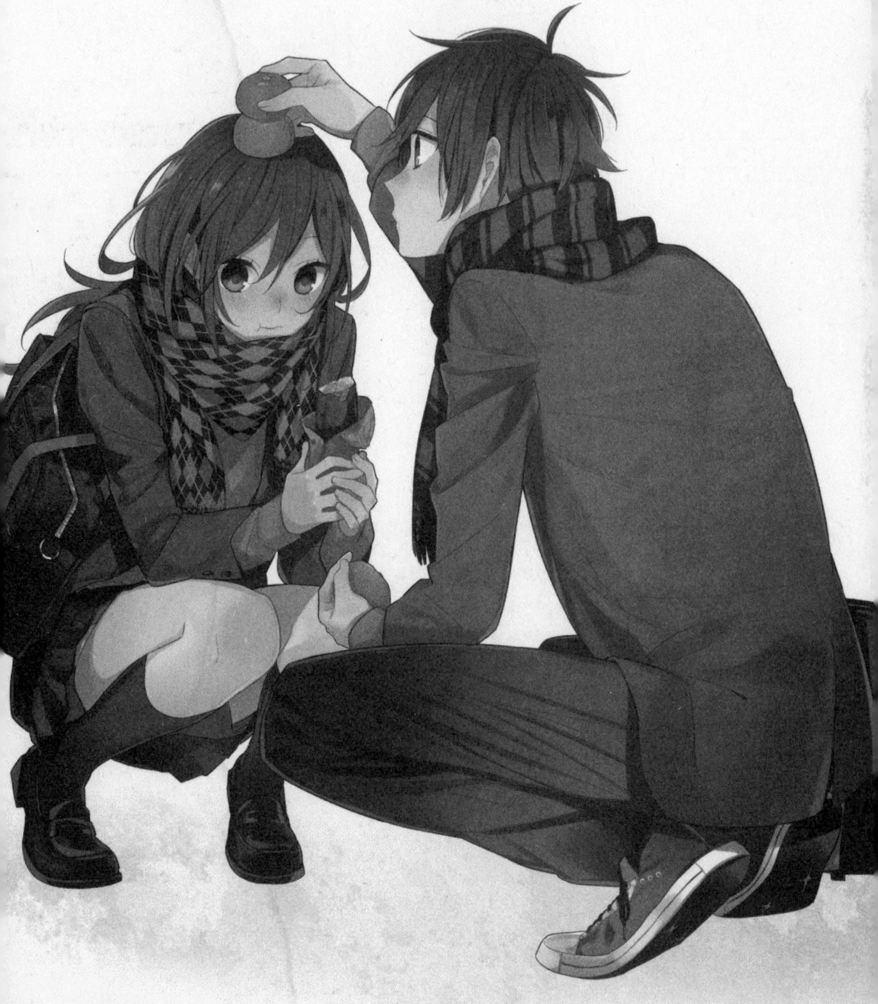

HORIMIYA

KOTATSU MEDLEY ①

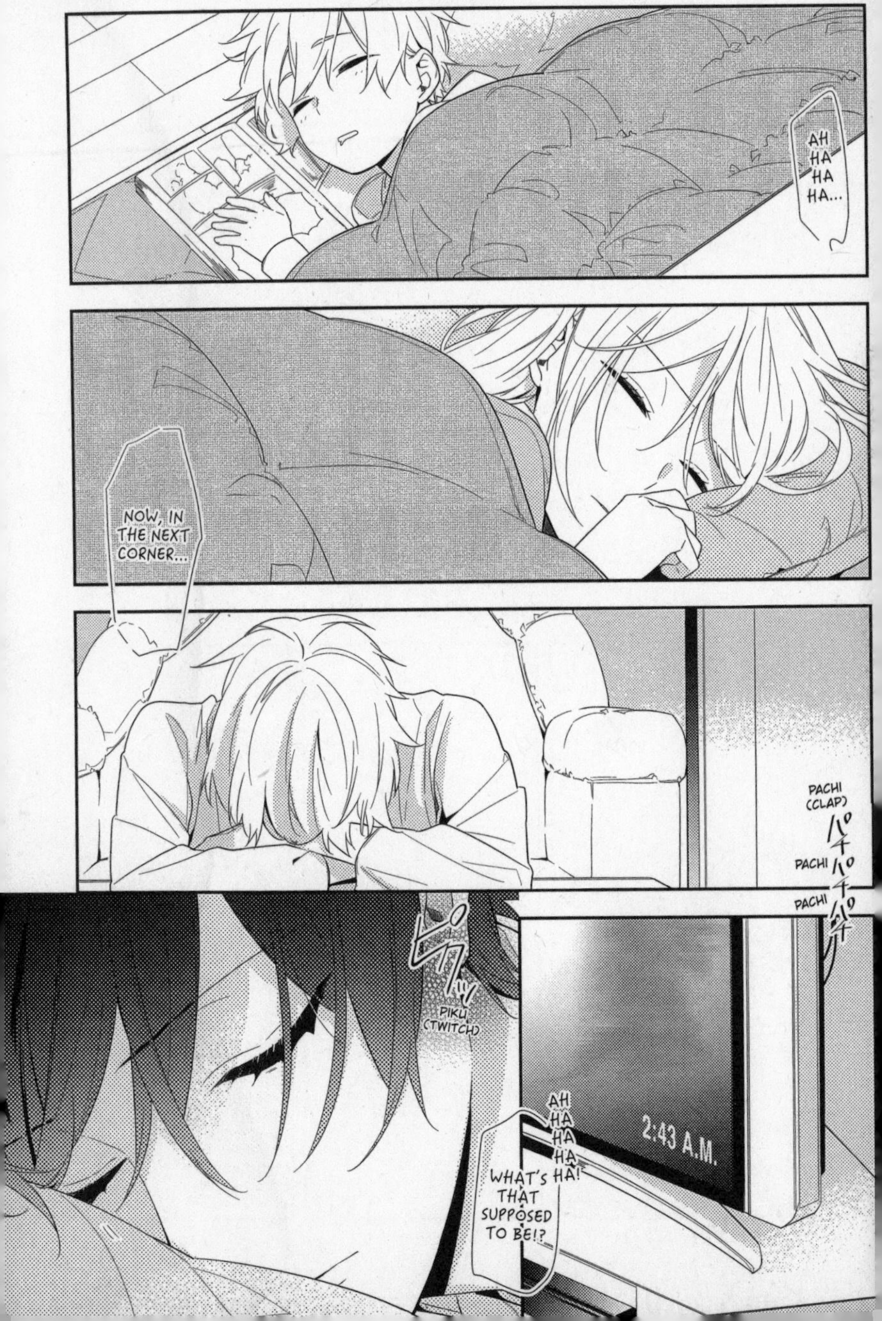
AH HA HA HA...
NOW, IN THE NEXT CORNER...
PACHI (CLAP)
パチ
PACHI
パチ
PACHI
パチ
ピクッ
PIKU (TWITCH)
AH HA HA HA HA!
WHAT'S THAT SUPPOSED TO BE!?
2:43 A.M.

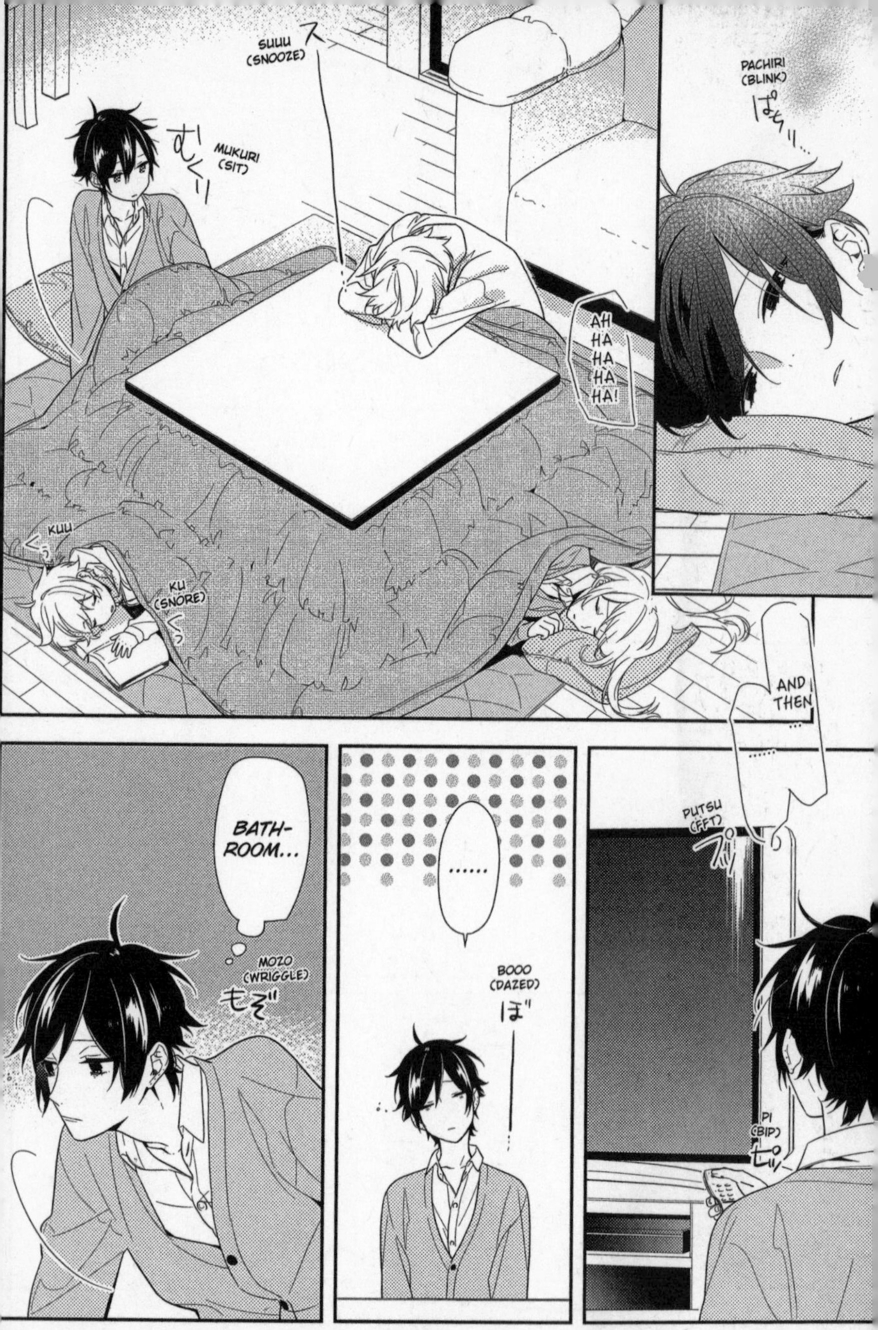
PACHIRI (BLINK)
ぱちり…
SUUU (SNOOZE)
ス
AH HA HA HA HA!
MUKURI (SIT)
むくり
KUU
くぅ
KU (SNORE)
くぅ
AND THEN...
......
PUTSU (FFT)
プツ
PI (BIP)
ピッ
......
BOOO (DAZED)
ぼー
BATH-ROOM...
MOZO (WRIGGLE)
もぞ

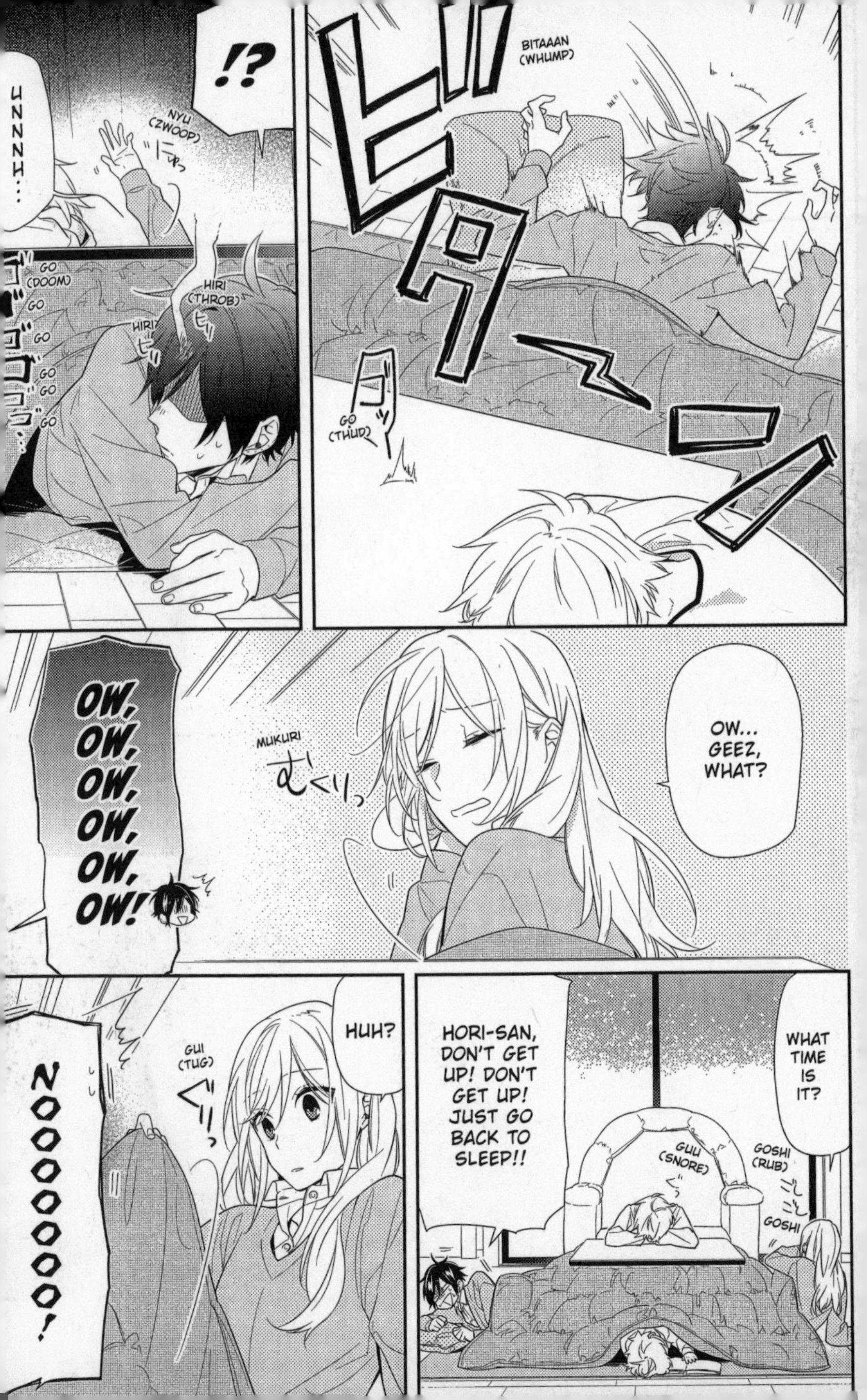
BITAAN (WHUMP)
GO (THUD)
!?
UNNNNH...
NYU (ZWOOP)
GO (DOOM)
GO
GO
GO
GO
GO
HIRI (THROB)
HIRI
OW... GEEZ, WHAT?
MUKURI
OW, OW, OW, OW, OW, OW!
WHAT TIME IS IT?
GOSHI (RUB)
GOSHI
HORI-SAN, DON'T GET UP! DON'T GET UP! JUST GO BACK TO SLEEP!!
GUU (SNORE)
HUH?
GUI (TUG)
NOOOOOOOO!

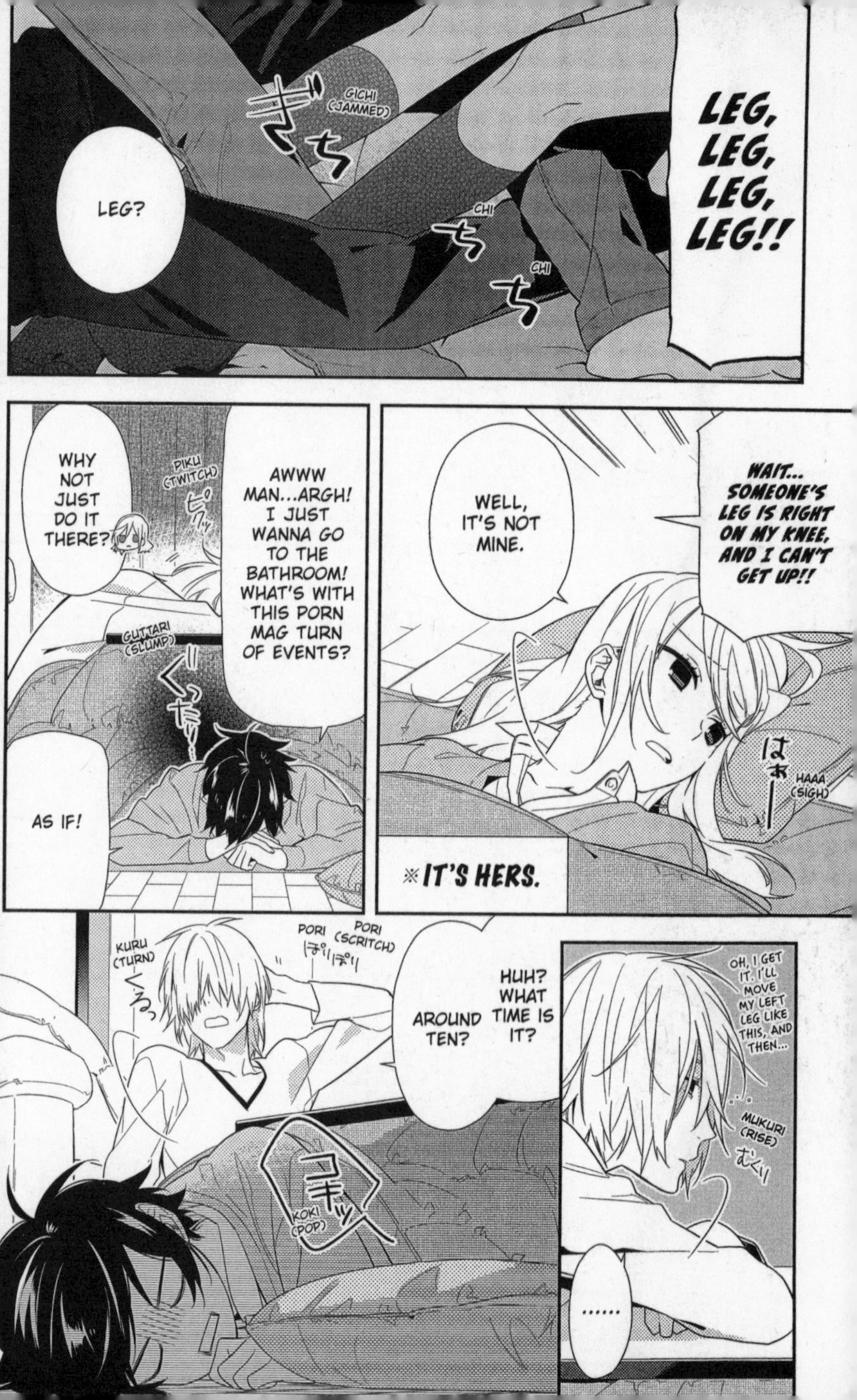
LEG, LEG, LEG, LEG!!
GICHI (JAMMED)
CHI
CHI
LEG?
WAIT... SOMEONE'S LEG IS RIGHT ON MY KNEE, AND I CAN'T GET UP!!
WELL, IT'S NOT MINE.
HAAA (SIGH)
※IT'S HERS.
AWWW MAN...ARGH! I JUST WANNA GO TO THE BATHROOM! WHAT'S WITH THIS PORN MAG TURN OF EVENTS?
PIKU (TWITCH)
WHY NOT JUST DO IT THERE?
GUTTARI (SLUMP)
AS IF!
OH, I GET IT. I'LL MOVE MY LEFT LEG LIKE THIS, AND THEN...
MUKURI (RISE)
......
HUH? WHAT TIME IS IT?
AROUND TEN?
PORI PORI (SCRITCH)
KURU (TURN)
KOKI (POP)

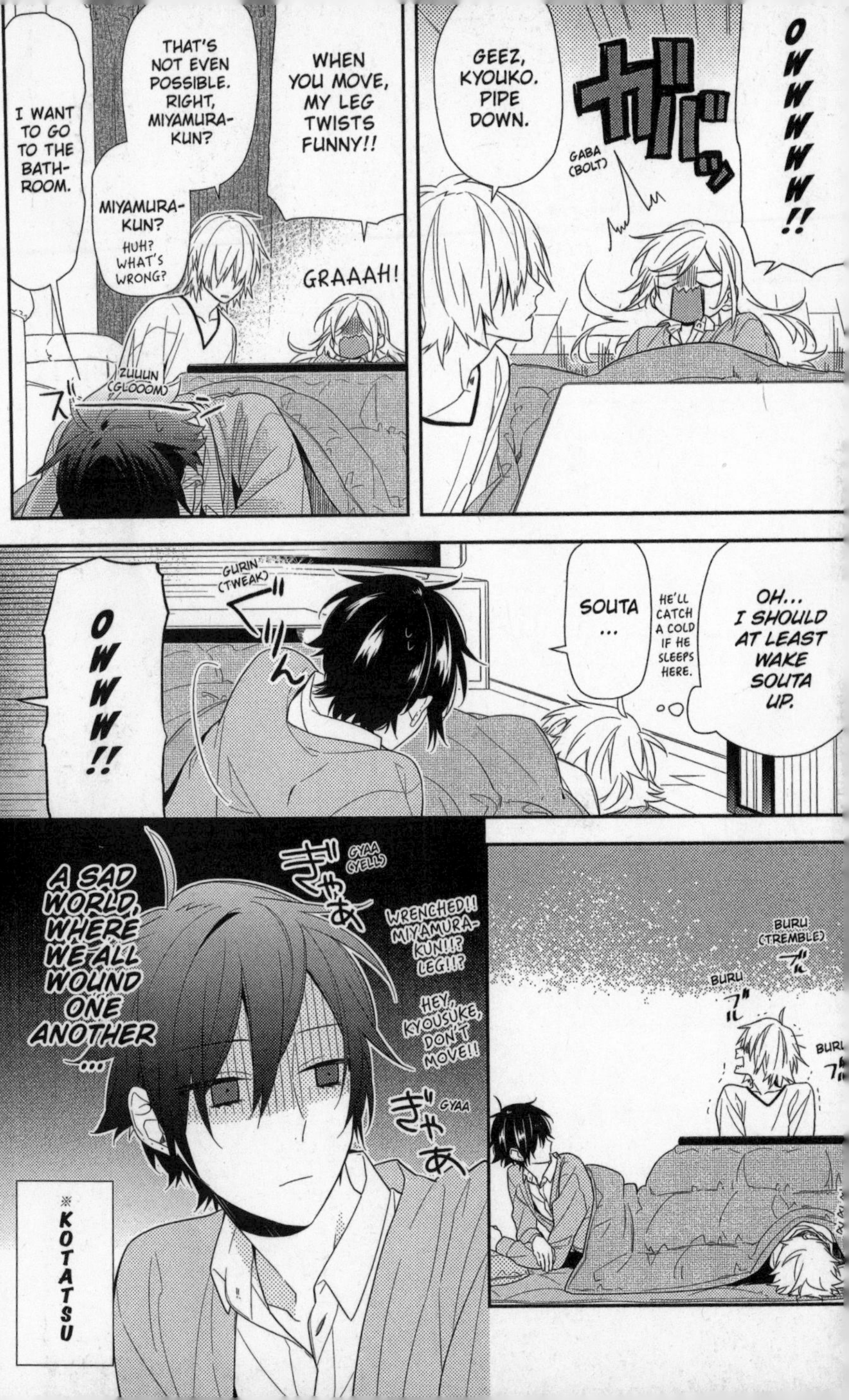
OWWWWWWW!!
GABA (BOLT)
GEEZ, KYOUKO. PIPE DOWN.
WHEN YOU MOVE, MY LEG TWISTS FUNNY!!
GRAAAH!
THAT'S NOT EVEN POSSIBLE. RIGHT, MIYAMURA-KUN?
MIYAMURA-KUN?
HUH? WHAT'S WRONG?
ZUUUN (GLOOOM)
I WANT TO GO TO THE BATH-ROOM.
OH... I SHOULD AT LEAST WAKE SOUTA UP.
HE'LL CATCH A COLD IF HE SLEEPS HERE.
SOUTA ...
GURIN (TWEAK)
OWWWW!!
BURU (TREMBLE)
BURU
BURU
GYAA (YELL)
WRENCHED!! MIYAMURA-KUN!!? LEG!!?
HEY, KYOUSUKE, DON'T MOVE!!
GYAA
A SAD WORLD, WHERE WE ALL WOUND ONE ANOTHER ...
※KOTATSU

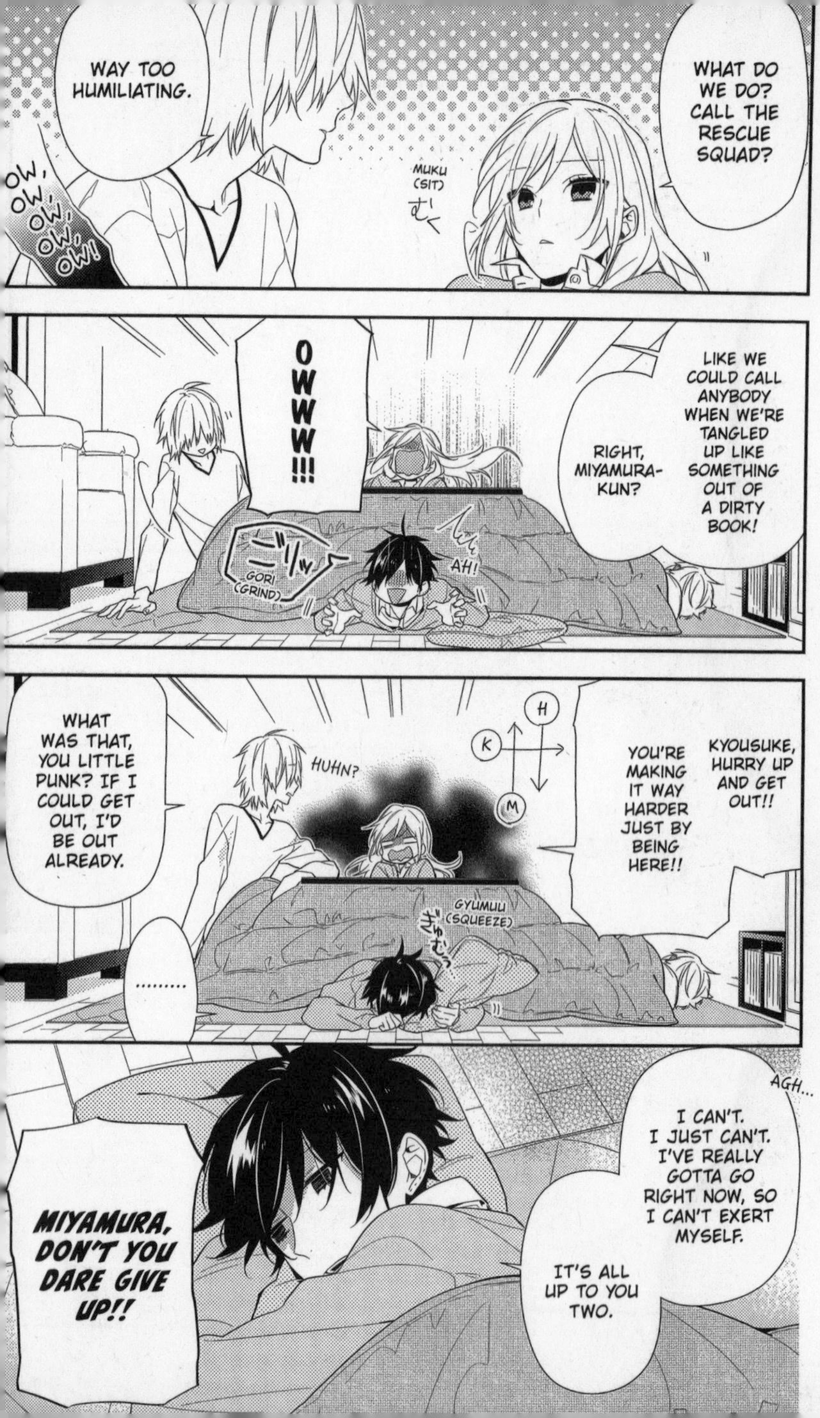
WHAT DO WE DO? CALL THE RESCUE SQUAD?
MUKU (SIT)
むく
WAY TOO HUMILIATING.
OW, OW, OW, OW, OW!
LIKE WE COULD CALL ANYBODY WHEN WE'RE TANGLED UP LIKE SOMETHING OUT OF A DIRTY BOOK!
RIGHT, MIYAMURA-KUN?
OWWW!!!
AH!
GORI (GRIND)
ごりッ
KYOUSUKE, HURRY UP AND GET OUT!!
YOU'RE MAKING IT WAY HARDER JUST BY BEING HERE!!
H
K
M
HUHN?
WHAT WAS THAT, YOU LITTLE PUNK? IF I COULD GET OUT, I'D BE OUT ALREADY.
GYUMUU (SQUEEZE)
....
AGH...
I CAN'T. I JUST CAN'T. I'VE REALLY GOTTA GO RIGHT NOW, SO I CAN'T EXERT MYSELF.
IT'S ALL UP TO YOU TWO.
MIYAMURA, DON'T YOU DARE GIVE UP!!

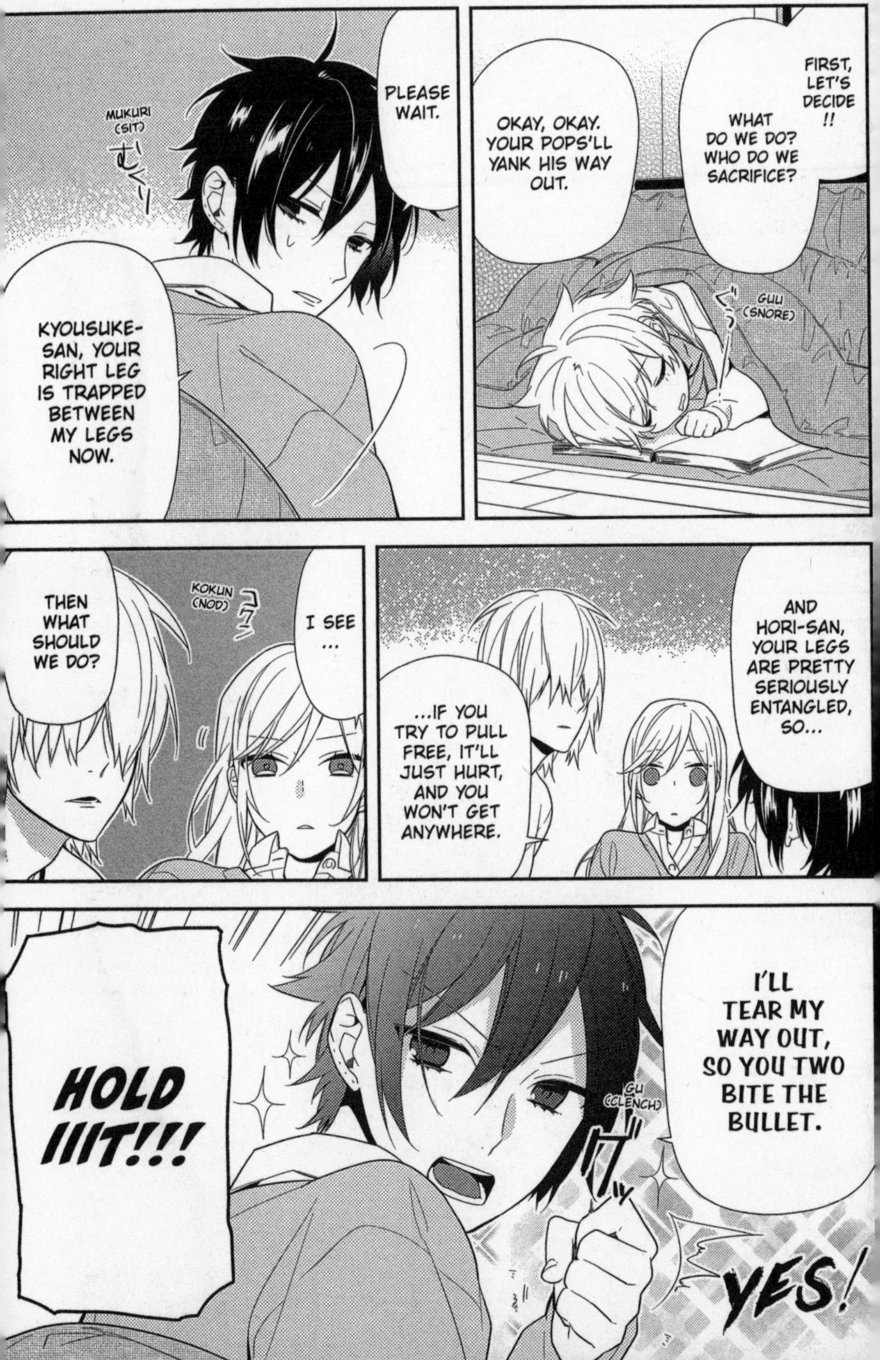
FIRST, LET'S DECIDE !!
WHAT DO WE DO? WHO DO WE SACRIFICE?
OKAY, OKAY. YOUR POPS'LL YANK HIS WAY OUT.
GUU (SNORE)
PLEASE WAIT.
MUKURI (SIT)
KYOUSUKE-SAN, YOUR RIGHT LEG IS TRAPPED BETWEEN MY LEGS NOW.
AND HORI-SAN, YOUR LEGS ARE PRETTY SERIOUSLY ENTANGLED, SO...
...IF YOU TRY TO PULL FREE, IT'LL JUST HURT, AND YOU WON'T GET ANYWHERE.
I SEE ...
KOKUN (NOD)
THEN WHAT SHOULD WE DO?
I'LL TEAR MY WAY OUT, SO YOU TWO BITE THE BULLET.
GU (CLENCH)
YES!
HOLD IIIT!!!

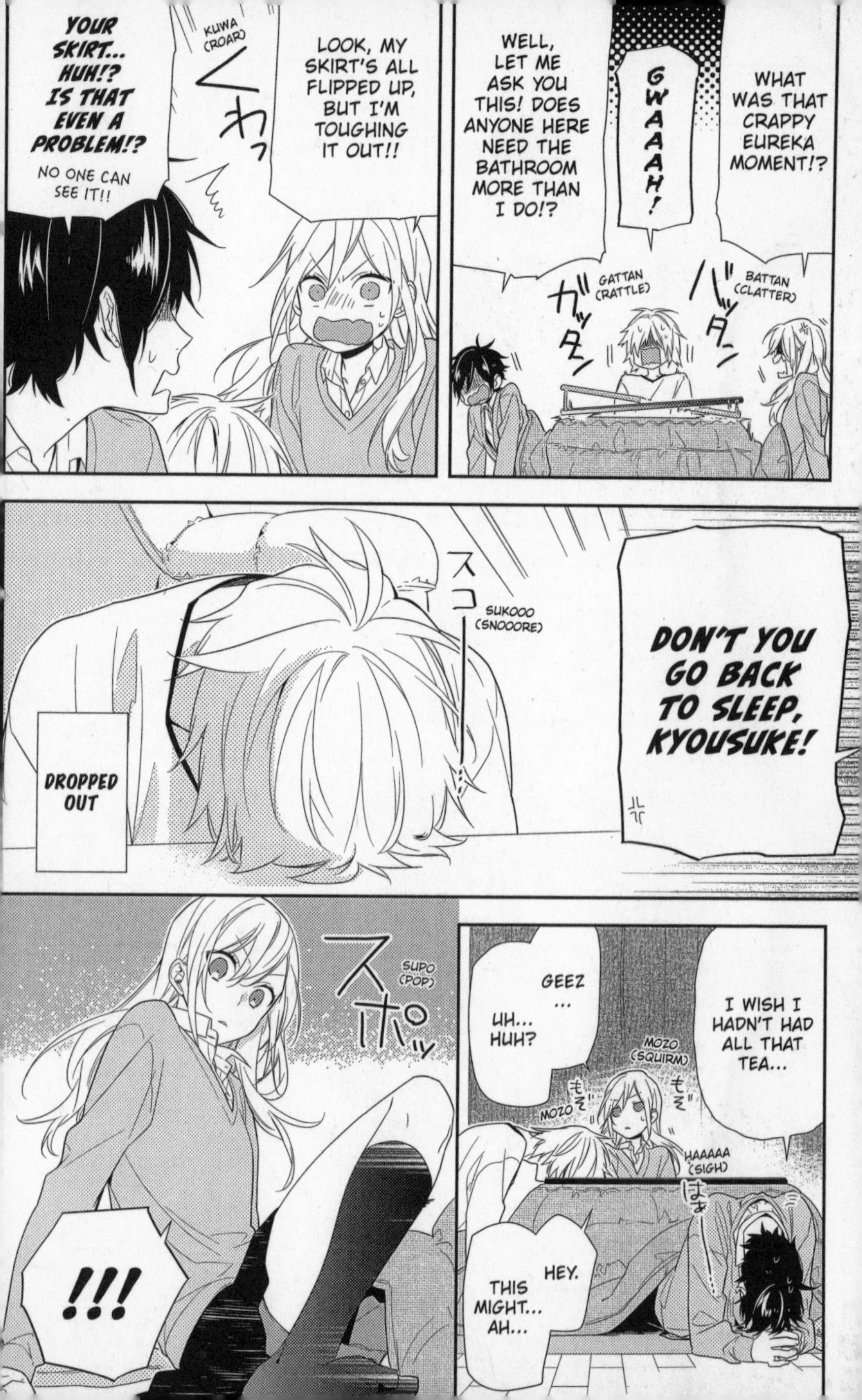
WHAT WAS THAT CRAPPY EUREKA MOMENT!?
GWAAAH!
WELL, LET ME ASK YOU THIS! DOES ANYONE HERE NEED THE BATHROOM MORE THAN I DO!?
BATTAN (CLATTER)
GATTAN (RATTLE)
LOOK, MY SKIRT'S ALL FLIPPED UP, BUT I'M TOUGHING IT OUT!!
KUWA (ROAR)
YOUR SKIRT... HUH!? IS THAT EVEN A PROBLEM!?
NO ONE CAN SEE IT!!
DON'T YOU GO BACK TO SLEEP, KYOUSUKE!
SUKOOO (SNOOORE)
DROPPED OUT
I WISH I HADN'T HAD ALL THAT TEA...
GEEZ...
UH... HUH?
MOZO (SQUIRM)
MOZO
HAAAAA (SIGH)
HEY.
THIS MIGHT... AH...
SUPO (POP)
!!!

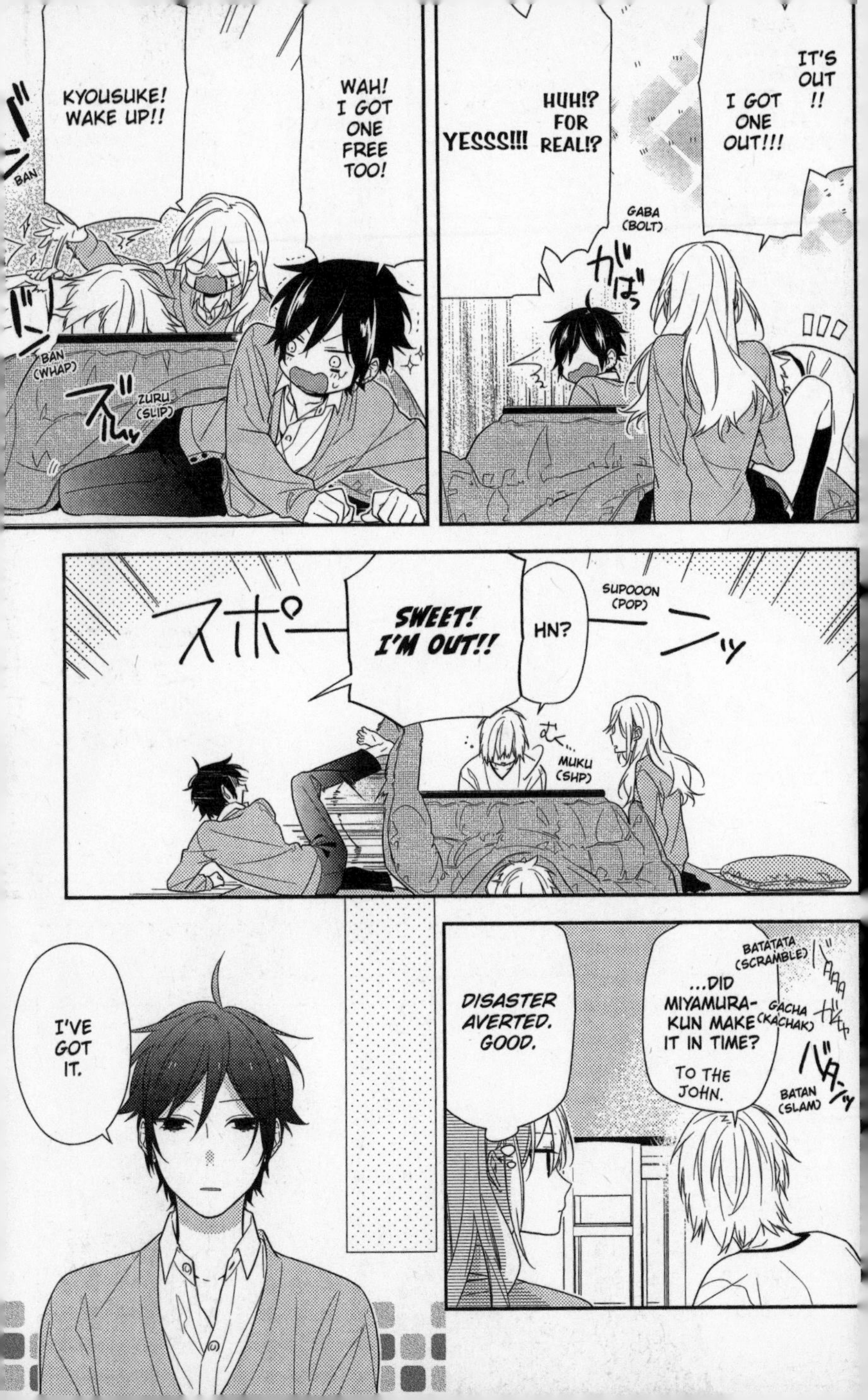
IT'S OUT !!
I GOT ONE OUT!!!
HUH!? FOR REAL!?
YESSS!!!
GABA (BOLT)
WAH! I GOT ONE FREE TOO!
KYOUSUKE! WAKE UP!!
BAN
BAN (WHAP)
ZURU (SLIP)
SUPOOON (POP)
HN?
SWEET! I'M OUT!!
MUKU (SHP)
BATATATA (SCRAMBLE)
GACHA (KACHAK)
...DID MIYAMURA-KUN MAKE IT IN TIME?
TO THE JOHN.
BATAN (SLAM)
DISASTER AVERTED. GOOD.
I'VE GOT IT.

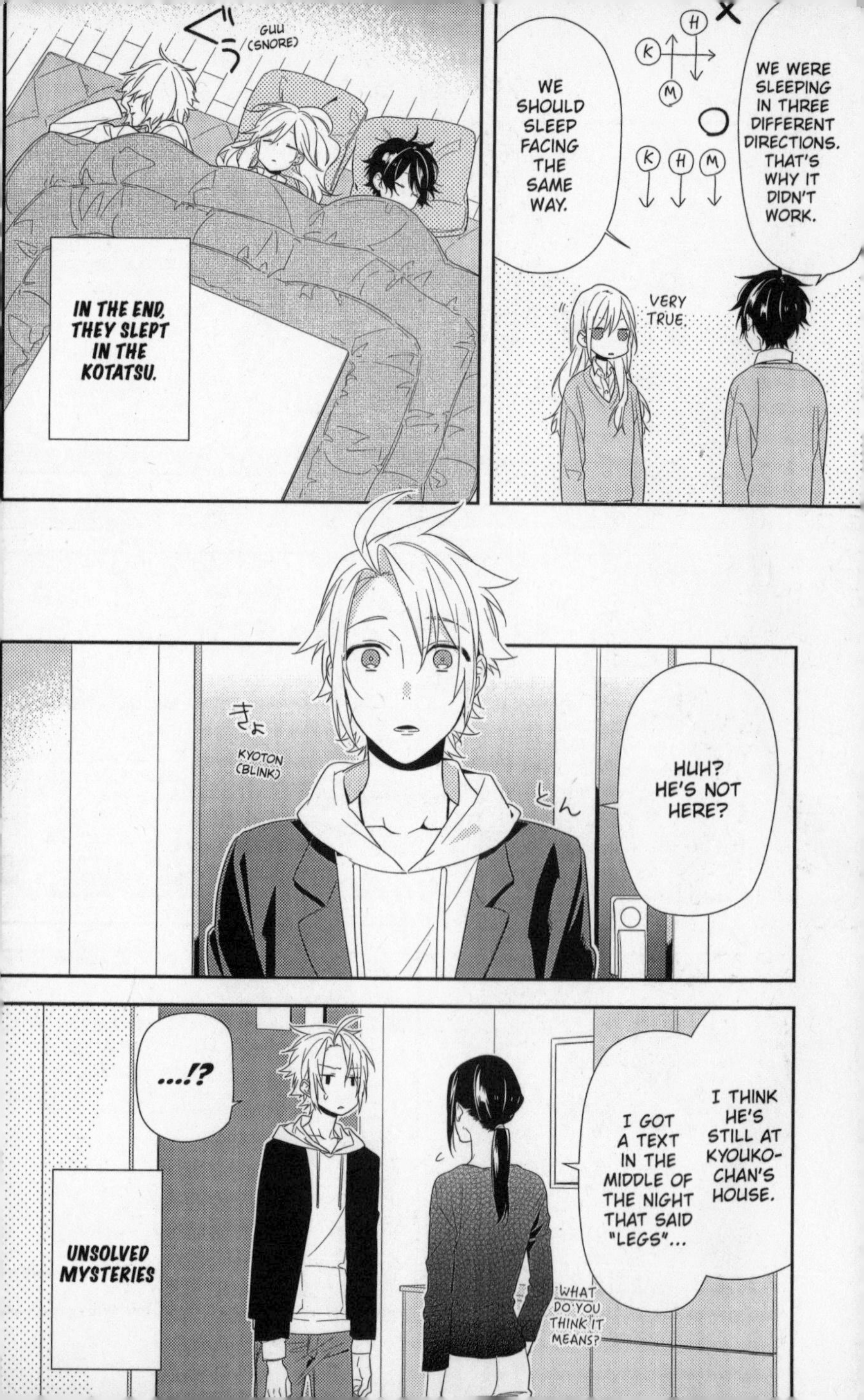
WE WERE SLEEPING IN THREE DIFFERENT DIRECTIONS. THAT'S WHY IT DIDN'T WORK.
K H M
WE SHOULD SLEEP FACING THE SAME WAY.
K H M
VERY TRUE.
ぐう
GUU (SNORE)
IN THE END, THEY SLEPT IN THE KOTATSU.
HUH? HE'S NOT HERE?
きょとん
KYOTON (BLINK)
I THINK HE'S STILL AT KYOUKO-CHAN'S HOUSE.
I GOT A TEXT IN THE MIDDLE OF THE NIGHT THAT SAID "LEGS"...
WHAT DO YOU THINK IT MEANS?
...!?
UNSOLVED MYSTERIES

KOTATSU MEDLEY ②

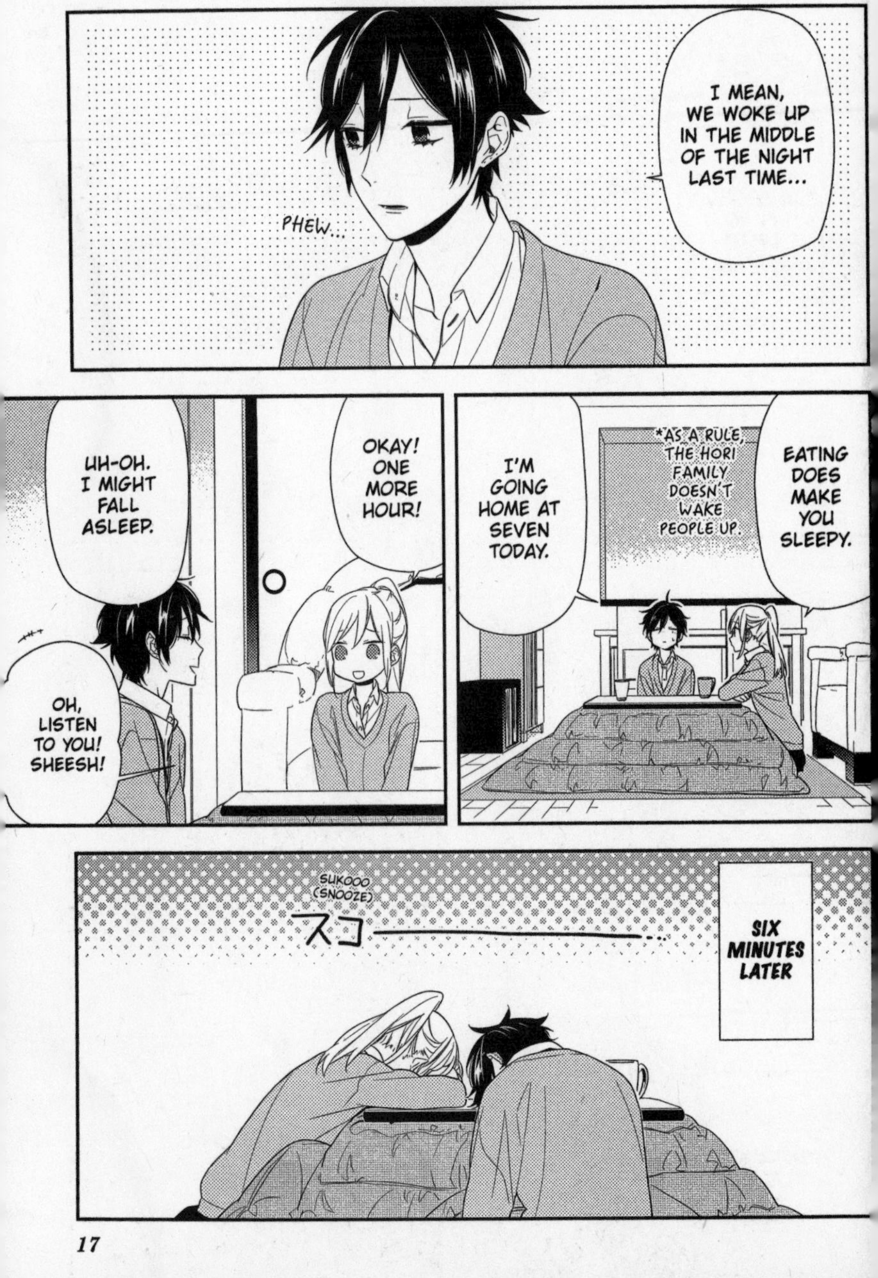

I MEAN, WE WOKE UP IN THE MIDDLE OF THE NIGHT LAST TIME...
PHEW...
EATING DOES MAKE YOU SLEEPY.
*AS A RULE, THE HORI FAMILY DOESN'T WAKE PEOPLE UP.
I'M GOING HOME AT SEVEN TODAY.
OKAY! ONE MORE HOUR!
UH-OH. I MIGHT FALL ASLEEP.
OH, LISTEN TO YOU! SHEESH!
SIX MINUTES LATER
SUKOOO (SNOOZE)
スコ——...

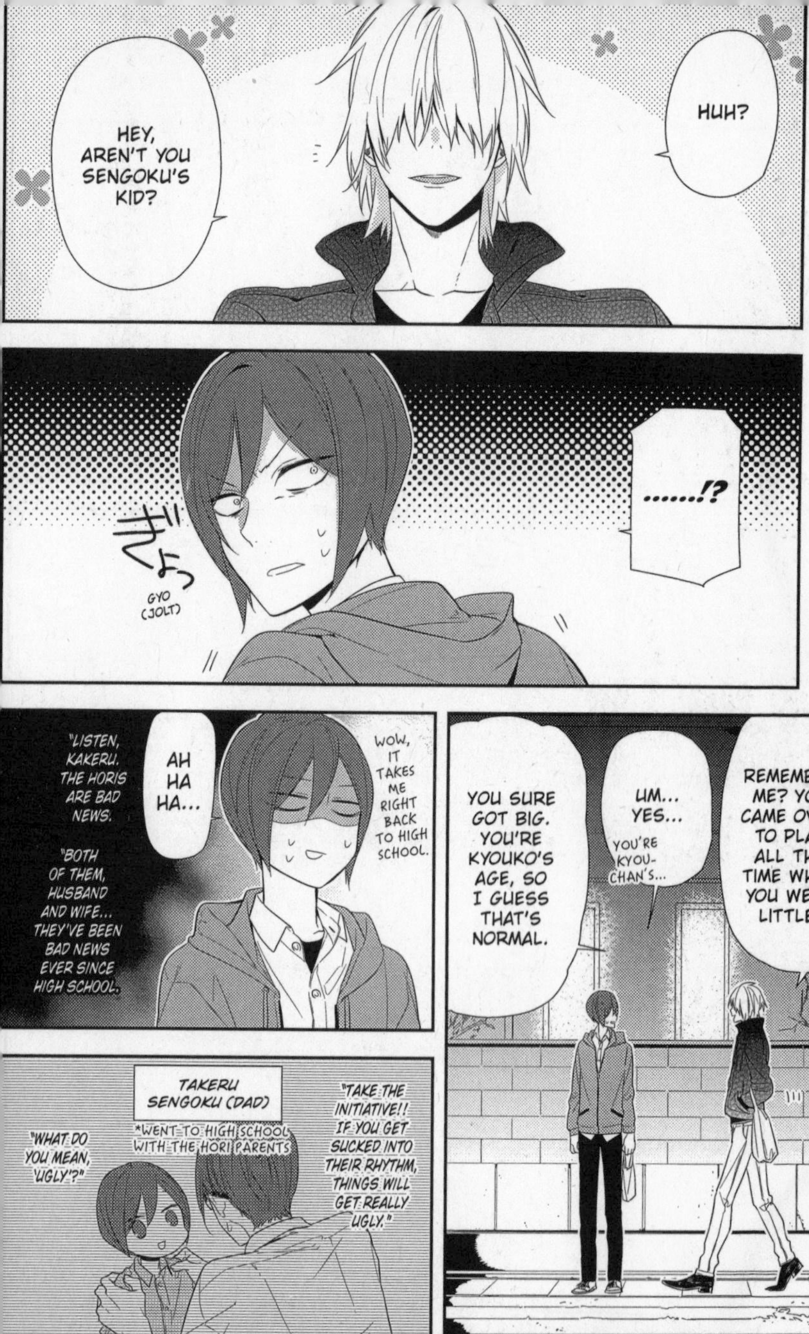
HUH?
HEY, AREN'T YOU SENGOKU'S KID?
......!?
ぎょっ
GYO (JOLT)
REMEMBER ME? YOU CAME OVER TO PLAY ALL THE TIME WHEN YOU WERE LITTLE.
UM... YES...
YOU'RE KYOU-CHAN'S...
YOU SURE GOT BIG. YOU'RE KYOUKO'S AGE, SO I GUESS THAT'S NORMAL.
WOW, IT TAKES ME RIGHT BACK TO HIGH SCHOOL.
AH HA HA...
"LISTEN, KAKERU. THE HORIS ARE BAD NEWS.
"BOTH OF THEM, HUSBAND AND WIFE... THEY'VE BEEN BAD NEWS EVER SINCE HIGH SCHOOL.
"TAKE THE INITIATIVE!! IF YOU GET SUCKED INTO THEIR RHYTHM, THINGS WILL GET REALLY UGLY."
TAKERU SENGOKU (DAD)
*WENT TO HIGH SCHOOL WITH THE HORI PARENTS
"WHAT DO YOU MEAN, 'UGLY'?"

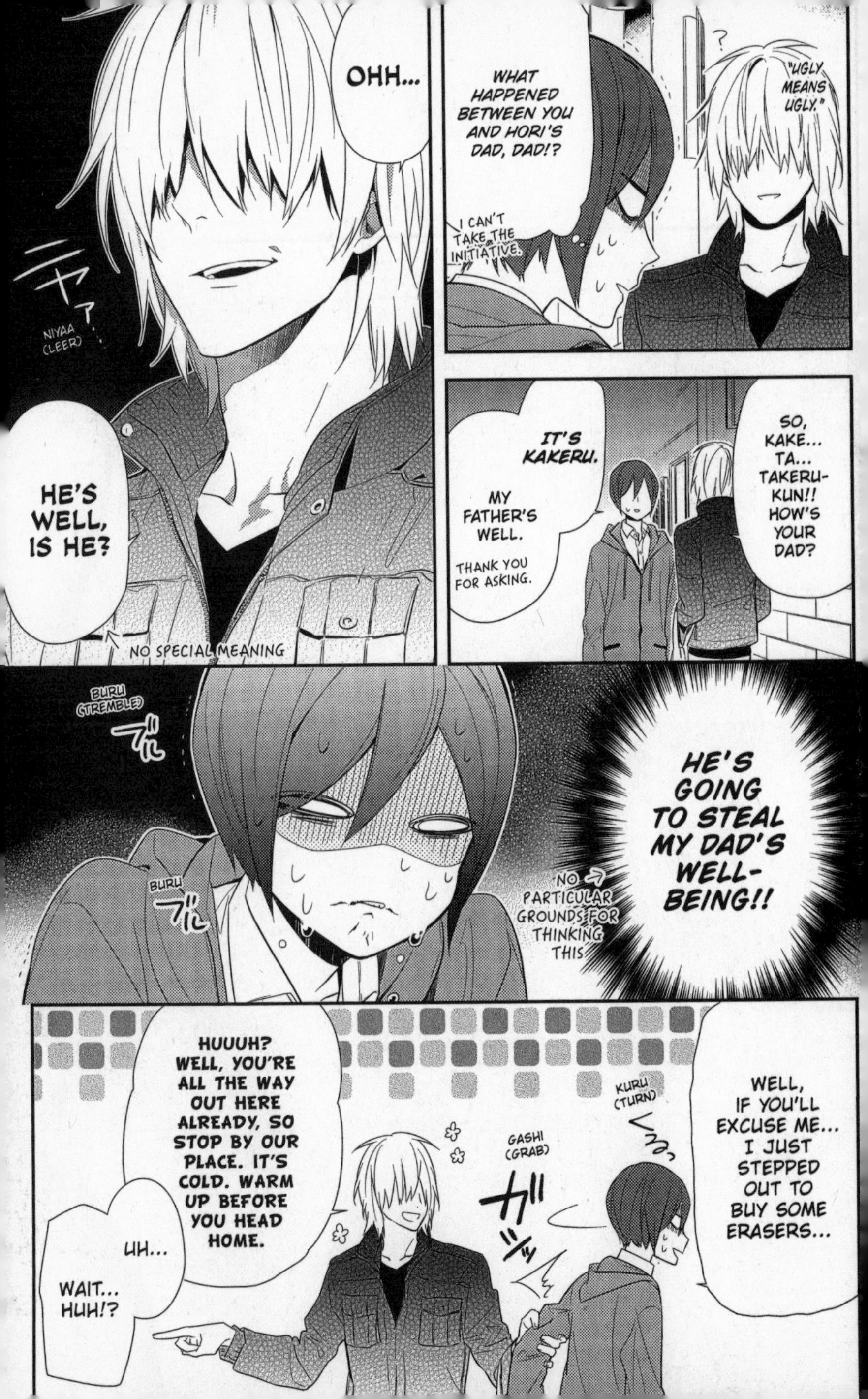
?
"UGLY MEANS UGLY."
WHAT HAPPENED BETWEEN YOU AND HORI'S DAD, DAD!?
I CAN'T TAKE THE INITIATIVE.
SO, KAKE... TA... TAKERU-KUN!! HOW'S YOUR DAD?
IT'S KAKERU.
MY FATHER'S WELL.
THANK YOU FOR ASKING.
OHH...
NIYAA (LEER)
HE'S WELL, IS HE?
NO SPECIAL MEANING
HE'S GOING TO STEAL MY DAD'S WELL-BEING!!
NO PARTICULAR GROUNDS FOR THINKING THIS
BURU (TREMBLE)
BURU
WELL, IF YOU'LL EXCUSE ME... I JUST STEPPED OUT TO BUY SOME ERASERS...
KURU (TURN)
GASHI (GRAB)
HUUUH? WELL, YOU'RE ALL THE WAY OUT HERE ALREADY, SO STOP BY OUR PLACE. IT'S COLD. WARM UP BEFORE YOU HEAD HOME.
UH...
WAIT... HUH!?

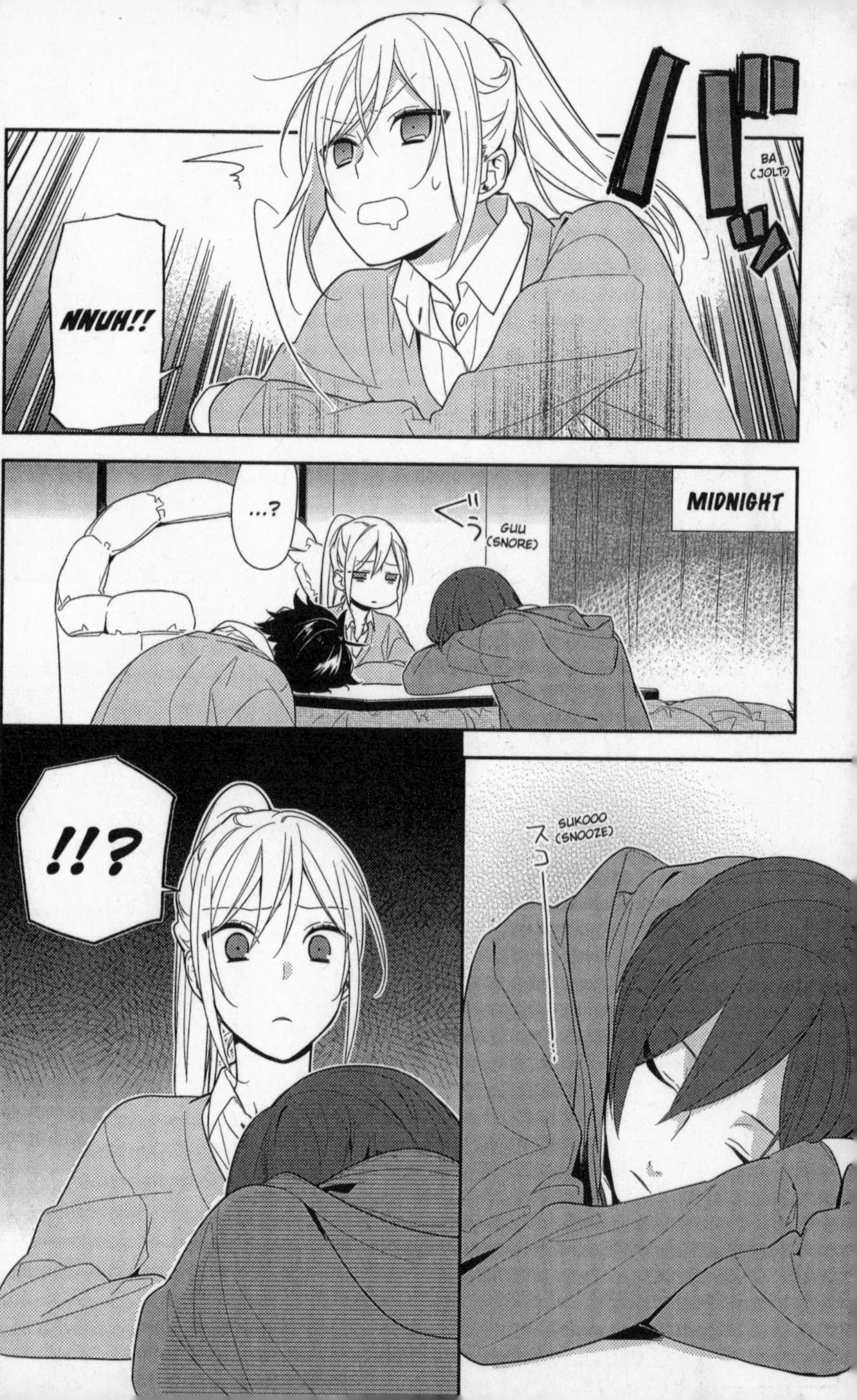
バッ
BA (JOLT)
NNUH!!
MIDNIGHT
ぐぅ
GUU (SNORE)
...?
スコー
SUKOOO (SNOOZE)
!!?

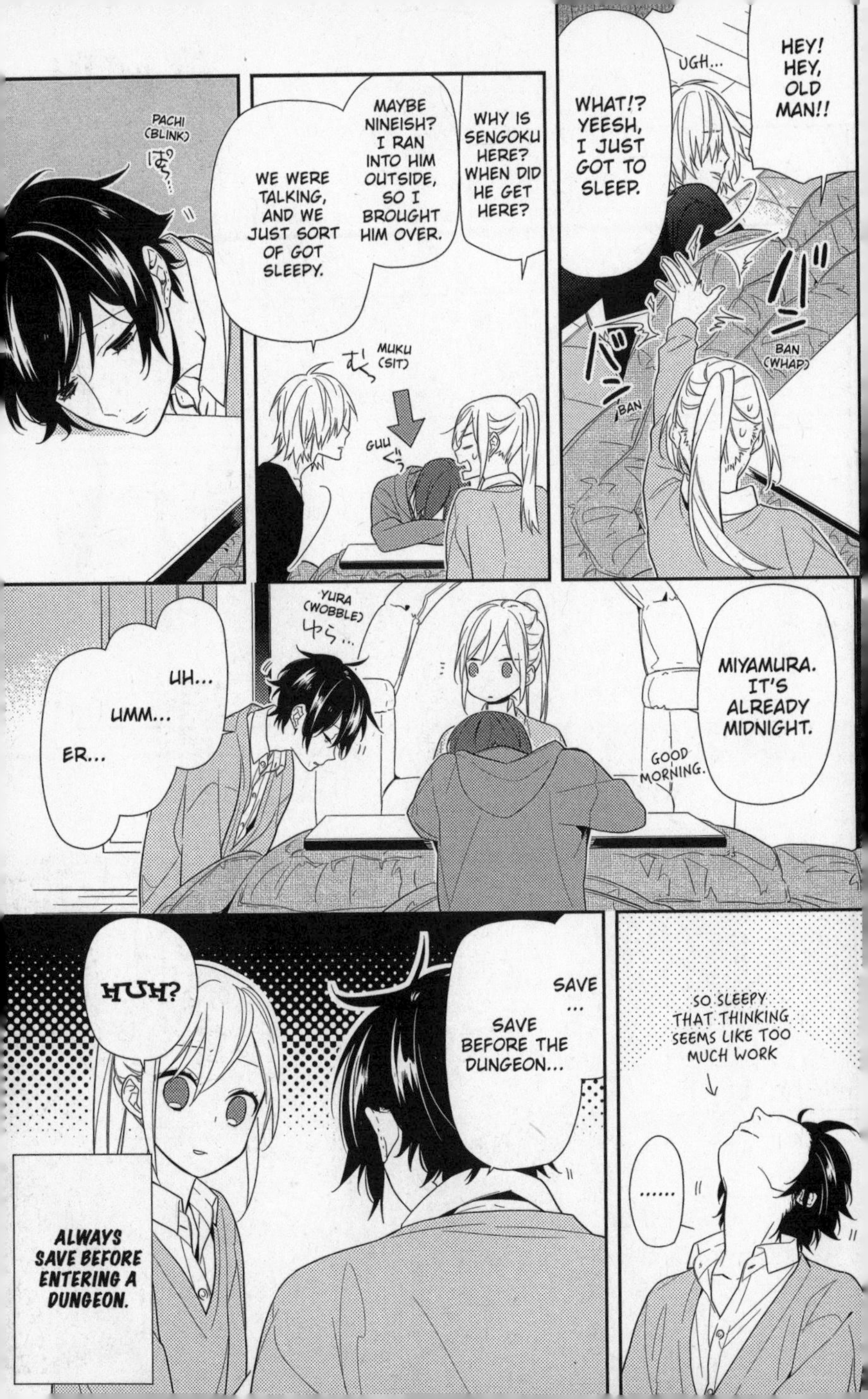

HEY! HEY, OLD MAN!!
UGH...
WHAT!? YEESH, I JUST GOT TO SLEEP.
BAN (WHAP)
BAN
WHY IS SENGOKU HERE? WHEN DID HE GET HERE?
MAYBE NINEISH? I RAN INTO HIM OUTSIDE, SO I BROUGHT HIM OVER.
WE WERE TALKING, AND WE JUST SORT OF GOT SLEEPY.
MUKU (SIT)
GUU
PACHI (BLINK)
MIYAMURA. IT'S ALREADY MIDNIGHT.
GOOD MORNING.
YURA (WOBBLE)
UH...
UMM...
ER...
SO SLEEPY THAT THINKING SEEMS LIKE TOO MUCH WORK
......
SAVE ...
SAVE BEFORE THE DUNGEON...
HUH?
ALWAYS SAVE BEFORE ENTERING A DUNGEON.

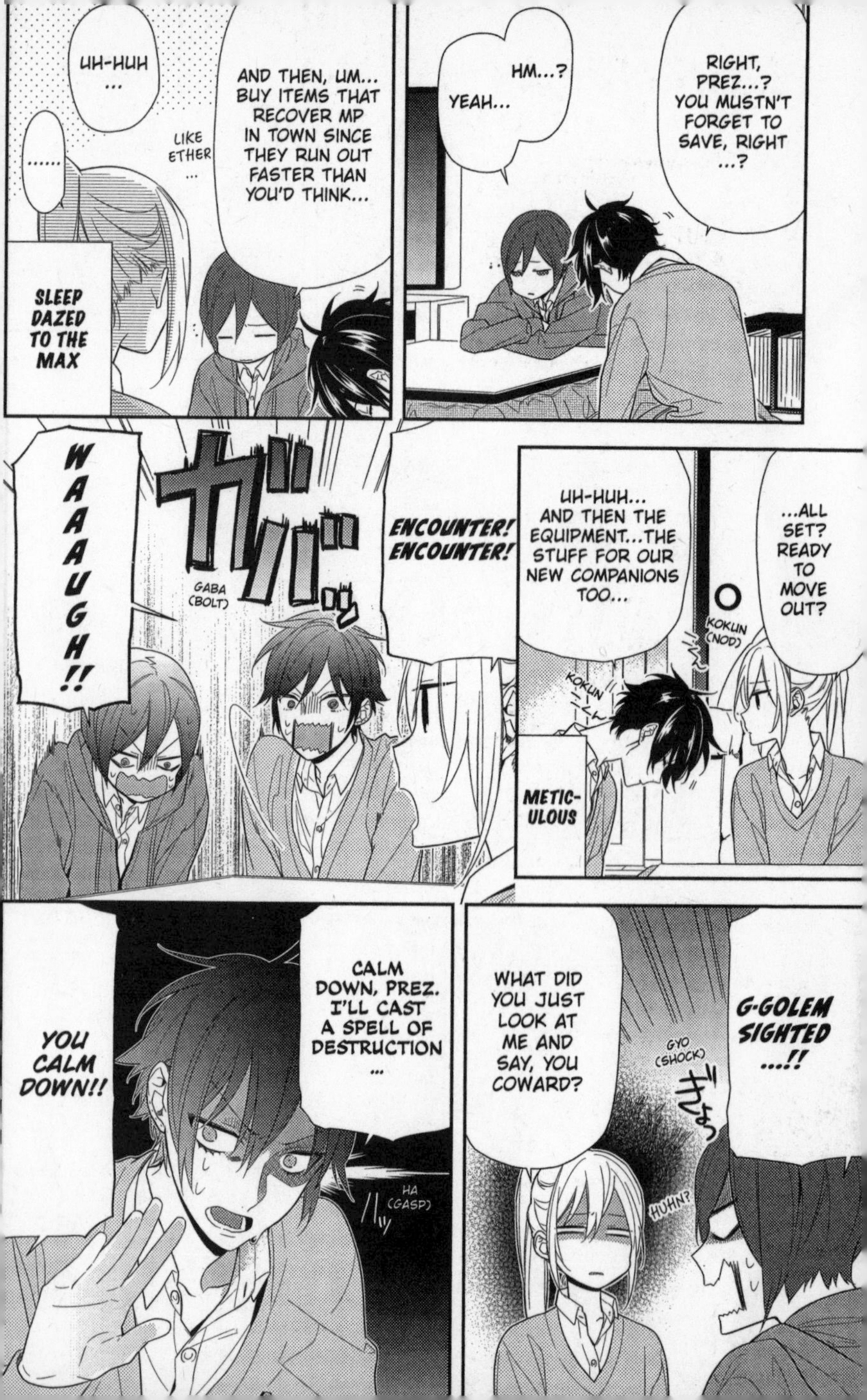
RIGHT, PREZ...? YOU MUSTN'T FORGET TO SAVE, RIGHT...?
HM...?
YEAH...
AND THEN, UM... BUY ITEMS THAT RECOVER MP IN TOWN SINCE THEY RUN OUT FASTER THAN YOU'D THINK...
LIKE ETHER...
UH-HUH...
......
SLEEP DAZED TO THE MAX
...ALL SET? READY TO MOVE OUT?
UH-HUH... AND THEN THE EQUIPMENT...THE STUFF FOR OUR NEW COMPANIONS TOO...
KOKUN (NOD)
KOKUN
METICULOUS
ENCOUNTER! ENCOUNTER!
GABA (BOLT)
WAAAAUGH!!
G-GOLEM SIGHTED...!!
WHAT DID YOU JUST LOOK AT ME AND SAY, YOU COWARD?
GYO (SHOCK)
HUHN?
CALM DOWN, PREZ. I'LL CAST A SPELL OF DESTRUCTION...
HA (GASP)
YOU CALM DOWN!!

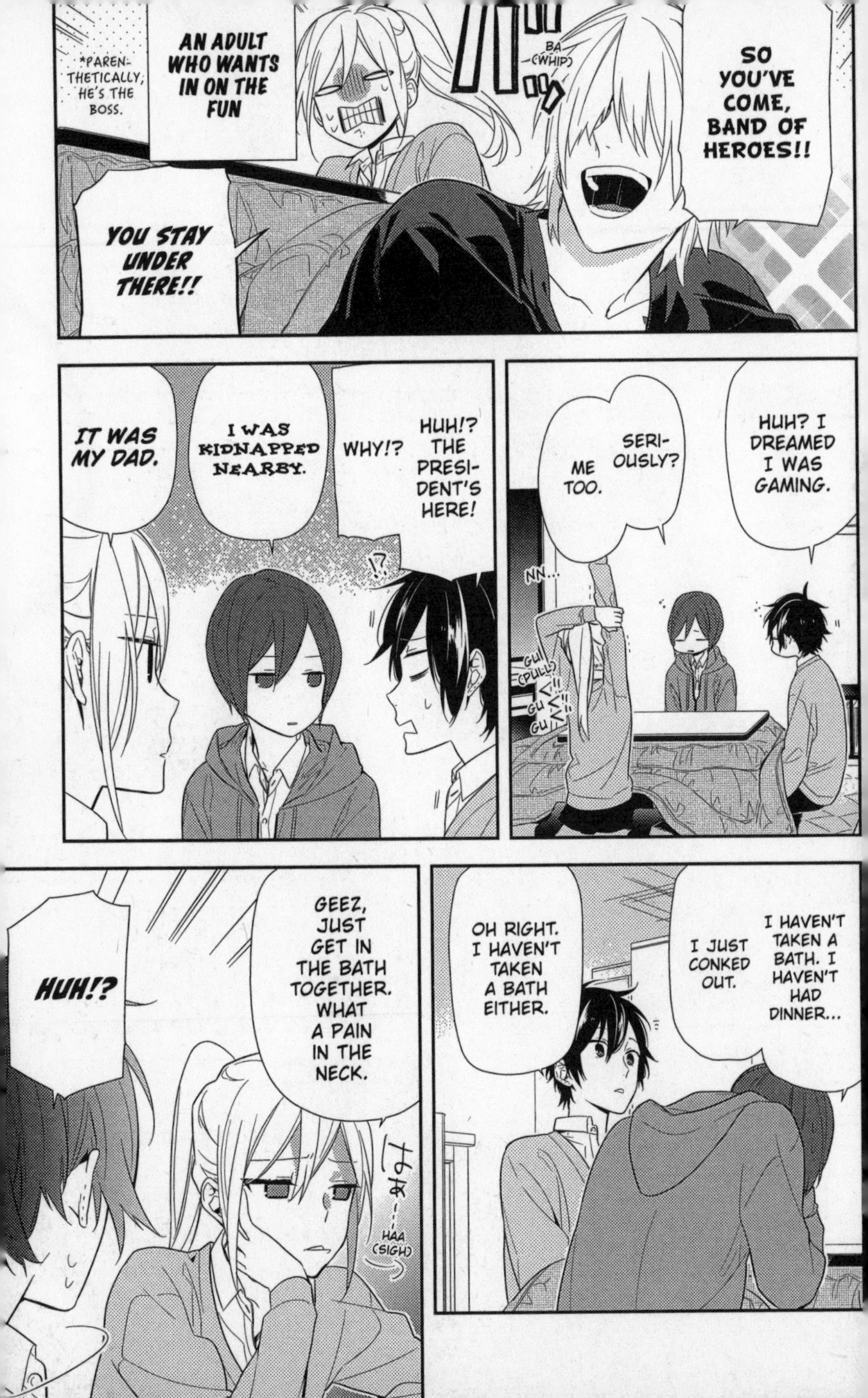
SO YOU'VE COME, BAND OF HEROES!!
BA (WHIP)
AN ADULT WHO WANTS IN ON THE FUN
*PARENTHETICALLY, HE'S THE BOSS.
YOU STAY UNDER THERE!!
HUH? I DREAMED I WAS GAMING.
SERIOUSLY?
ME TOO.
NN...
GUI (PULL)
GU
GU
HUH!? THE PRESIDENT'S HERE!
WHY!?
I WAS KIDNAPPED NEARBY.
IT WAS MY DAD.
!?
I HAVEN'T TAKEN A BATH. I HAVEN'T HAD DINNER...
I JUST CONKED OUT.
OH RIGHT. I HAVEN'T TAKEN A BATH EITHER.
GEEZ, JUST GET IN THE BATH TOGETHER. WHAT A PAIN IN THE NECK.
はぁ…
HAA (SIGH)
HUH!?

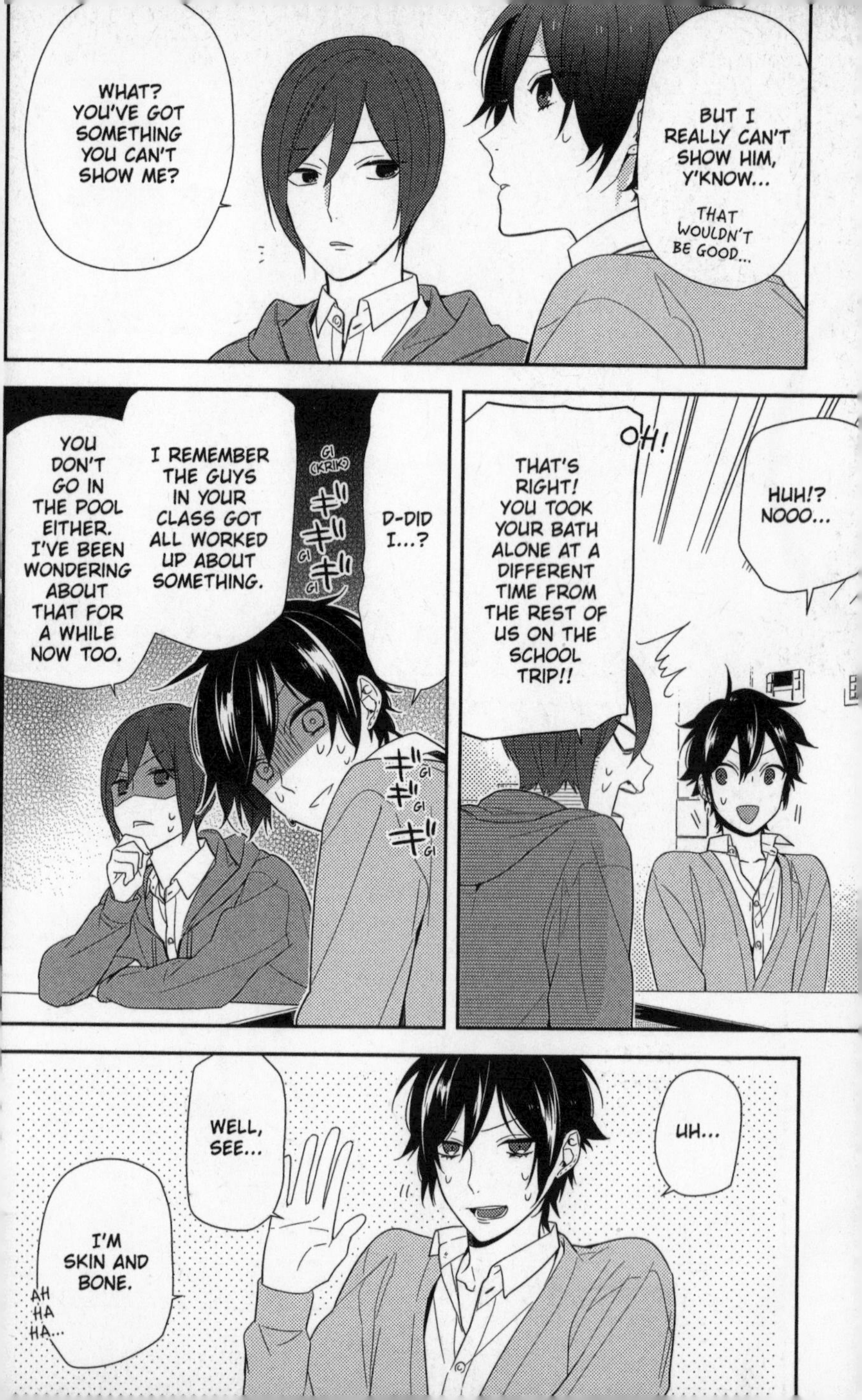
BUT I REALLY CAN'T SHOW HIM, Y'KNOW...
THAT WOULDN'T BE GOOD...
WHAT? YOU'VE GOT SOMETHING YOU CAN'T SHOW ME?
HUH!? NOOO...
OH!
THAT'S RIGHT! YOU TOOK YOUR BATH ALONE AT A DIFFERENT TIME FROM THE REST OF US ON THE SCHOOL TRIP!!
D-DID I...?
GI (KRIK) GI GI
I REMEMBER THE GUYS IN YOUR CLASS GOT ALL WORKED UP ABOUT SOMETHING.
YOU DON'T GO IN THE POOL EITHER. I'VE BEEN WONDERING ABOUT THAT FOR A WHILE NOW TOO.
GI GI GI
UH...
WELL, SEE...
I'M SKIN AND BONE.
AH HA HA...

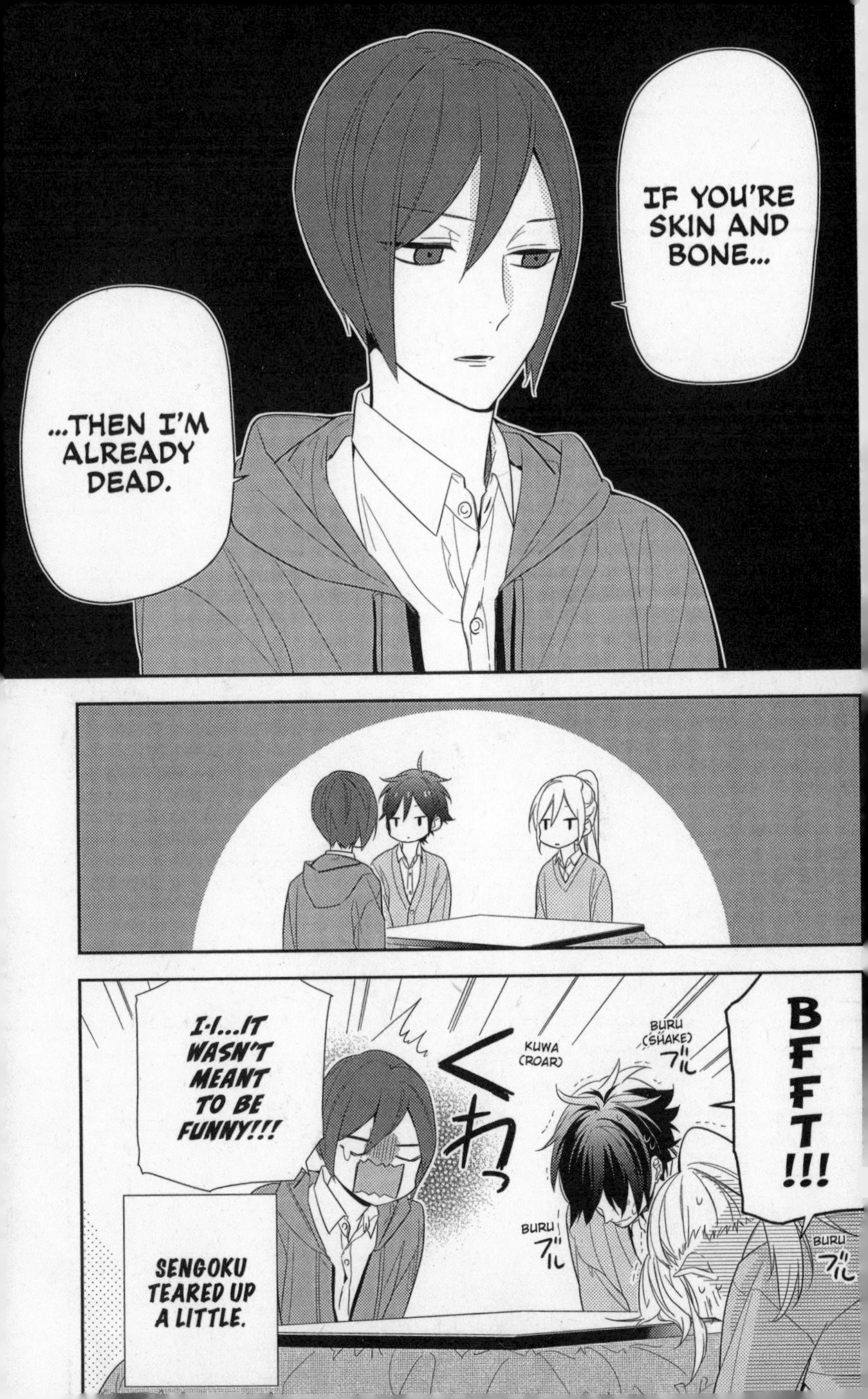
IF YOU'RE SKIN AND BONE...
...THEN I'M ALREADY DEAD.
BFFT!!!
BURU (SHAKE)
ブル
KUWA (ROAR)
くわっ
I-I...IT WASN'T MEANT TO BE FUNNY!!!
BURU
ブル
BURU
ブル
SENGOKU TEARED UP A LITTLE.

KOTATSU MEDLEY ③

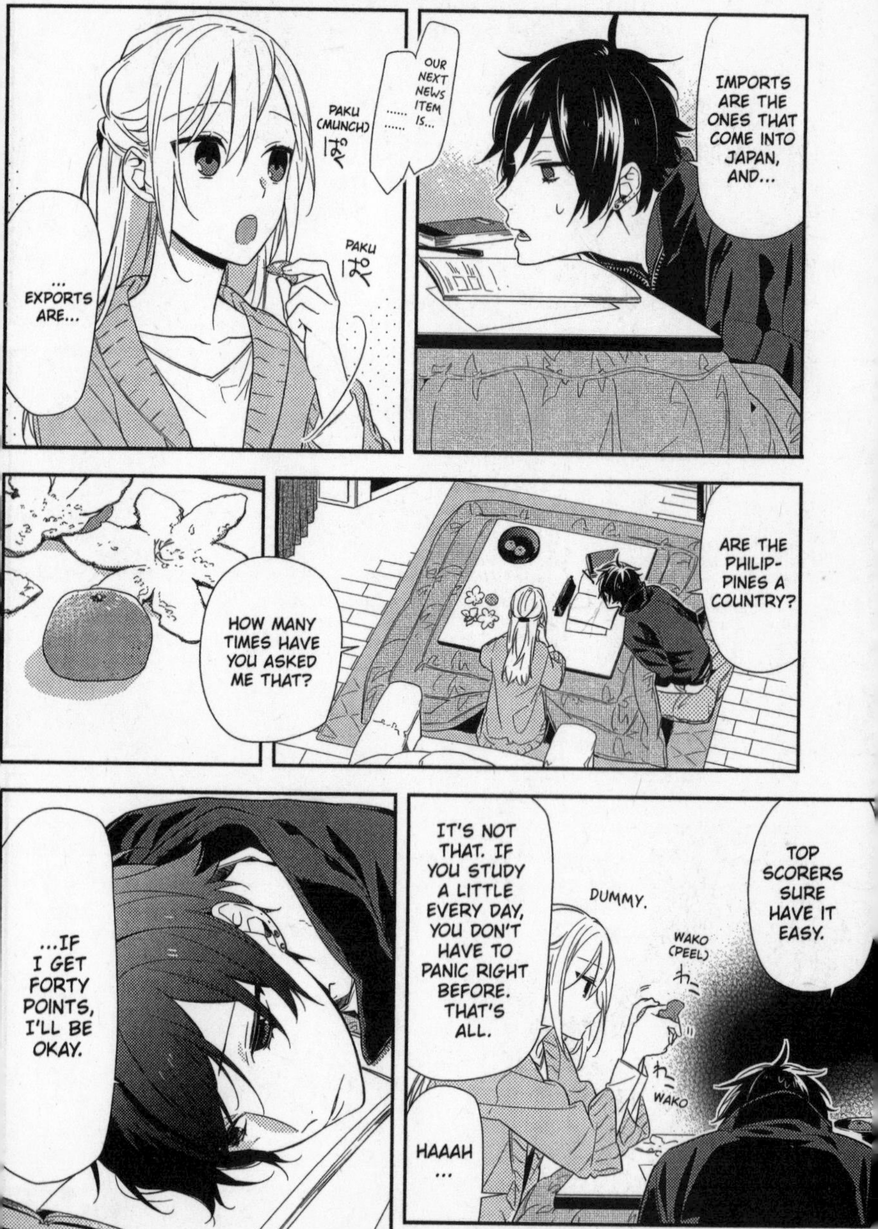
IMPORTS ARE THE ONES THAT COME INTO JAPAN, AND...
OUR NEXT NEWS ITEM IS...
......
......
PAKU (MUNCH)
ぱく
PAKU
ぱく
... EXPORTS ARE...
ARE THE PHILIP-PINES A COUNTRY?
HOW MANY TIMES HAVE YOU ASKED ME THAT?
TOP SCORERS SURE HAVE IT EASY.
IT'S NOT THAT. IF YOU STUDY A LITTLE EVERY DAY, YOU DON'T HAVE TO PANIC RIGHT BEFORE. THAT'S ALL.
DUMMY.
WAKO (PEEL)
わ
WAKO
わ
HAAAH ...
...IF I GET FORTY POINTS, I'LL BE OKAY.

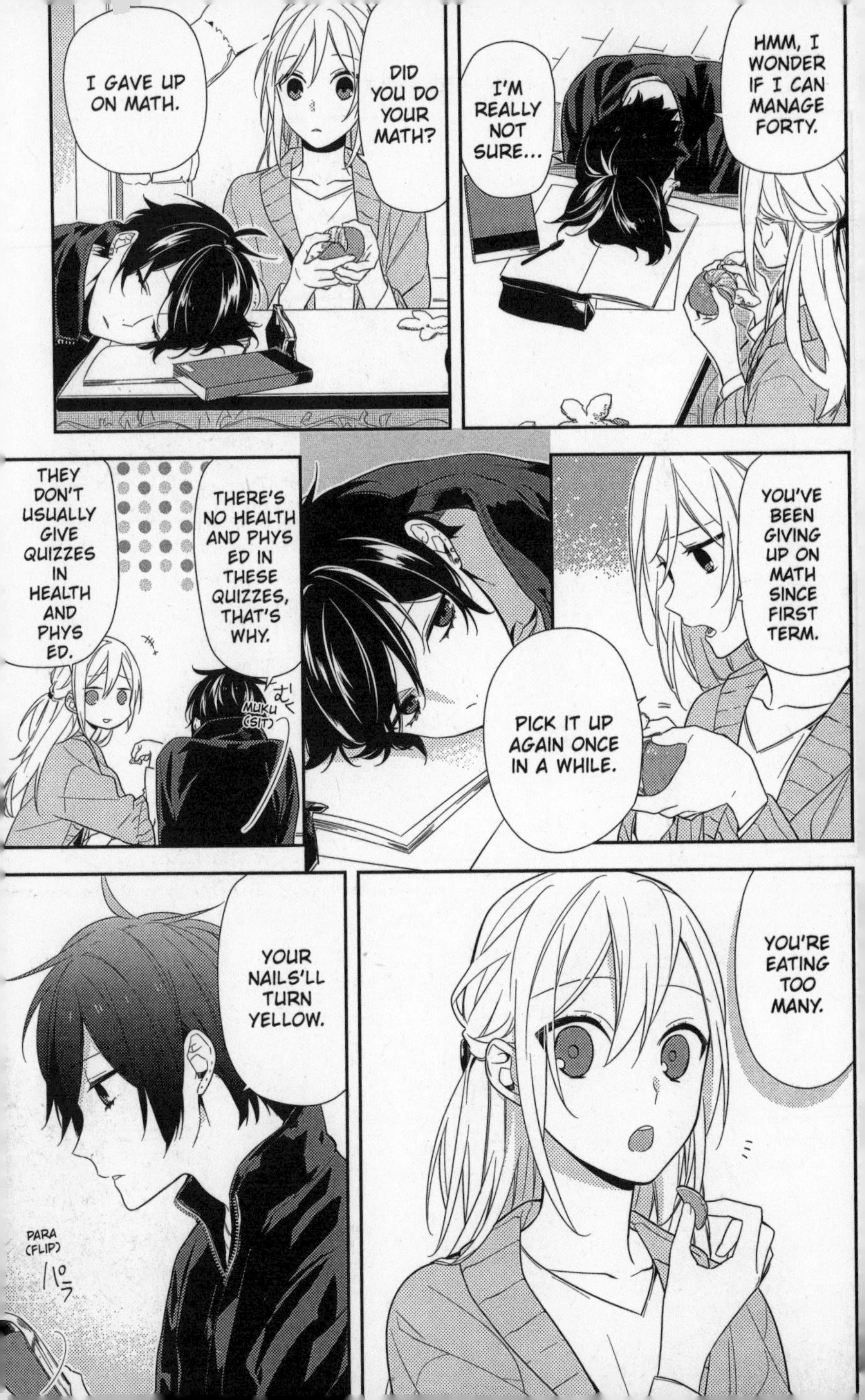
HMM, I WONDER IF I CAN MANAGE FORTY.
I'M REALLY NOT SURE...
DID YOU DO YOUR MATH?
I GAVE UP ON MATH.
YOU'VE BEEN GIVING UP ON MATH SINCE FIRST TERM.
PICK IT UP AGAIN ONCE IN A WHILE.
THERE'S NO HEALTH AND PHYS ED IN THESE QUIZZES, THAT'S WHY.
MUKU (SIT)
THEY DON'T USUALLY GIVE QUIZZES IN HEALTH AND PHYS ED.
YOU'RE EATING TOO MANY.
YOUR NAILS'LL TURN YELLOW.
PARA (FLIP)

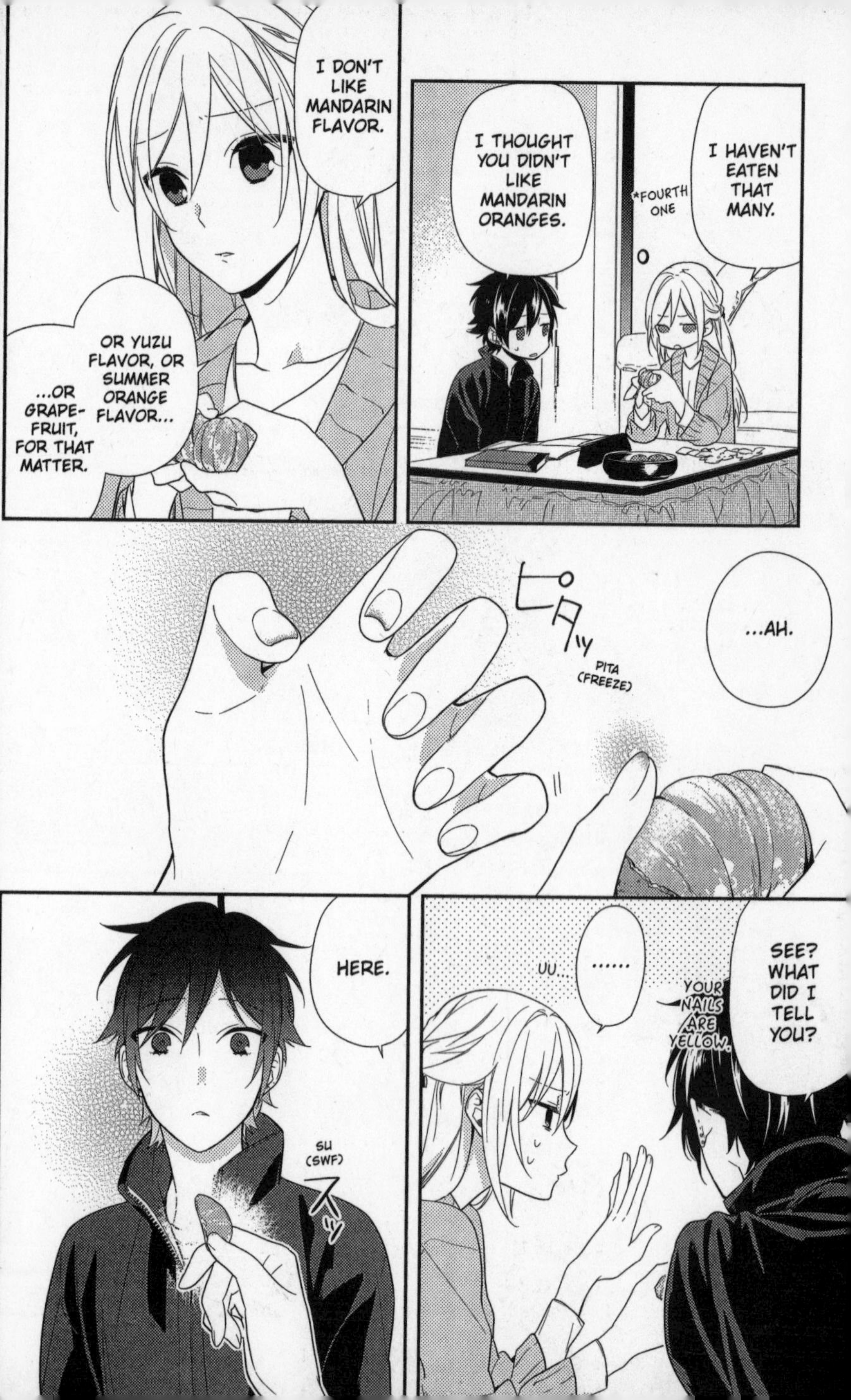
I HAVEN'T EATEN THAT MANY.
*FOURTH ONE
I THOUGHT YOU DIDN'T LIKE MANDARIN ORANGES.
I DON'T LIKE MANDARIN FLAVOR.
OR YUZU FLAVOR, OR SUMMER ORANGE FLAVOR...
...OR GRAPEFRUIT, FOR THAT MATTER.
...AH.
PITA (FREEZE)
SEE? WHAT DID I TELL YOU?
YOUR NAILS ARE YELLOW.
......
UU...
HERE.
SU (SWF)

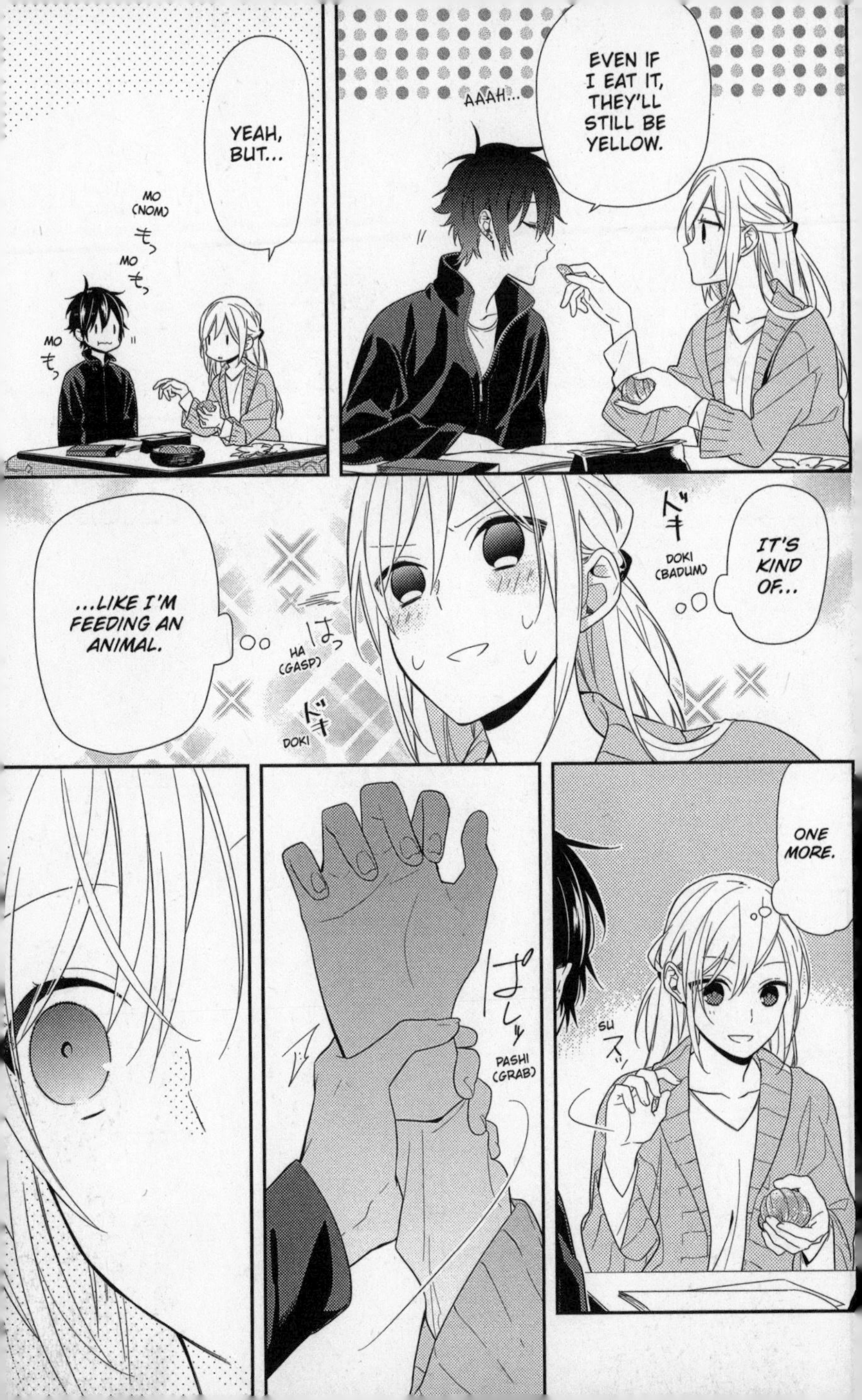
AAAH...
EVEN IF I EAT IT, THEY'LL STILL BE YELLOW.
YEAH, BUT...
MO (NOM)
もっ
MO
もっ
MO
もっ
ドキ
DOKI (BADUM)
IT'S KIND OF...
はっ
HA (GASP)
...LIKE I'M FEEDING AN ANIMAL.
ドキ
DOKI
ONE MORE.
SU
スッ
ぱしッ
PASHI (GRAB)

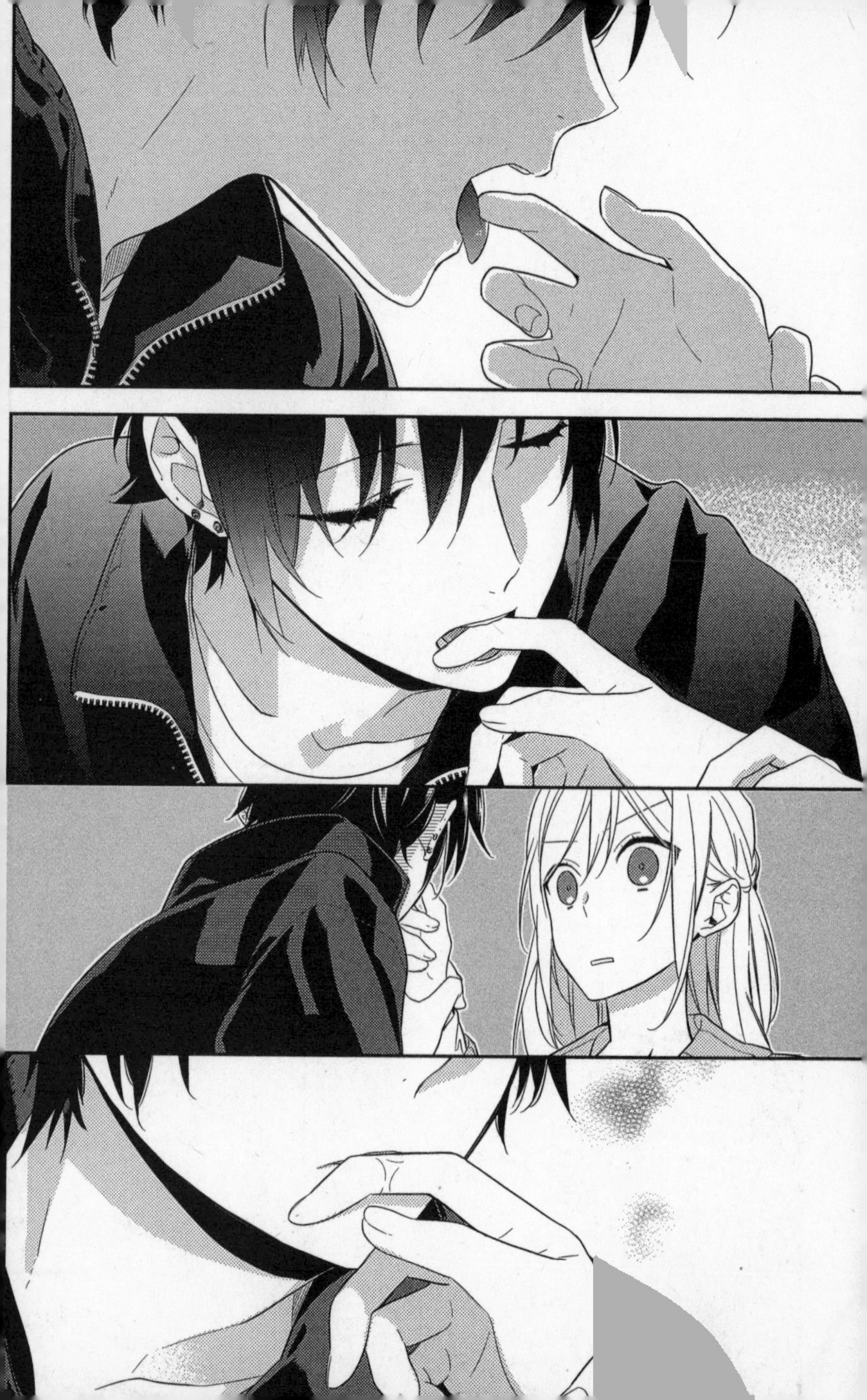

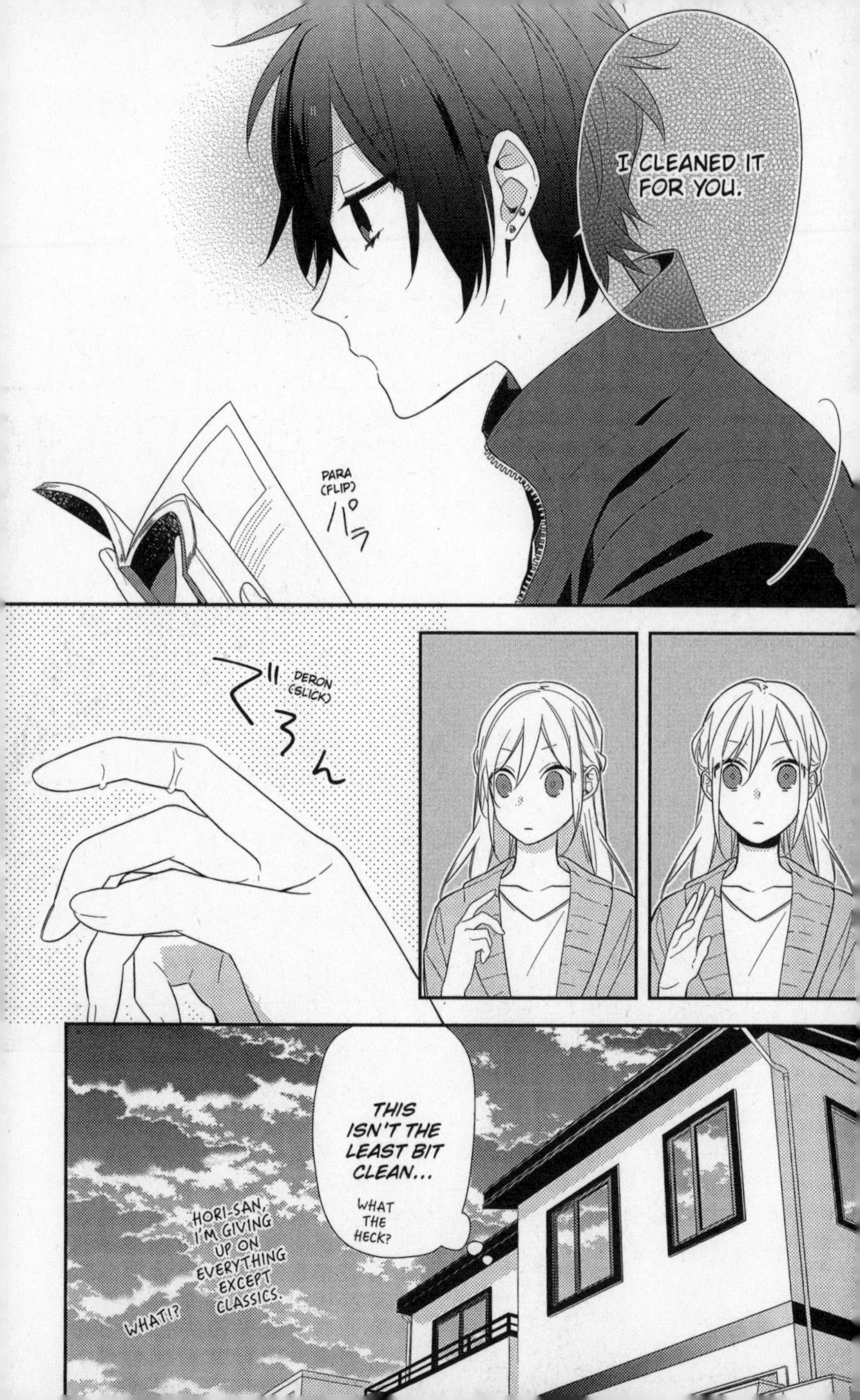
I CLEANED IT FOR YOU.
PARA (FLIP)
パラ
でろん
DERON (SLICK)
THIS ISN'T THE LEAST BIT CLEAN...
WHAT THE HECK?
HORI-SAN, I'M GIVING UP ON EVERYTHING EXCEPT CLASSICS.
WHAT!?

HORIMIYA

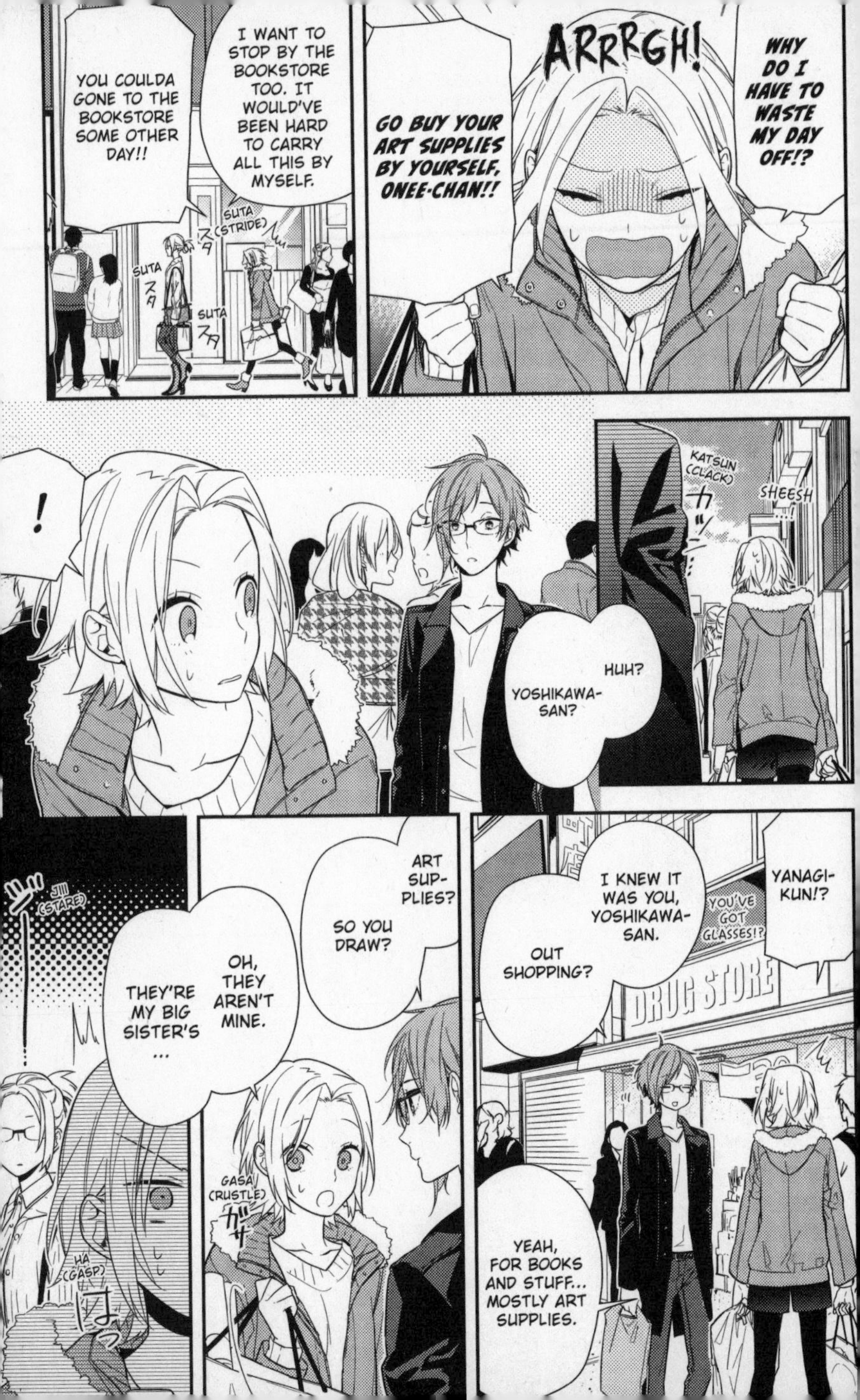
ARRRGH!
WHY DO I HAVE TO WASTE MY DAY OFF!?
GO BUY YOUR ART SUPPLIES BY YOURSELF, ONEE-CHAN!!
I WANT TO STOP BY THE BOOKSTORE TOO. IT WOULD'VE BEEN HARD TO CARRY ALL THIS BY MYSELF.
YOU COULDA GONE TO THE BOOKSTORE SOME OTHER DAY!!
SUTA (STRIDE)
SUTA
SUTA
KATSUN (CLACK)
SHEESH
HUH?
YOSHIKAWA-SAN?
!
YANAGI-KUN!?
YOU'VE GOT GLASSES!?
I KNEW IT WAS YOU, YOSHIKAWA-SAN.
OUT SHOPPING?
YEAH, FOR BOOKS AND STUFF... MOSTLY ART SUPPLIES.
DRUG STORE
ART SUP-PLIES?
SO YOU DRAW?
OH, THEY AREN'T MINE.
THEY'RE MY BIG SISTER'S...
GASA (RUSTLE)
JIII (STARE)
HA (GASP)

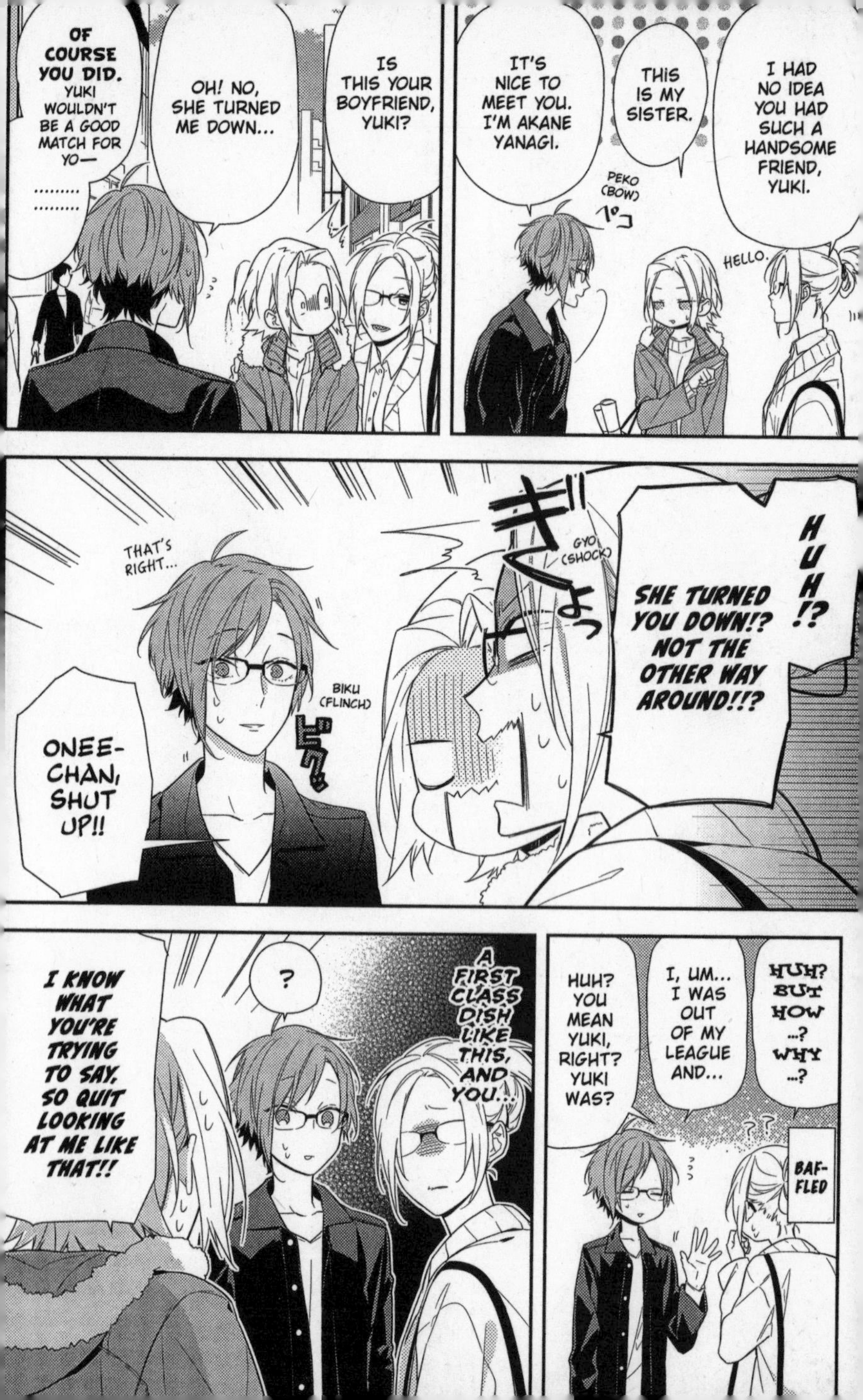
I HAD NO IDEA YOU HAD SUCH A HANDSOME FRIEND, YUKI.
HELLO.
THIS IS MY SISTER.
PEKO (BOW)
IT'S NICE TO MEET YOU. I'M AKANE YANAGI.
IS THIS YOUR BOYFRIEND, YUKI?
OH! NO, SHE TURNED ME DOWN...
OF COURSE YOU DID. YUKI WOULDN'T BE A GOOD MATCH FOR YO—
....
....
HUH!?
SHE TURNED YOU DOWN!? NOT THE OTHER WAY AROUND!!?
GYO (SHOCK)
THAT'S RIGHT...
BIKU (FLINCH)
ONEE-CHAN, SHUT UP!!
HUH? BUT HOW ...? WHY ...?
I, UM... I WAS OUT OF MY LEAGUE AND...
HUH? YOU MEAN YUKI, RIGHT? YUKI WAS?
BAFFLED
A FIRST CLASS DISH LIKE THIS, AND YOU...
?
I KNOW WHAT YOU'RE TRYING TO SAY, SO QUIT LOOKING AT ME LIKE THAT!!

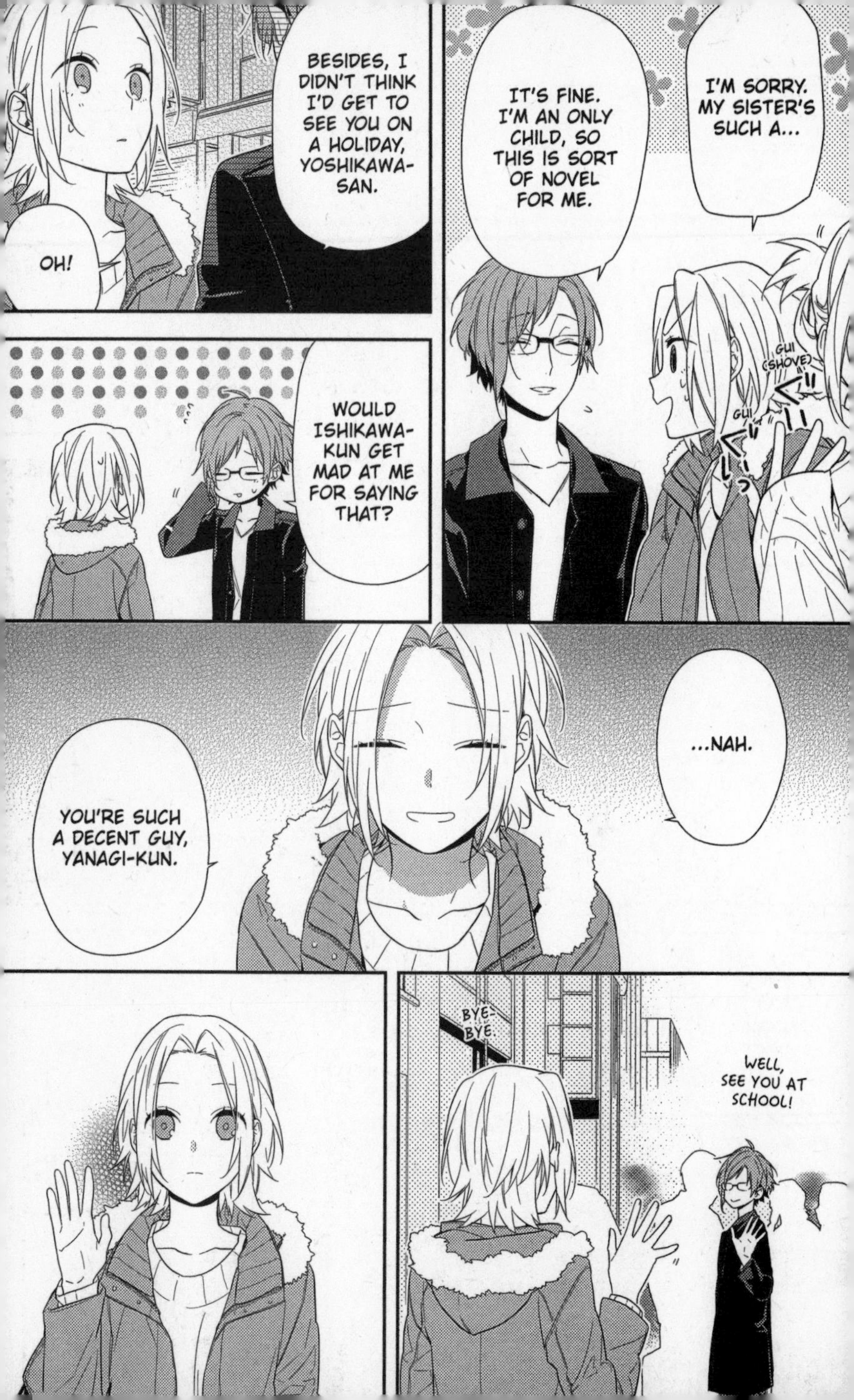
I'M SORRY. MY SISTER'S SUCH A...
IT'S FINE. I'M AN ONLY CHILD, SO THIS IS SORT OF NOVEL FOR ME.
GUI (SHOVE)
GUI
BESIDES, I DIDN'T THINK I'D GET TO SEE YOU ON A HOLIDAY, YOSHIKAWA-SAN.
OH!
WOULD ISHIKAWA-KUN GET MAD AT ME FOR SAYING THAT?
...NAH.
YOU'RE SUCH A DECENT GUY, YANAGI-KUN.
WELL, SEE YOU AT SCHOOL!
BYE-BYE

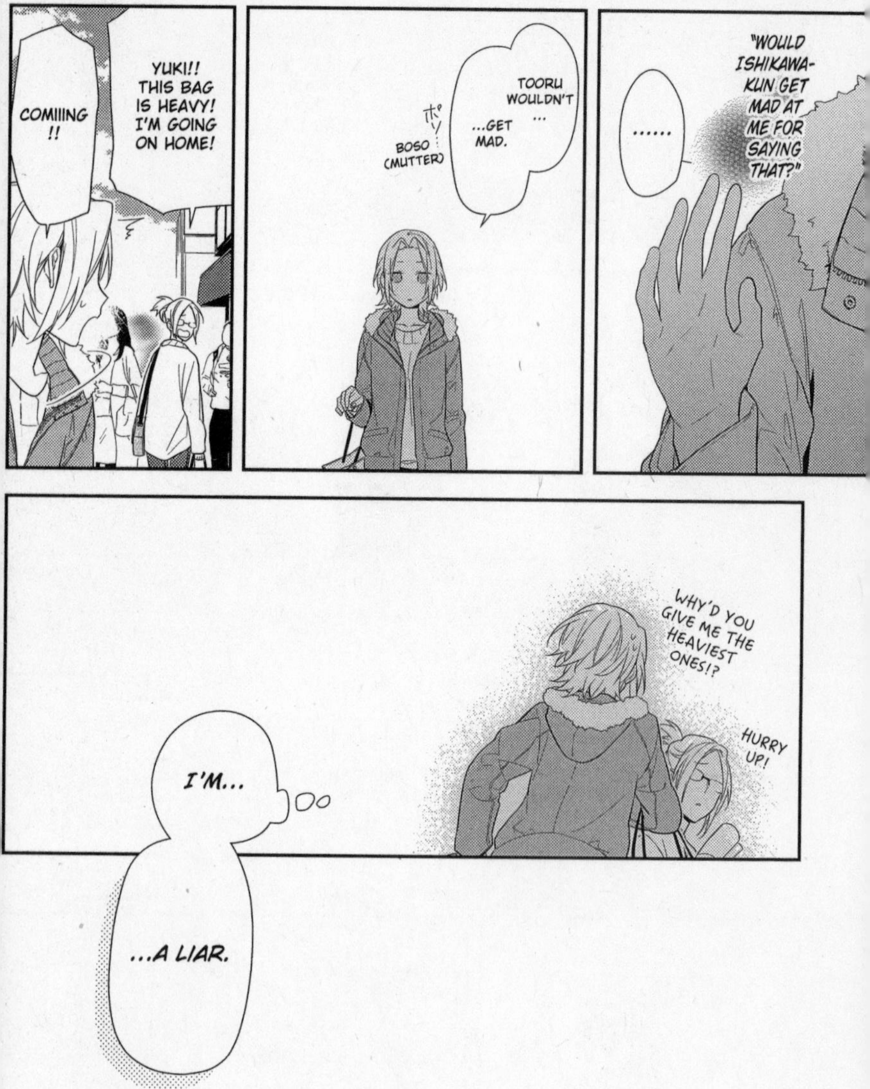
"WOULD ISHIKAWA-KUN GET MAD AT ME FOR SAYING THAT?"
......
TOORU WOULDN'T ...
...GET MAD.
ポソ
BOSO (MUTTER)
YUKI!! THIS BAG IS HEAVY! I'M GOING ON HOME!
COMIIING!!
WHY'D YOU GIVE ME THE HEAVIEST ONES!?
HURRY UP!
I'M...
...A LIAR.

Page·58

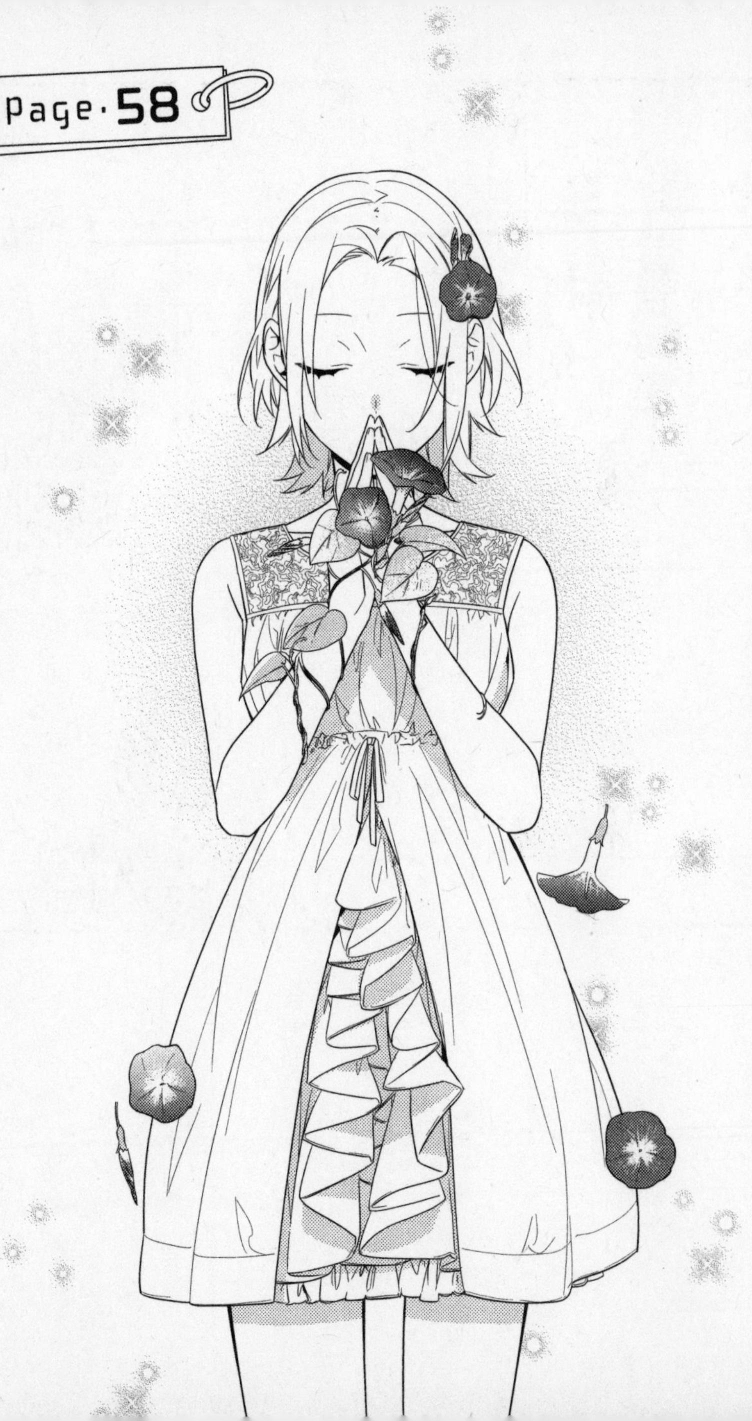

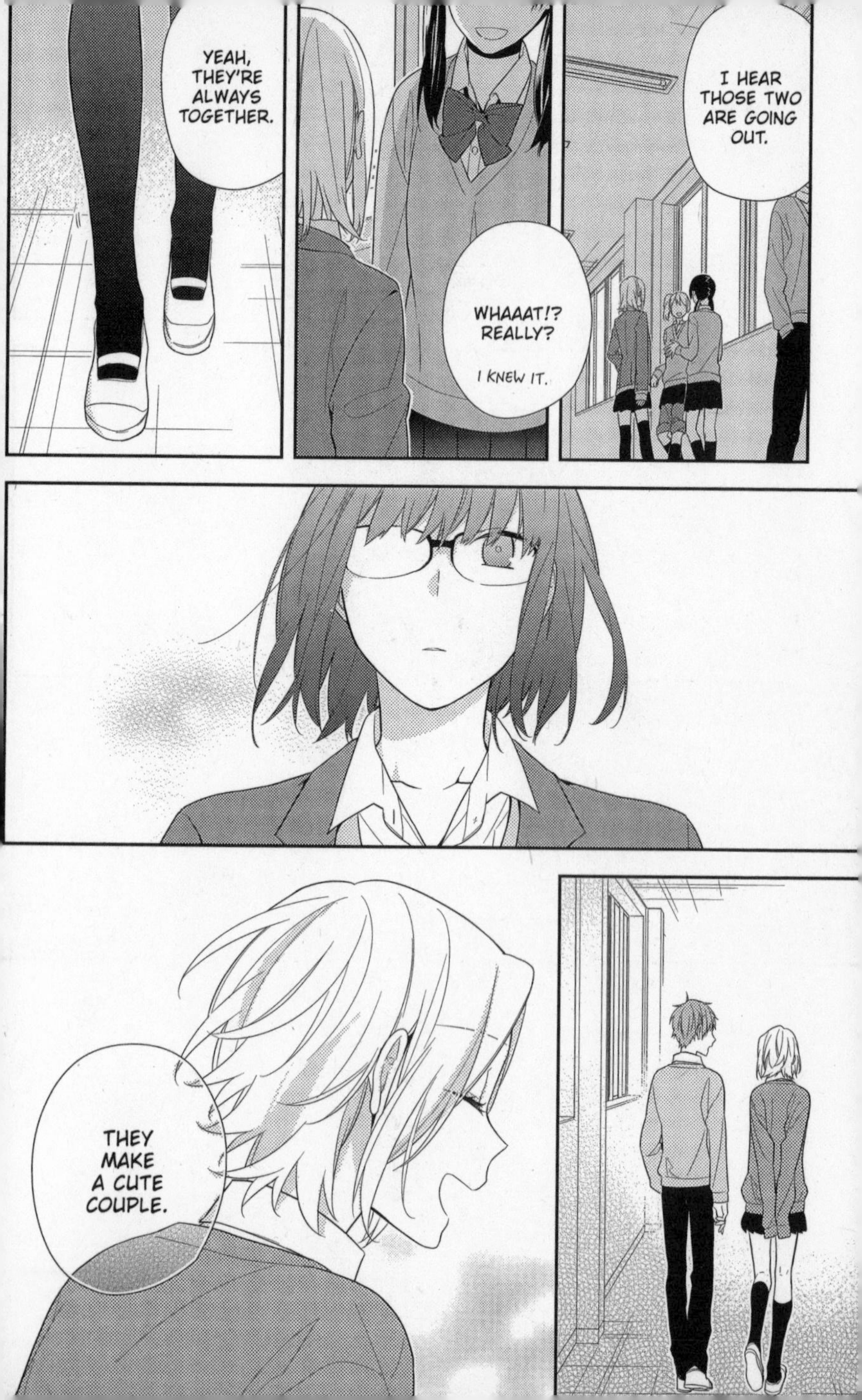
I HEAR THOSE TWO ARE GOING OUT.
WHAAAT!? REALLY?
I KNEW IT.
YEAH, THEY'RE ALWAYS TOGETHER.
THEY MAKE A CUTE COUPLE.

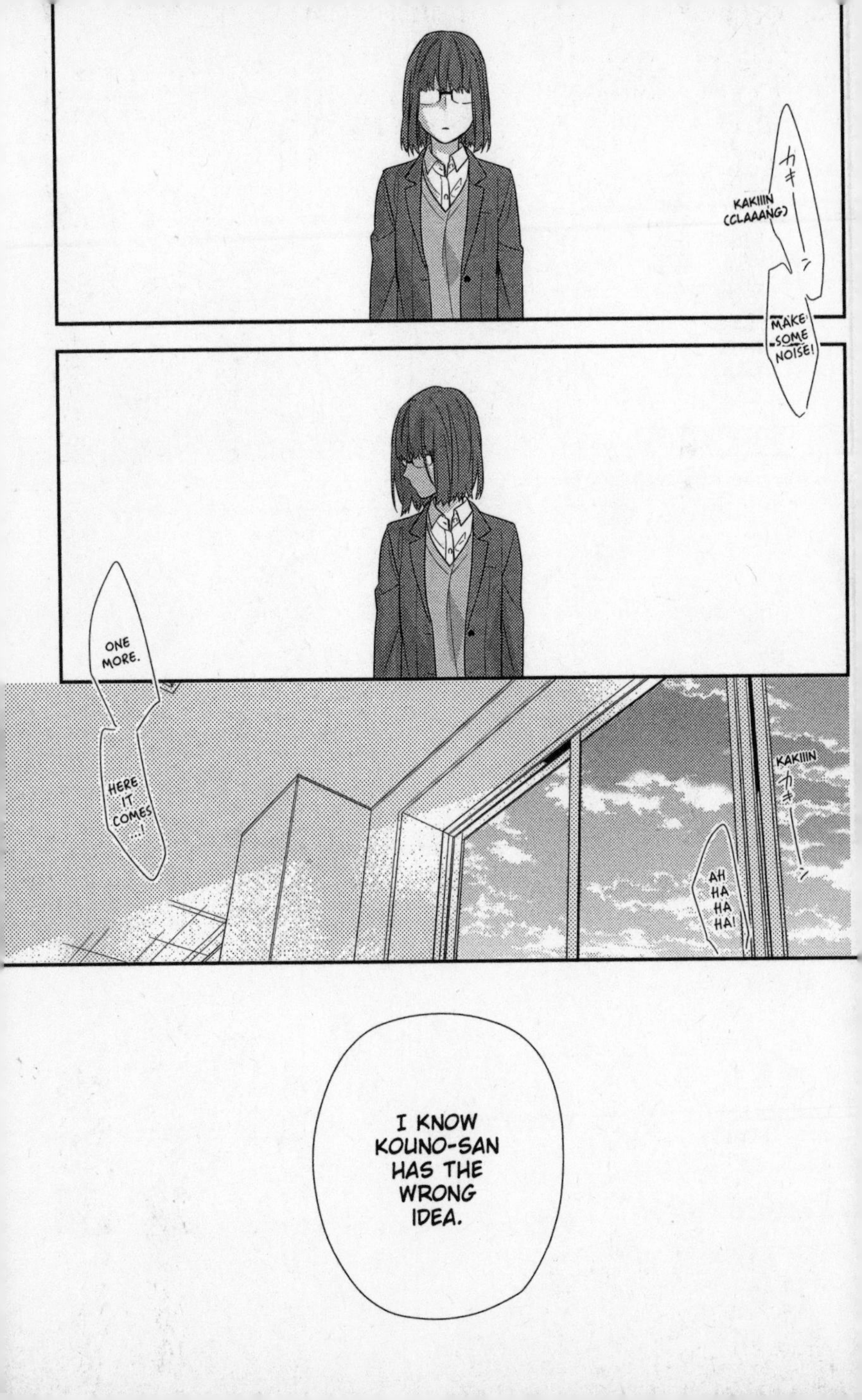
KAKIIIN (CLAAANG)
カキーン
MAKE SOME NOISE!
ONE MORE.
KAKIIIN
カキーン
AH HA HA HA!
HERE IT COMES...!
I KNOW KOUNO-SAN HAS THE WRONG IDEA.

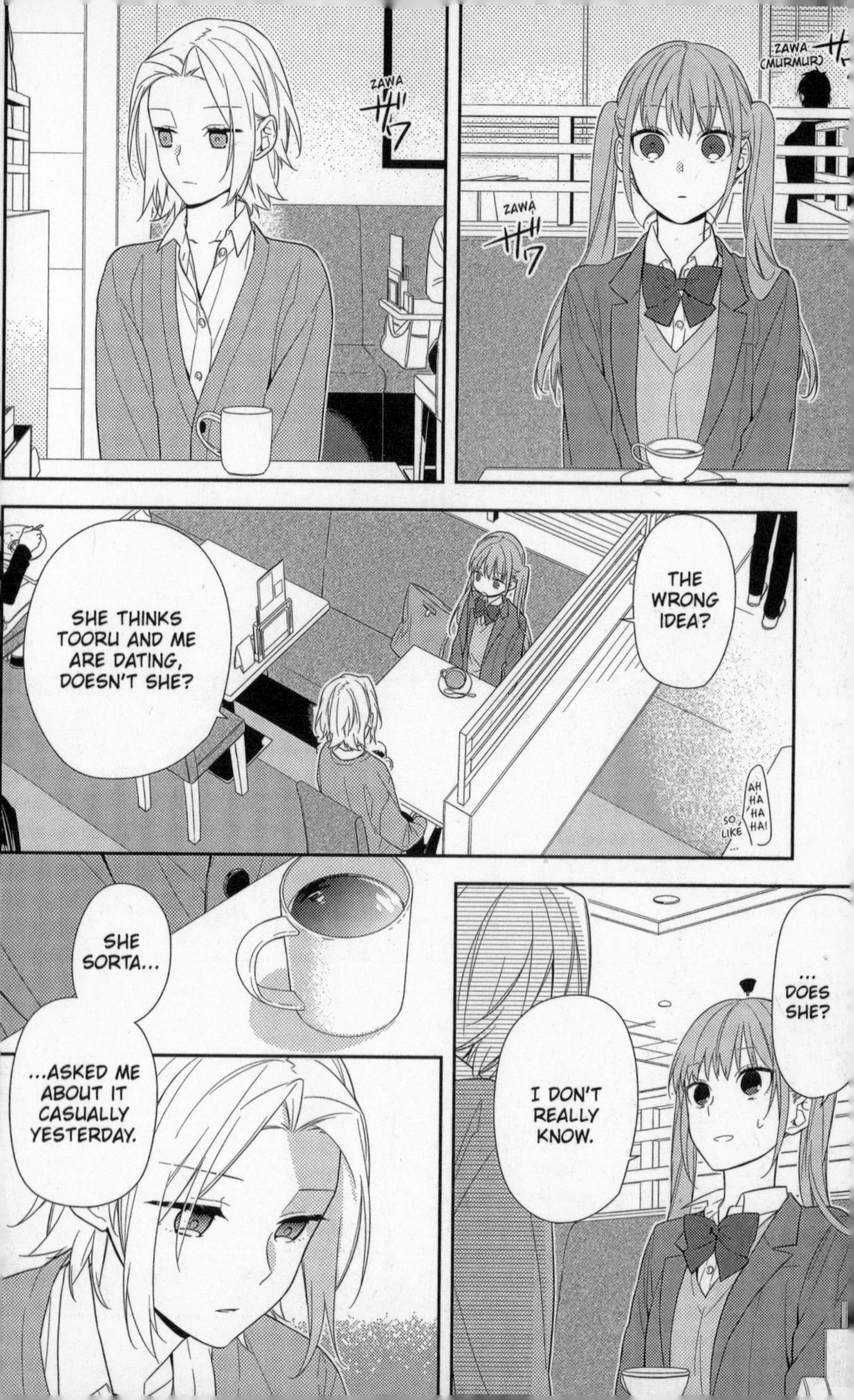

ZAWA (MURMUR)
ザワ
ZAWA
ザワ
ZAWA
ザワ
THE WRONG IDEA?
AH HA HA HA!
SO, LIKE ...
SHE THINKS TOORU AND ME ARE DATING, DOESN'T SHE?
... DOES SHE?
I DON'T REALLY KNOW.
SHE SORTA...
...ASKED ME ABOUT IT CASUALLY YESTERDAY.

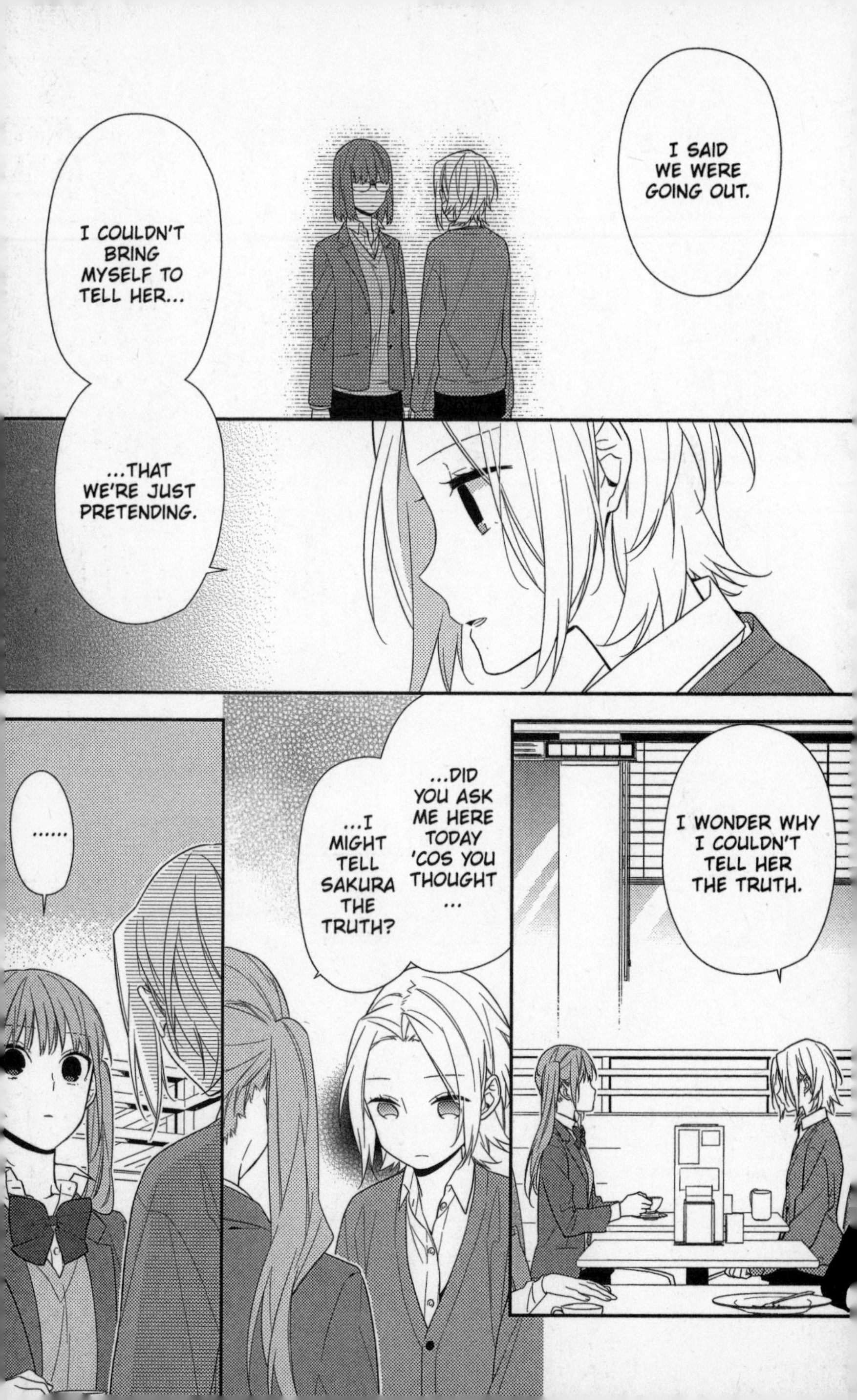
I SAID WE WERE GOING OUT.
I COULDN'T BRING MYSELF TO TELL HER...
...THAT WE'RE JUST PRETENDING.
I WONDER WHY I COULDN'T TELL HER THE TRUTH.
...DID YOU ASK ME HERE TODAY 'COS YOU THOUGHT ...
...I MIGHT TELL SAKURA THE TRUTH?
......

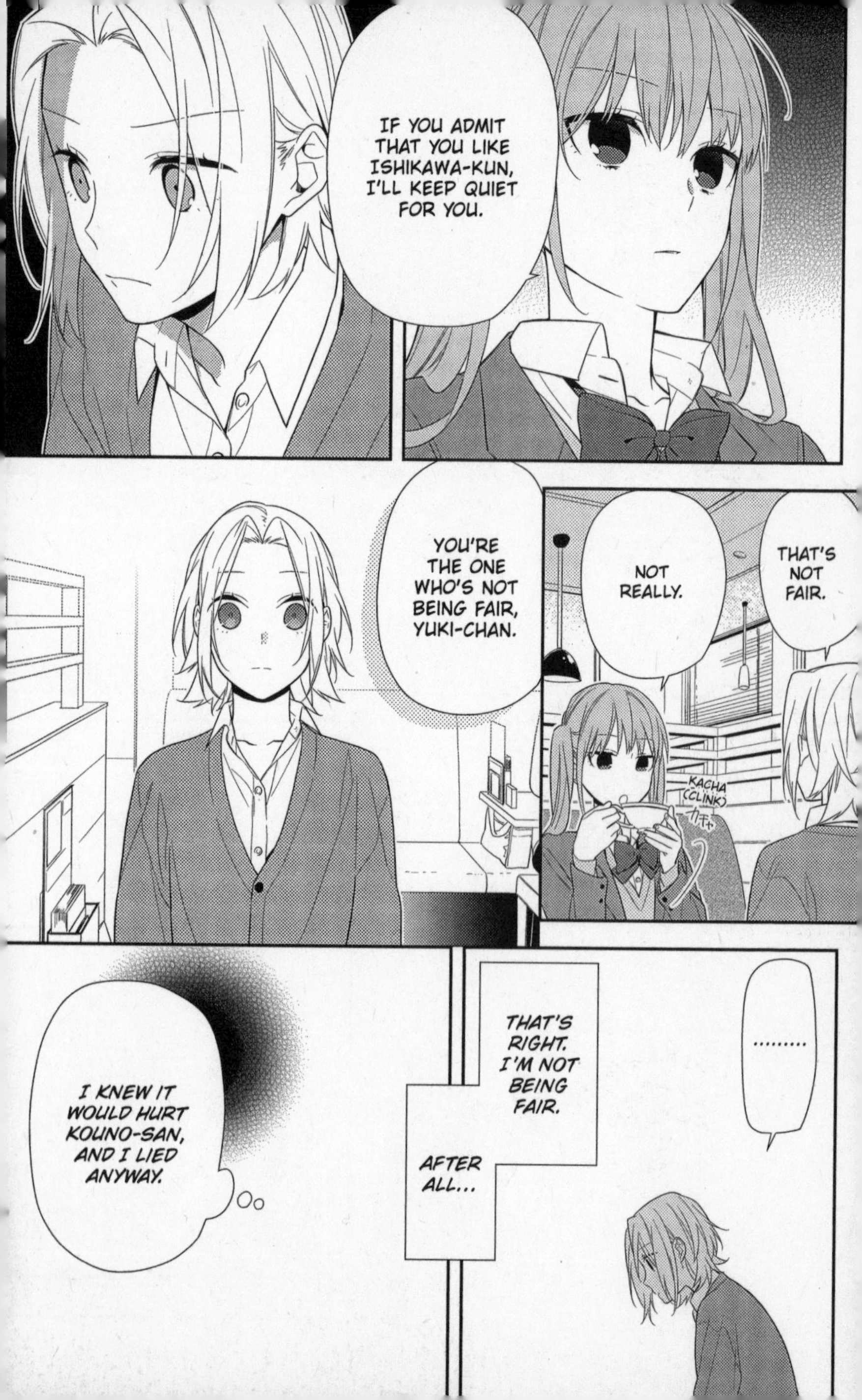
IF YOU ADMIT THAT YOU LIKE ISHIKAWA-KUN, I'LL KEEP QUIET FOR YOU.
THAT'S NOT FAIR.
NOT REALLY.
KACHA (CLINK)
カチャ
YOU'RE THE ONE WHO'S NOT BEING FAIR, YUKI-CHAN.
....
THAT'S RIGHT. I'M NOT BEING FAIR.
AFTER ALL...
I KNEW IT WOULD HURT KOUNO-SAN, AND I LIED ANYWAY.

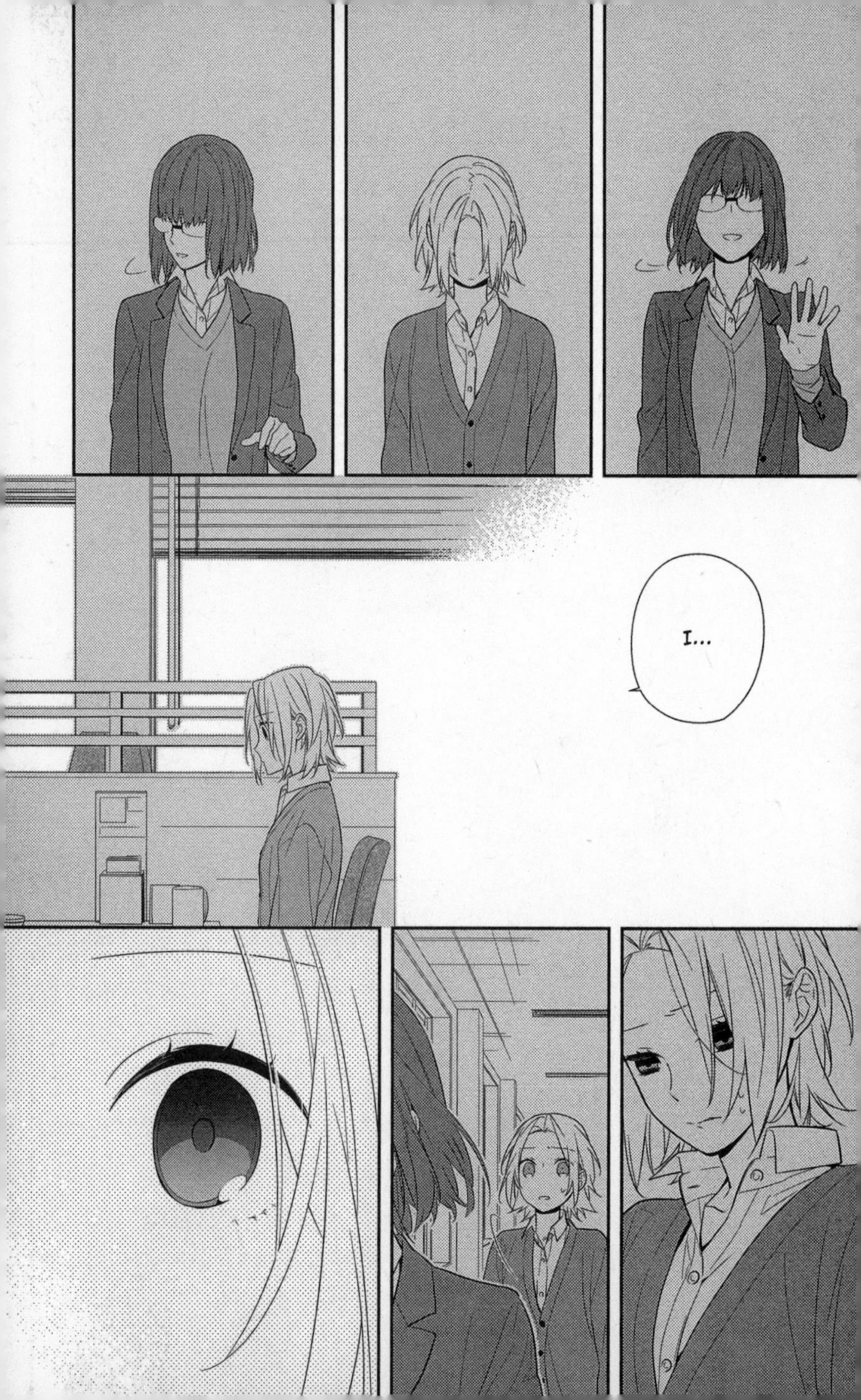
I...

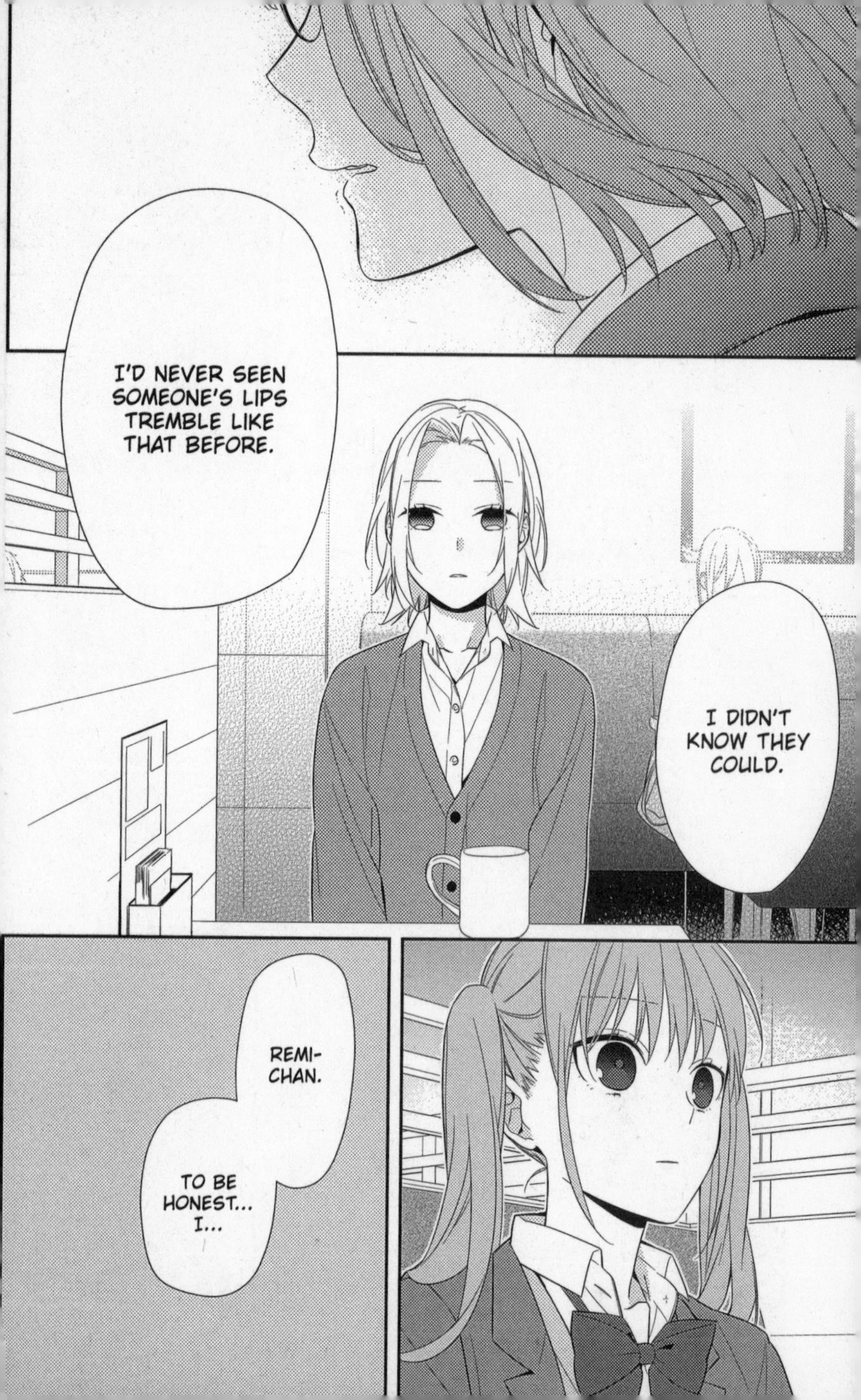
I'D NEVER SEEN SOMEONE'S LIPS TREMBLE LIKE THAT BEFORE.
I DIDN'T KNOW THEY COULD.
REMI-CHAN.
TO BE HONEST... I...

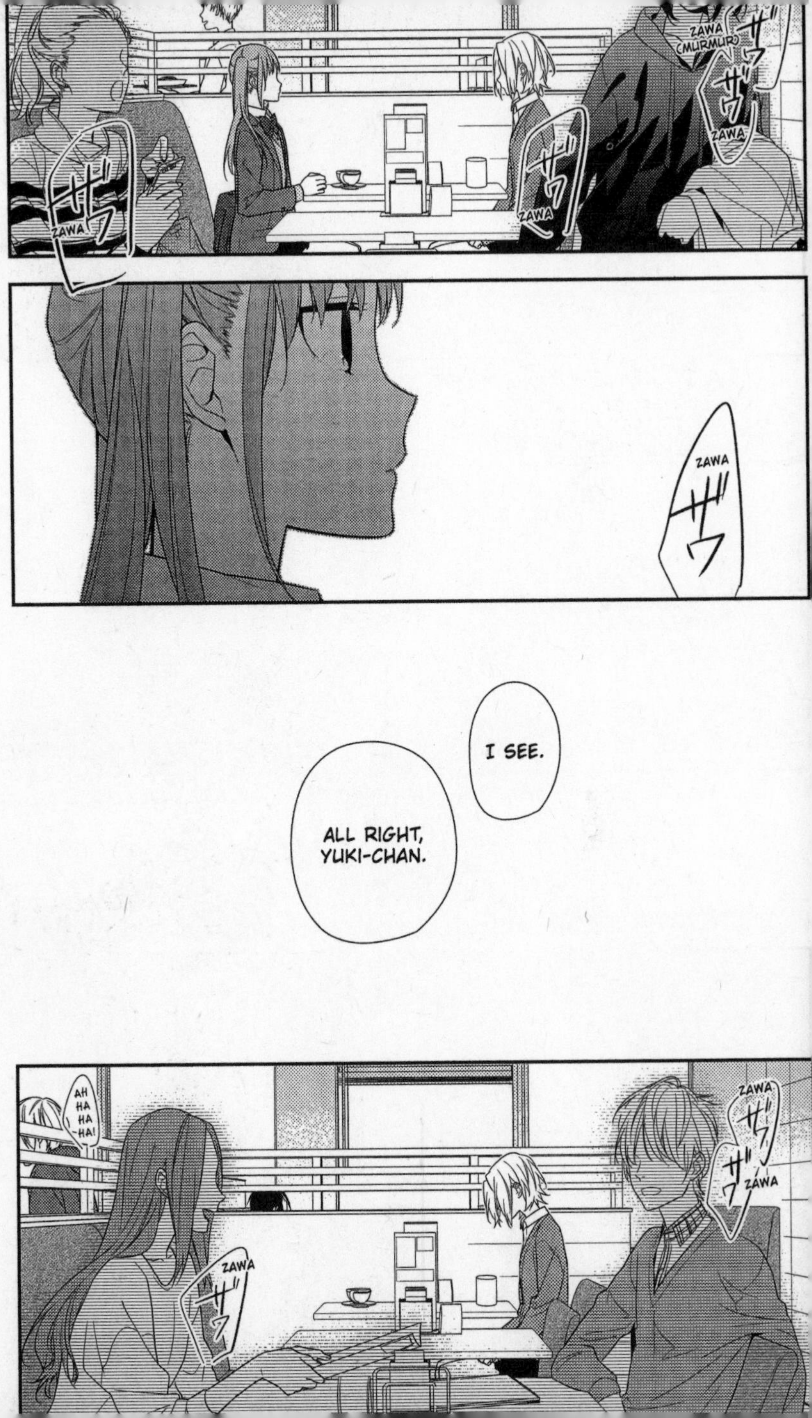

ZAWA (MURMUR)
ザワ
ザワ
ZAWA
ザワ
ZAWA
ザワ
ZAWA
ZAWA
ザワ
I SEE.
ALL RIGHT, YUKI-CHAN.
ZAWA
ザワ
ザワ
ZAWA
AH HA HA HA!
ZAWA
ザワ

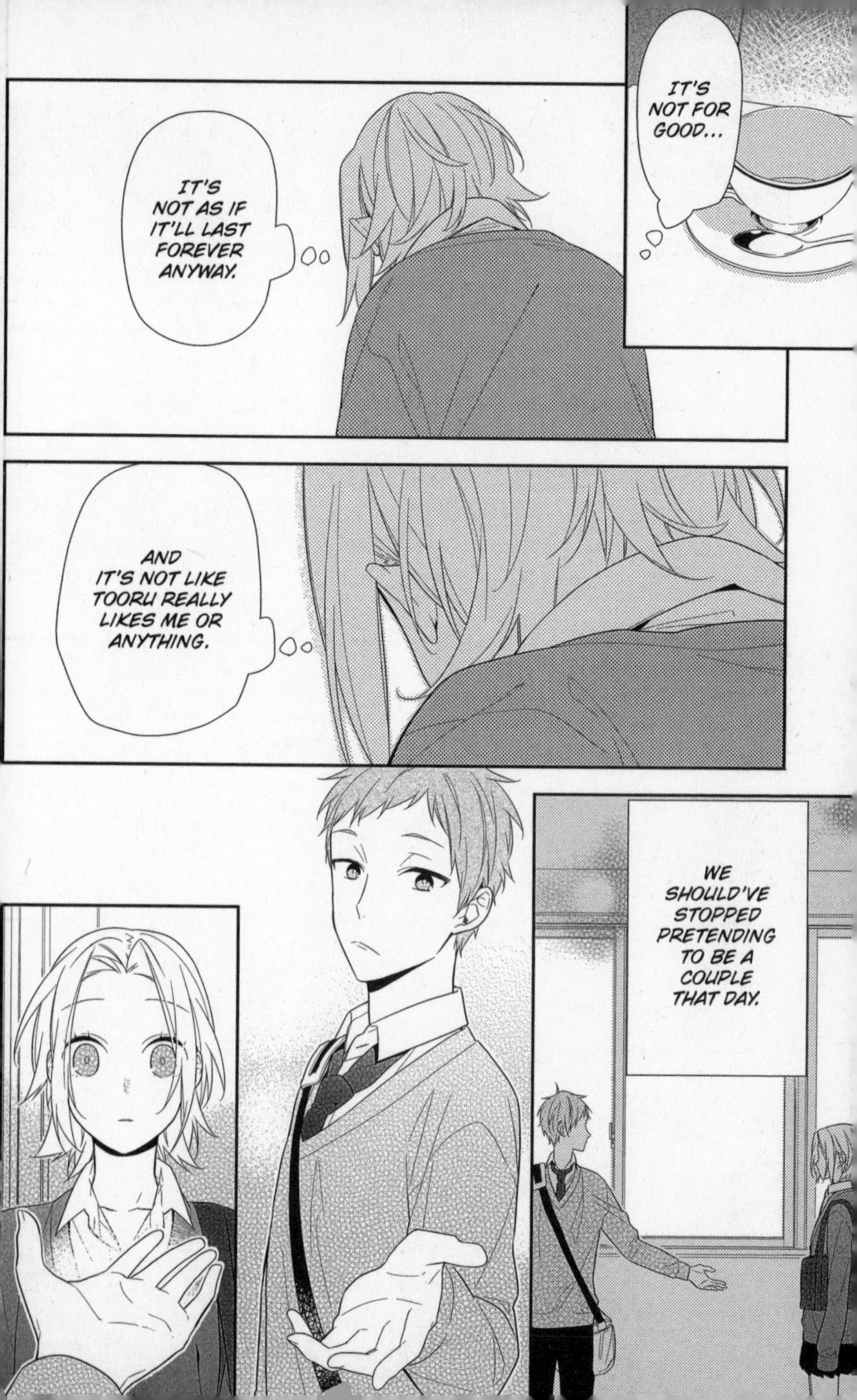
IT'S NOT FOR GOOD...
IT'S NOT AS IF IT'LL LAST FOREVER ANYWAY.
AND IT'S NOT LIKE TOORU REALLY LIKES ME OR ANYTHING.
WE SHOULD'VE STOPPED PRETENDING TO BE A COUPLE THAT DAY.

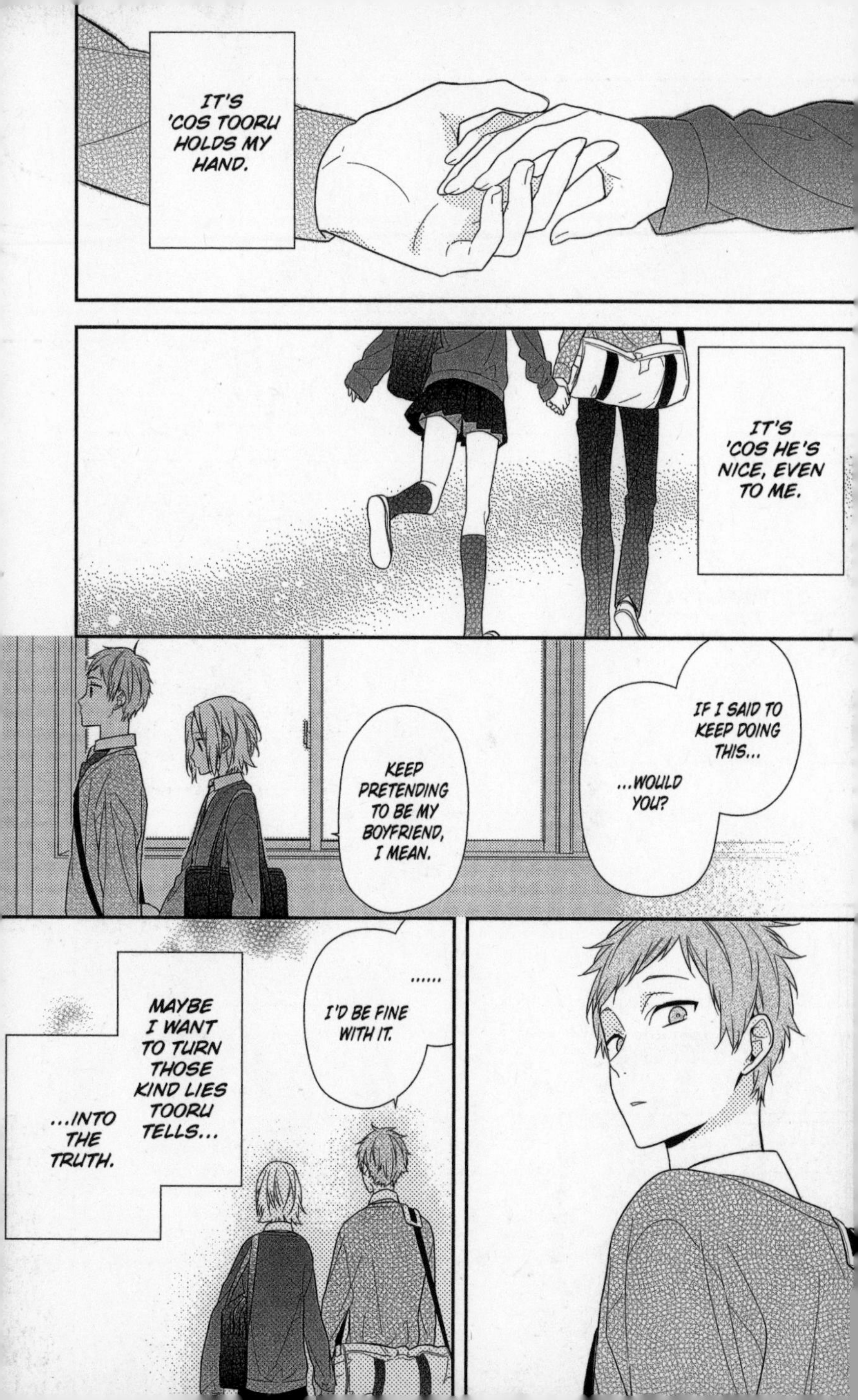
IT'S 'COS TOORU HOLDS MY HAND.
IT'S 'COS HE'S NICE, EVEN TO ME.
IF I SAID TO KEEP DOING THIS...
...WOULD YOU?
KEEP PRETENDING TO BE MY BOYFRIEND, I MEAN.
......
I'D BE FINE WITH IT.
MAYBE I WANT TO TURN THOSE KIND LIES TOORU TELLS...
...INTO THE TRUTH.

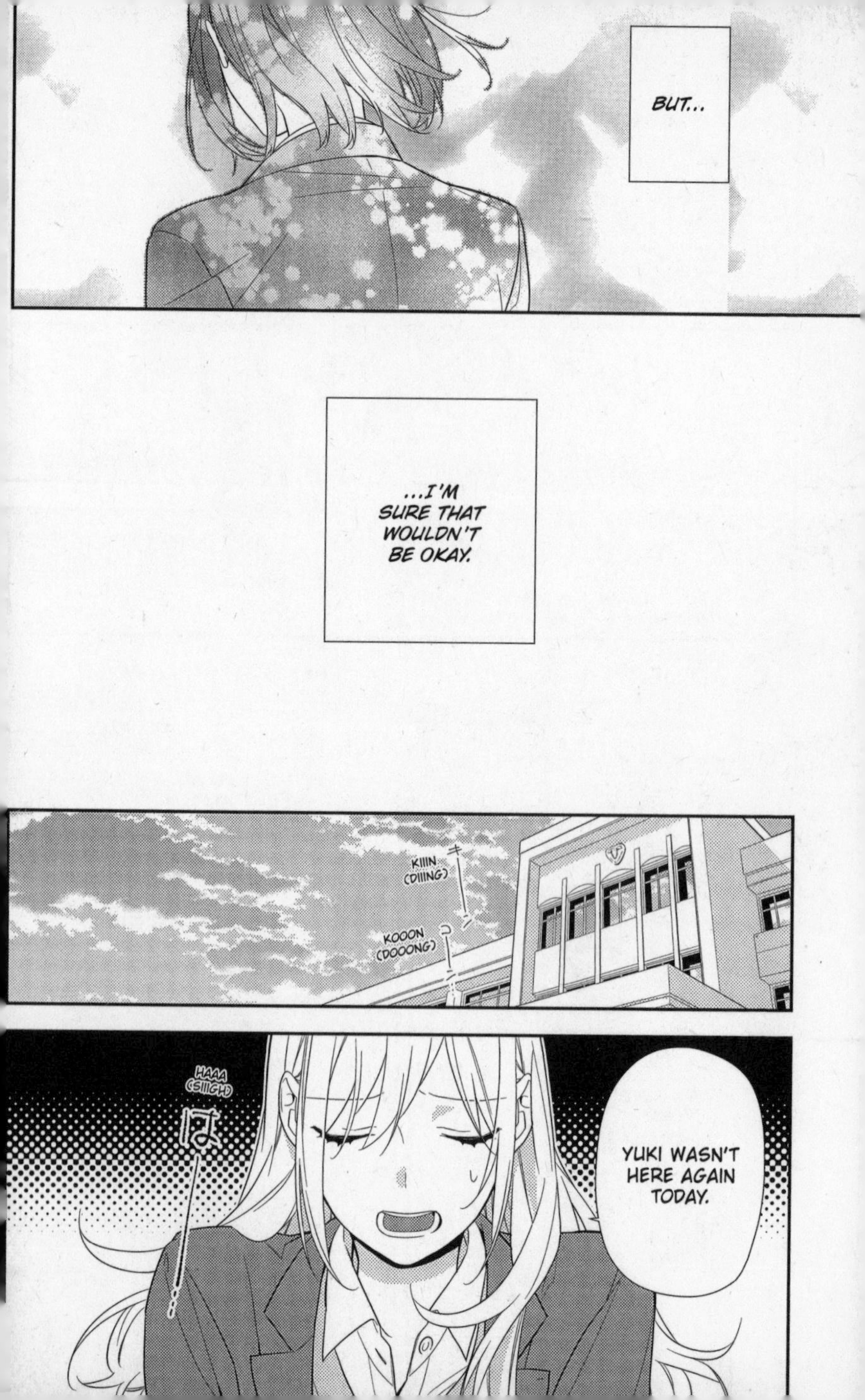

BUT...
...I'M SURE THAT WOULDN'T BE OKAY.
KIIN (DIIING)
KOOON (DOOONG)
HAAA (SIIIGH)
YUKI WASN'T HERE AGAIN TODAY.

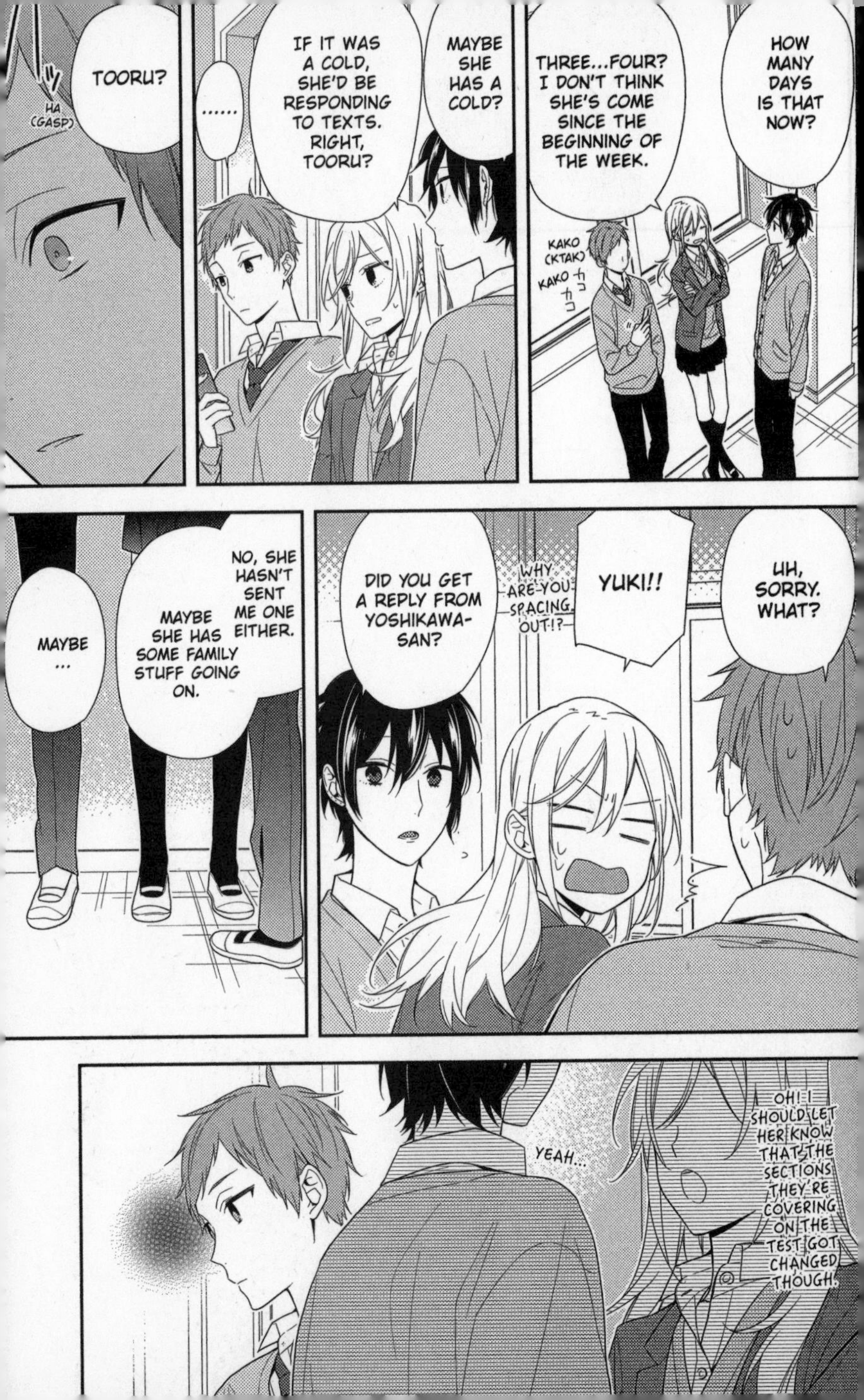
HOW MANY DAYS IS THAT NOW?
THREE...FOUR? I DON'T THINK SHE'S COME SINCE THE BEGINNING OF THE WEEK.
KAKO (KTAK) KAKO
カコ カコ
MAYBE SHE HAS A COLD?
IF IT WAS A COLD, SHE'D BE RESPONDING TO TEXTS. RIGHT, TOORU?
......
ハッ
HA (GASP)
TOORU?
UH, SORRY. WHAT?
YUKI!!
WHY ARE YOU SPACING OUT!?
DID YOU GET A REPLY FROM YOSHIKAWA-SAN?
NO, SHE HASN'T SENT ME ONE EITHER.
MAYBE SHE HAS SOME FAMILY STUFF GOING ON.
MAYBE...
OH! I SHOULD LET HER KNOW THAT THE SECTIONS THEY'RE COVERING ON THE TEST GOT CHANGED THOUGH.
YEAH...

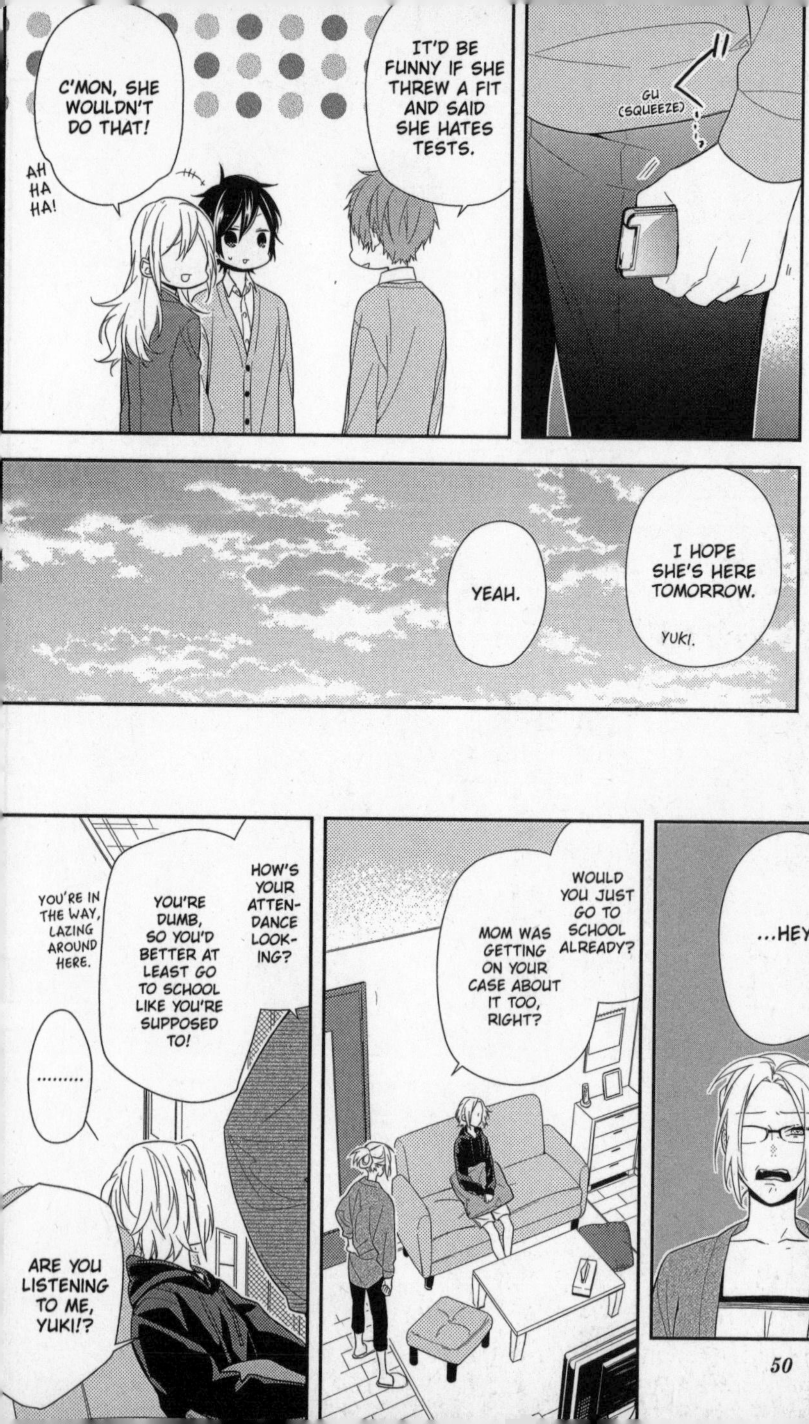
GU (SQUEEZE)
IT'D BE FUNNY IF SHE THREW A FIT AND SAID SHE HATES TESTS.
C'MON, SHE WOULDN'T DO THAT!
AH HA HA!
I HOPE SHE'S HERE TOMORROW.
YUKI.
YEAH.
...HEY.
WOULD YOU JUST GO TO SCHOOL ALREADY?
MOM WAS GETTING ON YOUR CASE ABOUT IT TOO, RIGHT?
HOW'S YOUR ATTEN-DANCE LOOK-ING?
YOU'RE DUMB, SO YOU'D BETTER AT LEAST GO TO SCHOOL LIKE YOU'RE SUPPOSED TO!
YOU'RE IN THE WAY, LAZING AROUND HERE.
....
ARE YOU LISTENING TO ME, YUKI!?

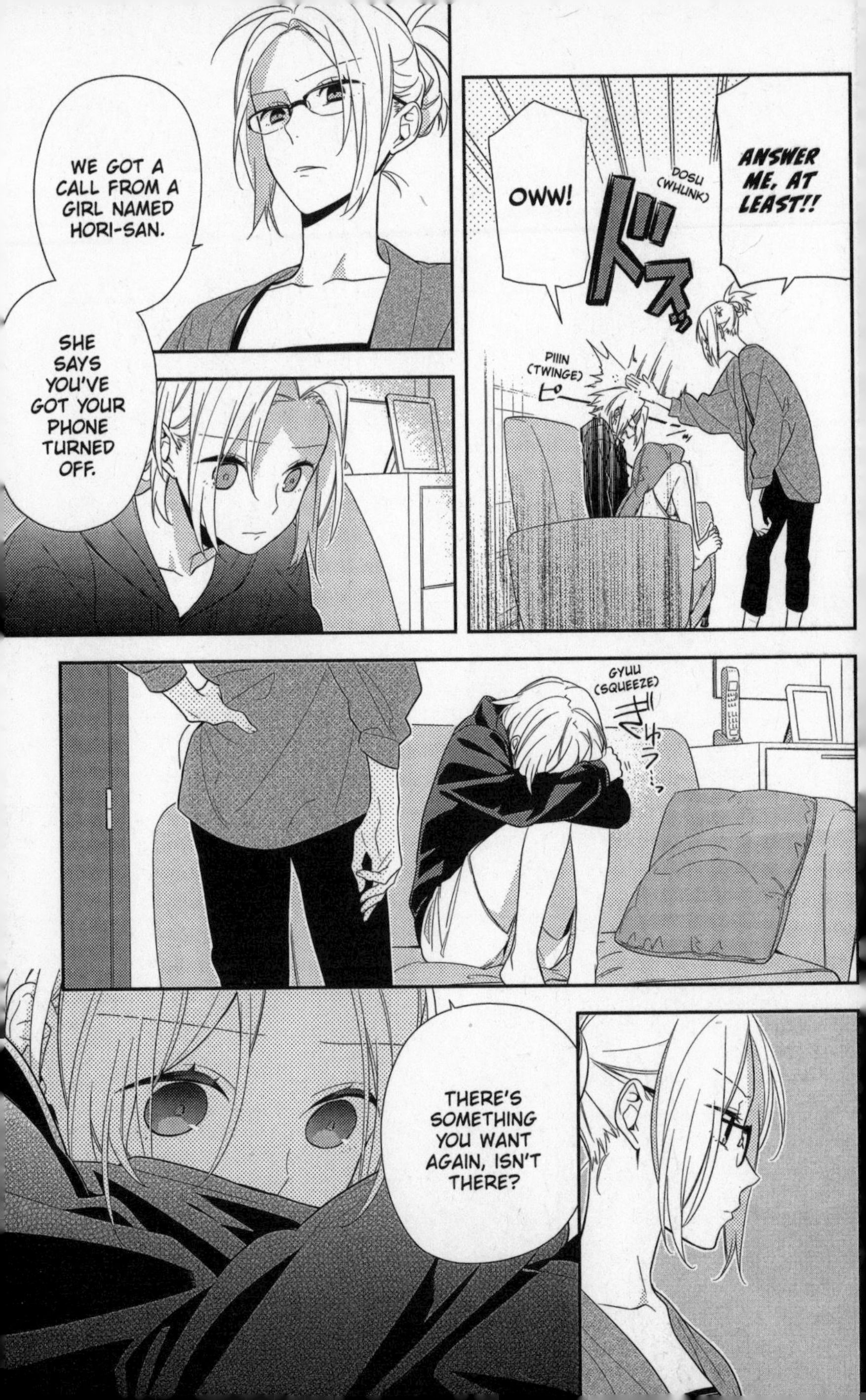
WE GOT A CALL FROM A GIRL NAMED HORI-SAN.
SHE SAYS YOU'VE GOT YOUR PHONE TURNED OFF.
ANSWER ME, AT LEAST!!
DOSU (WHUNK)
OWW!
PIIIN (TWINGE)
GYUU (SQUEEZE)
THERE'S SOMETHING YOU WANT AGAIN, ISN'T THERE?

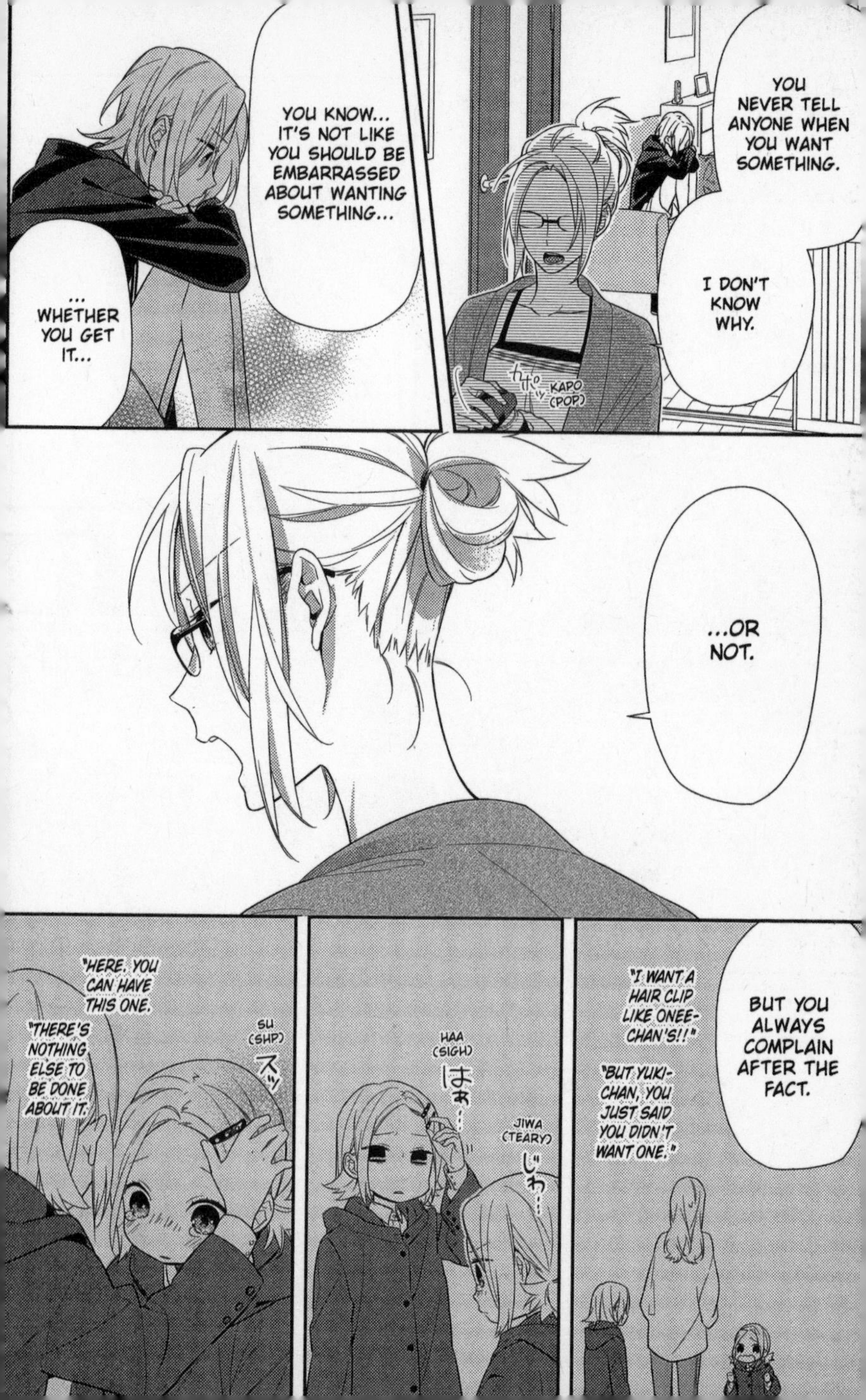
YOU NEVER TELL ANYONE WHEN YOU WANT SOMETHING.
I DON'T KNOW WHY.
カポッ KAPO (POP)
YOU KNOW... IT'S NOT LIKE YOU SHOULD BE EMBARRASSED ABOUT WANTING SOMETHING...
...WHETHER YOU GET IT...
...OR NOT.
BUT YOU ALWAYS COMPLAIN AFTER THE FACT.
"I WANT A HAIR CLIP LIKE ONEE-CHAN'S!!"
"BUT YUKI-CHAN, YOU JUST SAID YOU DIDN'T WANT ONE."
じわ… JIWA (TEARY)
はぁ… HAA (SIGH)
スッ SU (SHP)
"HERE. YOU CAN HAVE THIS ONE.
"THERE'S NOTHING ELSE TO BE DONE ABOUT IT.

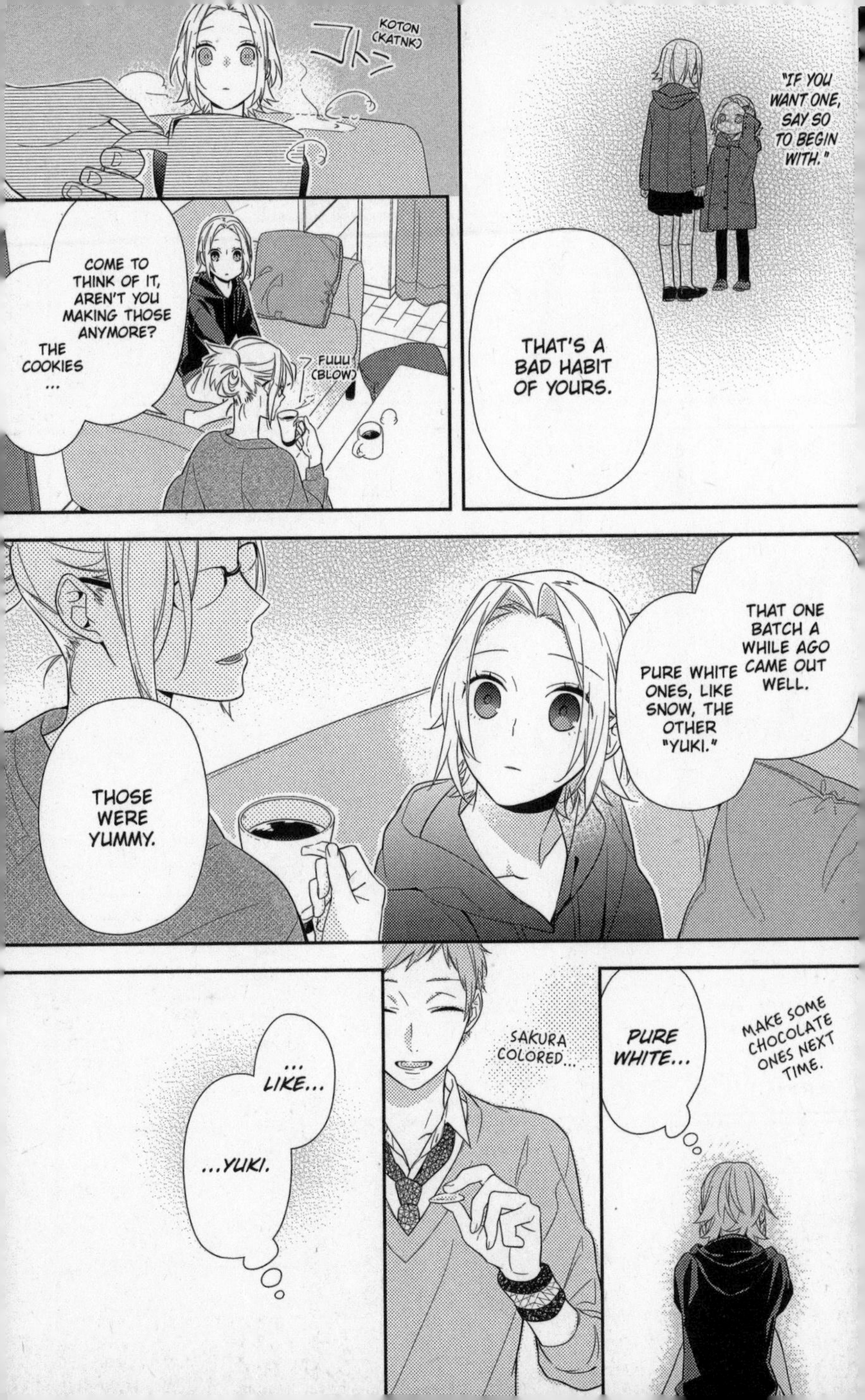
"IF YOU WANT ONE, SAY SO TO BEGIN WITH."
THAT'S A BAD HABIT OF YOURS.
KOTON (KATNK)
COME TO THINK OF IT, AREN'T YOU MAKING THOSE ANYMORE?
THE COOKIES ...
FUUU (BLOW)
THAT ONE BATCH A WHILE AGO CAME OUT WELL.
PURE WHITE ONES, LIKE SNOW, THE OTHER "YUKI."
THOSE WERE YUMMY.
MAKE SOME CHOCOLATE ONES NEXT TIME.
PURE WHITE...
SAKURA COLORED...
... LIKE...
...YUKI.

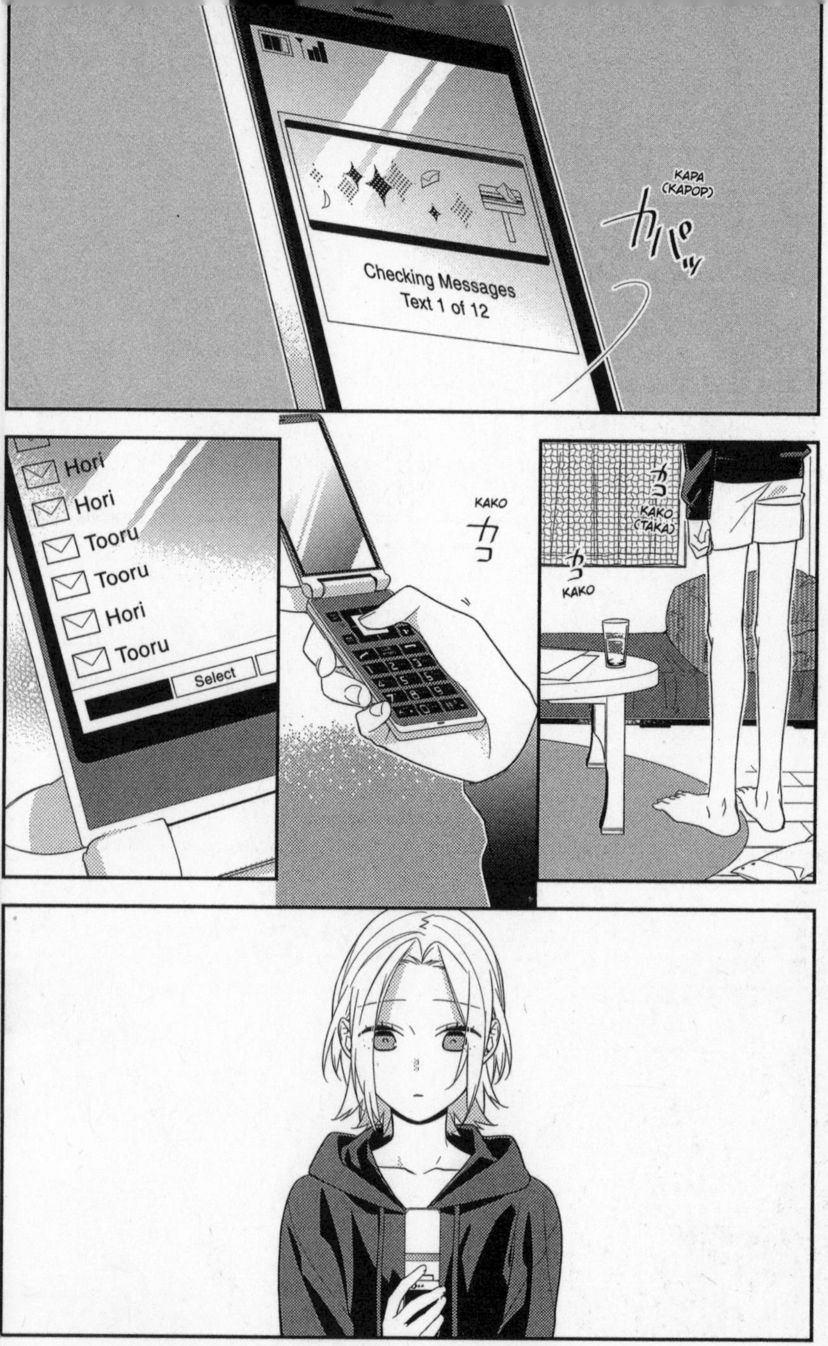
Checking Messages
Text 1 of 12
カパッ
KAPA (KAPOP)
カコ
KAKO (TAKA)
カコ
KAKO
カコ
KAKO
Hori
Hori
Tooru
Tooru
Hori
Tooru
Select

...and got now... ...mura today, but the ...me out a little...I thought they might be okay, so I gave some of them to Miyamura, but I didn't think he'd actually eat them, you know!?

| Function | Select |

KAKO カコ

KAKO カコ

New message
From Tooru
Sub.

I sent you a text. Did you get it? You don't pick up when we call, and Hori and everyone are worried. Even if you don't want to ...at home, at least ...now if you're oka

KAKO カコ

...old or somethin

I hope everything's okay. Today was almost all self-study, so you don't have to worry about what we covered in class. If you're nervous, you can look at my notes next time.

...nction | Select | Reply

HEH.

KAKO カコ

CLR MEMO

KAKO カコ

KAKO カコ

KAKO カコ

KAKO カコ

You don't have to... Just show up. Ther... a ton I want to tell y... I'll listen to anythi...

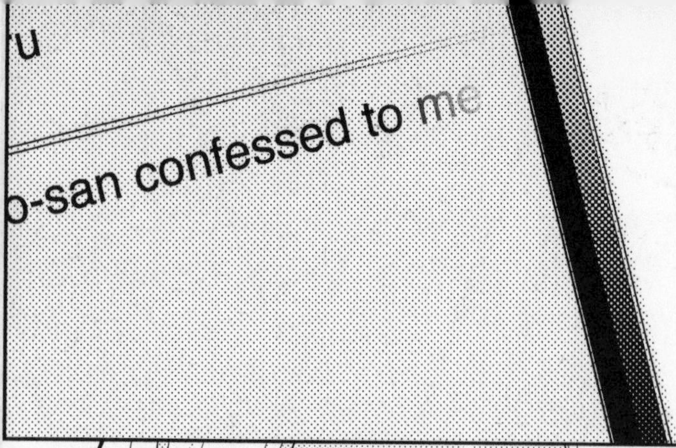
ru
o-san confessed to me

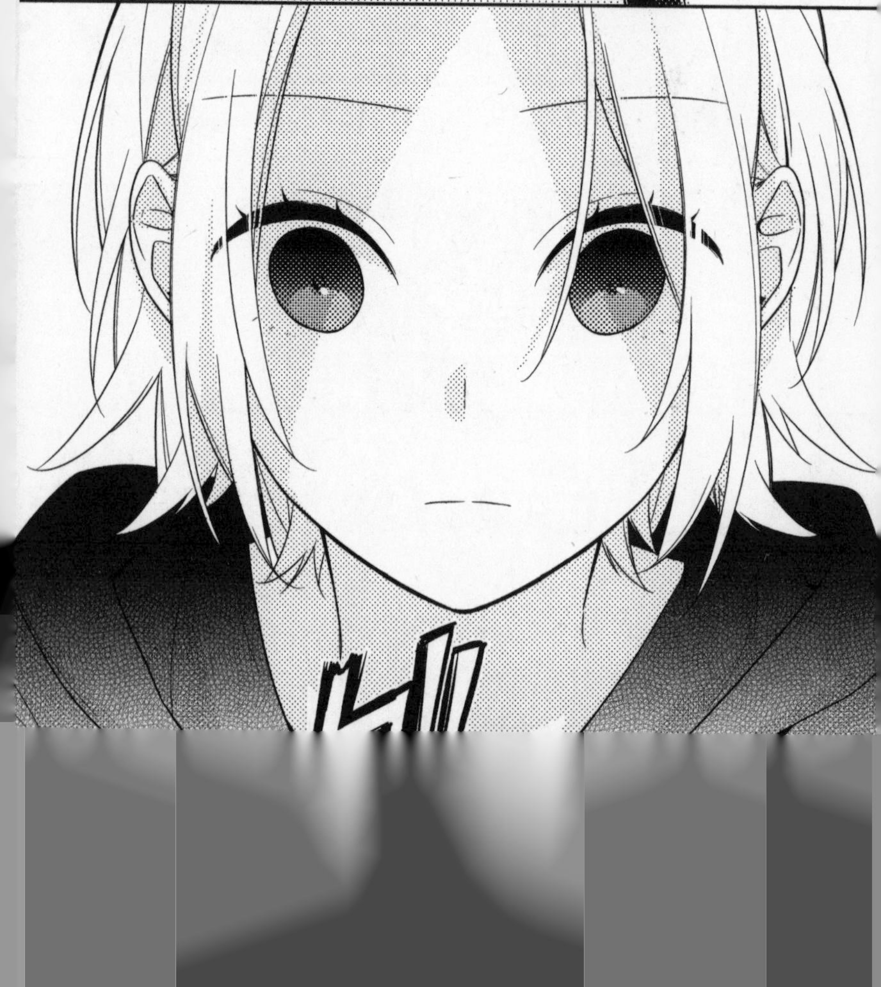

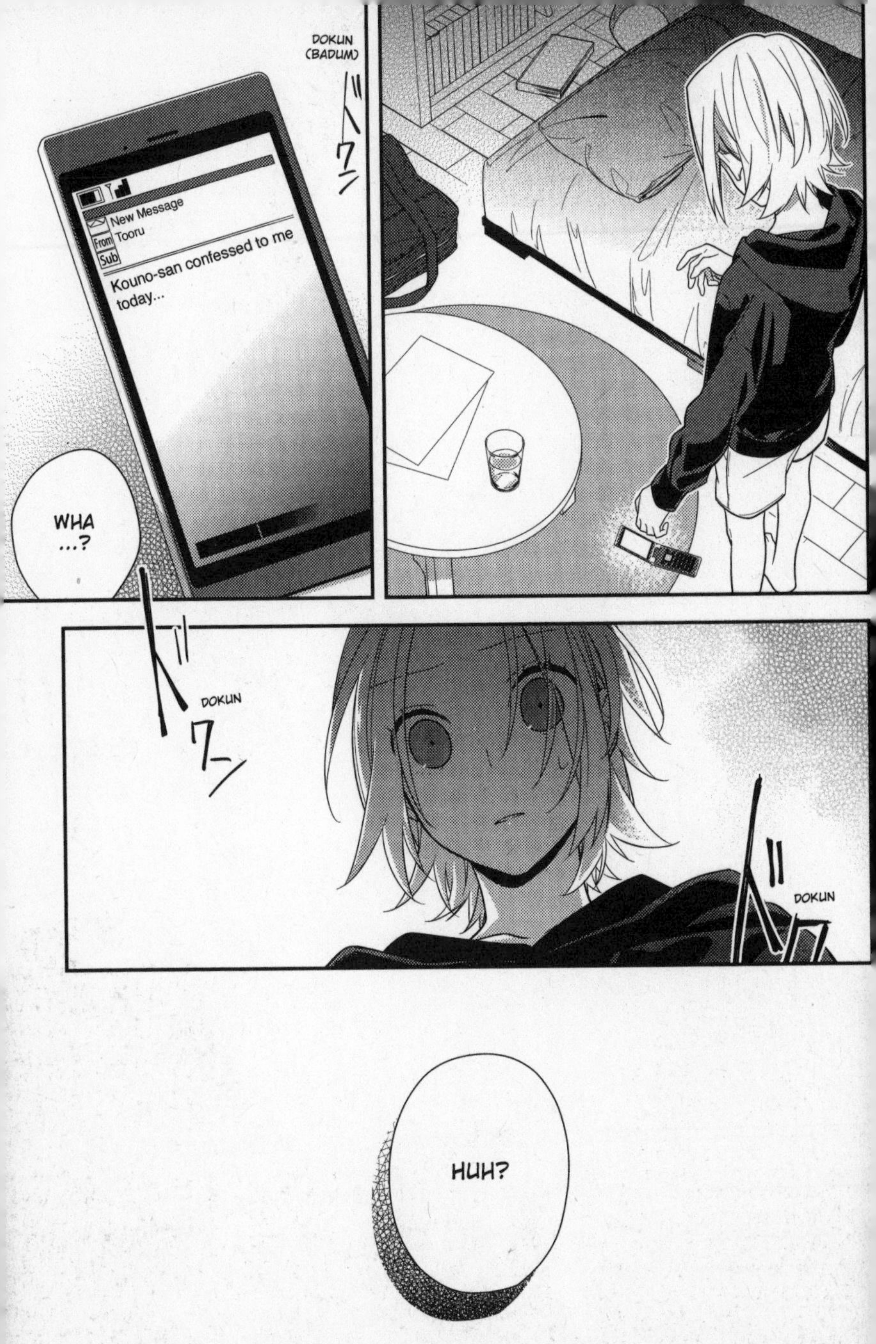
DOKUN (BADUM)
New Message
From Tooru
Sub
Kouno-san confessed to me today...
WHA ...?
DOKUN
DOKUN
HUH?

HORIMIYA

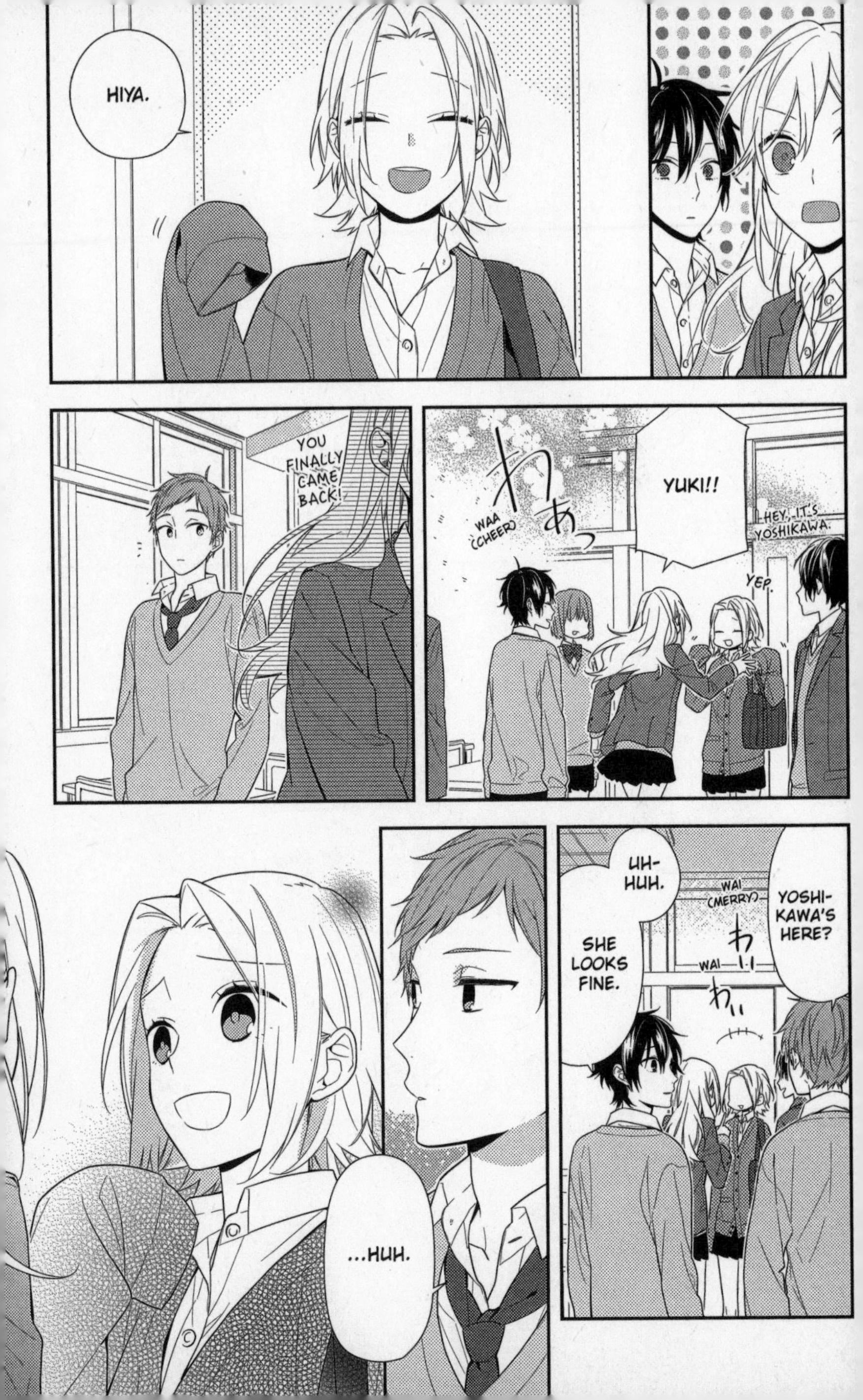
HIYA.
WAA (CHEER)
わあっ
YUKI!!
HEY, IT'S YOSHIKAWA.
YEP.
YOU FINALLY CAME BACK!
YOSHI-KAWA'S HERE?
UH-HUH.
WAI (MERRY)
わ
SHE LOOKS FINE.
WAI
わい
...HUH.

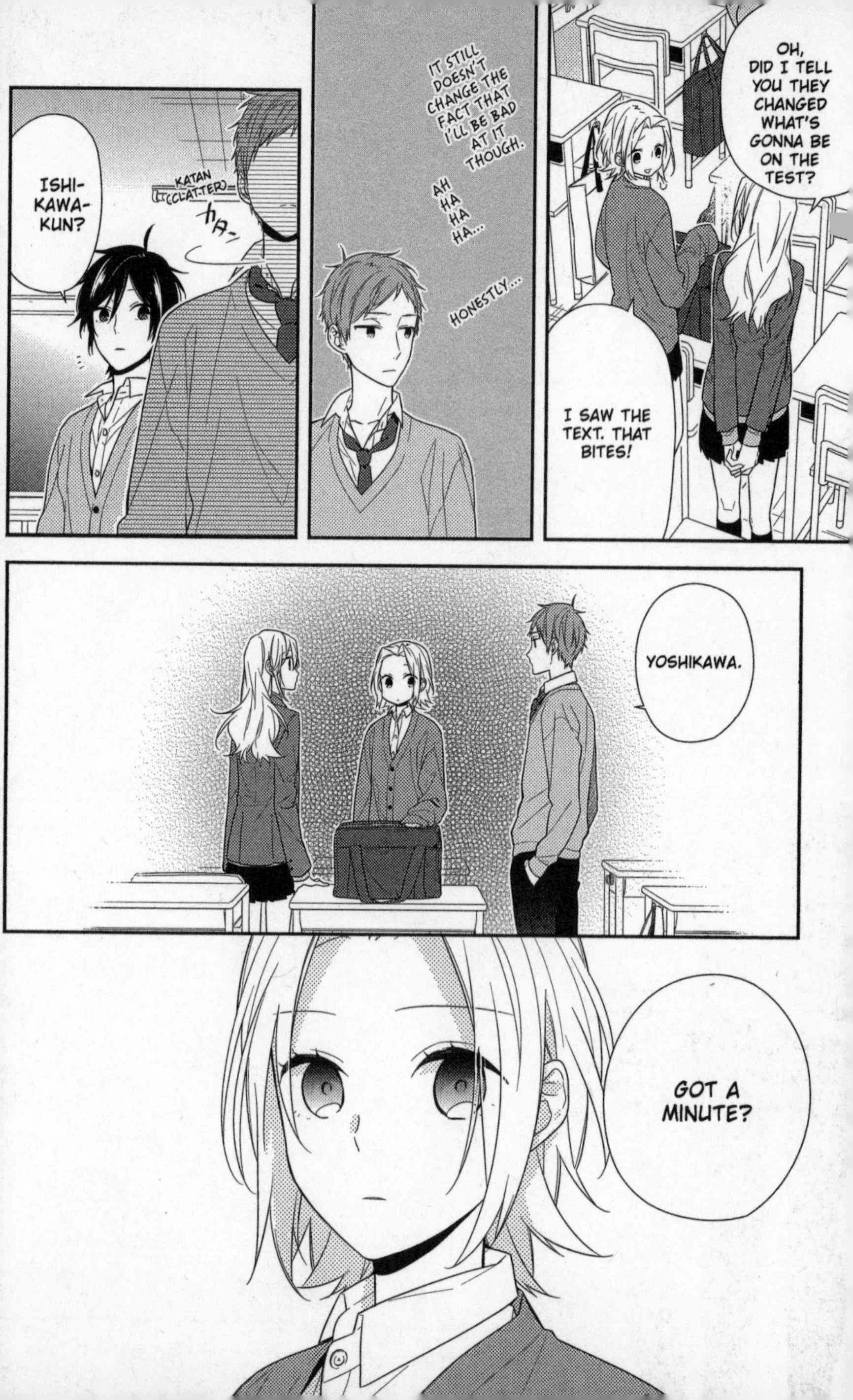
OH, DID I TELL YOU THEY CHANGED WHAT'S GONNA BE ON THE TEST?
I SAW THE TEXT. THAT BITES!
IT STILL DOESN'T CHANGE THE FACT THAT I'LL BE BAD AT IT THOUGH.
AH HA HA HA...
HONESTLY...
KATAN (CLATTER)
ISHI-KAWA-KUN?
YOSHIKAWA.
GOT A MINUTE?

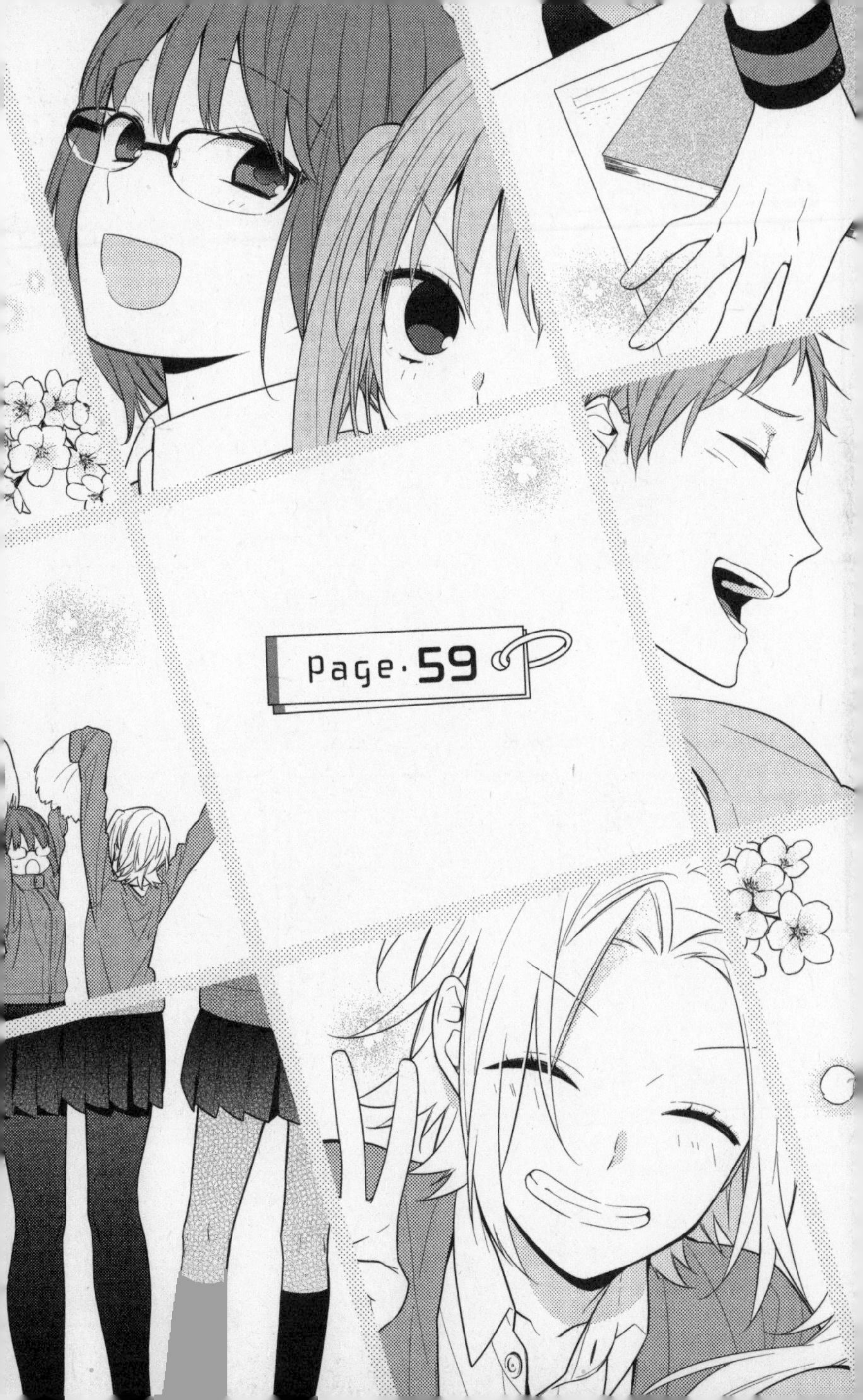
page·59

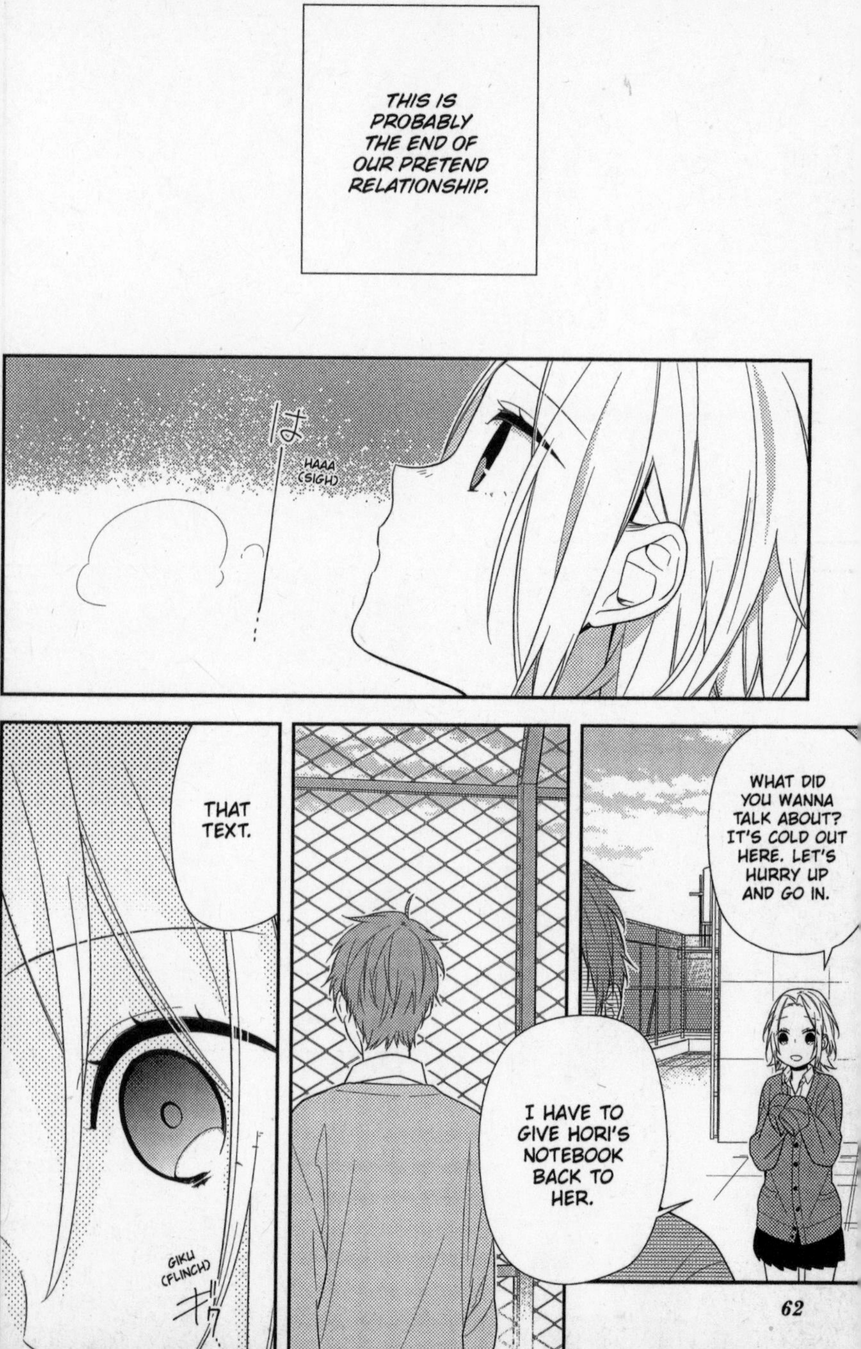
THIS IS PROBABLY THE END OF OUR PRETEND RELATIONSHIP.
は
HAAA (SIGH)
WHAT DID YOU WANNA TALK ABOUT? IT'S COLD OUT HERE. LET'S HURRY UP AND GO IN.
I HAVE TO GIVE HORI'S NOTEBOOK BACK TO HER.
THAT TEXT.
GIKU (FLINCH)
ギク

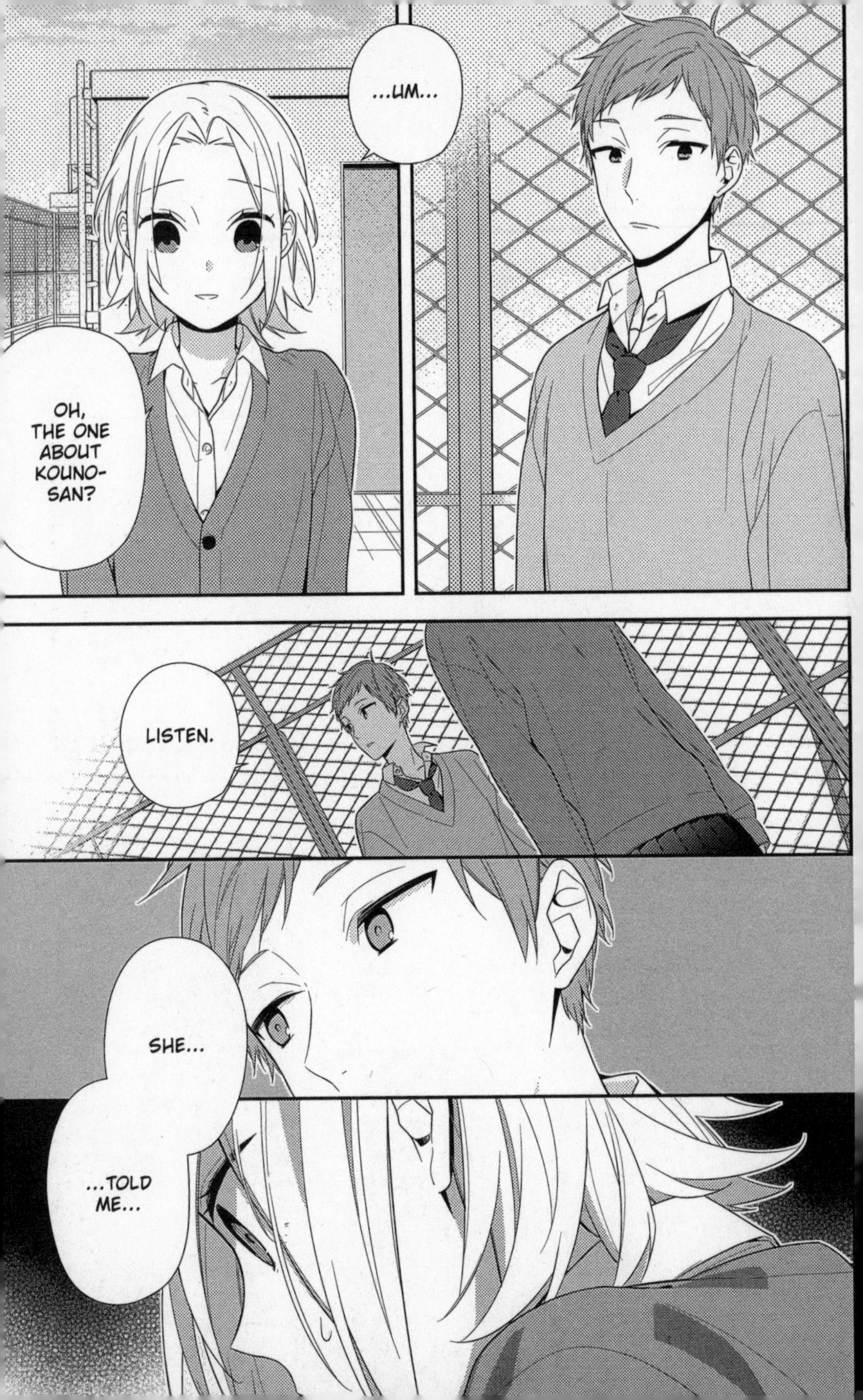
...UM...
OH, THE ONE ABOUT KOUNO-SAN?
LISTEN.
SHE...
...TOLD ME...

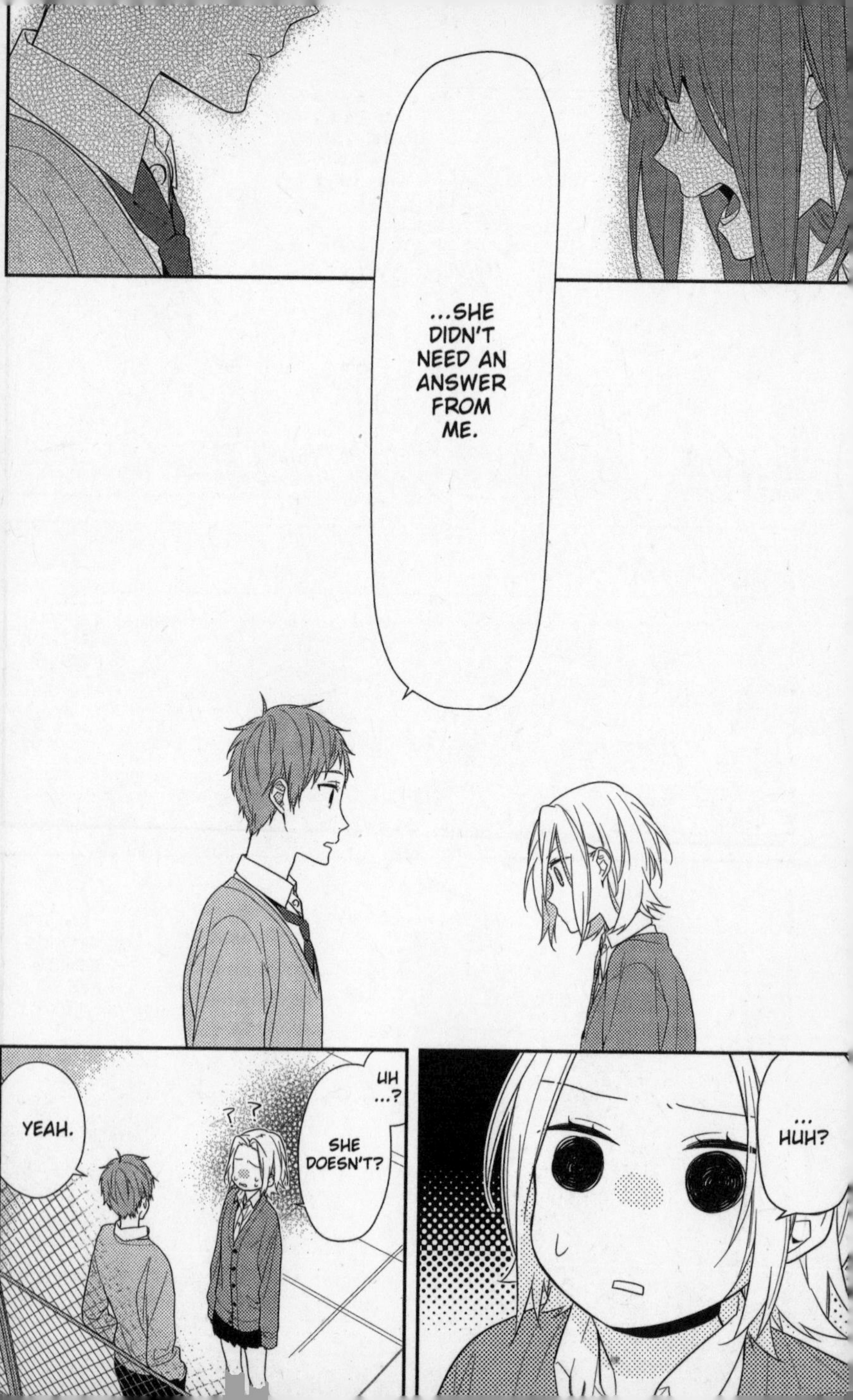
...SHE DIDN'T NEED AN ANSWER FROM ME.
... HUH?
UH ...?
SHE DOESN'T?
? ?
YEAH.

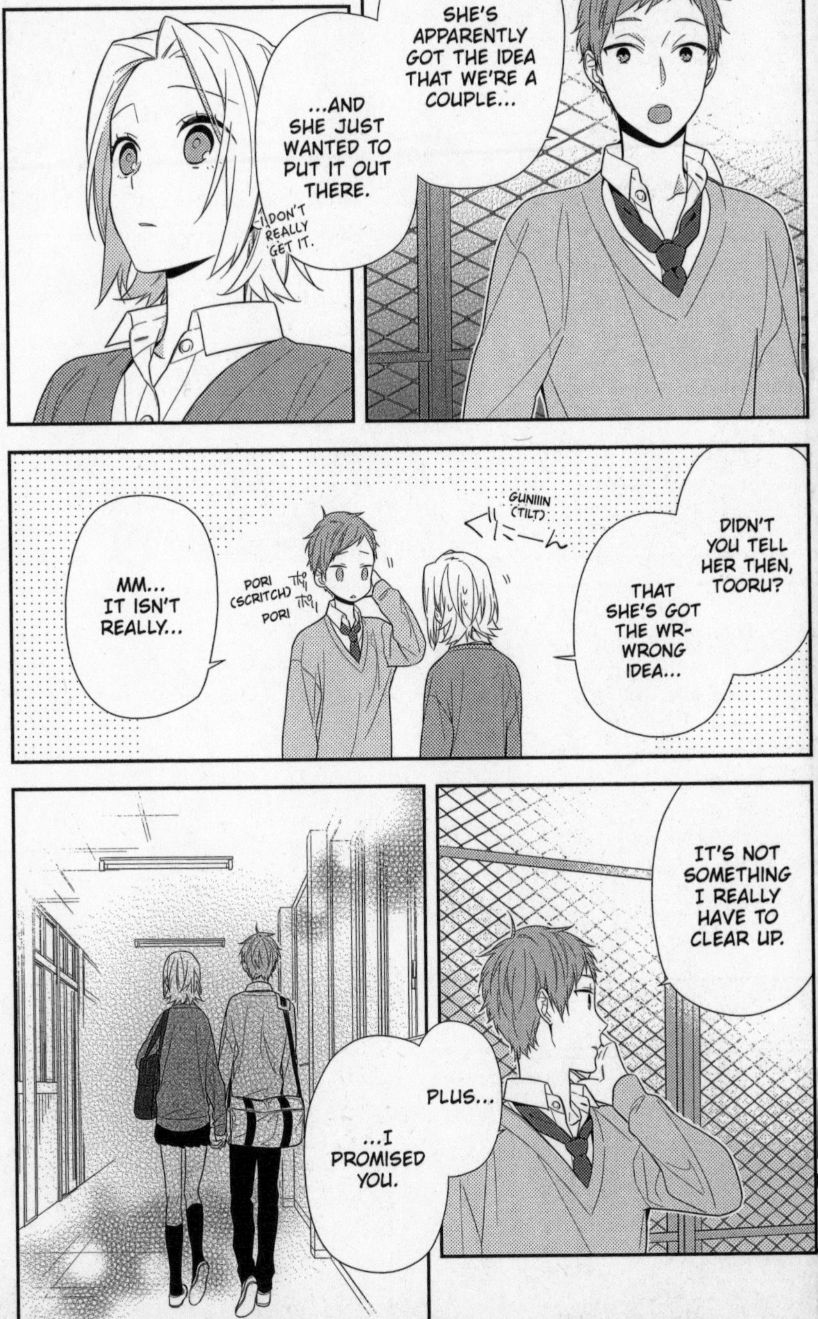
SHE'S APPARENTLY GOT THE IDEA THAT WE'RE A COUPLE...
...AND SHE JUST WANTED TO PUT IT OUT THERE.
I DON'T REALLY GET IT.
DIDN'T YOU TELL HER THEN, TOORU?
THAT SHE'S GOT THE WR-WRONG IDEA...
GUNIIIN (TILT)
ぐにーん
PORI (SCRITCH) PORI
MM... IT ISN'T REALLY...
IT'S NOT SOMETHING I REALLY HAVE TO CLEAR UP.
PLUS...
...I PROMISED YOU.

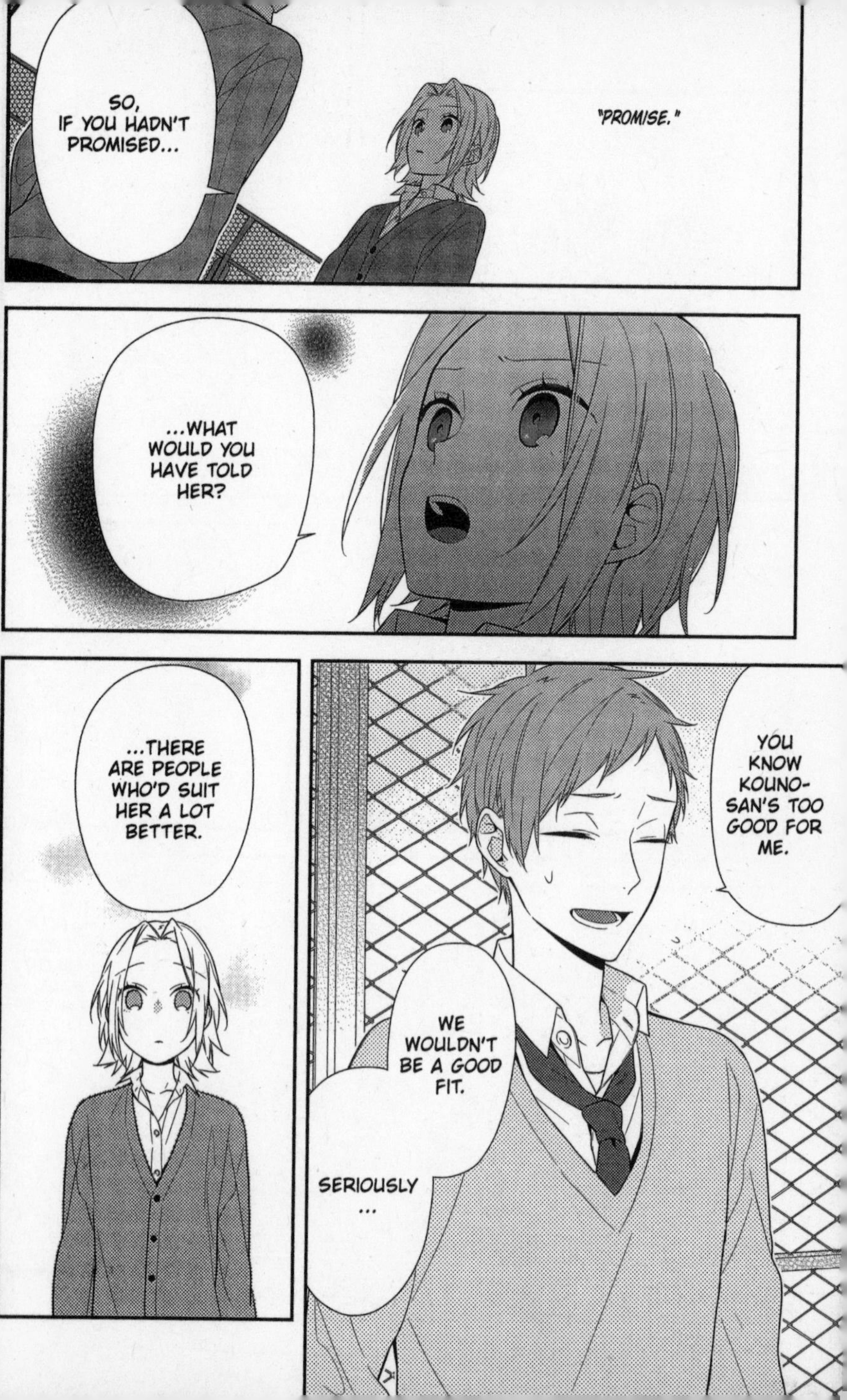
"PROMISE."
SO, IF YOU HADN'T PROMISED...
...WHAT WOULD YOU HAVE TOLD HER?
YOU KNOW KOUNO-SAN'S TOO GOOD FOR ME.
WE WOULDN'T BE A GOOD FIT.
SERIOUSLY...
...THERE ARE PEOPLE WHO'D SUIT HER A LOT BETTER.

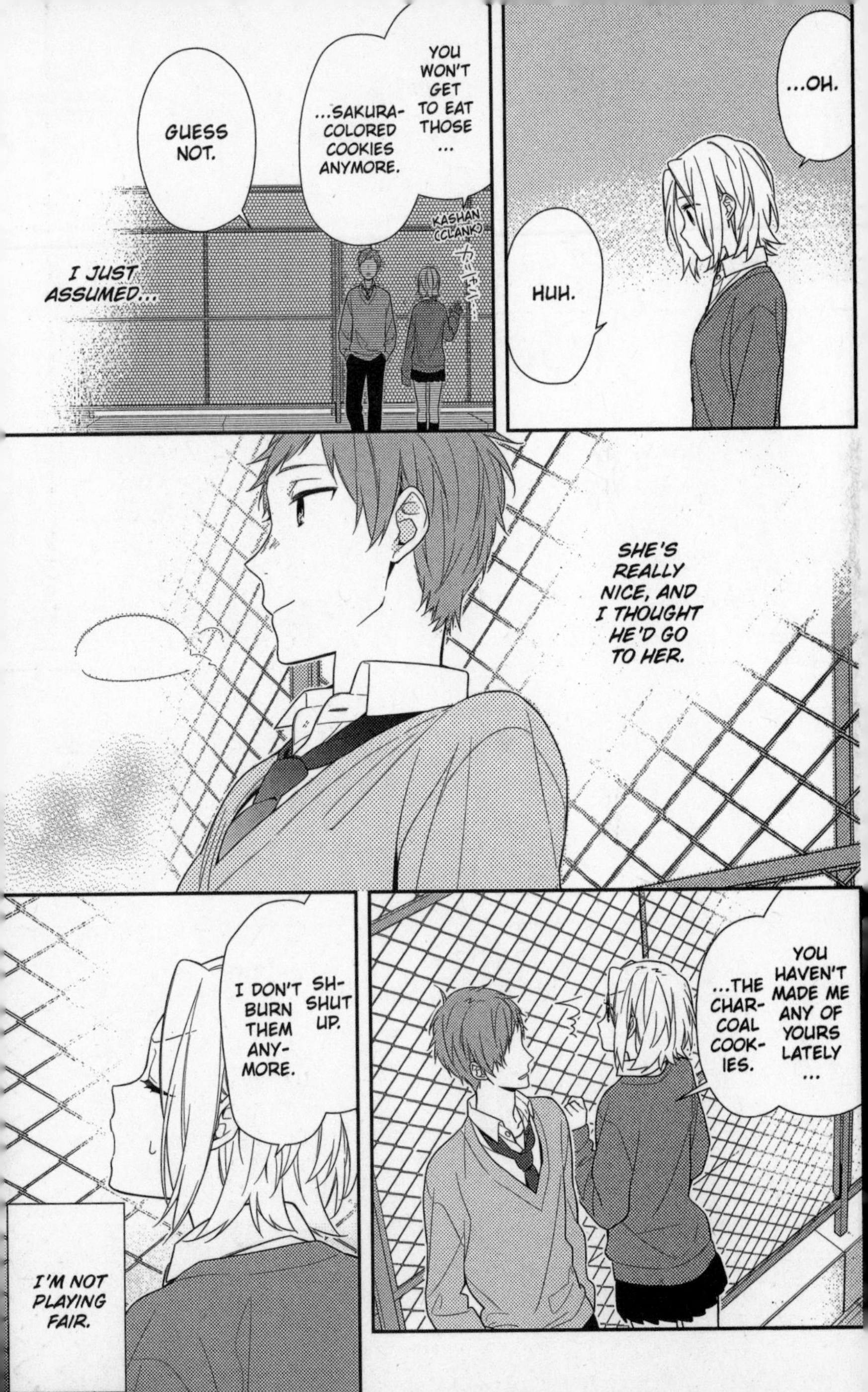
...OH.
HUH.
YOU WON'T GET TO EAT THOSE...
...SAKURA-COLORED COOKIES ANYMORE.
KASHAN (CLANK)
GUESS NOT.
I JUST ASSUMED...
SHE'S REALLY NICE, AND I THOUGHT HE'D GO TO HER.
YOU HAVEN'T MADE ME ANY OF YOURS LATELY...
...THE CHARCOAL COOKIES.
SH-SHUT UP.
I DON'T BURN THEM ANYMORE.
I'M NOT PLAYING FAIR.

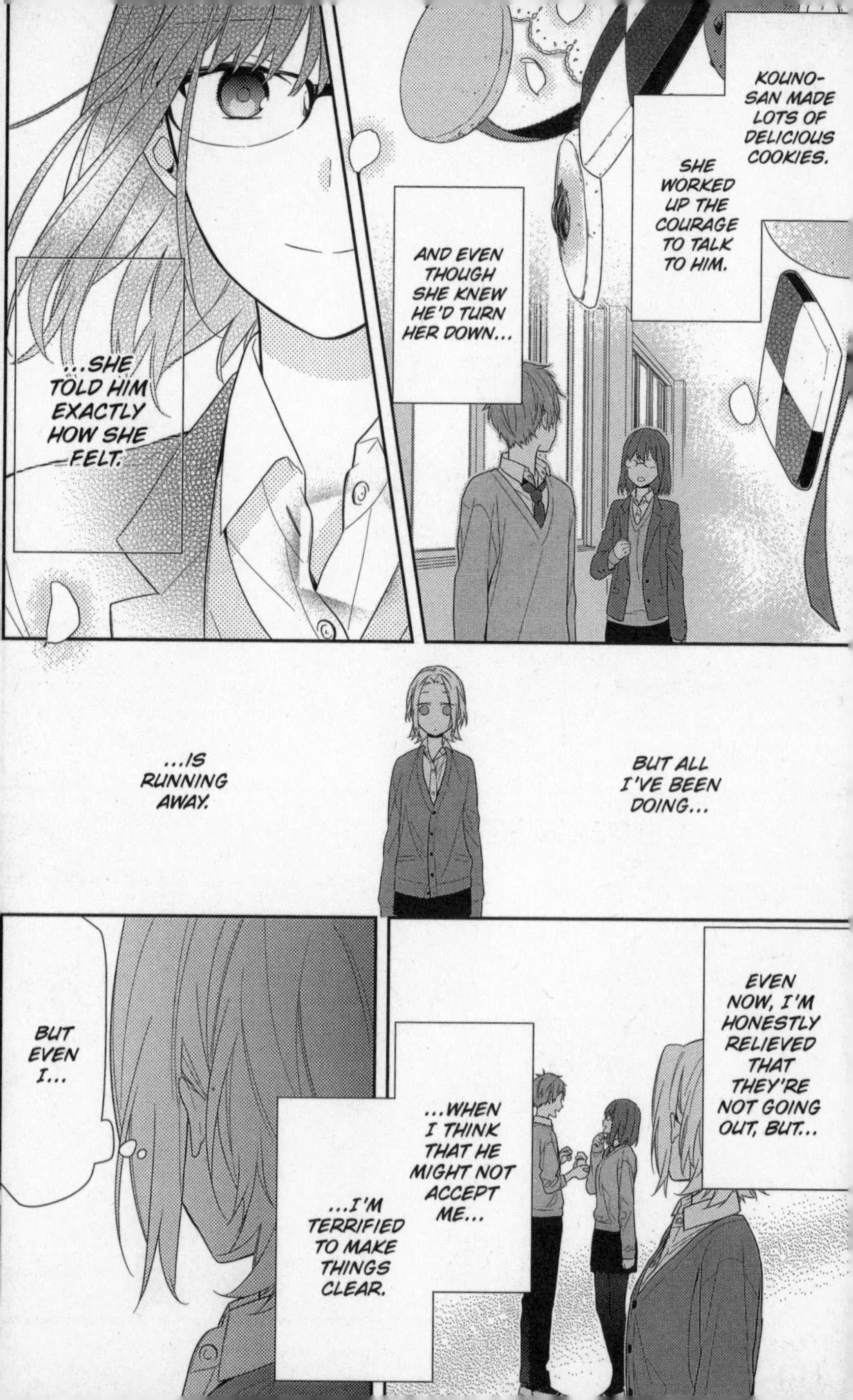
KOUNO-SAN MADE LOTS OF DELICIOUS COOKIES.
SHE WORKED UP THE COURAGE TO TALK TO HIM.
AND EVEN THOUGH SHE KNEW HE'D TURN HER DOWN...
...SHE TOLD HIM EXACTLY HOW SHE FELT.
BUT ALL I'VE BEEN DOING...
...IS RUNNING AWAY.
EVEN NOW, I'M HONESTLY RELIEVED THAT THEY'RE NOT GOING OUT, BUT...
...WHEN I THINK THAT HE MIGHT NOT ACCEPT ME...
...I'M TERRIFIED TO MAKE THINGS CLEAR.
BUT EVEN I...

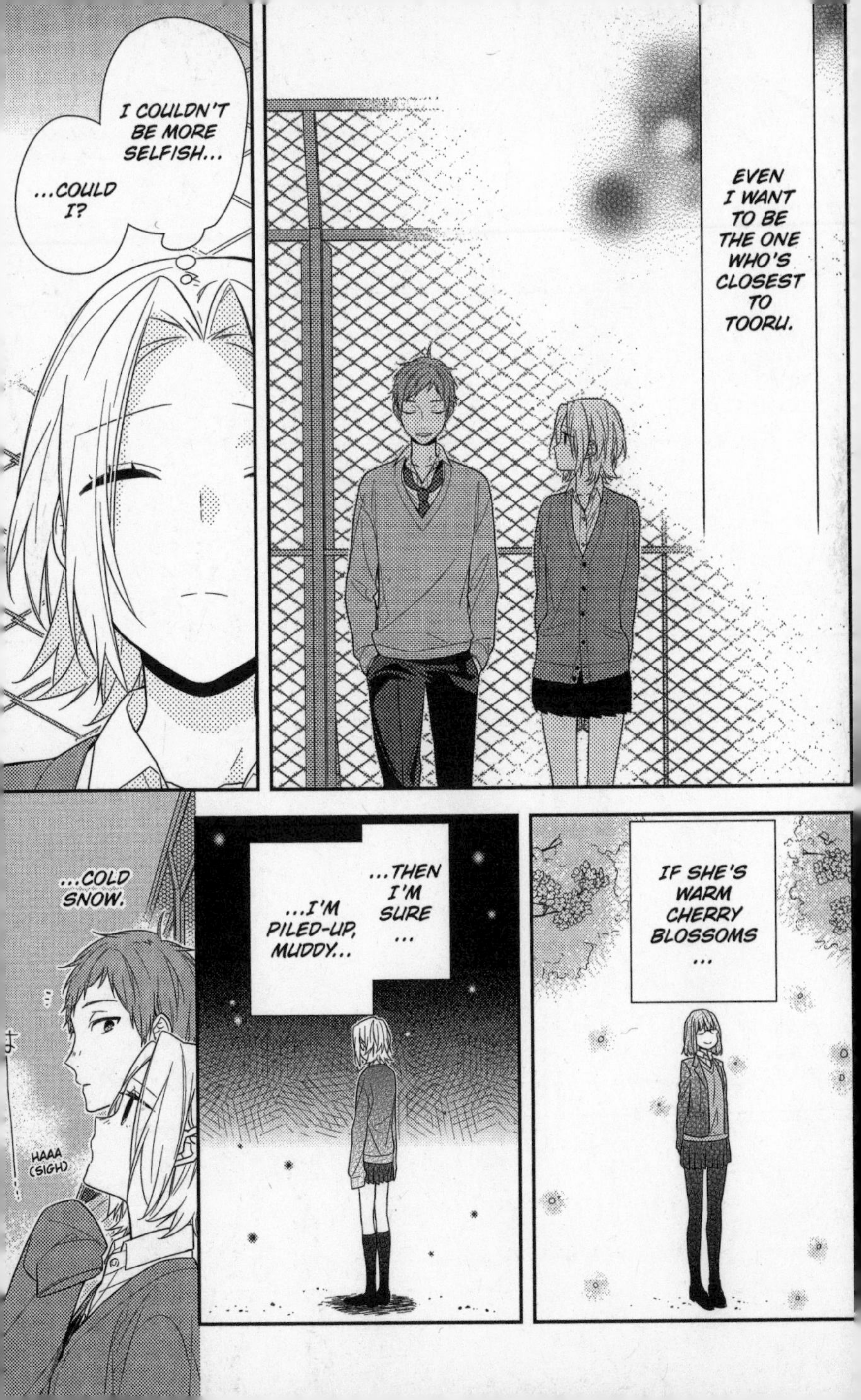
EVEN I WANT TO BE THE ONE WHO'S CLOSEST TO TOORU.
I COULDN'T BE MORE SELFISH...
...COULD I?
IF SHE'S WARM CHERRY BLOSSOMS...
...THEN I'M SURE...
...I'M PILED-UP, MUDDY...
...COLD SNOW.
HAAA (SIGH)

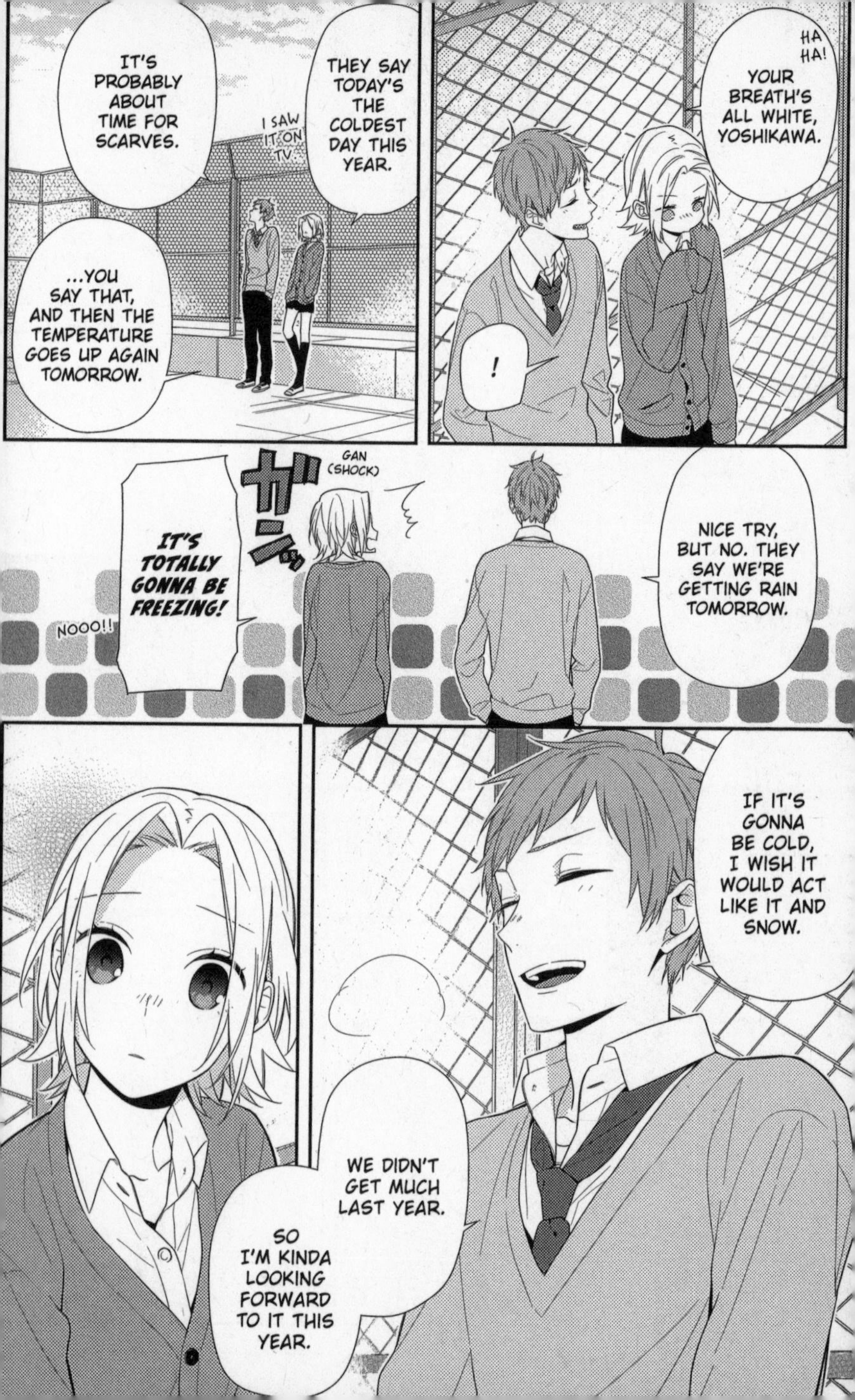
HA HA!
YOUR BREATH'S ALL WHITE, YOSHIKAWA.
!
THEY SAY TODAY'S THE COLDEST DAY THIS YEAR.
I SAW IT ON TV
IT'S PROBABLY ABOUT TIME FOR SCARVES.
...YOU SAY THAT, AND THEN THE TEMPERATURE GOES UP AGAIN TOMORROW.
NICE TRY, BUT NO. THEY SAY WE'RE GETTING RAIN TOMORROW.
GAN (SHOCK)
IT'S TOTALLY GONNA BE FREEZING!
NOOO!!
IF IT'S GONNA BE COLD, I WISH IT WOULD ACT LIKE IT AND SNOW.
WE DIDN'T GET MUCH LAST YEAR.
SO I'M KINDA LOOKING FORWARD TO IT THIS YEAR.

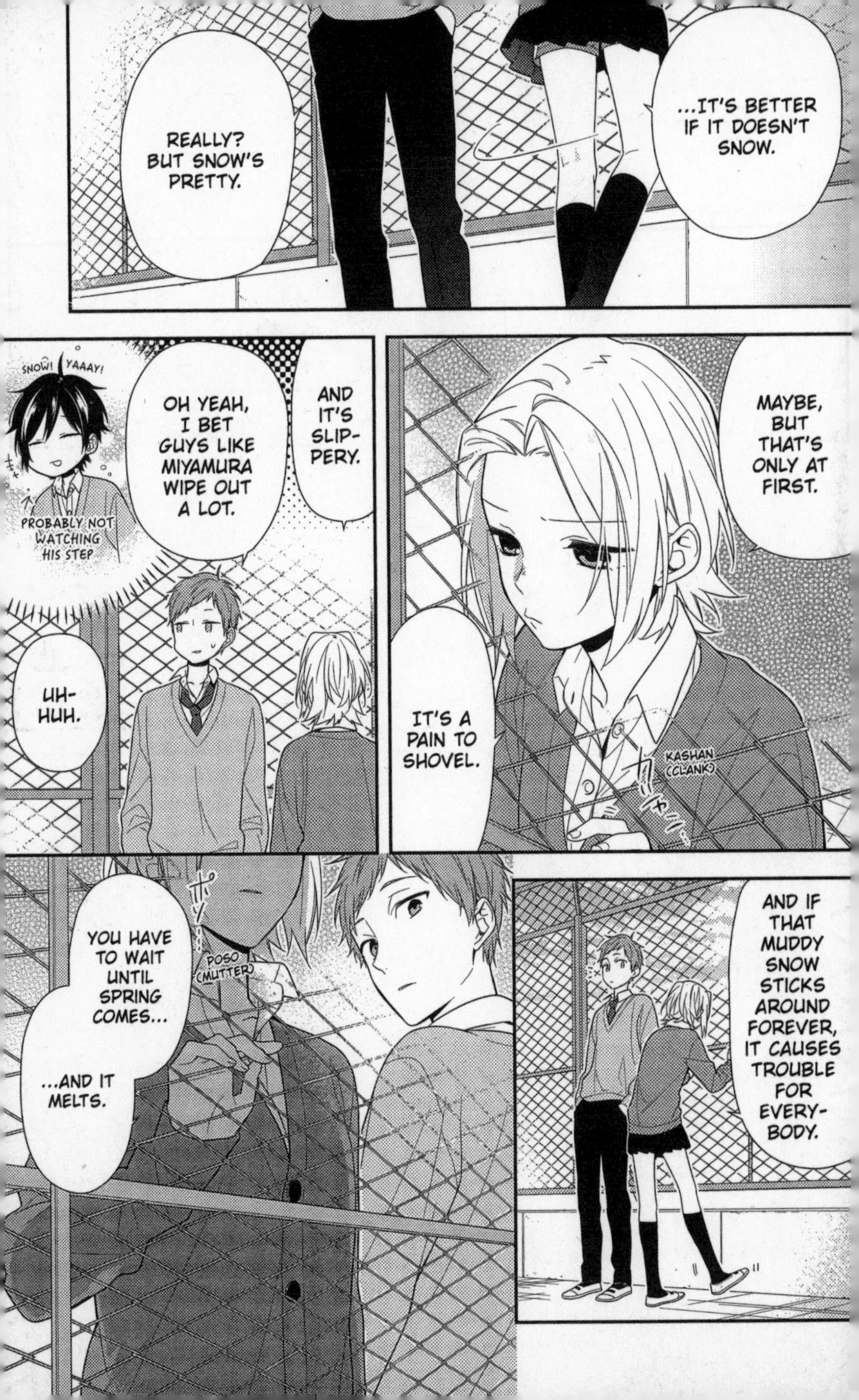
...IT'S BETTER IF IT DOESN'T SNOW.
REALLY? BUT SNOW'S PRETTY.
MAYBE, BUT THAT'S ONLY AT FIRST.
IT'S A PAIN TO SHOVEL.
KASHAN (CLANK)
AND IT'S SLIP-PERY.
OH YEAH, I BET GUYS LIKE MIYAMURA WIPE OUT A LOT.
SNOW! YAAAY!
PROBABLY NOT WATCHING HIS STEP
UH-HUH.
AND IF THAT MUDDY SNOW STICKS AROUND FOREVER, IT CAUSES TROUBLE FOR EVERY-BODY.
YOU HAVE TO WAIT UNTIL SPRING COMES...
POSO (MUTTER)
...AND IT MELTS.

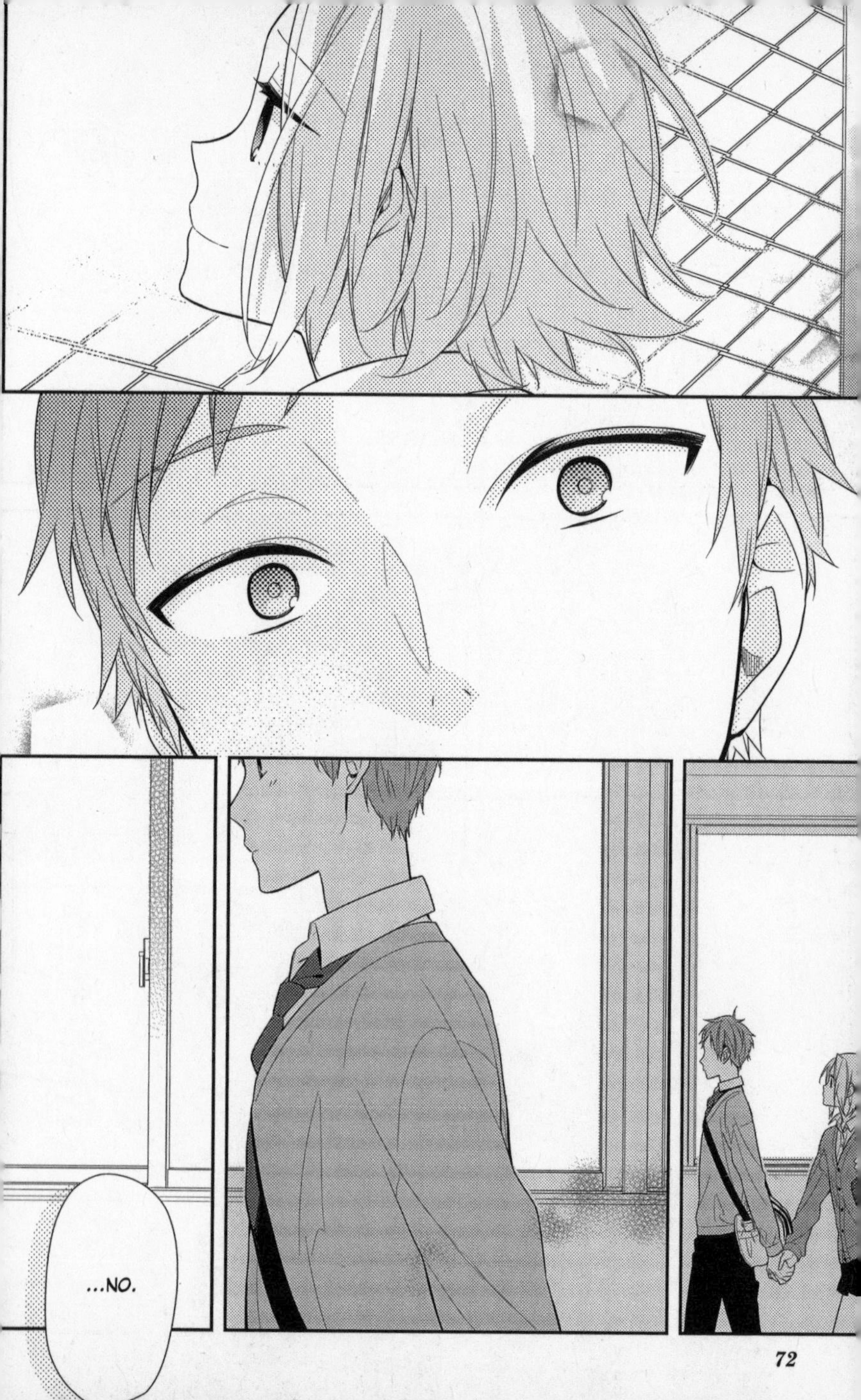
...NO.

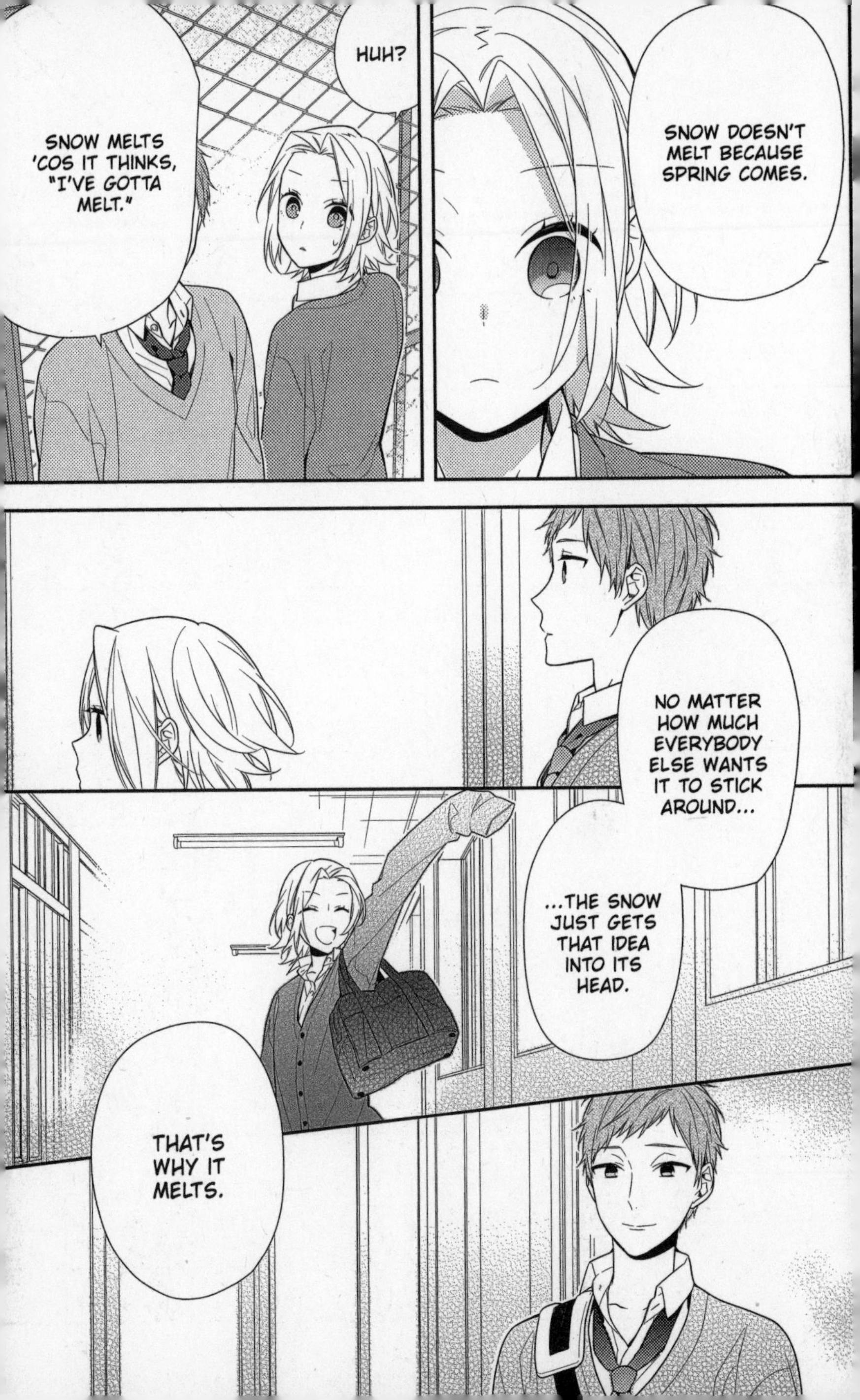
SNOW DOESN'T MELT BECAUSE SPRING COMES.
HUH?
SNOW MELTS 'COS IT THINKS, "I'VE GOTTA MELT."
NO MATTER HOW MUCH EVERYBODY ELSE WANTS IT TO STICK AROUND...
...THE SNOW JUST GETS THAT IDEA INTO ITS HEAD.
THAT'S WHY IT MELTS.

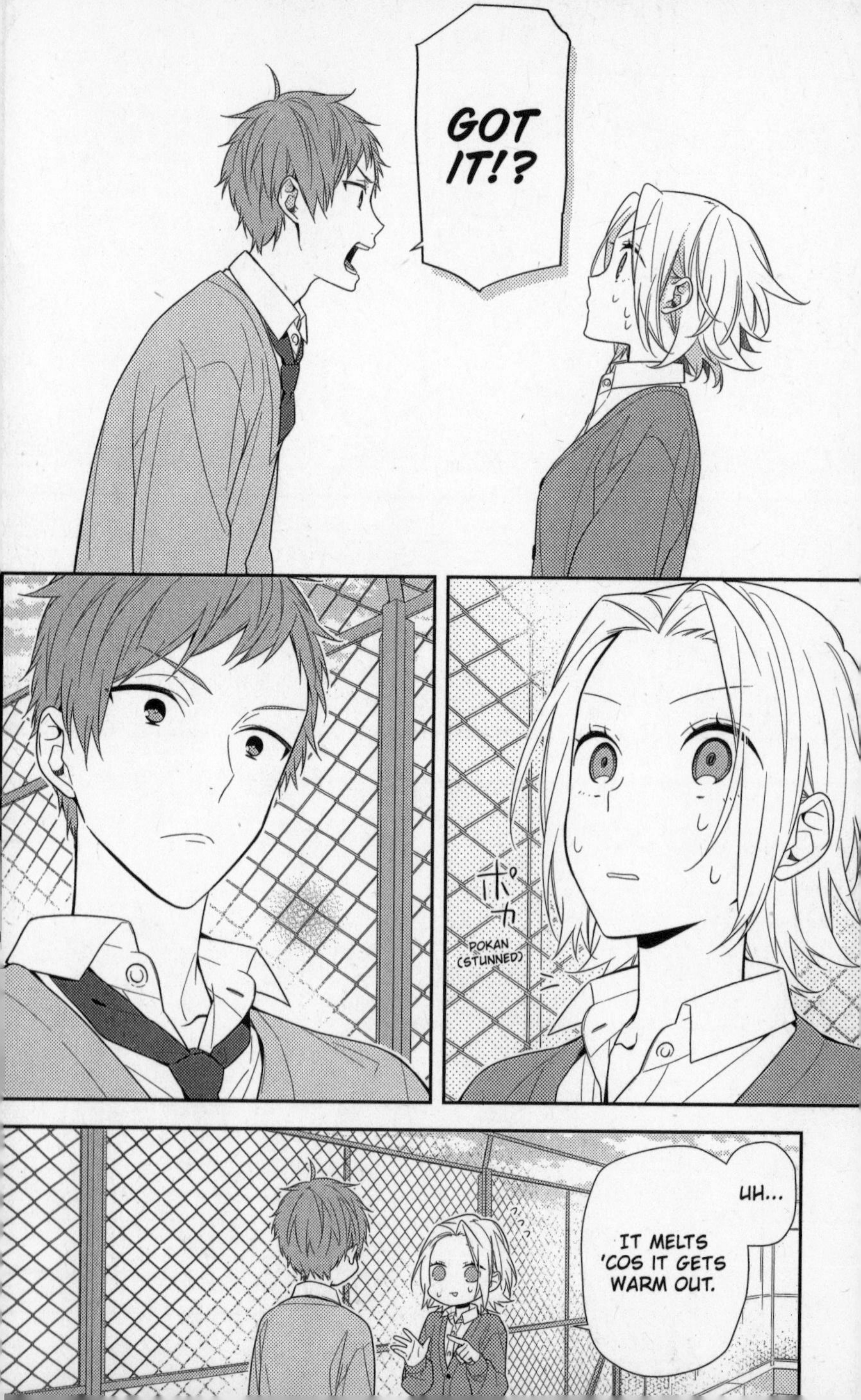
GOT IT!?
ポカ
POKAN (STUNNED)
UH...
IT MELTS 'COS IT GETS WARM OUT.

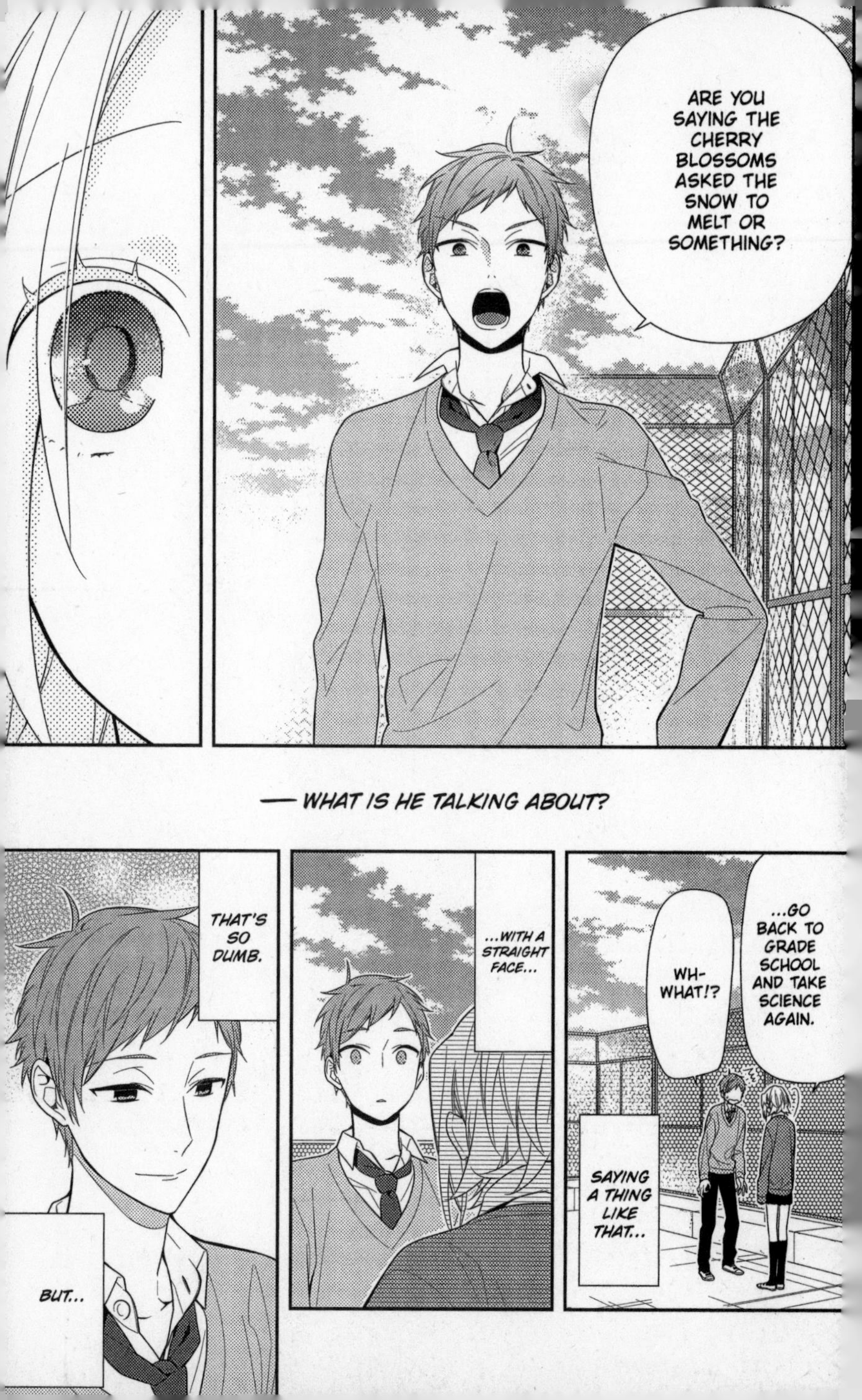
ARE YOU SAYING THE CHERRY BLOSSOMS ASKED THE SNOW TO MELT OR SOMETHING?
— WHAT IS HE TALKING ABOUT?
...GO BACK TO GRADE SCHOOL AND TAKE SCIENCE AGAIN.
WH-WHAT!?
SAYING A THING LIKE THAT...
...WITH A STRAIGHT FACE...
THAT'S SO DUMB.
BUT...

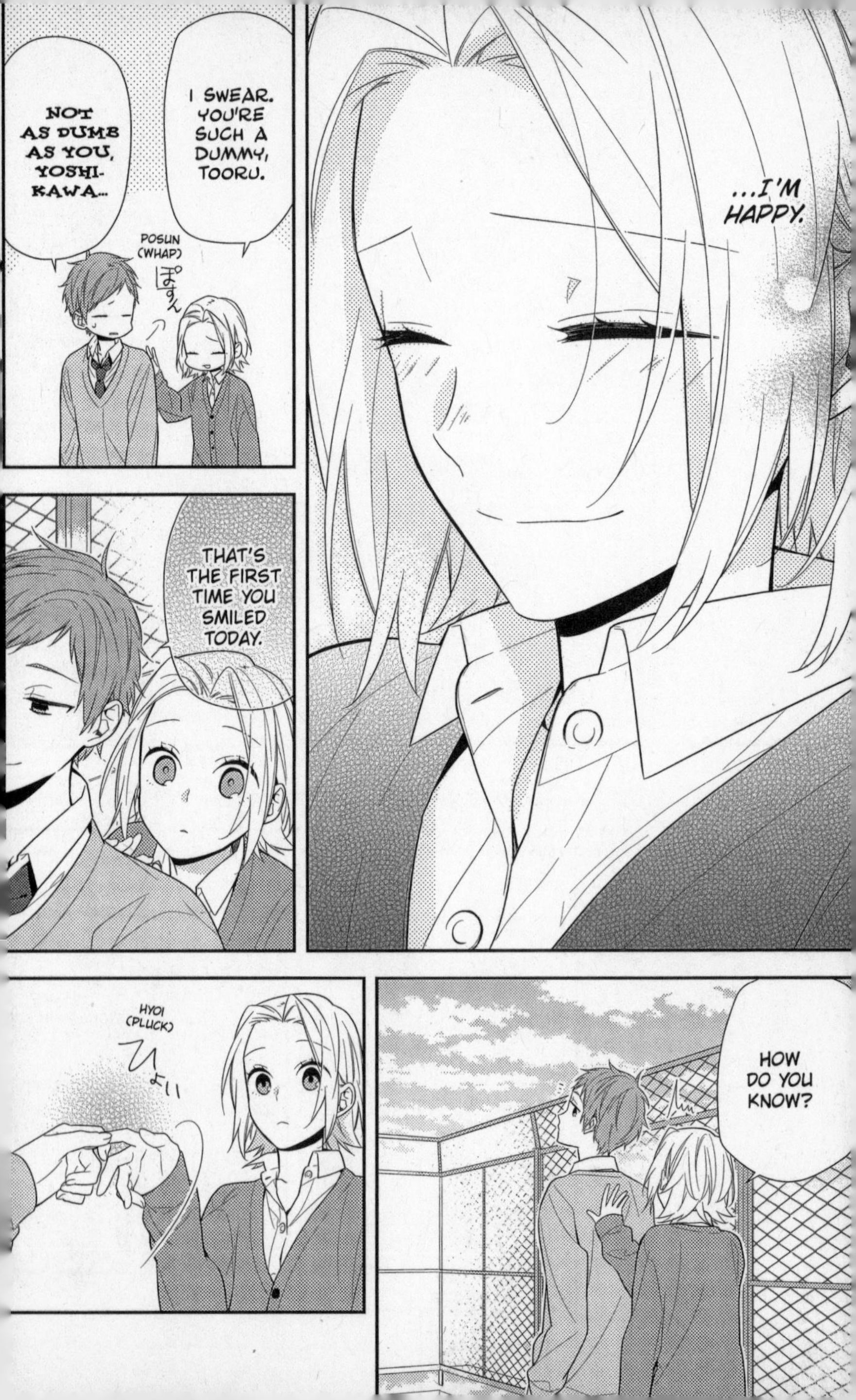
...I'M HAPPY.
I SWEAR. YOU'RE SUCH A DUMMY, TOORU.
NOT AS DUMB AS YOU, YOSHIKAWA...
POSUN (WHAP)
ぽすん
THAT'S THE FIRST TIME YOU SMILED TODAY.
HOW DO YOU KNOW?
HYOI (PLUCK)
ひょい

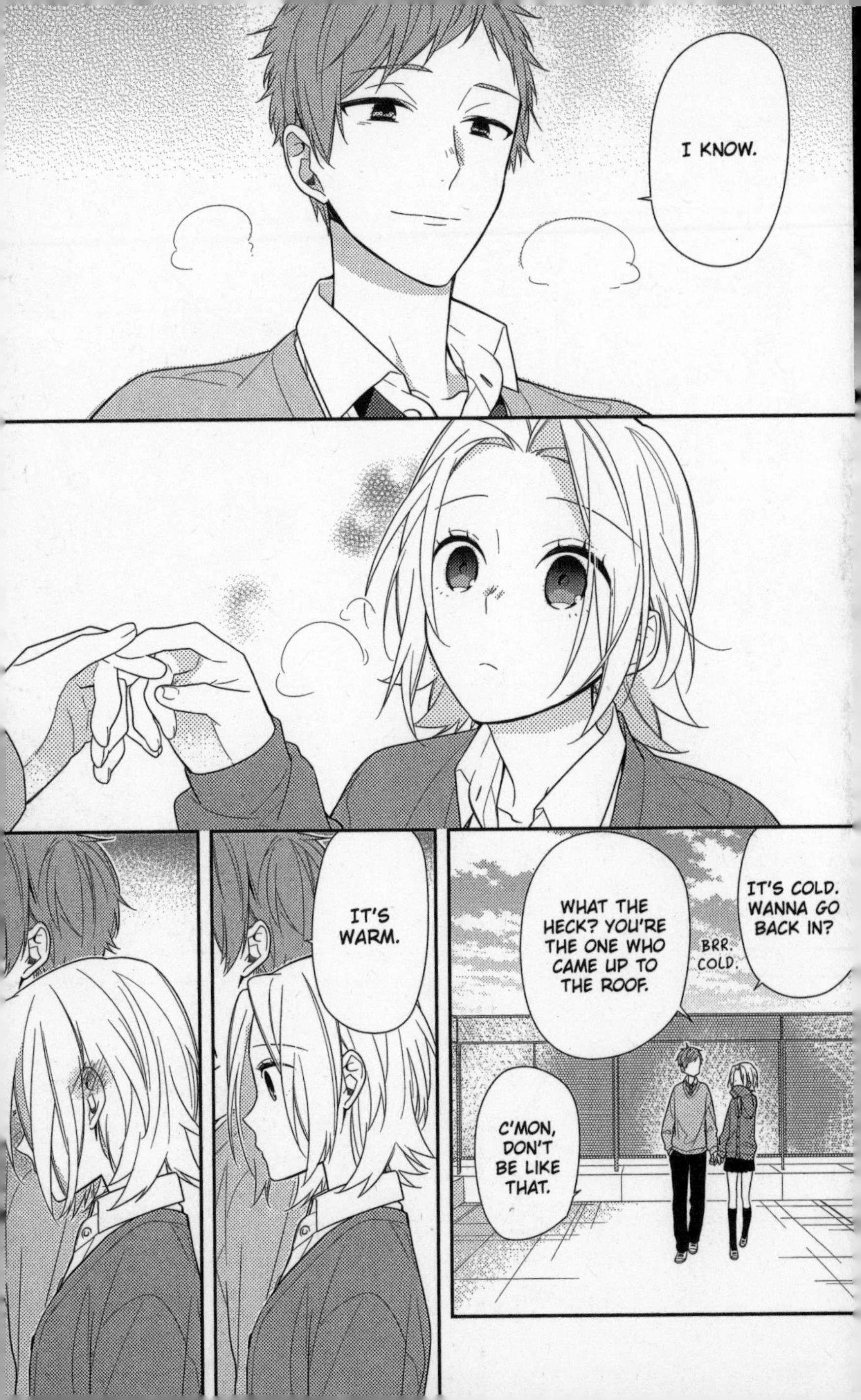
I KNOW.
IT'S COLD. WANNA GO BACK IN?
BRR. COLD.
WHAT THE HECK? YOU'RE THE ONE WHO CAME UP TO THE ROOF.
C'MON, DON'T BE LIKE THAT.
IT'S WARM.

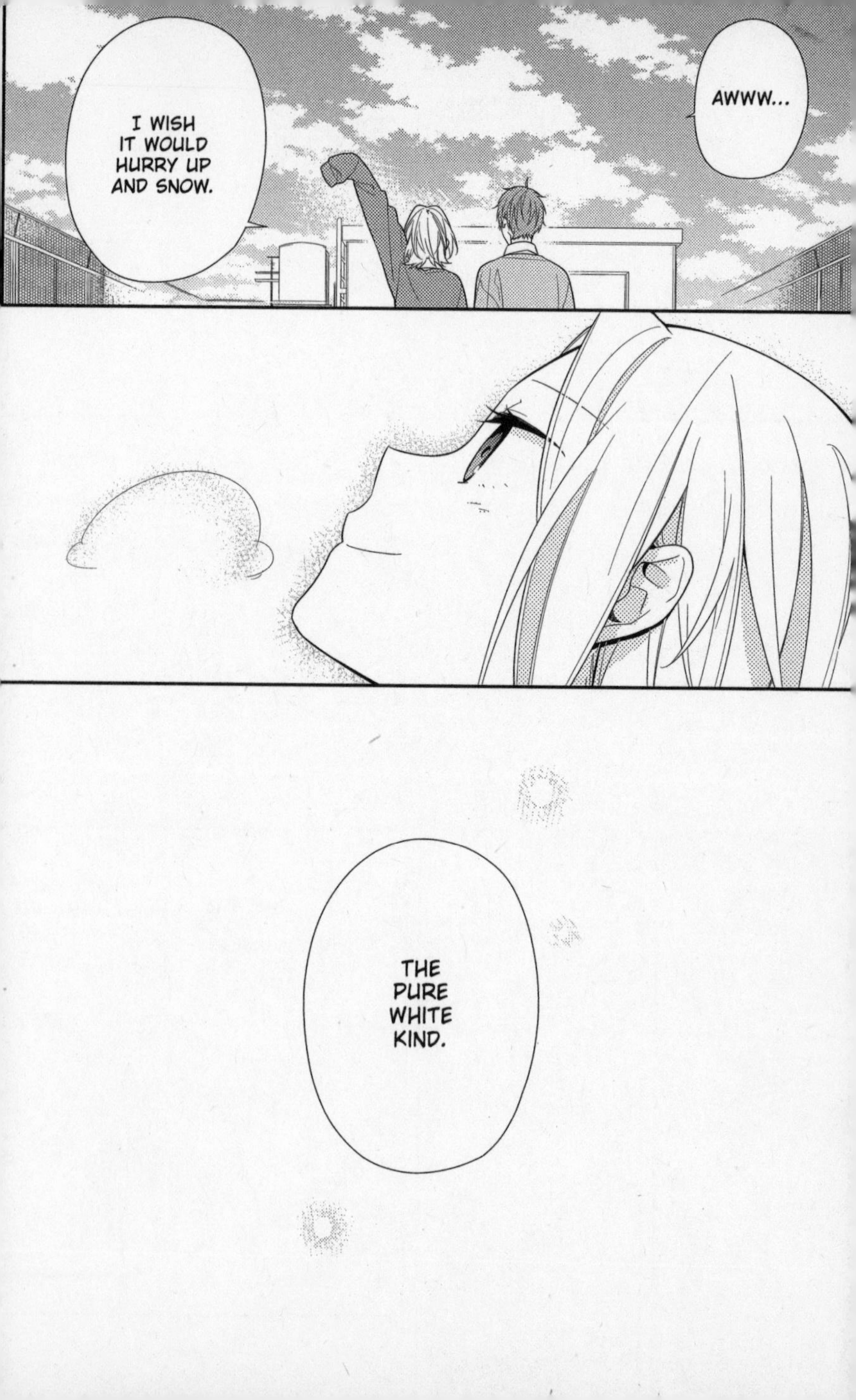
AWWW...
I WISH IT WOULD HURRY UP AND SNOW.
THE PURE WHITE KIND.

HORIMIYA

HORIMIYA

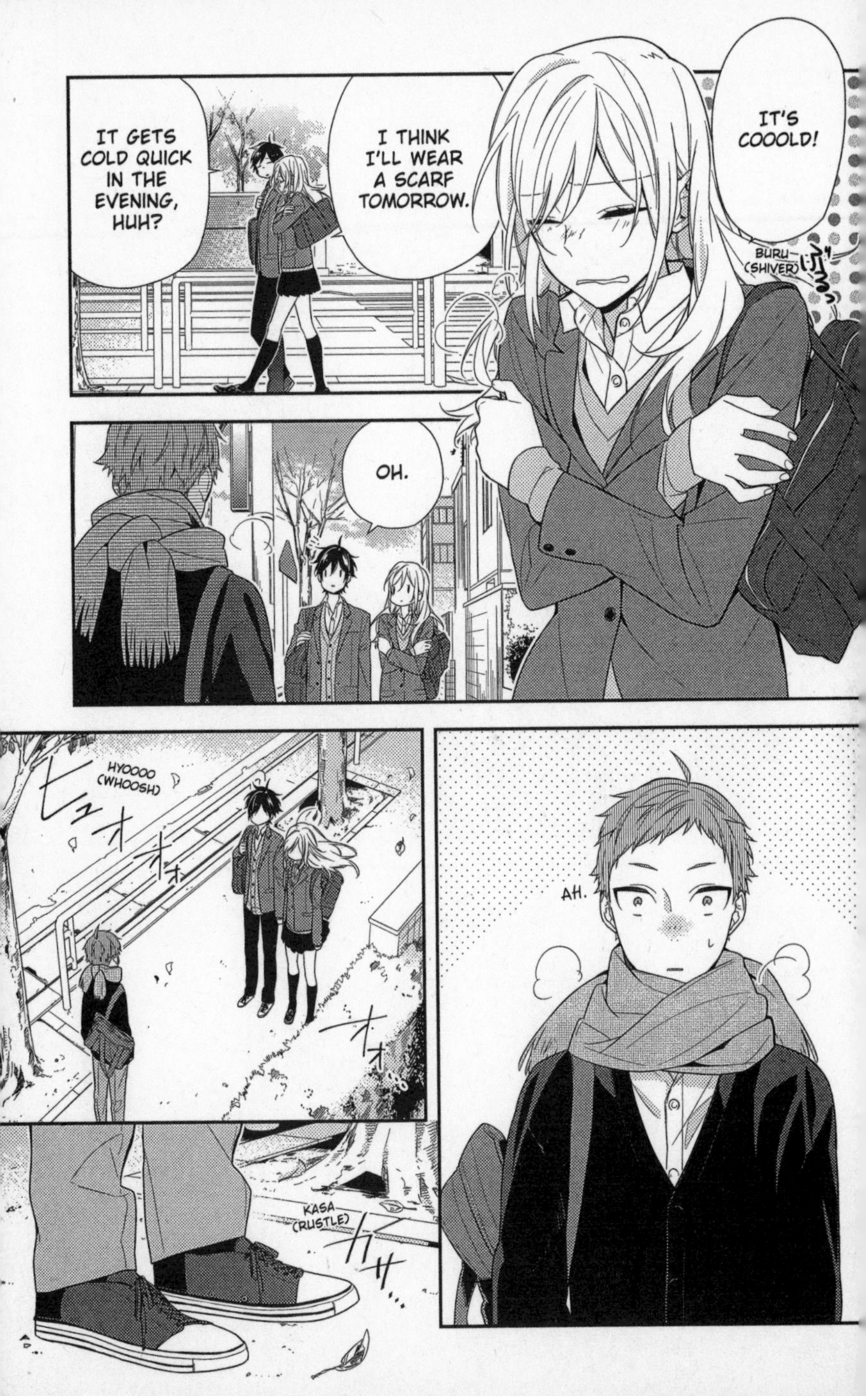
IT'S COOOLD!
BURU (SHIVER)
I THINK I'LL WEAR A SCARF TOMORROW.
IT GETS COLD QUICK IN THE EVENING, HUH?
OH.
AH.
HYOOOO (WHOOSH)
KASA (RUSTLE)

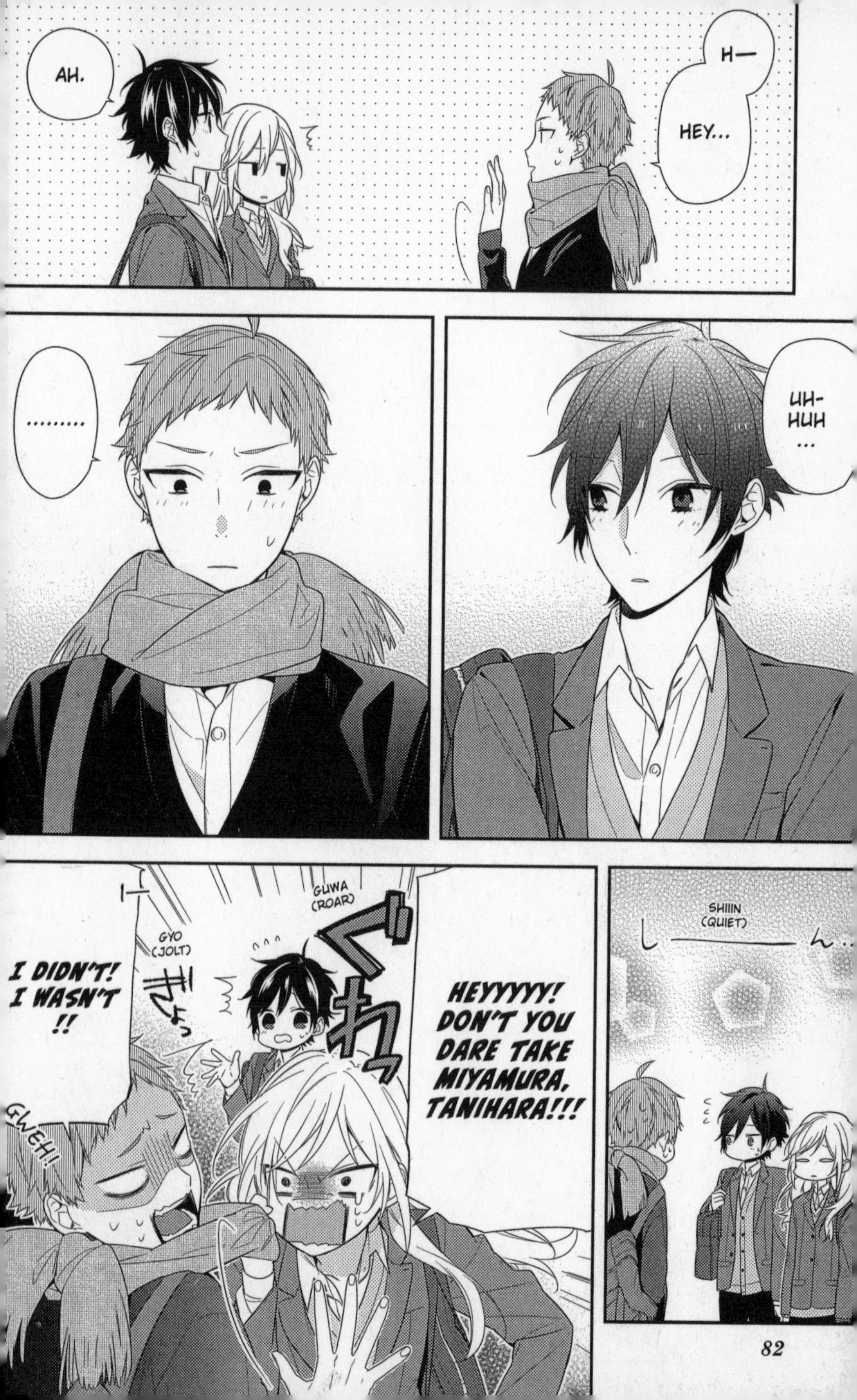
H—
HEY...
AH.
UH-HUH...
....
SHIIN (QUIET)
GUWA (ROAR)
HEYYYYY! DON'T YOU DARE TAKE MIYAMURA, TANIHARA!!!
GYO (JOLT)
I DIDN'T! I WASN'T!!
GWEH!!

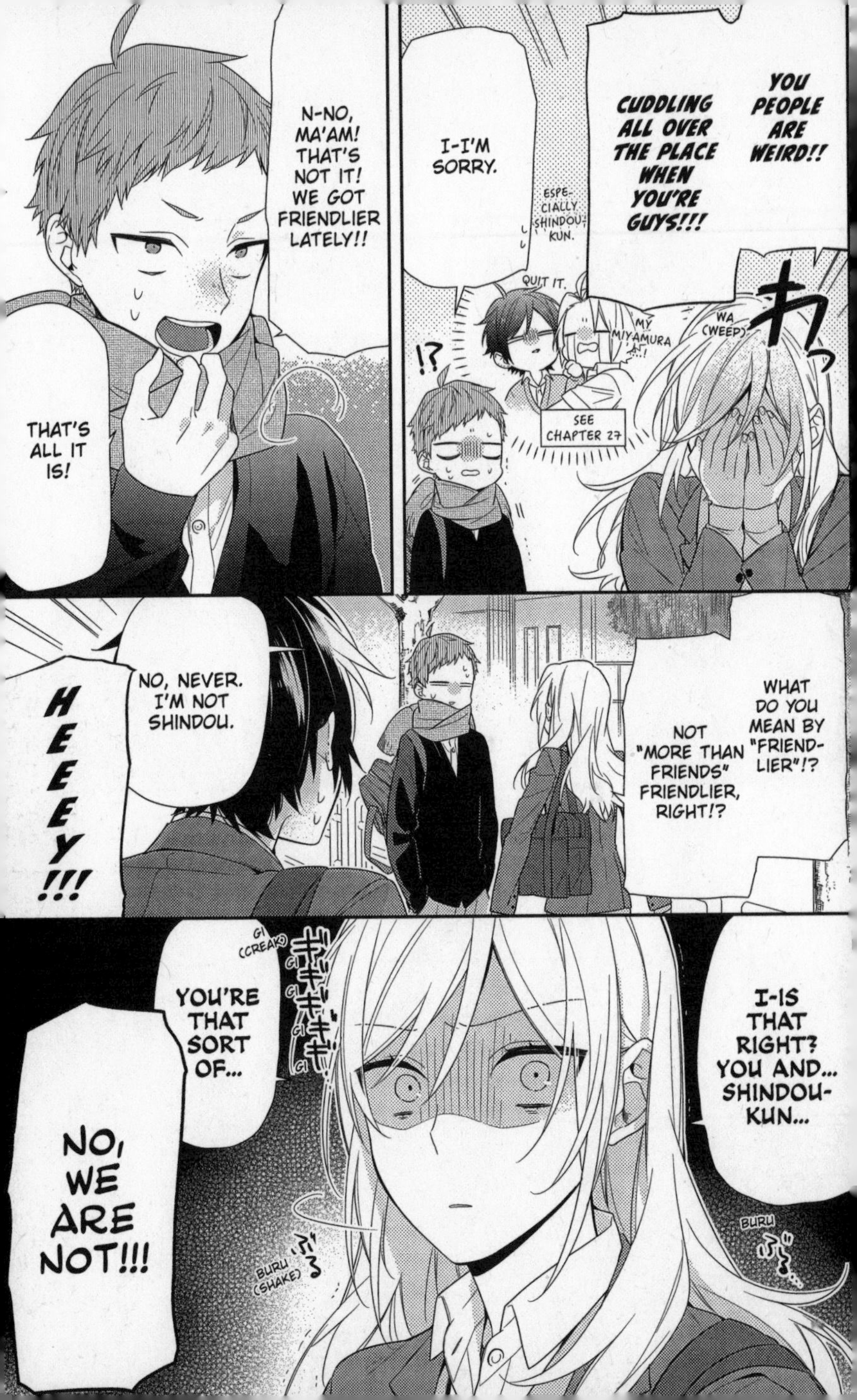
YOU PEOPLE ARE WEIRD!!
CUDDLING ALL OVER THE PLACE WHEN YOU'RE GUYS!!!
WA (WEEP)
わっ
I-I'M SORRY.
ESPE-CIALLY SHINDOU-KUN.
QUIT IT.
MY MIYAMURA...!
!?
SEE CHAPTER 27
N-NO, MA'AM! THAT'S NOT IT! WE GOT FRIENDLIER LATELY!!
THAT'S ALL IT IS!
WHAT DO YOU MEAN BY "FRIEND-LIER"!?
NOT "MORE THAN FRIENDS" FRIENDLIER, RIGHT!?
NO, NEVER. I'M NOT SHINDOU.
HEEEY!!!
I-IS THAT RIGHT? YOU AND... SHINDOU-KUN...
BURU
ぶる…
YOU'RE THAT SORT OF...
GI (CREAK) GI GI GI GI
ぎぎぎぎぎ
BURU (SHAKE)
ぶる
NO, WE ARE NOT!!!

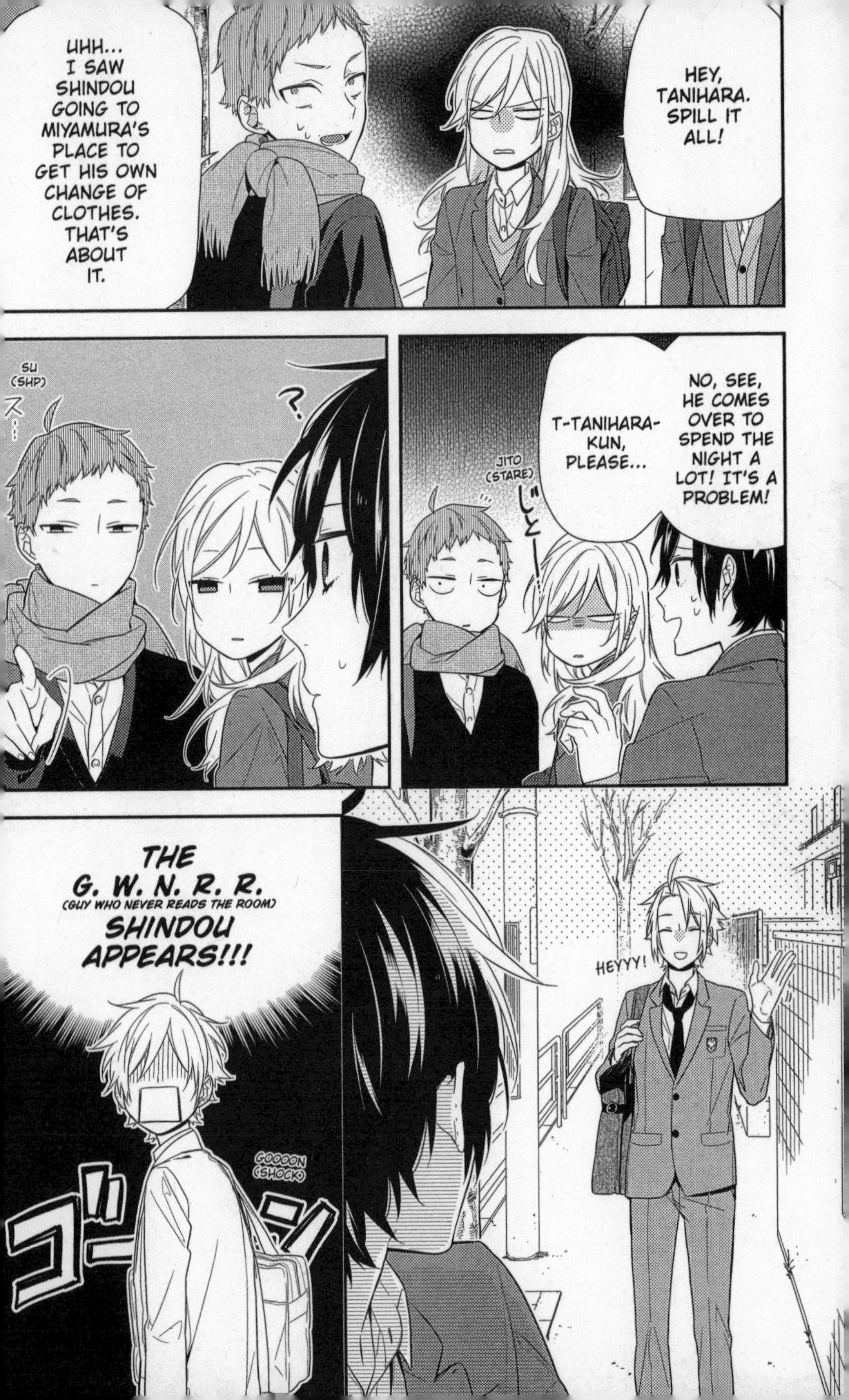
HEY, TANIHARA. SPILL IT ALL!
UHH... I SAW SHINDOU GOING TO MIYAMURA'S PLACE TO GET HIS OWN CHANGE OF CLOTHES. THAT'S ABOUT IT.
NO, SEE, HE COMES OVER TO SPEND THE NIGHT A LOT! IT'S A PROBLEM!
T-TANIHARA-KUN, PLEASE...
JITO (STARE)
?
SU (SHP)
HEYYY!
THE G. W. N. R. R. (GUY WHO NEVER READS THE ROOM) SHINDOU APPEARS!!!
GOOOON (SHOCK)

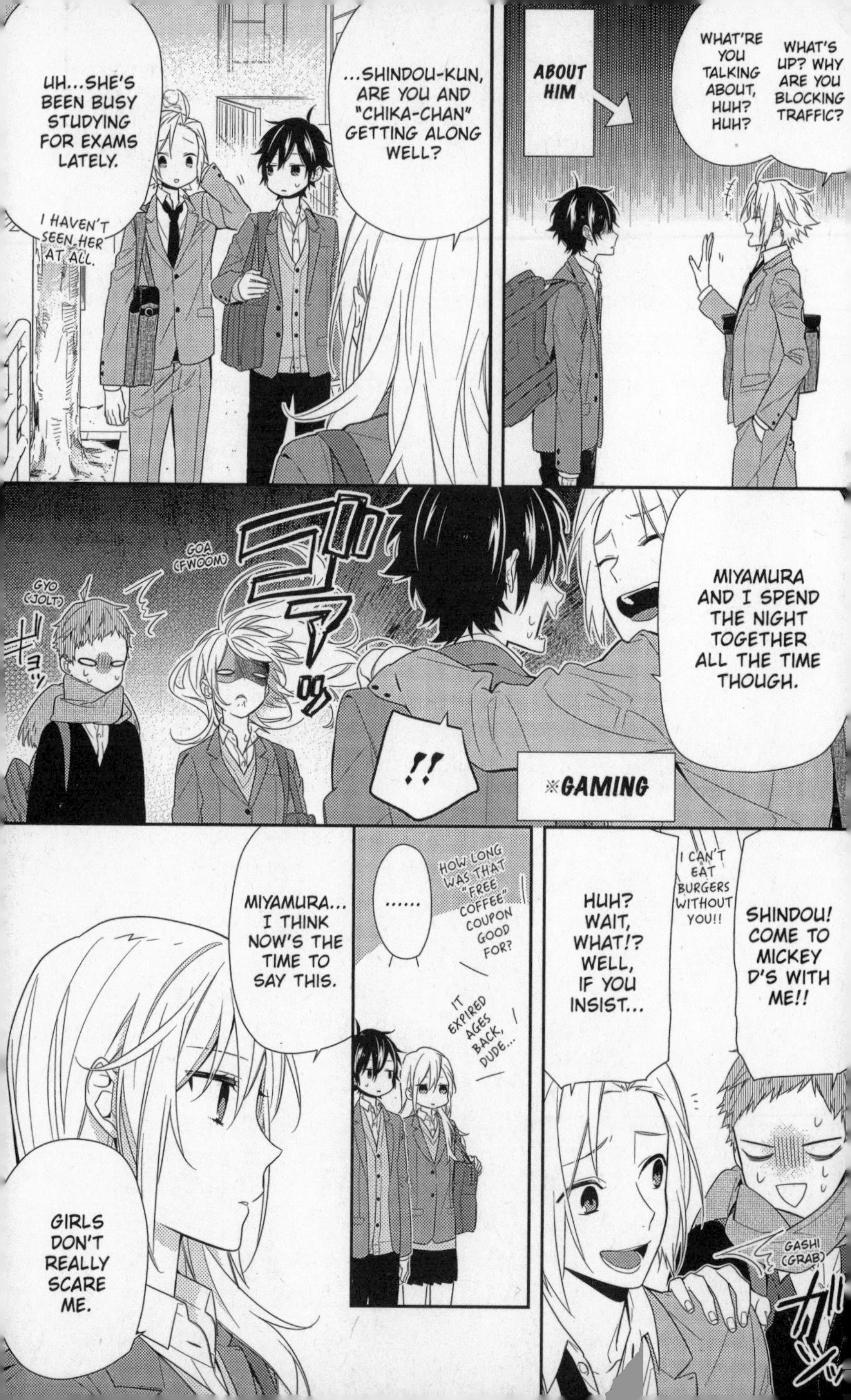
WHAT'S UP? WHY ARE YOU BLOCKING TRAFFIC?
WHAT'RE YOU TALKING ABOUT, HUH? HUH?
ABOUT HIM
...SHINDOU-KUN, ARE YOU AND "CHIKA-CHAN" GETTING ALONG WELL?
UH...SHE'S BEEN BUSY STUDYING FOR EXAMS LATELY.
I HAVEN'T SEEN HER AT ALL.
MIYAMURA AND I SPEND THE NIGHT TOGETHER ALL THE TIME THOUGH.
※GAMING
!!
GOA (FWOOM)
GYO (JOLT)
SHINDOU! COME TO MICKEY D'S WITH ME!!
I CAN'T EAT BURGERS WITHOUT YOU!!
HUH? WAIT, WHAT!? WELL, IF YOU INSIST...
GASHI (GRAB)
HOW LONG WAS THAT "FREE COFFEE" COUPON GOOD FOR?
......
IT EXPIRED AGES BACK, DUDE...
MIYAMURA... I THINK NOW'S THE TIME TO SAY THIS.
GIRLS DON'T REALLY SCARE ME.

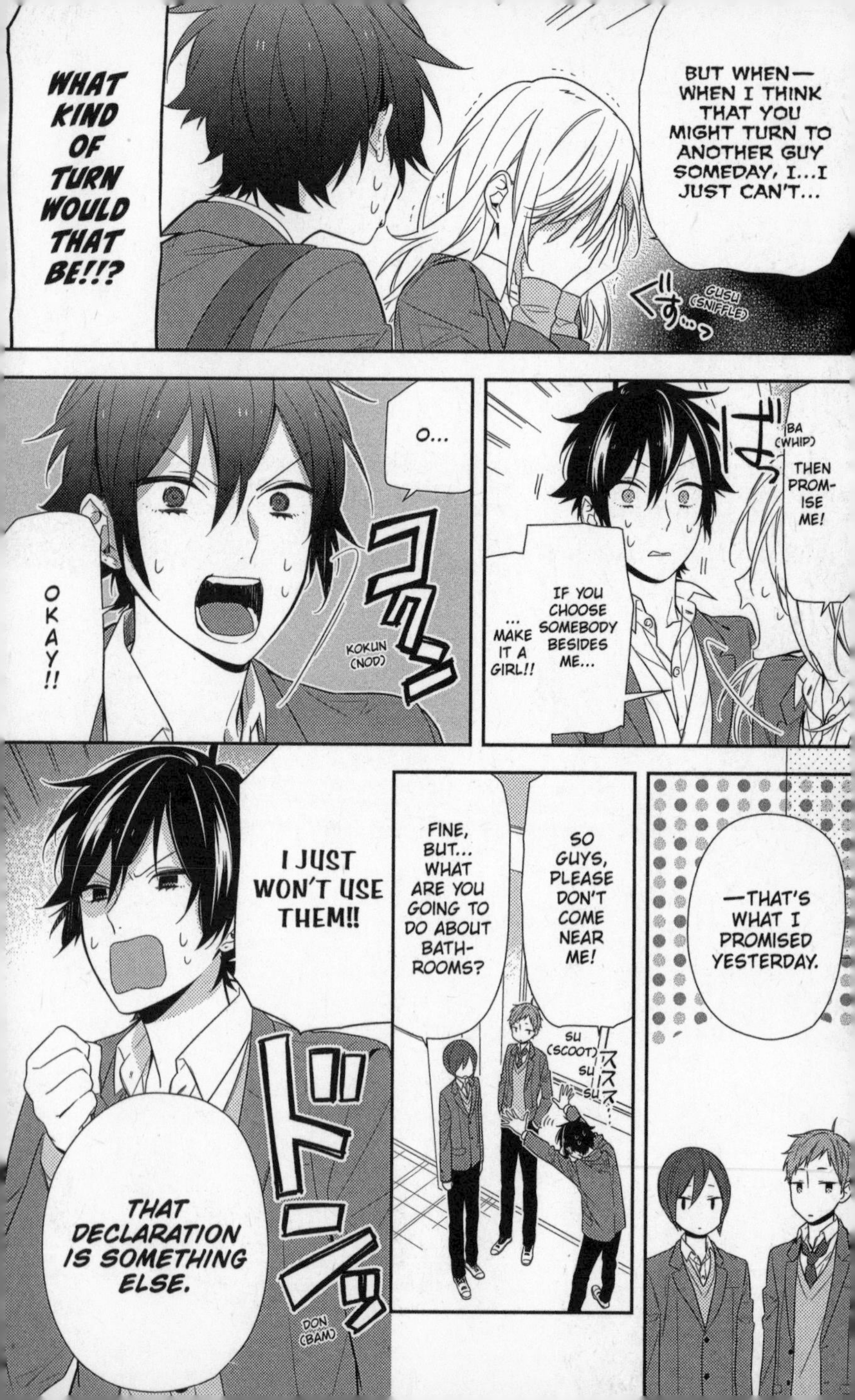
BUT WHEN— WHEN I THINK THAT YOU MIGHT TURN TO ANOTHER GUY SOMEDAY, I...I JUST CAN'T...
GUSU (SNIFFLE)
WHAT KIND OF TURN WOULD THAT BE!!?
BA (WHIP)
THEN PROMISE ME!
IF YOU CHOOSE SOMEBODY BESIDES ME...
...MAKE IT A GIRL!!
O...
KOKUN (NOD)
OKAY!!
—THAT'S WHAT I PROMISED YESTERDAY.
SO GUYS, PLEASE DON'T COME NEAR ME!
FINE, BUT... WHAT ARE YOU GOING TO DO ABOUT BATH-ROOMS?
SU (SCOOT) SU SU
I JUST WON'T USE THEM!!
DON (BAM)
THAT DECLARATION IS SOMETHING ELSE.

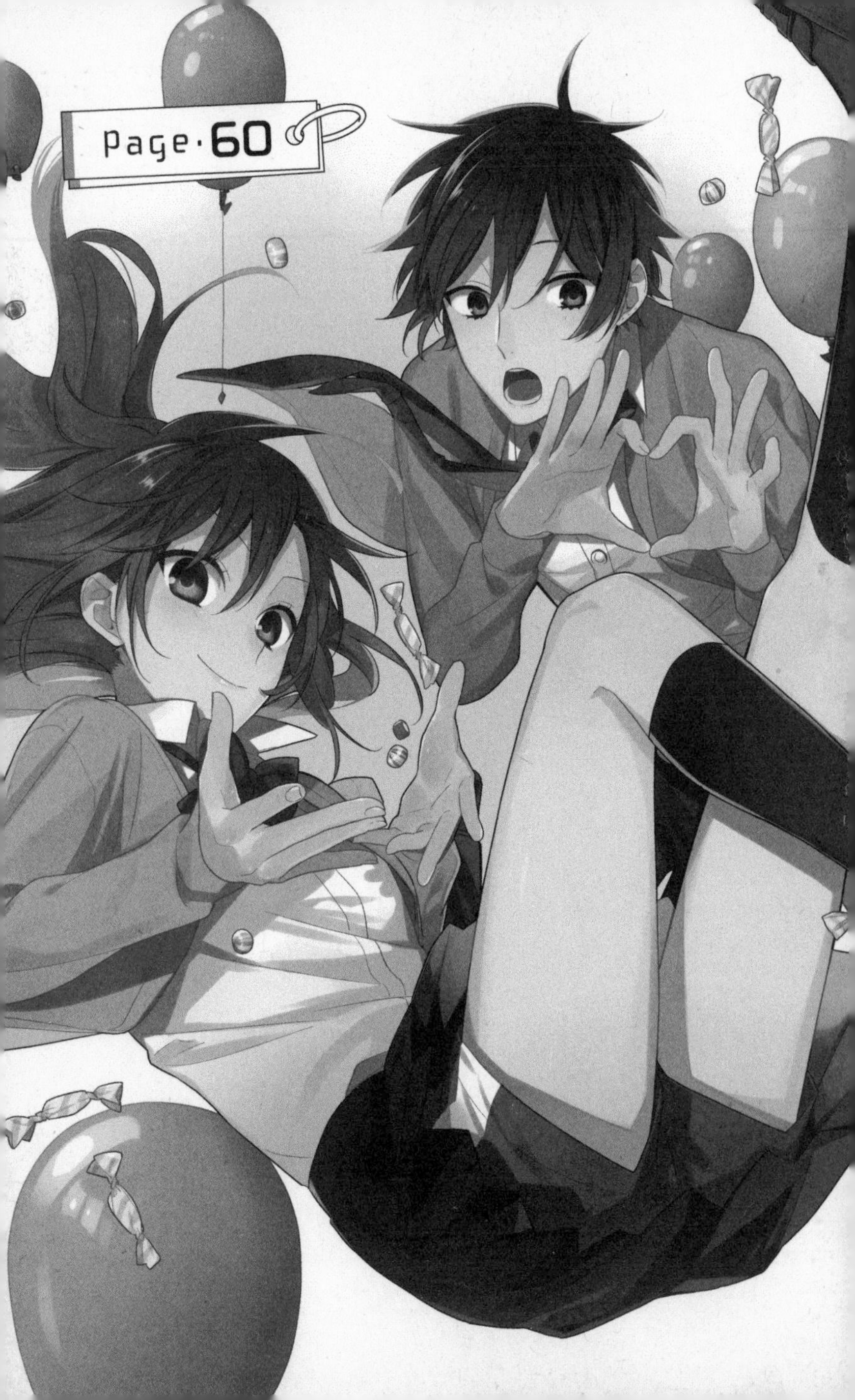
page·60

HORIMIYA

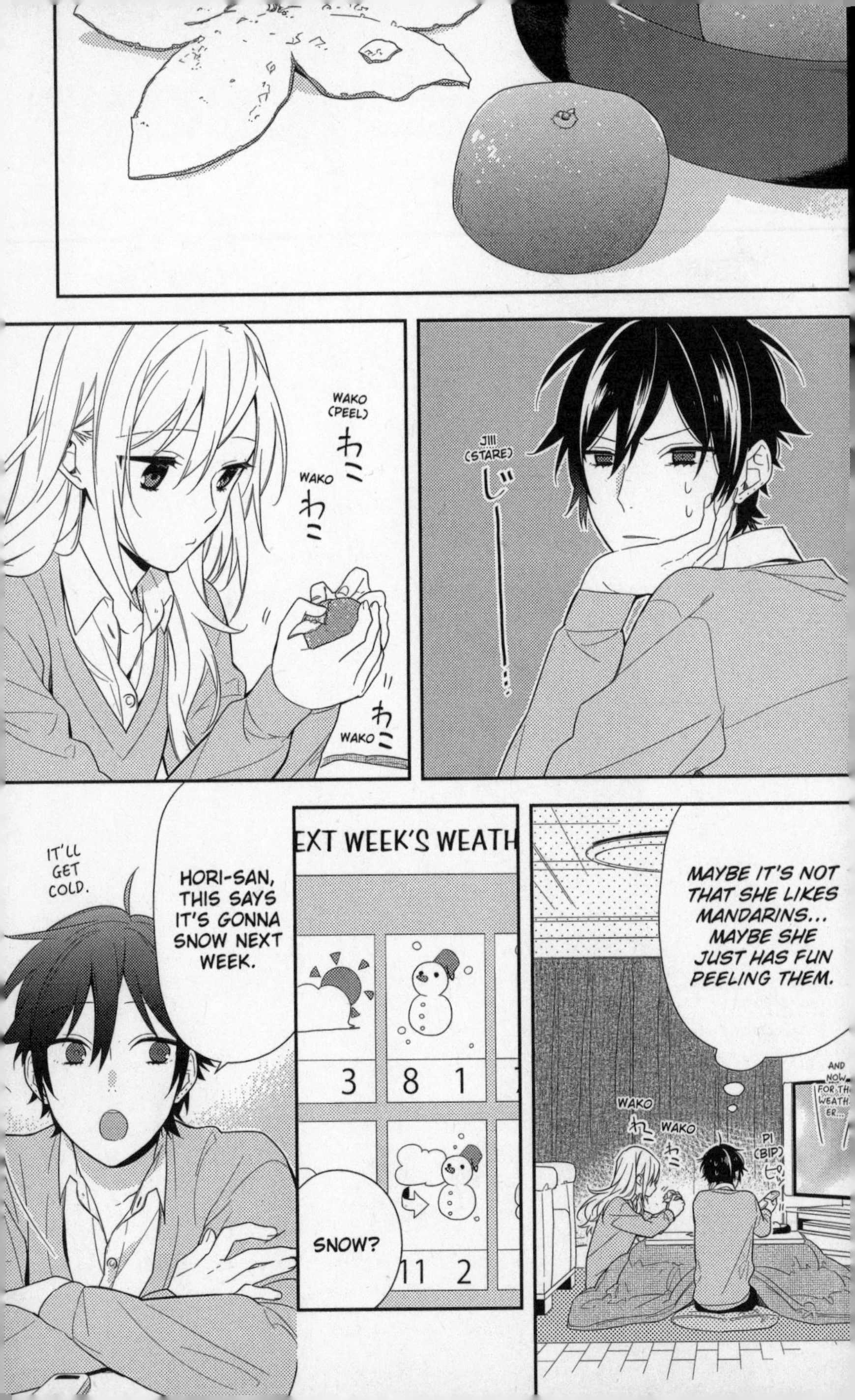
JIII (STARE)
じーー……
WAKO (PEEL)
わこ
WAKO
わこ
WAKO
わこ
MAYBE IT'S NOT THAT SHE LIKES MANDARINS... MAYBE SHE JUST HAS FUN PEELING THEM.
AND NOW FOR THE WEATHER...
WAKO
わこ
WAKO
わこ
PI (BIP)
ピッ
EXT WEEK'S WEATH
3 8 1
11 2
SNOW?
HORI-SAN, THIS SAYS IT'S GONNA SNOW NEXT WEEK.
IT'LL GET COLD.

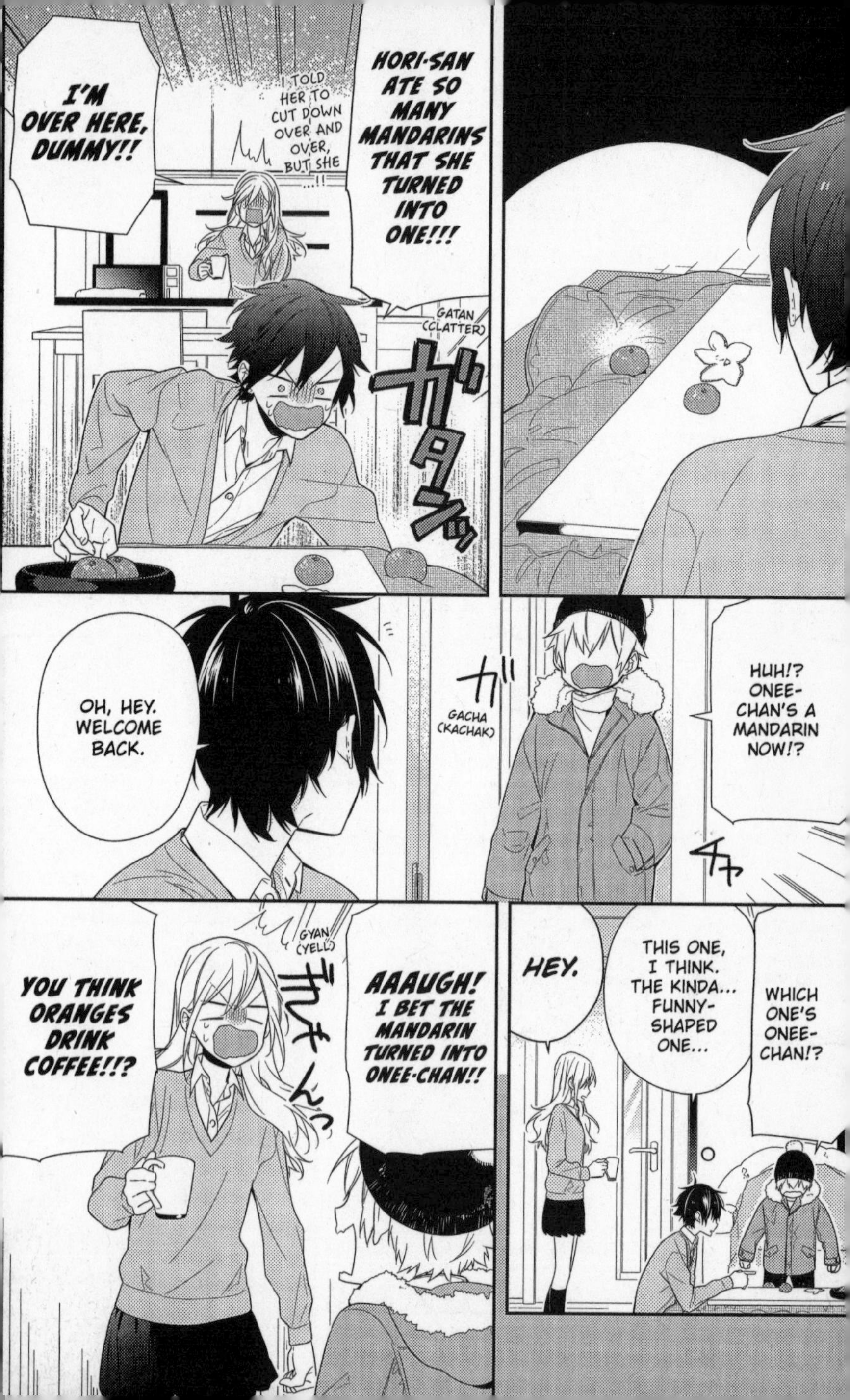
HORI-SAN ATE SO MANY MANDARINS THAT SHE TURNED INTO ONE!!!
GATAN (CLATTER)
I TOLD HER TO CUT DOWN OVER AND OVER, BUT SHE ...!!
I'M OVER HERE, DUMMY!!
HUH!? ONEE-CHAN'S A MANDARIN NOW!?
GACHA (KACHAK)
OH, HEY. WELCOME BACK.
WHICH ONE'S ONEE-CHAN!?
THIS ONE, I THINK. THE KINDA... FUNNY-SHAPED ONE...
HEY.
AAAUGH! I BET THE MANDARIN TURNED INTO ONEE-CHAN!!
GYAN (YELL)
YOU THINK ORANGES DRINK COFFEE!!?

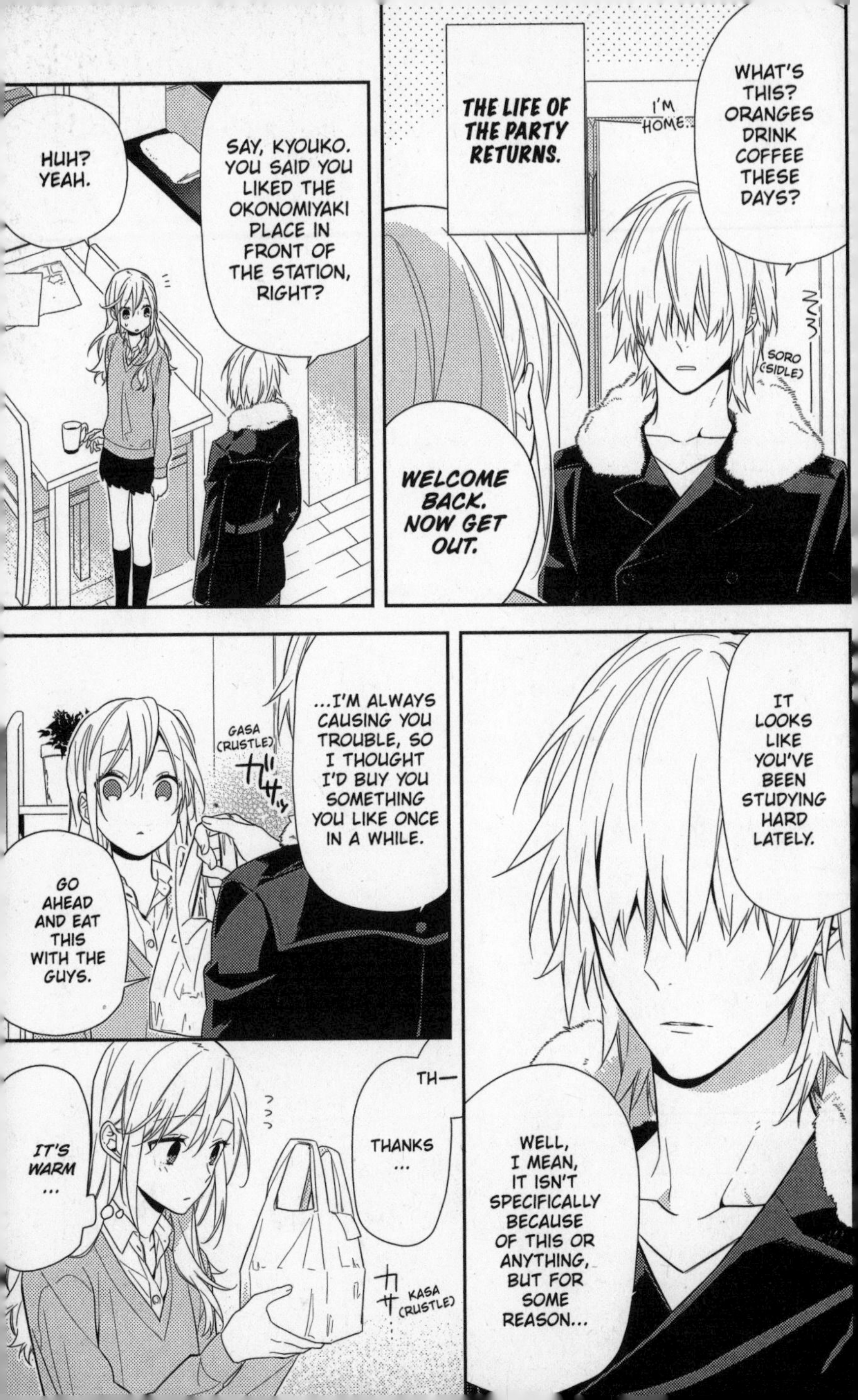
WHAT'S THIS? ORANGES DRINK COFFEE THESE DAYS?
I'M HOME..
THE LIFE OF THE PARTY RETURNS.
SORO (SIDLE)
WELCOME BACK. NOW GET OUT.
SAY, KYOUKO. YOU SAID YOU LIKED THE OKONOMIYAKI PLACE IN FRONT OF THE STATION, RIGHT?
HUH? YEAH.
IT LOOKS LIKE YOU'VE BEEN STUDYING HARD LATELY.
WELL, I MEAN, IT ISN'T SPECIFICALLY BECAUSE OF THIS OR ANYTHING, BUT FOR SOME REASON...
...I'M ALWAYS CAUSING YOU TROUBLE, SO I THOUGHT I'D BUY YOU SOMETHING YOU LIKE ONCE IN A WHILE.
GASA (RUSTLE)
GO AHEAD AND EAT THIS WITH THE GUYS.
TH—
THANKS...
KASA (RUSTLE)
IT'S WARM...

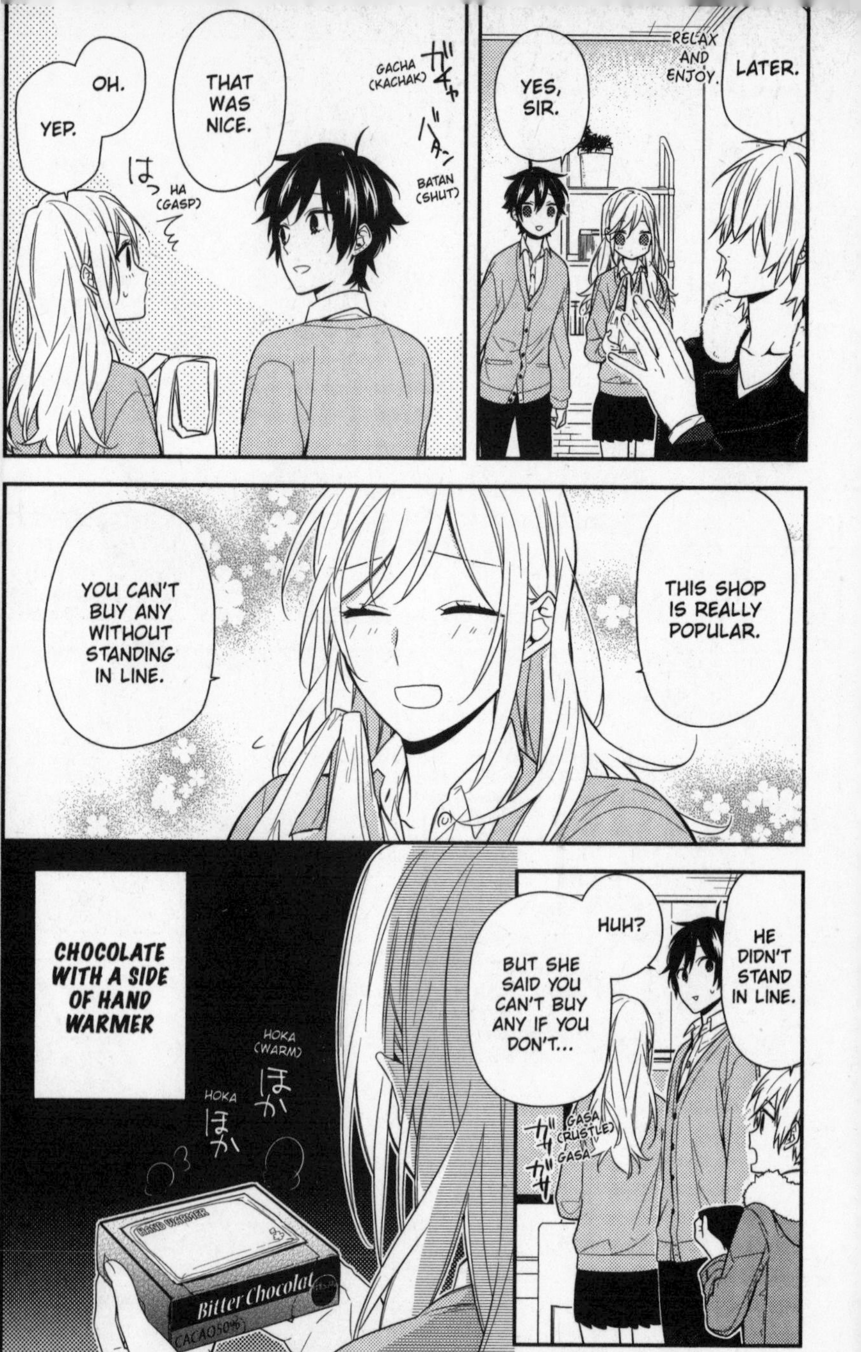
LATER.
RELAX AND ENJOY.
YES, SIR.
GACHA (KACHAK) ガチャ
THAT WAS NICE.
バタン BATAN (SHUT)
OH.
YEP.
はっ HA (GASP)
THIS SHOP IS REALLY POPULAR.
YOU CAN'T BUY ANY WITHOUT STANDING IN LINE.
HE DIDN'T STAND IN LINE.
HUH?
BUT SHE SAID YOU CAN'T BUY ANY IF YOU DON'T...
ガサガサ GASA (RUSTLE) GASA
CHOCOLATE WITH A SIDE OF HAND WARMER
ほか HOKA (WARM)
ほか HOKA
HAND WARMER
Bitter Chocolat
CACAO50%

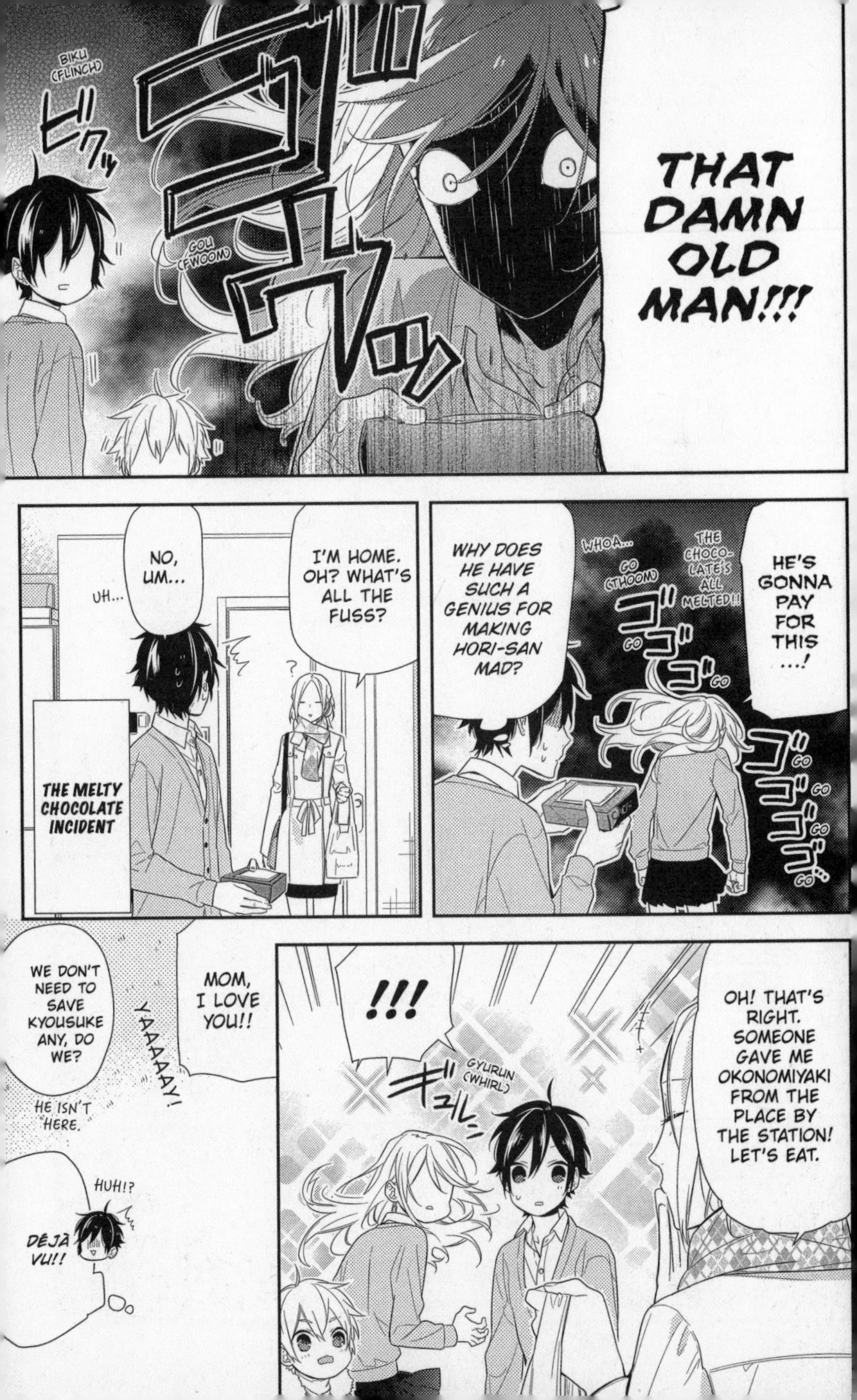

THAT DAMN OLD MAN!!!
GOU (FWOOM)
BIKU (FLINCH)
HE'S GONNA PAY FOR THIS ...!
THE CHOCO-LATE'S ALL MELTED!!
WHOA...
GO (THOOM)
WHY DOES HE HAVE SUCH A GENIUS FOR MAKING HORI-SAN MAD?
GO GO GO GO GO GO
I'M HOME. OH? WHAT'S ALL THE FUSS?
NO, UM...
UH...
THE MELTY CHOCOLATE INCIDENT
OH! THAT'S RIGHT. SOMEONE GAVE ME OKONOMIYAKI FROM THE PLACE BY THE STATION! LET'S EAT.
!!!
GYURUN (WHIRL)
MOM, I LOVE YOU!!
YAAAAAY!
WE DON'T NEED TO SAVE KYOUSUKE ANY, DO WE?
HE ISN'T HERE.
HUH!?
DÉJÀ VU!!

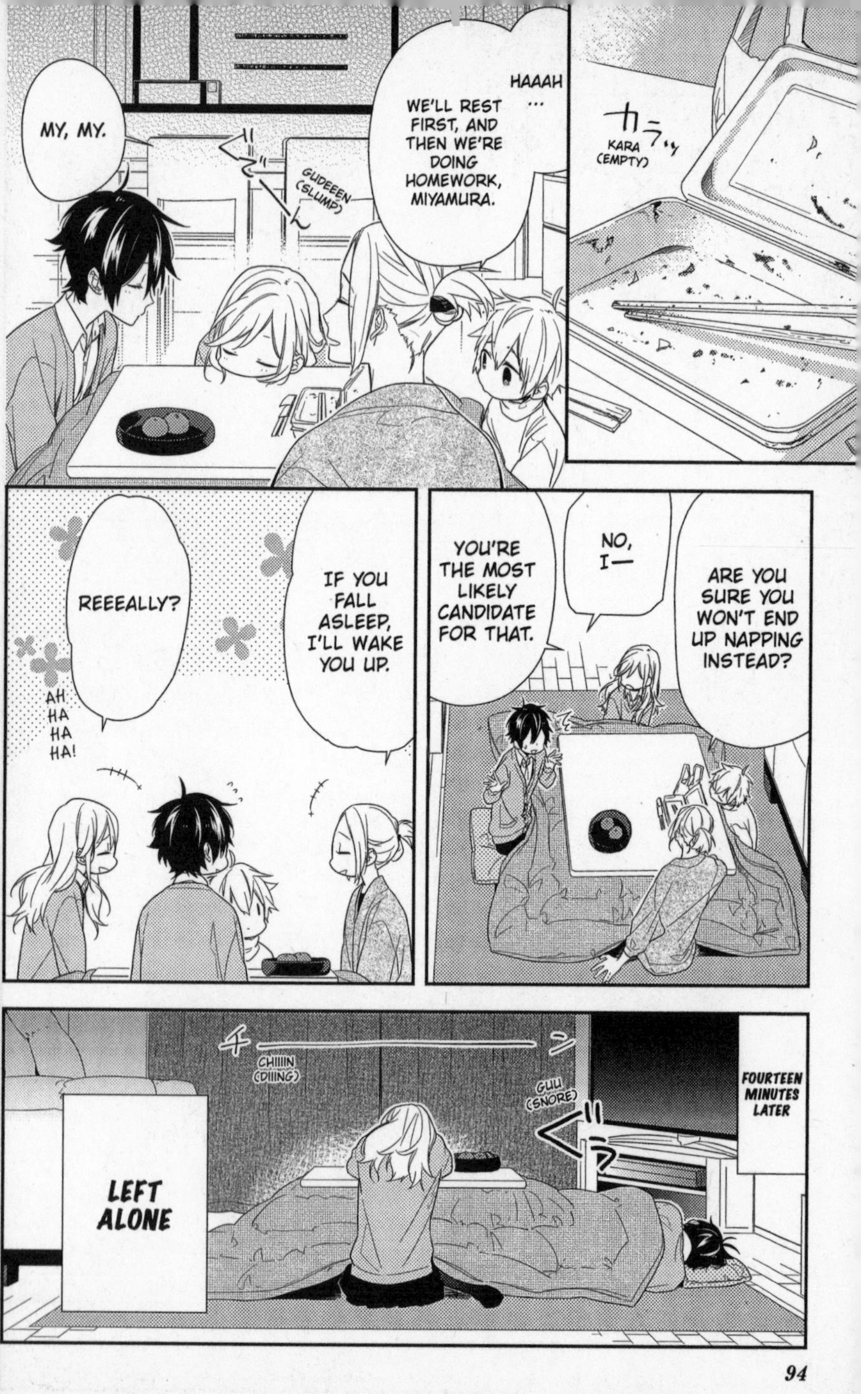
KARA (EMPTY)
HAAAH ...
WE'LL REST FIRST, AND THEN WE'RE DOING HOMEWORK, MIYAMURA.
GUDEEEN (SLUMP)
MY, MY.
ARE YOU SURE YOU WON'T END UP NAPPING INSTEAD?
NO, I—
YOU'RE THE MOST LIKELY CANDIDATE FOR THAT.
IF YOU FALL ASLEEP, I'LL WAKE YOU UP.
REEEALLY?
AH HA HA HA!
FOURTEEN MINUTES LATER
GUU (SNORE)
CHIIIN (DIIING)
LEFT ALONE

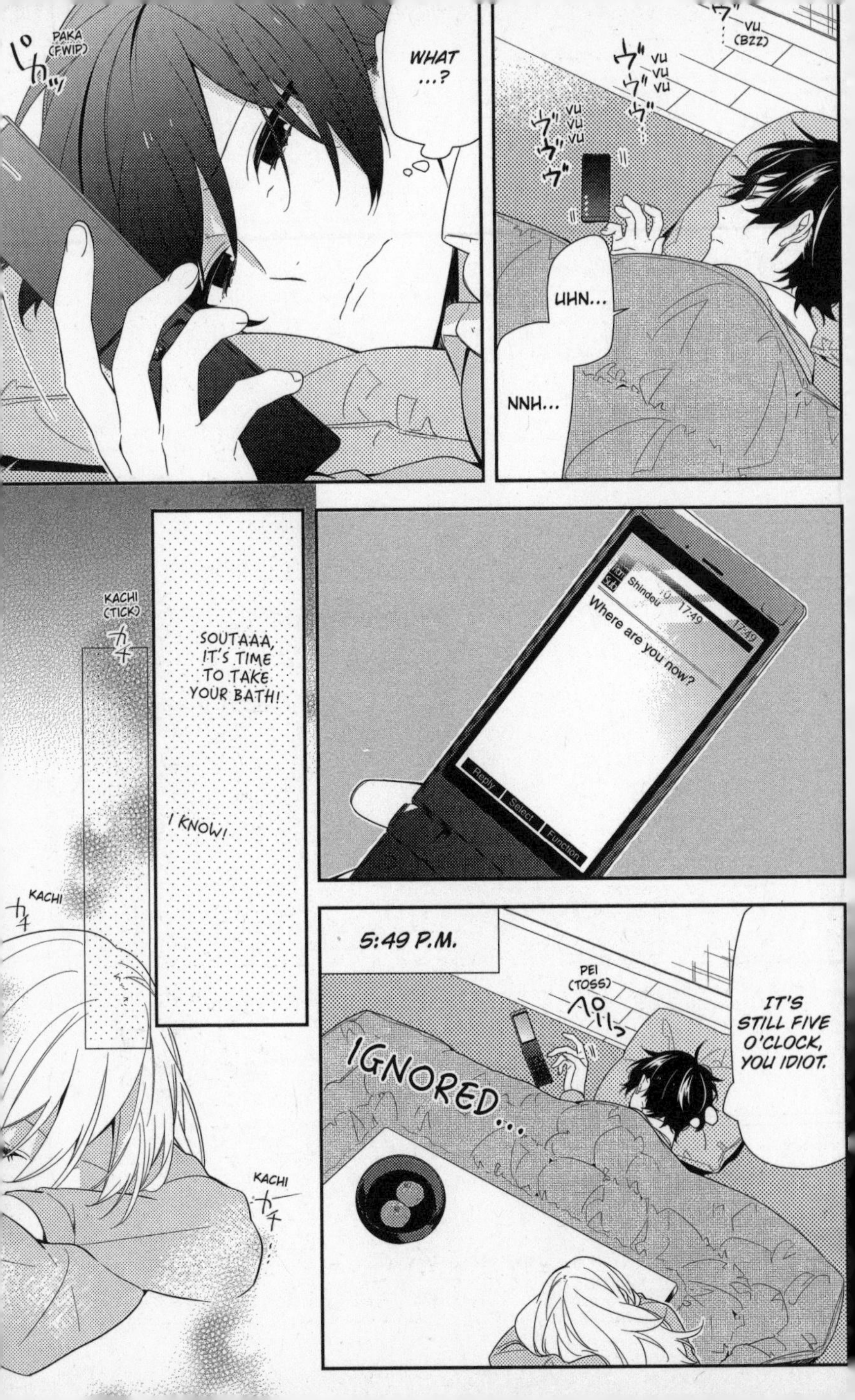
VU (BZZ)
VU VU VU
VU VU VU
UHN...
NNH...
PAKA (F.WIP)
WHAT ...?
Shindou
17:49
Where are you now?
Reply
Select
Function
5:49 P.M.
IT'S STILL FIVE O'CLOCK, YOU IDIOT.
PEI (TOSS)
IGNORED...
KACHI (TICK)
SOUTAAA, IT'S TIME TO TAKE YOUR BATH!
I KNOW!
KACHI
KACHI

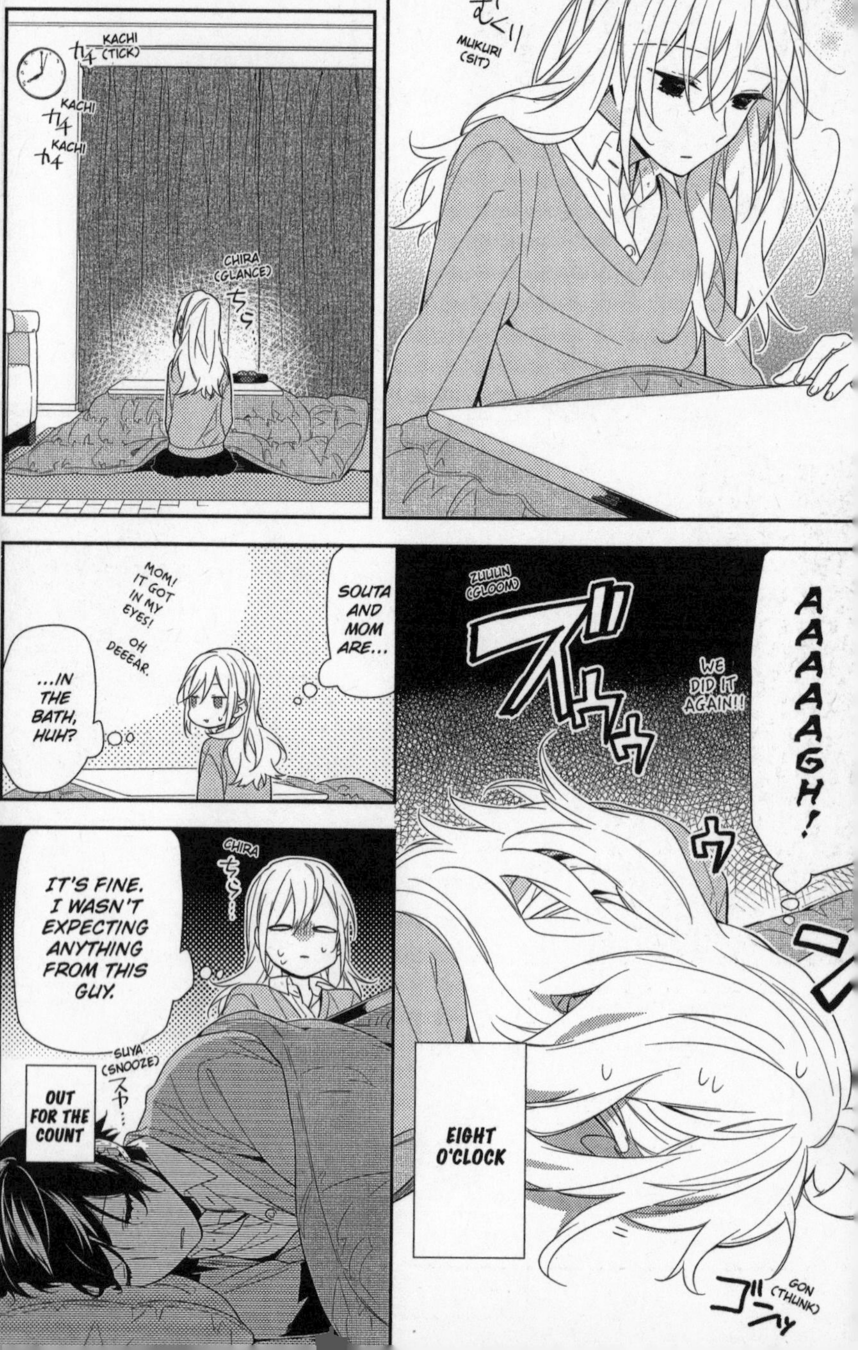
むくり
MUKURI (SIT)
カチ
KACHI (TICK)
カチ
KACHI
カチ
KACHI
CHIRA (GLANCE)
ちら…
AAAAAGH!
WE DID IT AGAIN!!
ZUUUN (GLOOM)
ズゥゥゥゥ
EIGHT O'CLOCK
GON (THUNK)
ゴンッ
SOUTA AND MOM ARE…
MOM! IT GOT IN MY EYES!
OH DEEEAR.
…IN THE BATH, HUH?
CHIRA
ちら…
IT'S FINE. I WASN'T EXPECTING ANYTHING FROM THIS GUY.
SUYA (SNOOZE)
スヤ…
OUT FOR THE COUNT

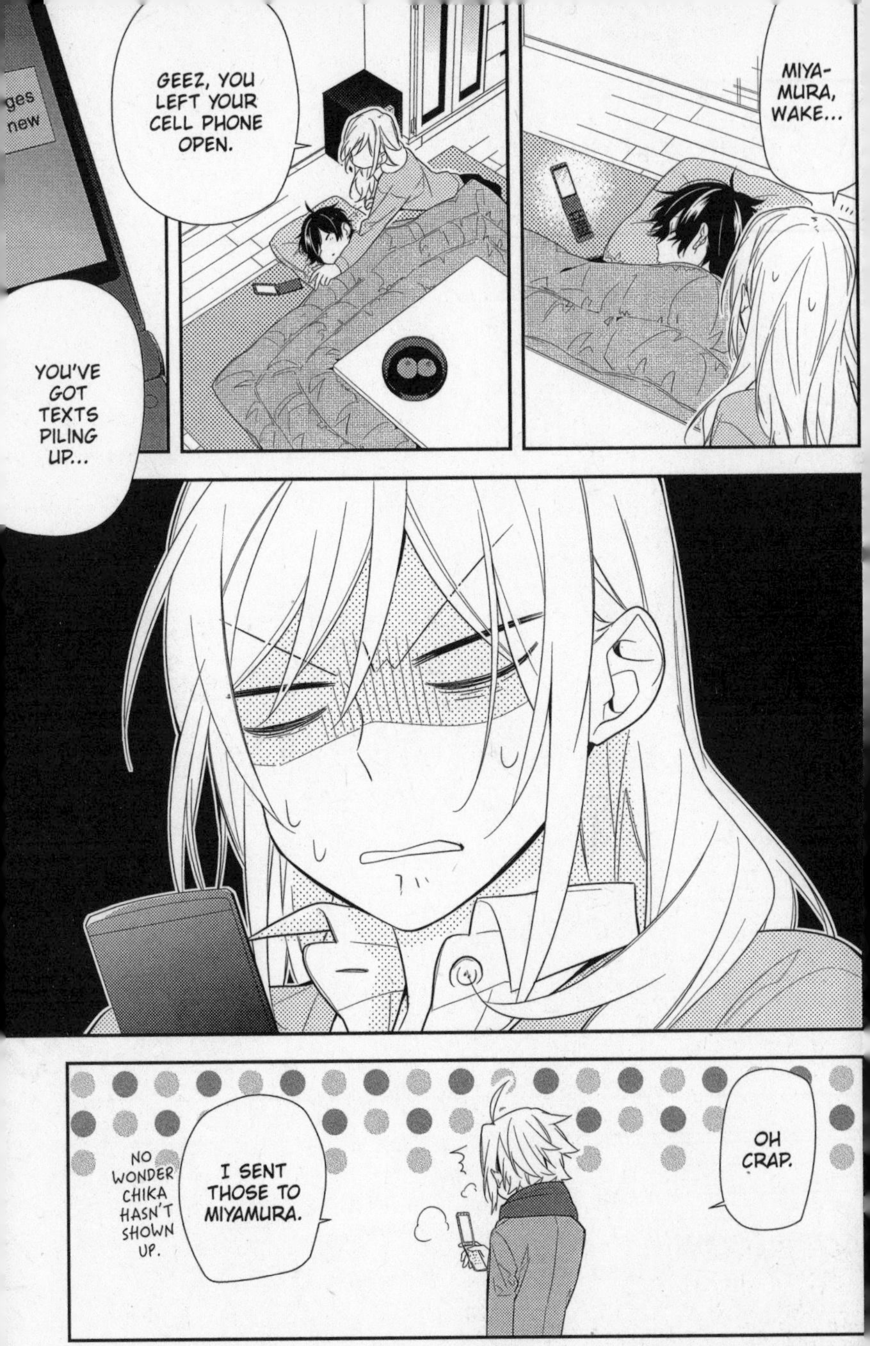
MIYA-MURA, WAKE...
GEEZ, YOU LEFT YOUR CELL PHONE OPEN.
YOU'VE GOT TEXTS PILING UP...
OH CRAP.
I SENT THOSE TO MIYAMURA.
NO WONDER CHIKA HASN'T SHOWN UP.

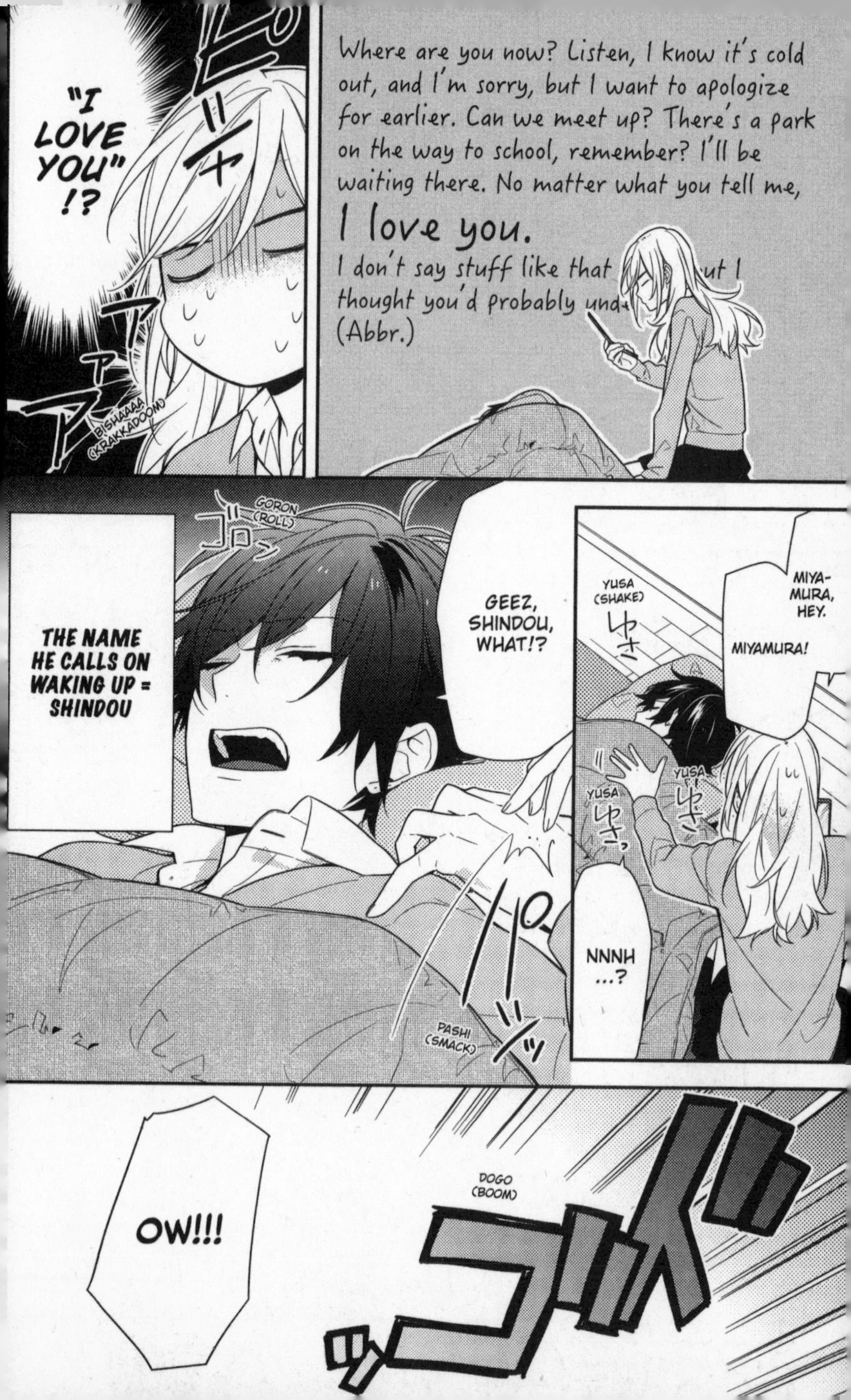
Where are you now? Listen, I know it's cold out, and I'm sorry, but I want to apologize for earlier. Can we meet up? There's a park on the way to school, remember? I'll be waiting there. No matter what you tell me,
I love you.
I don't say stuff like that
ut I
thought you'd probably und
(Abbr.)
"I LOVE YOU"!?
BISHAAAA (KRAKKADOOM)
MIYA-MURA, HEY.
MIYAMURA!
YUSA (SHAKE)
YUSA
YUSA
NNNH ...?
GEEZ, SHINDOU, WHAT!?
GORON (ROLL)
THE NAME HE CALLS ON WAKING UP = SHINDOU
PASHI (SMACK)
DOGO (BOOM)
OW!!!

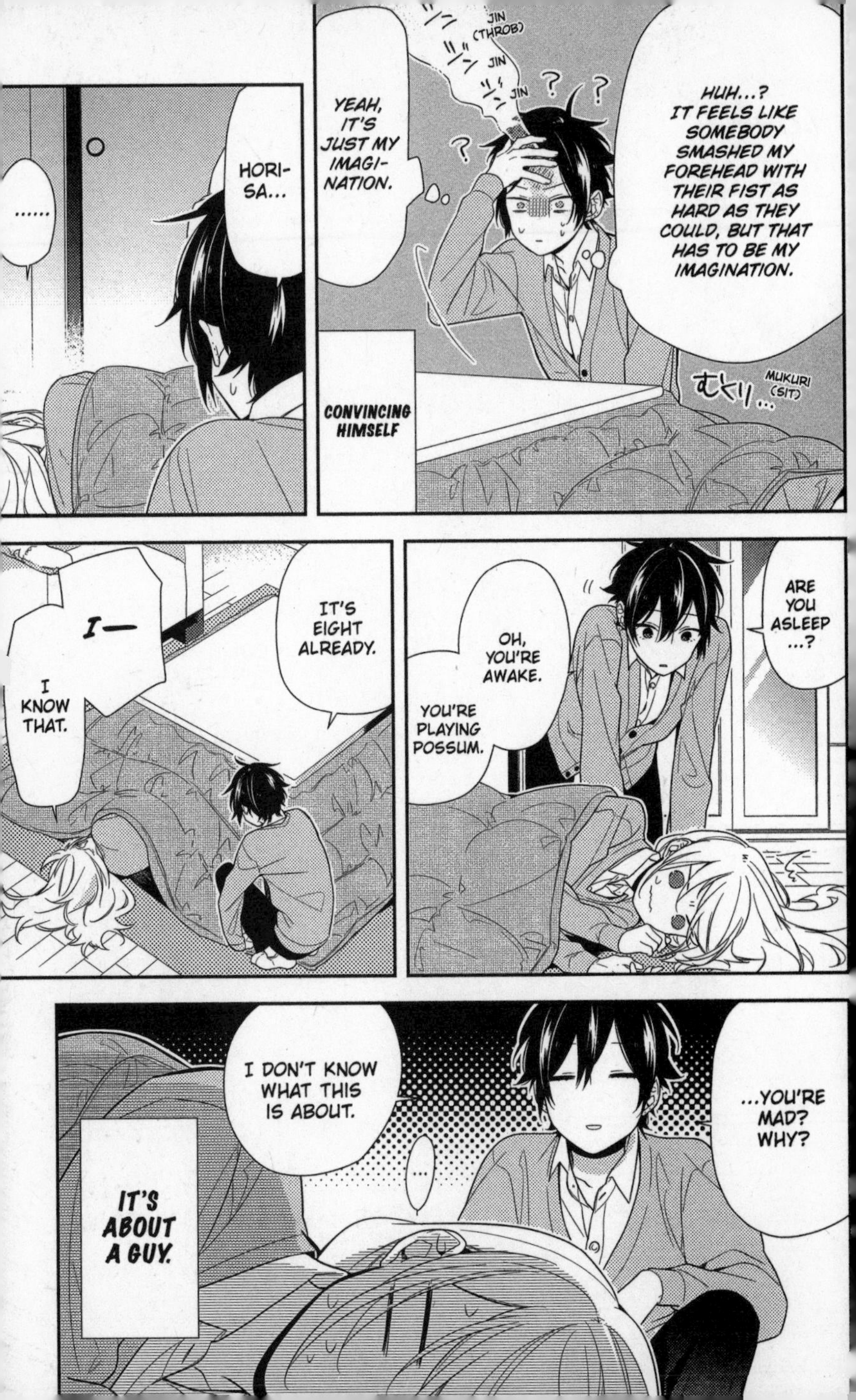
JIN (THROB)
JIN
JIN
HUH...? IT FEELS LIKE SOMEBODY SMASHED MY FOREHEAD WITH THEIR FIST AS HARD AS THEY COULD, BUT THAT HAS TO BE MY IMAGINATION.
YEAH, IT'S JUST MY IMAGI-NATION.
むくり... MUKURI (SIT)
CONVINCING HIMSELF
HORI-SA...
......
ARE YOU ASLEEP ...?
OH, YOU'RE AWAKE.
YOU'RE PLAYING POSSUM.
IT'S EIGHT ALREADY.
I—
I KNOW THAT.
...YOU'RE MAD? WHY?
I DON'T KNOW WHAT THIS IS ABOUT.
...
IT'S ABOUT A GUY.

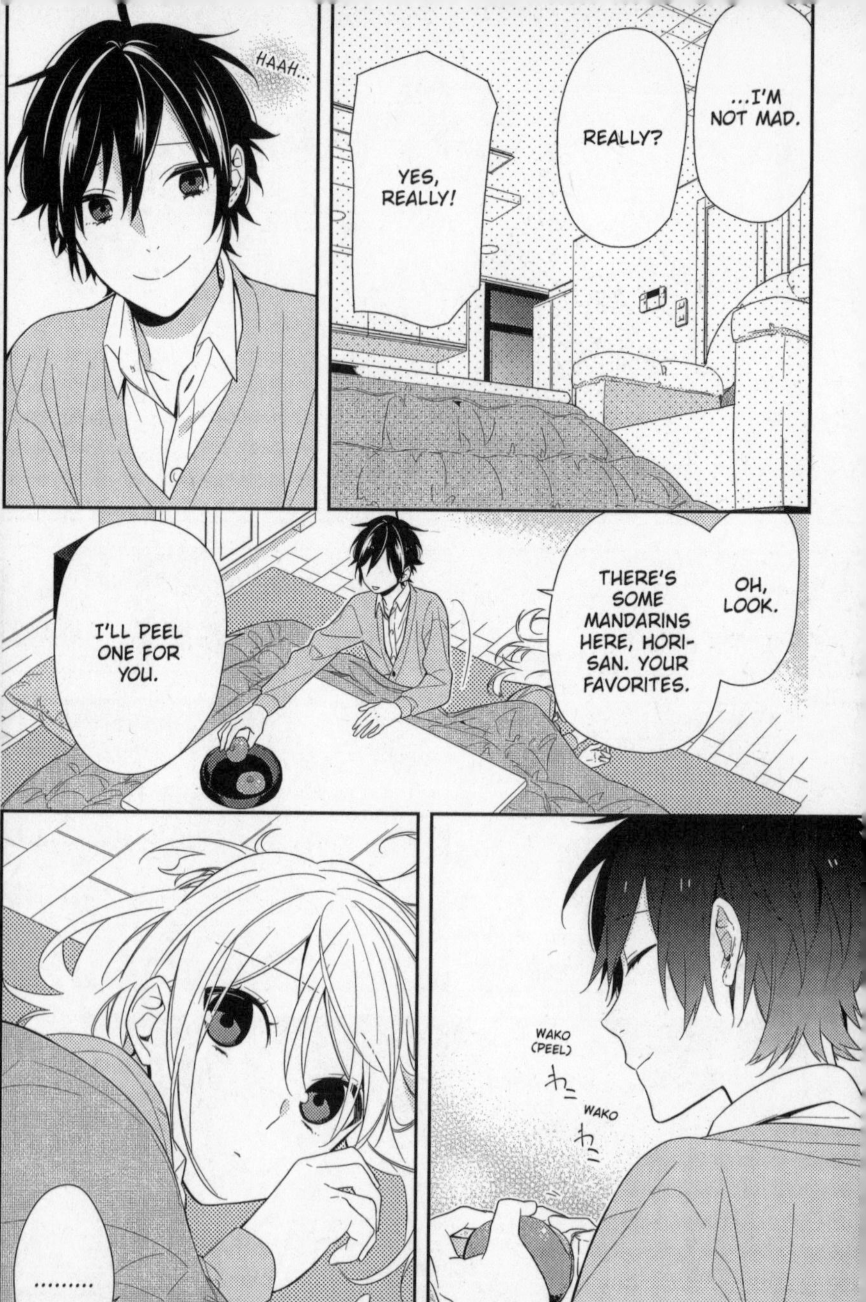
...I'M NOT MAD.
REALLY?
YES, REALLY!
HAAAH...
OH, LOOK.
THERE'S SOME MANDARINS HERE, HORI-SAN. YOUR FAVORITES.
I'LL PEEL ONE FOR YOU.
WAKO (PEEL)
WAKO
....

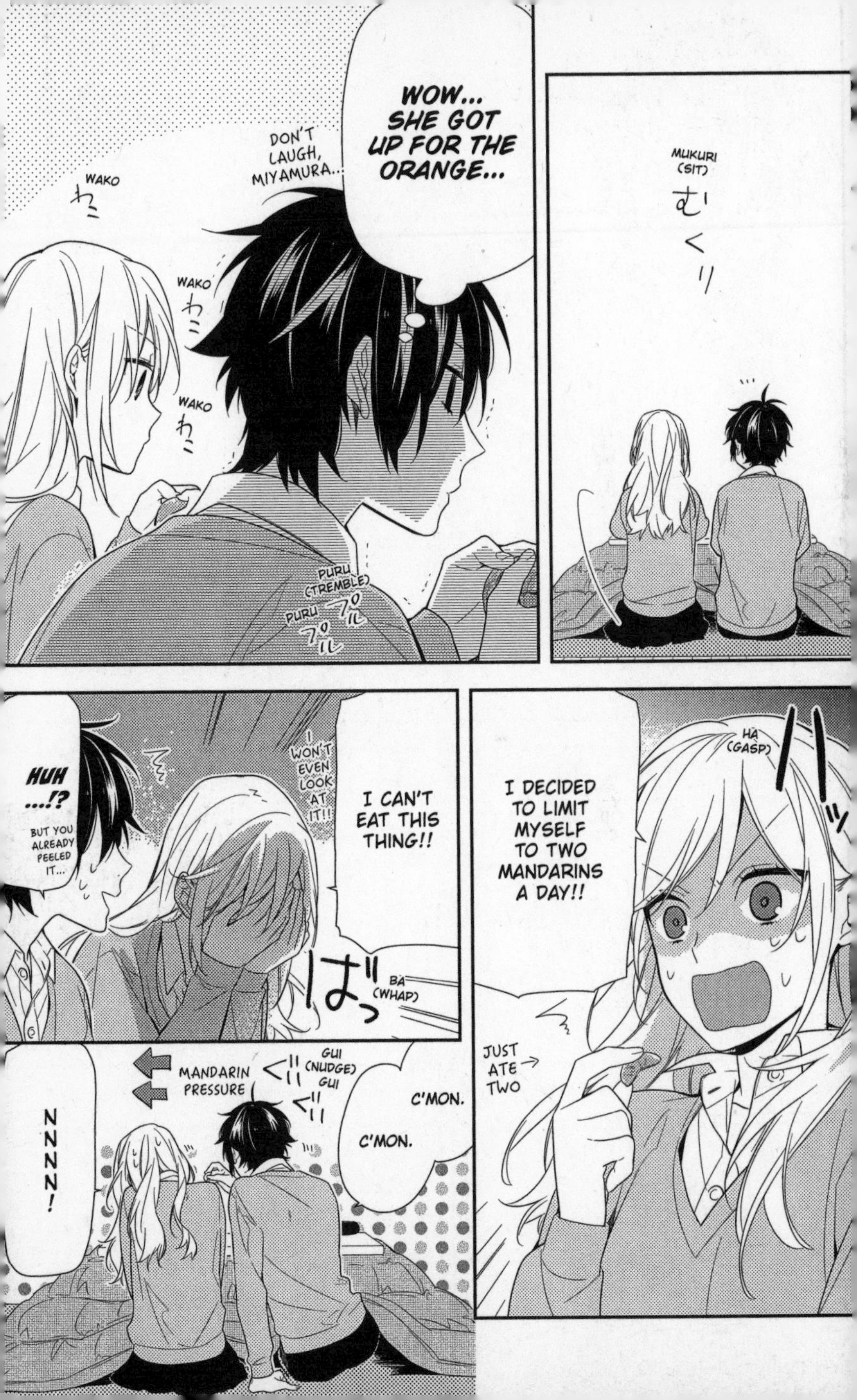
MUKURI (SIT)
むくり
...
WOW... SHE GOT UP FOR THE ORANGE...
DON'T LAUGH, MIYAMURA...
WAKO
わ
WAKO
わ
WAKO
わ
PURU (TREMBLE)
PURU
プル
プル
HA (GASP)
ッ
I DECIDED TO LIMIT MYSELF TO TWO MANDARINS A DAY!!
JUST ATE TWO
I CAN'T EAT THIS THING!!
I WON'T EVEN LOOK AT IT!!
ばっ
BA (WHAP)
HUH ...!?
BUT YOU ALREADY PEELED IT...
C'MON.
C'MON.
GUI (NUDGE) GUI
ぐい
ぐい
MANDARIN PRESSURE
NNNN!

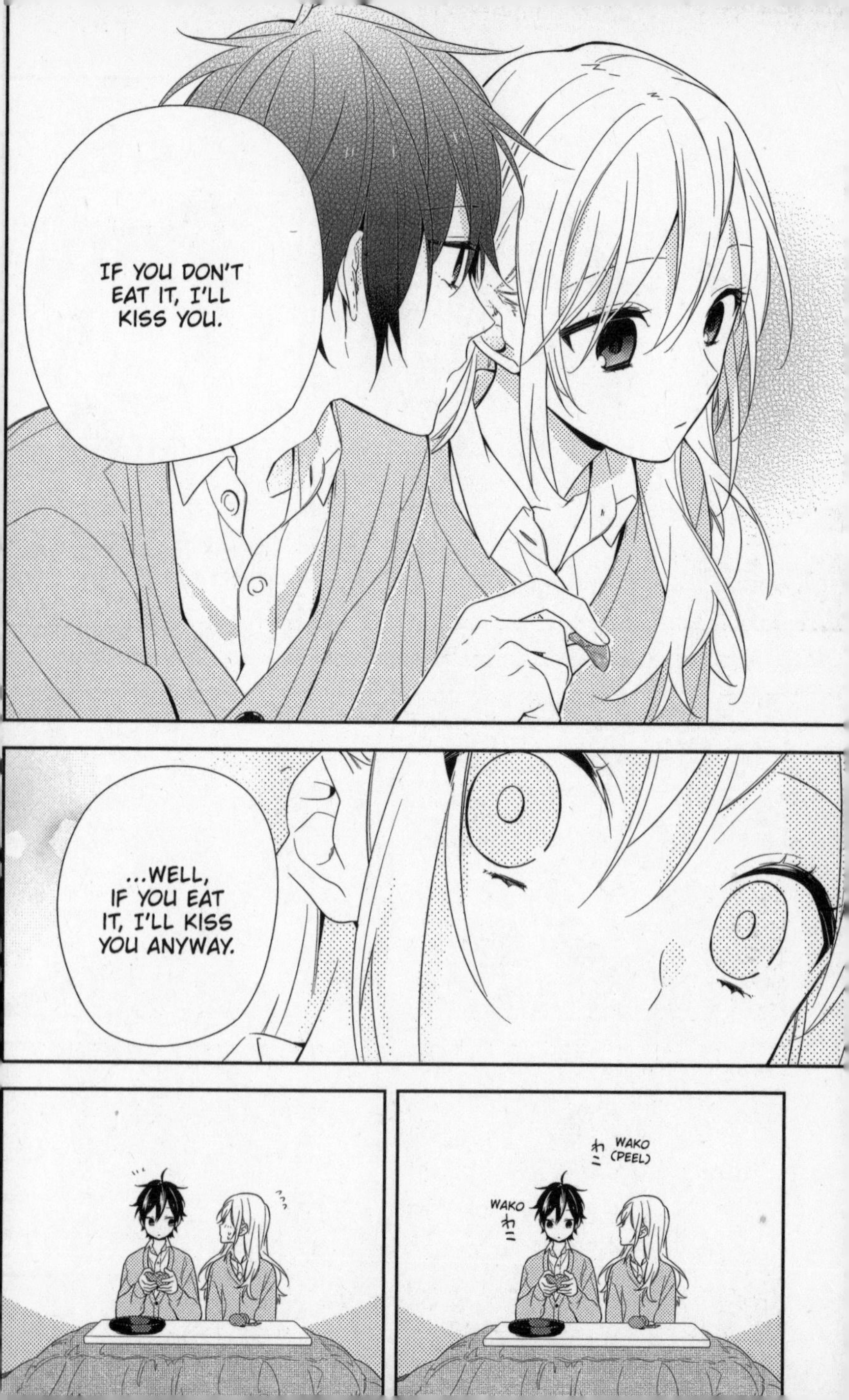
IF YOU DON'T EAT IT, I'LL KISS YOU.
...WELL, IF YOU EAT IT, I'LL KISS YOU ANYWAY.
WAKO (PEEL)
WAKO

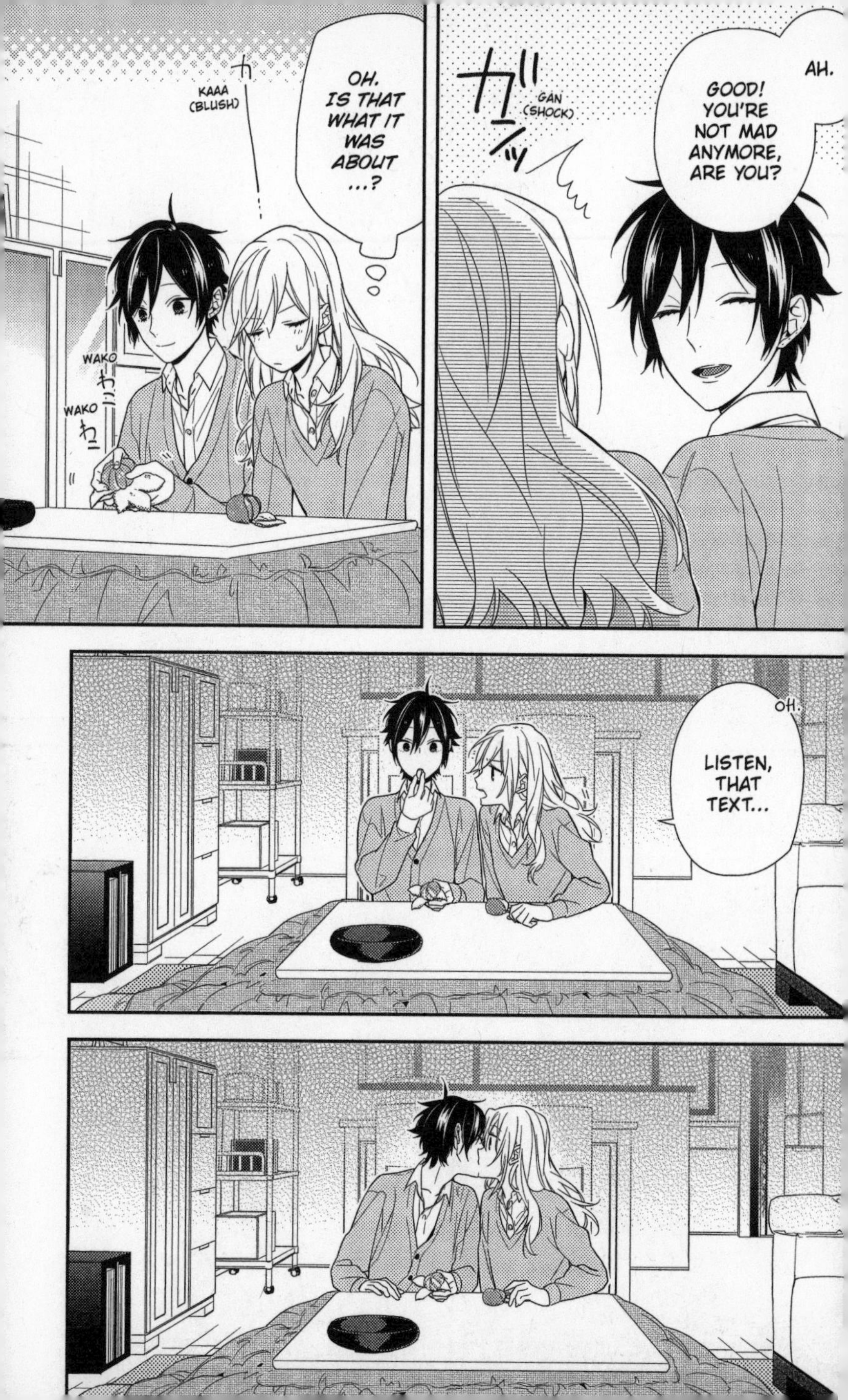
AH.
GOOD! YOU'RE NOT MAD ANYMORE, ARE YOU?
GAN (SHOCK)
OH. IS THAT WHAT IT WAS ABOUT ...?
KAAA (BLUSH)
WAKO
WAKO
OH.
LISTEN, THAT TEXT...

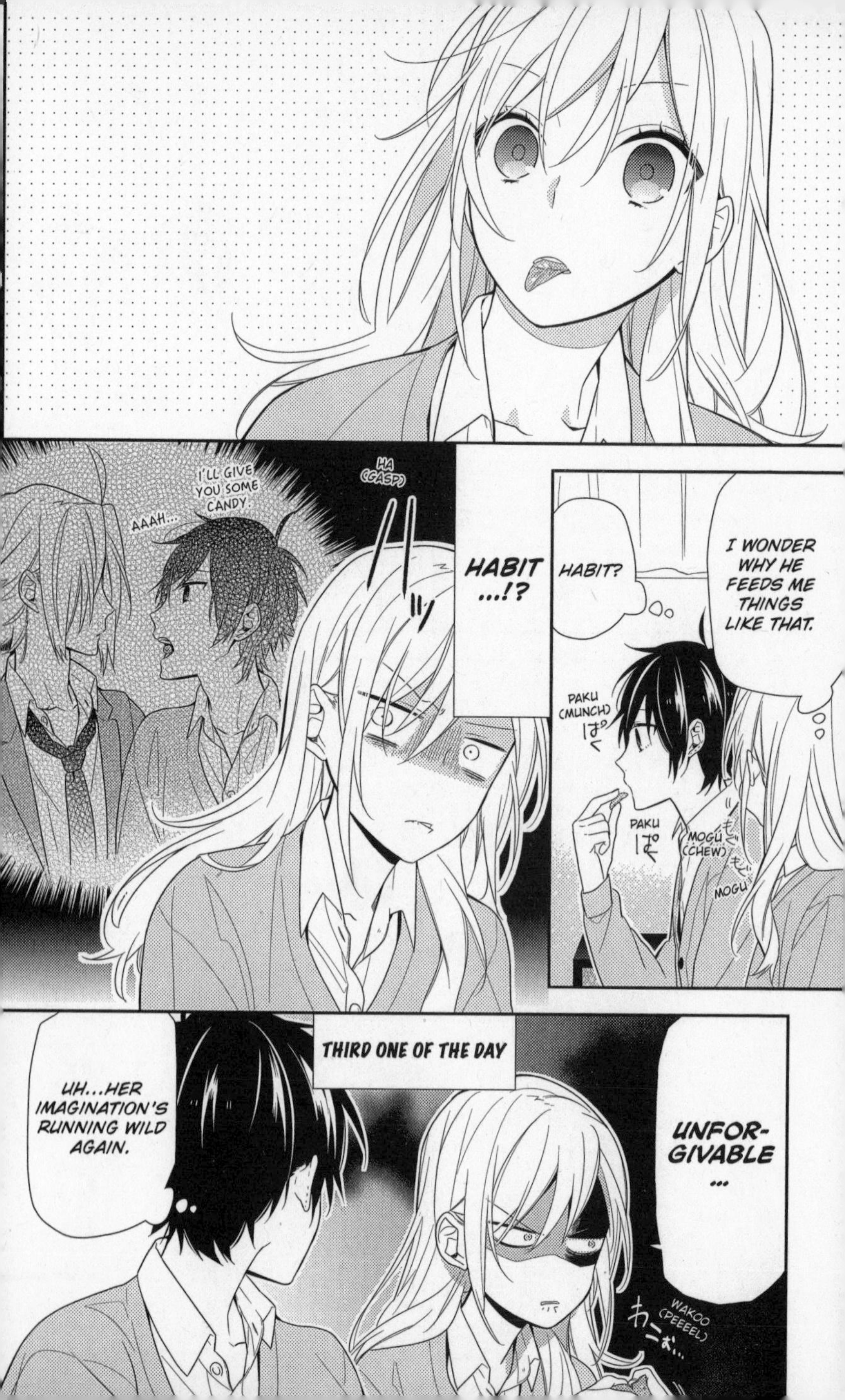
I WONDER WHY HE FEEDS ME THINGS LIKE THAT.
HABIT?
PAKU (MUNCH) ぱく
PAKU ぱく
MOGU (CHEW) もぐ
MOGU もぐ
HABIT ...!?
HA (GASP)
I'LL GIVE YOU SOME CANDY.
AAAH...
THIRD ONE OF THE DAY
UNFORGIVABLE ...
WAKOO (PEEEEL) わこぉ...
UH...HER IMAGINATION'S RUNNING WILD AGAIN.

HORIMIYA

HORIMIYA

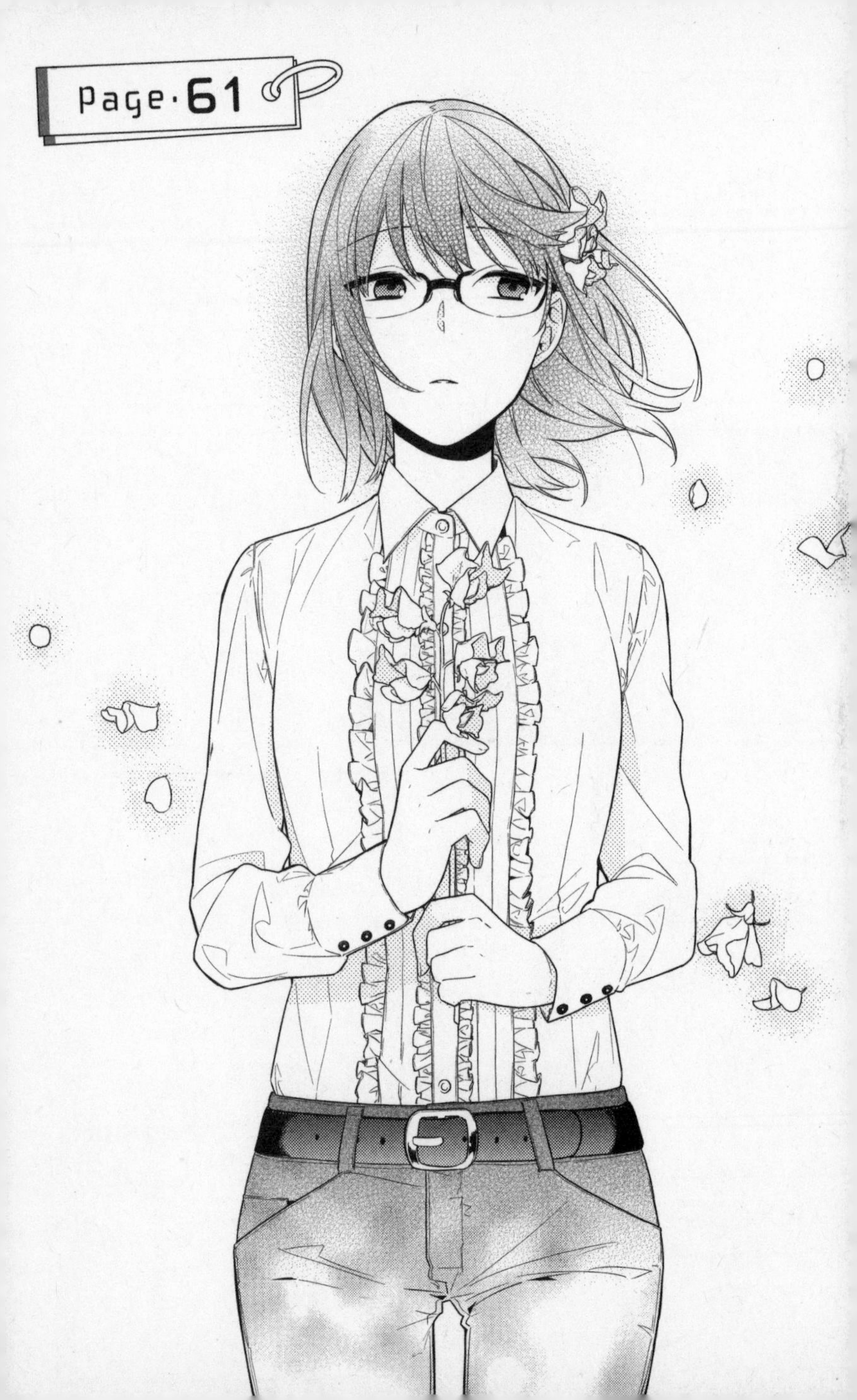
Page·61

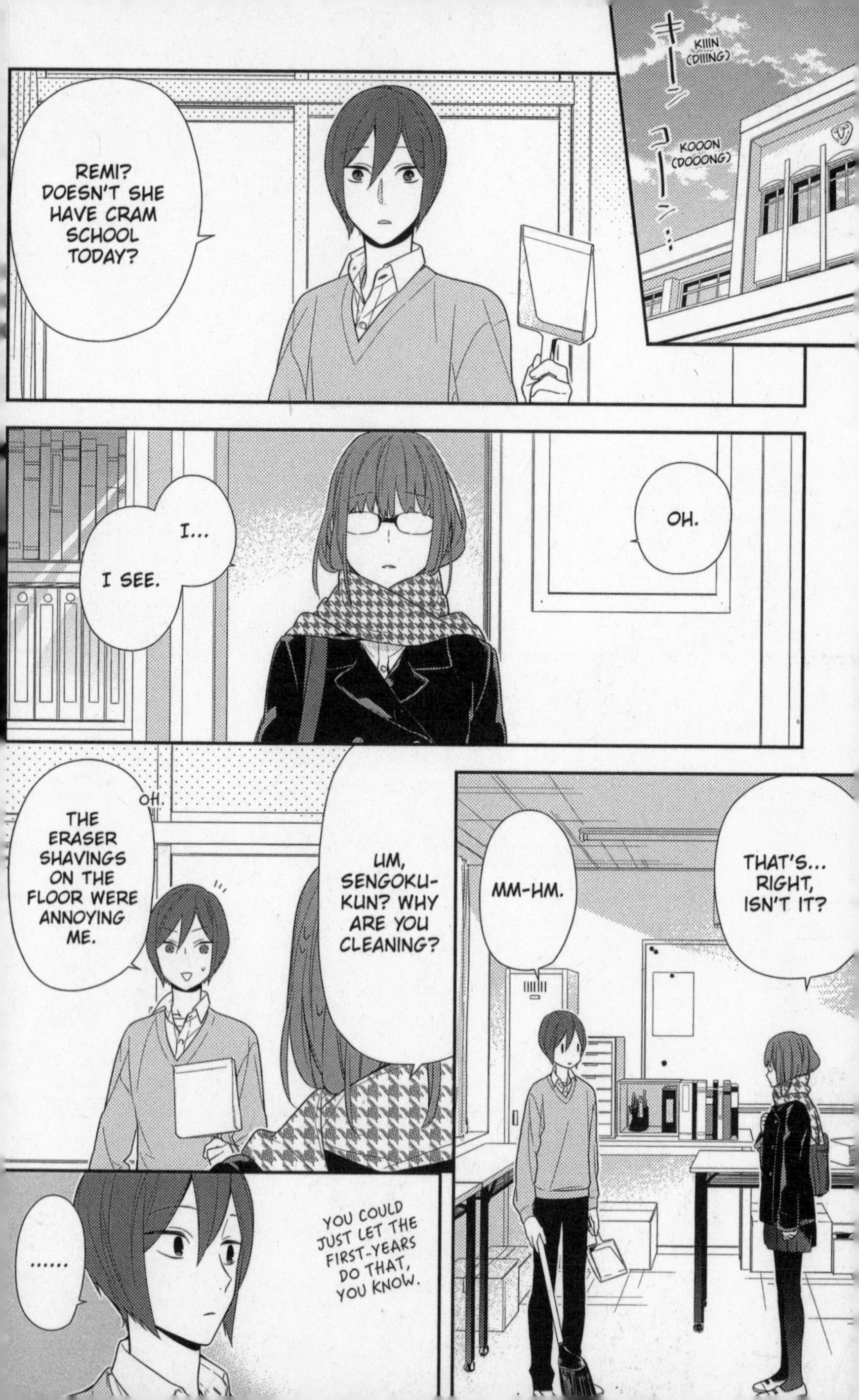
KIIN (DIIING)
KOOON (DOOONG)
REMI? DOESN'T SHE HAVE CRAM SCHOOL TODAY?
OH.
I... I SEE.
THAT'S... RIGHT, ISN'T IT?
MM-HM.
UM, SENGOKU-KUN? WHY ARE YOU CLEANING?
OH.
THE ERASER SHAVINGS ON THE FLOOR WERE ANNOYING ME.
YOU COULD JUST LET THE FIRST-YEARS DO THAT, YOU KNOW.
......

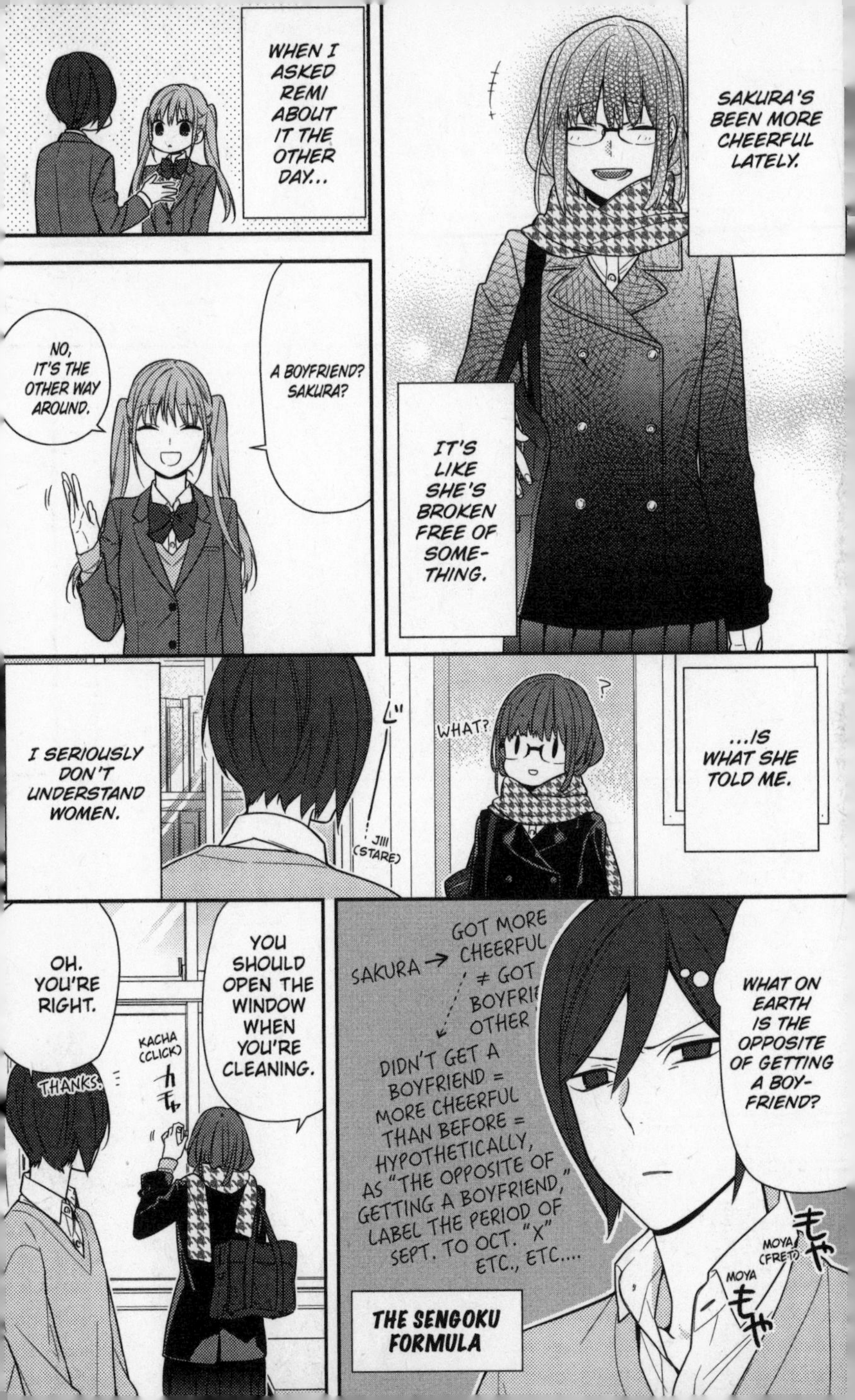
SAKURA'S BEEN MORE CHEERFUL LATELY.
IT'S LIKE SHE'S BROKEN FREE OF SOME-THING.
WHEN I ASKED REMI ABOUT IT THE OTHER DAY...
A BOYFRIEND? SAKURA?
NO, IT'S THE OTHER WAY AROUND.
...IS WHAT SHE TOLD ME.
?
WHAT?
JIII (STARE)
I SERIOUSLY DON'T UNDERSTAND WOMEN.
WHAT ON EARTH IS THE OPPOSITE OF GETTING A BOY-FRIEND?
MOYA (FRET)
MOYA
SAKURA → GOT MORE CHEERFUL
≠ GOT BOYFRI
OTHER
DIDN'T GET A BOYFRIEND = MORE CHEERFUL THAN BEFORE = HYPOTHETICALLY, AS "THE OPPOSITE OF GETTING A BOYFRIEND," LABEL THE PERIOD OF SEPT. TO OCT. "X" ETC., ETC....
THE SENGOKU FORMULA
YOU SHOULD OPEN THE WINDOW WHEN YOU'RE CLEANING.
OH. YOU'RE RIGHT.
KACHA (CLICK)
THANKS.

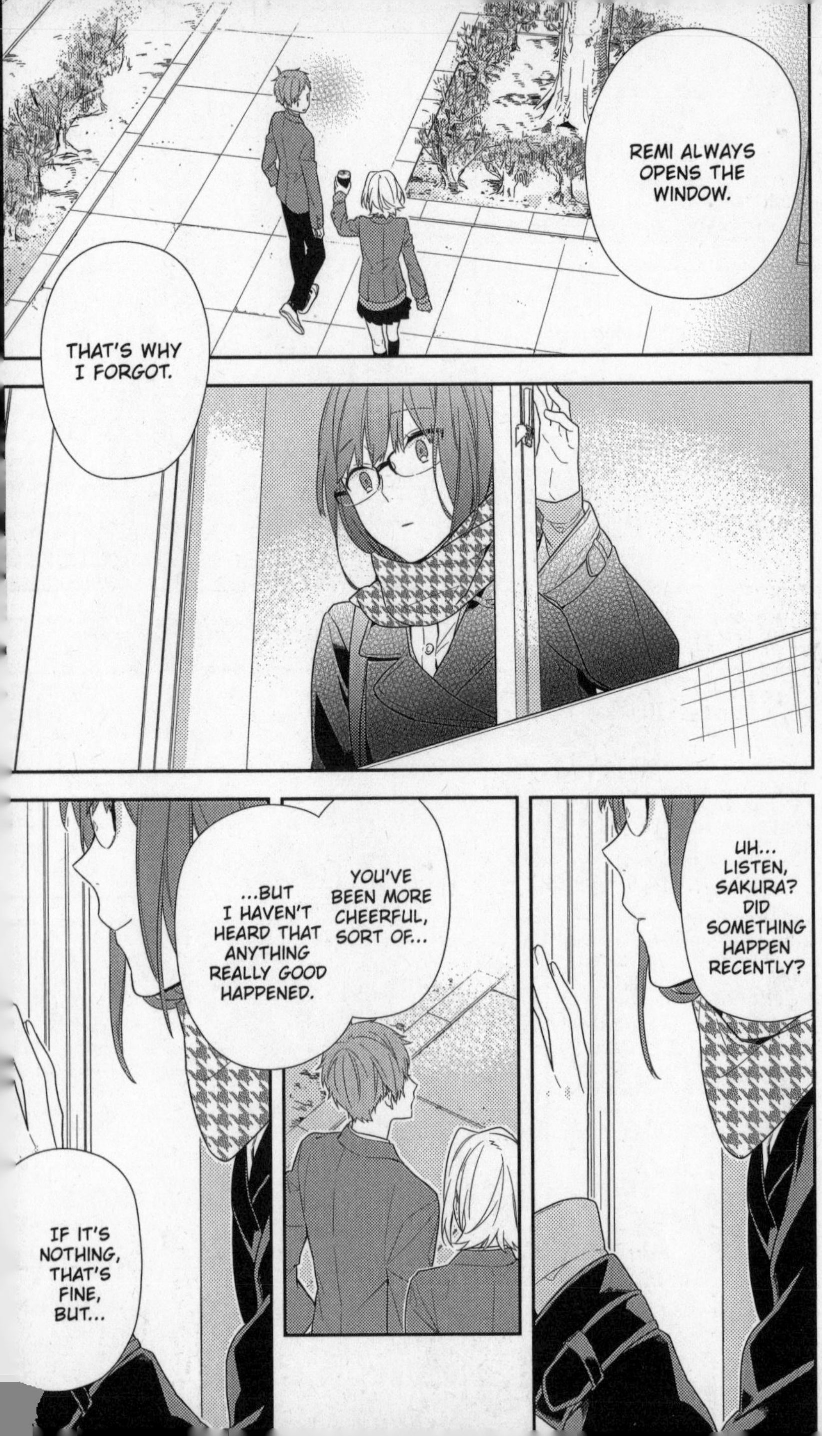
REMI ALWAYS OPENS THE WINDOW.
THAT'S WHY I FORGOT.
UH... LISTEN, SAKURA? DID SOMETHING HAPPEN RECENTLY?
YOU'VE BEEN MORE CHEERFUL, SORT OF...
...BUT I HAVEN'T HEARD THAT ANYTHING REALLY GOOD HAPPENED.
IF IT'S NOTHING, THAT'S FINE, BUT...

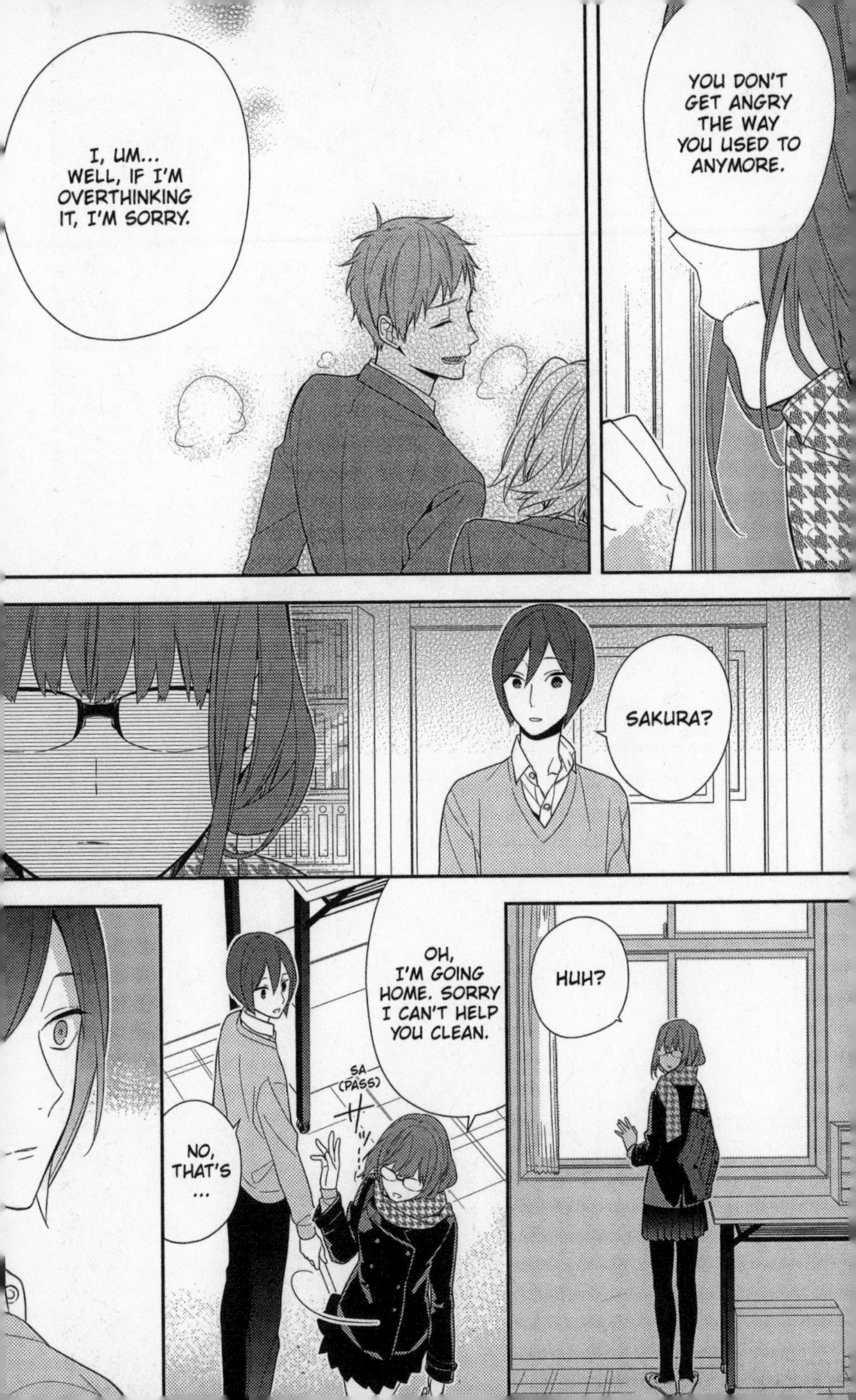
YOU DON'T GET ANGRY THE WAY YOU USED TO ANYMORE.
I, UM... WELL, IF I'M OVERTHINKING IT, I'M SORRY.
SAKURA?
HUH?
OH, I'M GOING HOME. SORRY I CAN'T HELP YOU CLEAN.
SA (PASS)
NO, THAT'S ...

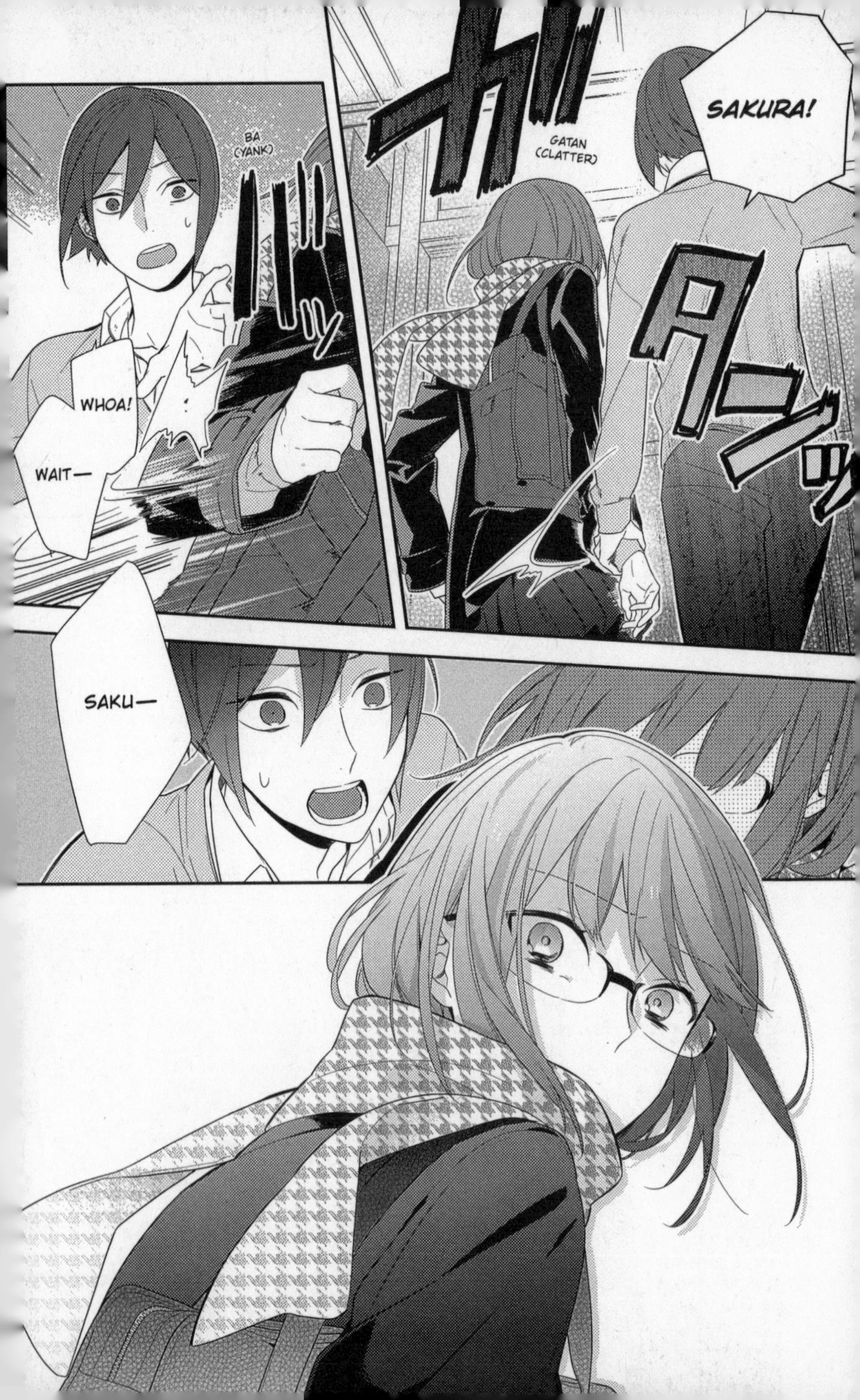
SAKURA!
GATAN (CLATTER)
BA (YANK)
WHOA!
WAIT—
SAKU—

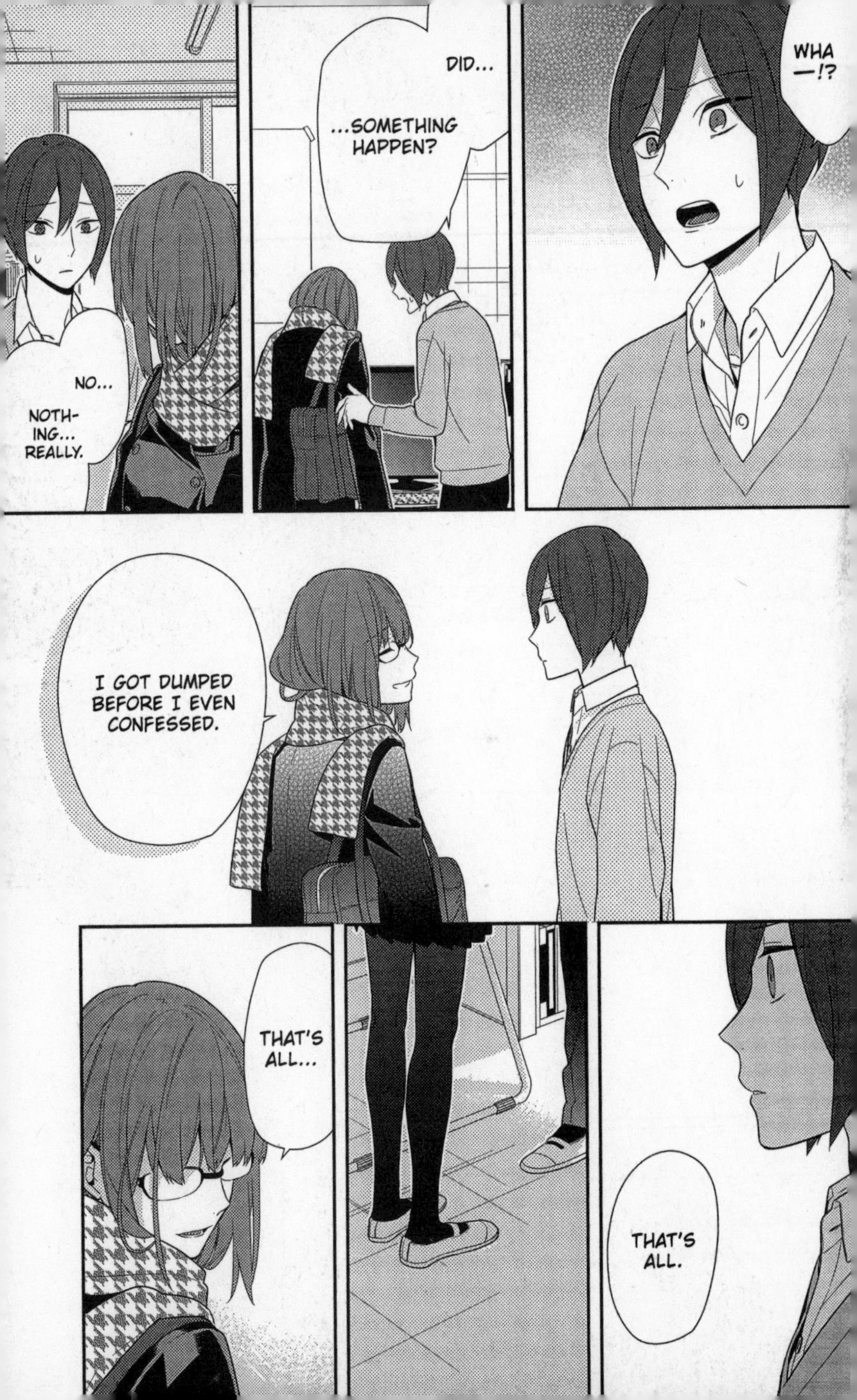
WHA—!?
DID…
…SOMETHING HAPPEN?
NO…
NOTH-ING… REALLY.
I GOT DUMPED BEFORE I EVEN CONFESSED.
THAT'S ALL.
THAT'S ALL…

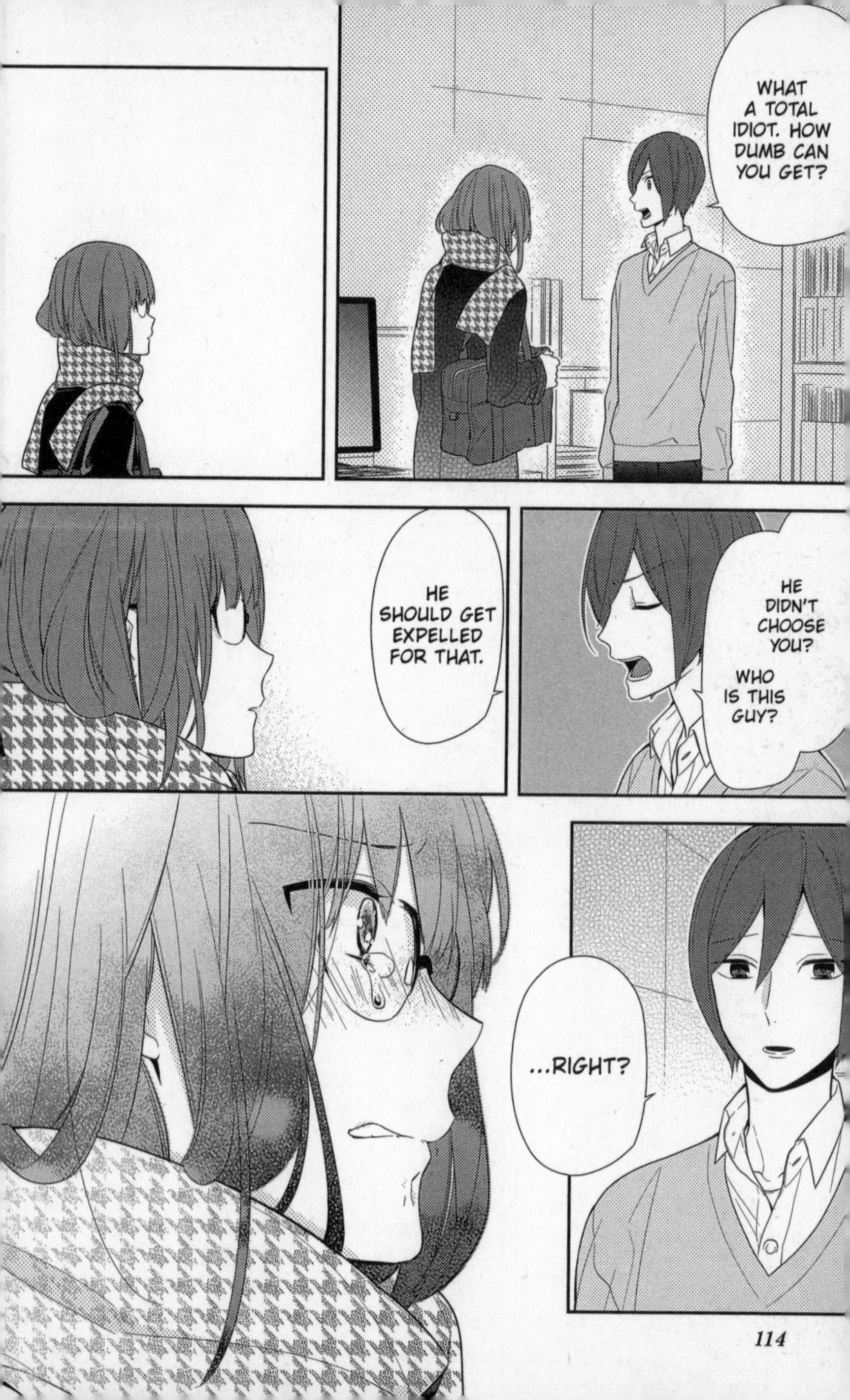
WHAT A TOTAL IDIOT. HOW DUMB CAN YOU GET?
HE DIDN'T CHOOSE YOU?
WHO IS THIS GUY?
HE SHOULD GET EXPELLED FOR THAT.
...RIGHT?

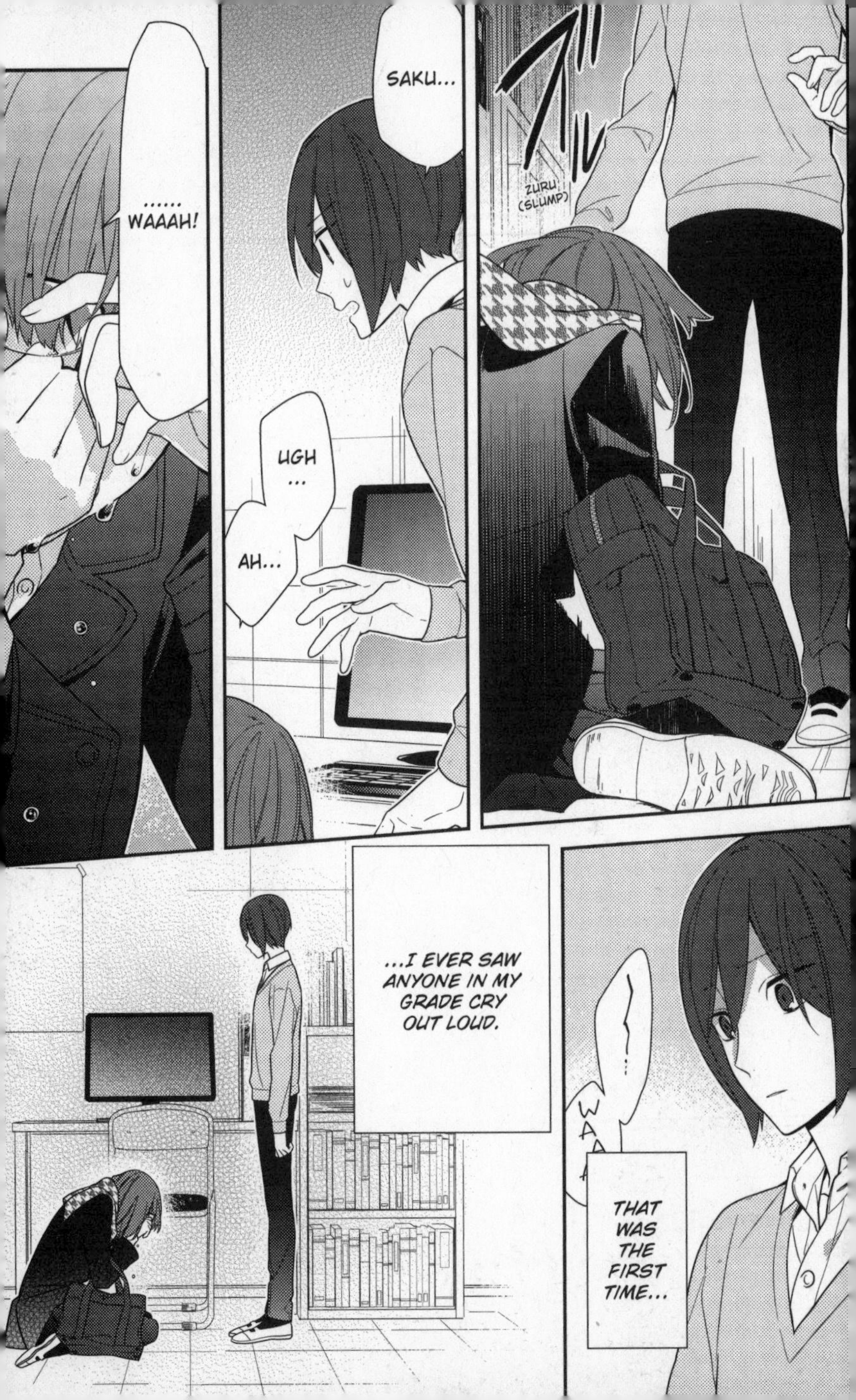
ZURU (SLUMP)
SAKU...
UGH ...
AH...
...... WAAAH!
THAT WAS THE FIRST TIME...
...I EVER SAW ANYONE IN MY GRADE CRY OUT LOUD.

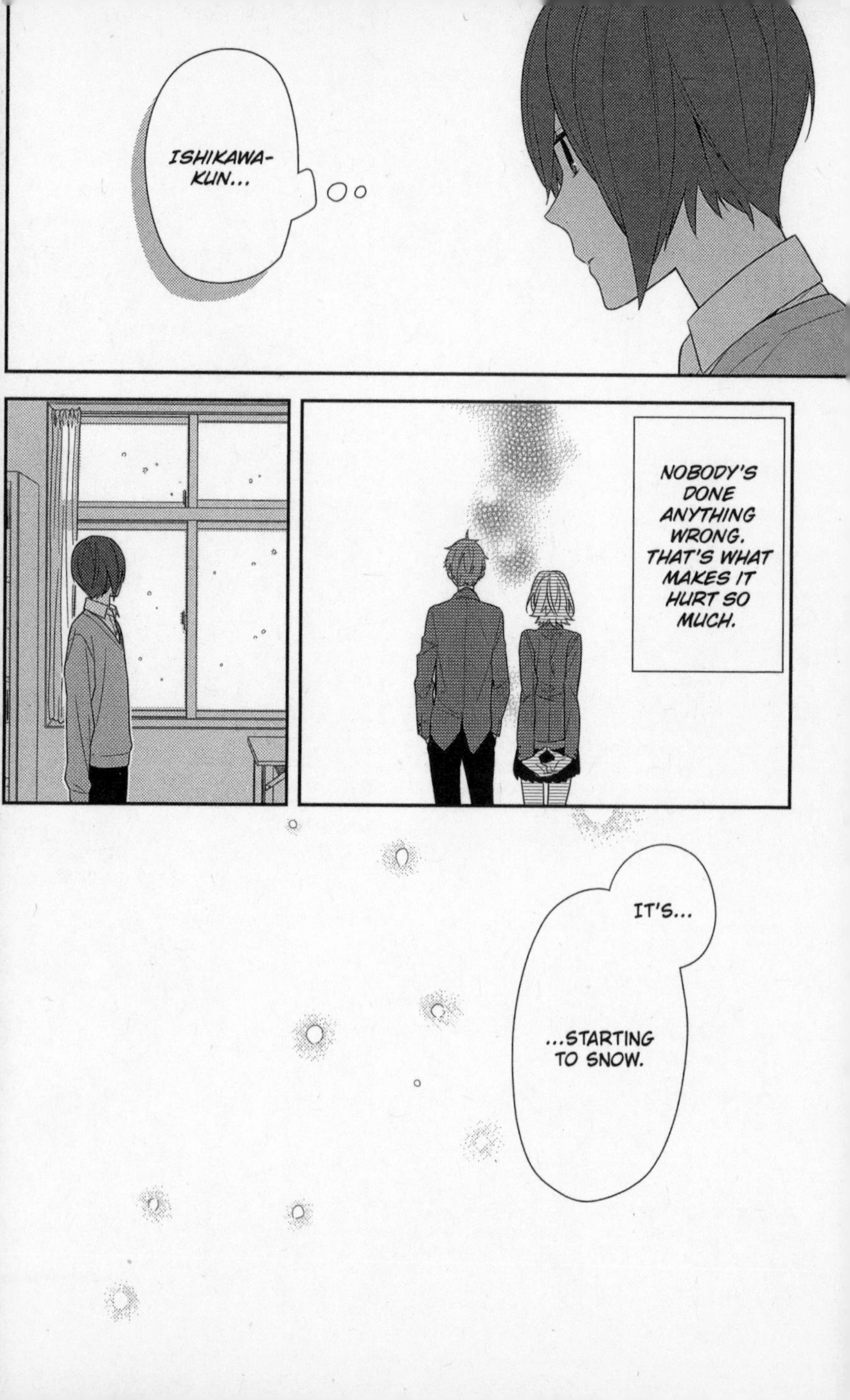
ISHIKAWA-KUN...
NOBODY'S DONE ANYTHING WRONG. THAT'S WHAT MAKES IT HURT SO MUCH.
IT'S...
...STARTING TO SNOW.

HORIMIYA

HORIMIYA

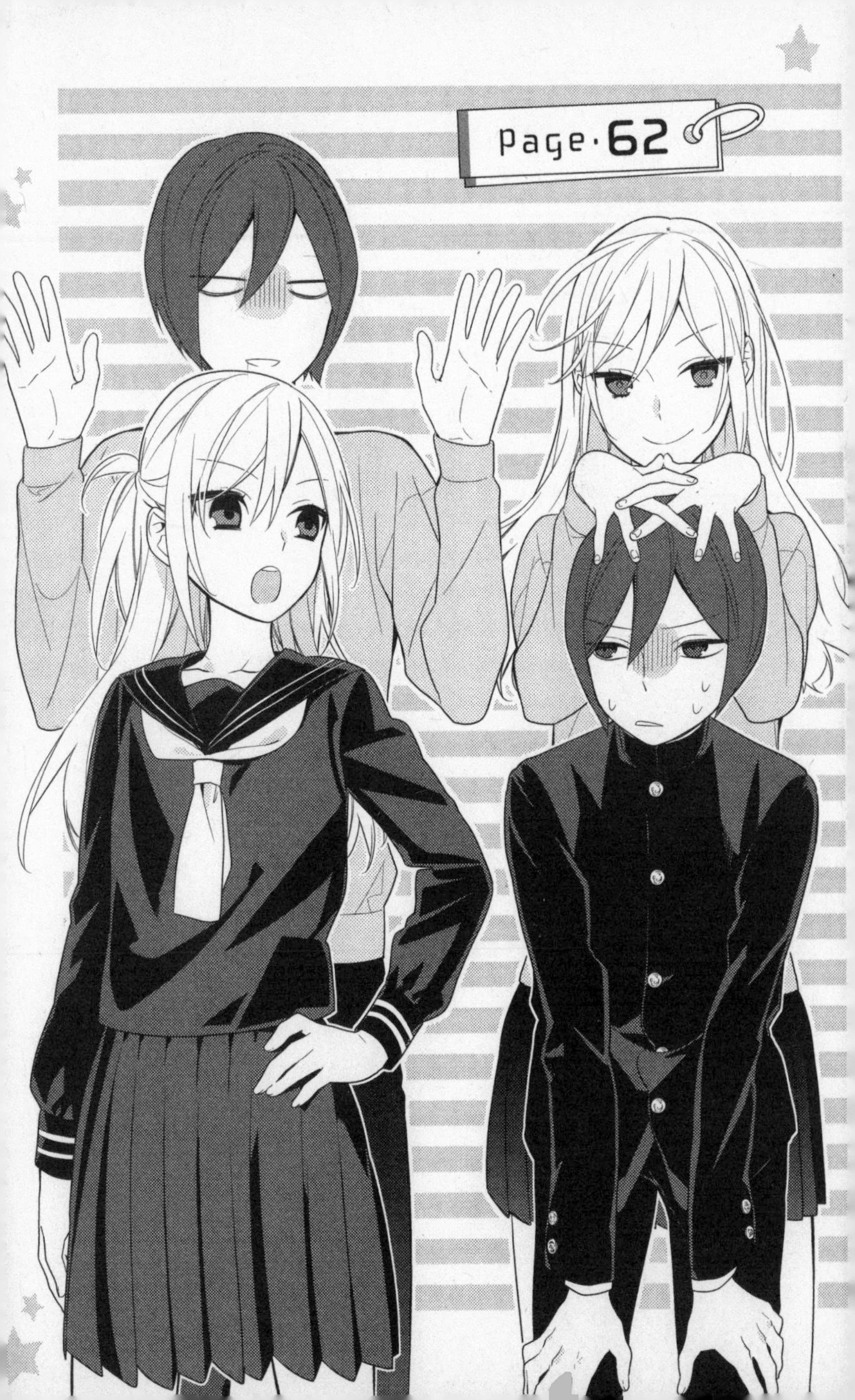
Page·62

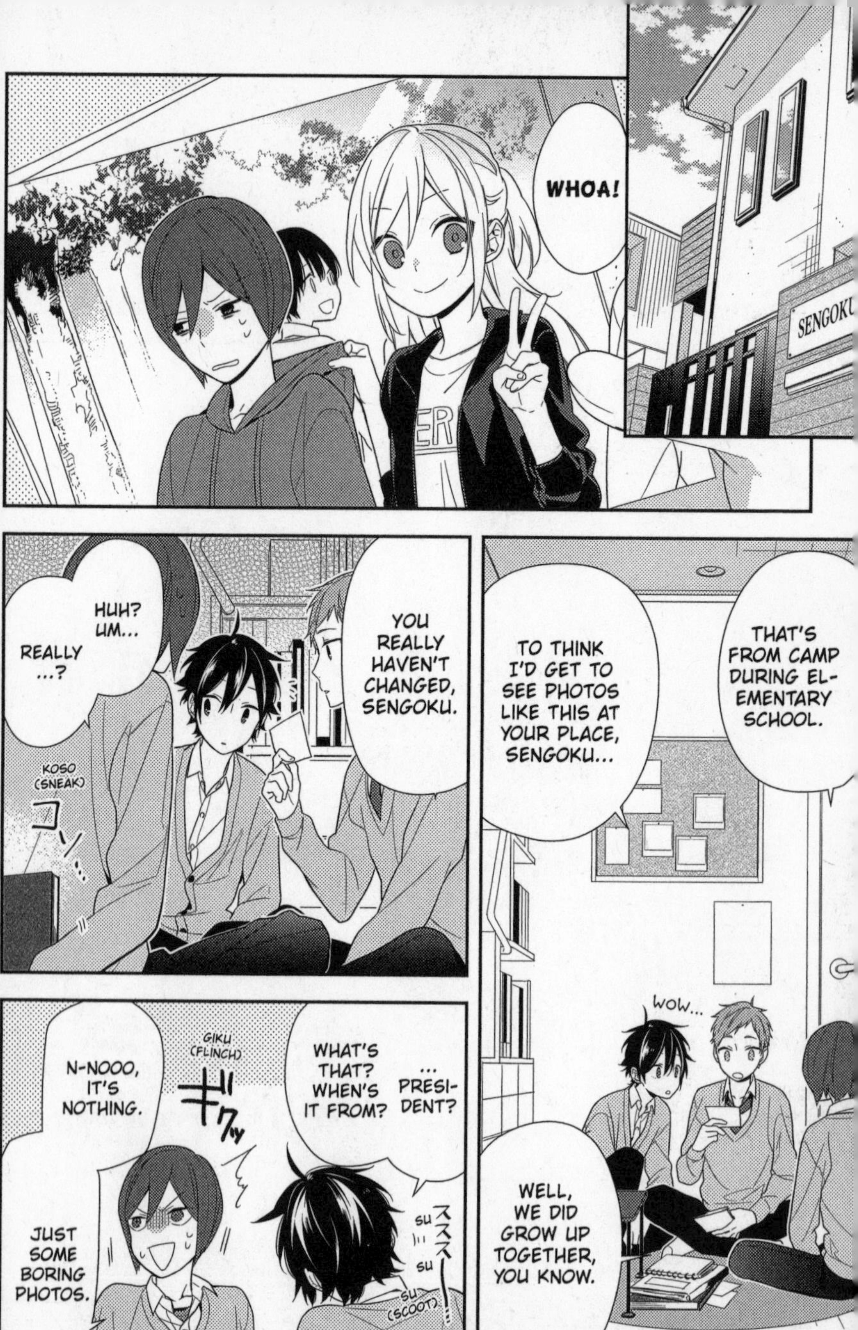
SENGOKU
WHOA!
THAT'S FROM CAMP DURING EL-EMENTARY SCHOOL.
TO THINK I'D GET TO SEE PHOTOS LIKE THIS AT YOUR PLACE, SENGOKU...
WOW...
WELL, WE DID GROW UP TOGETHER, YOU KNOW.
YOU REALLY HAVEN'T CHANGED, SENGOKU.
HUH? UM... REALLY ...?
KOSO (SNEAK)
コソ…
...PRESI-DENT?
WHAT'S THAT? WHEN'S IT FROM?
SU SU SU (SCOOT)
ススス—…
GIKU (FLINCH)
ギクッ
N-NOOO, IT'S NOTHING.
JUST SOME BORING PHOTOS.

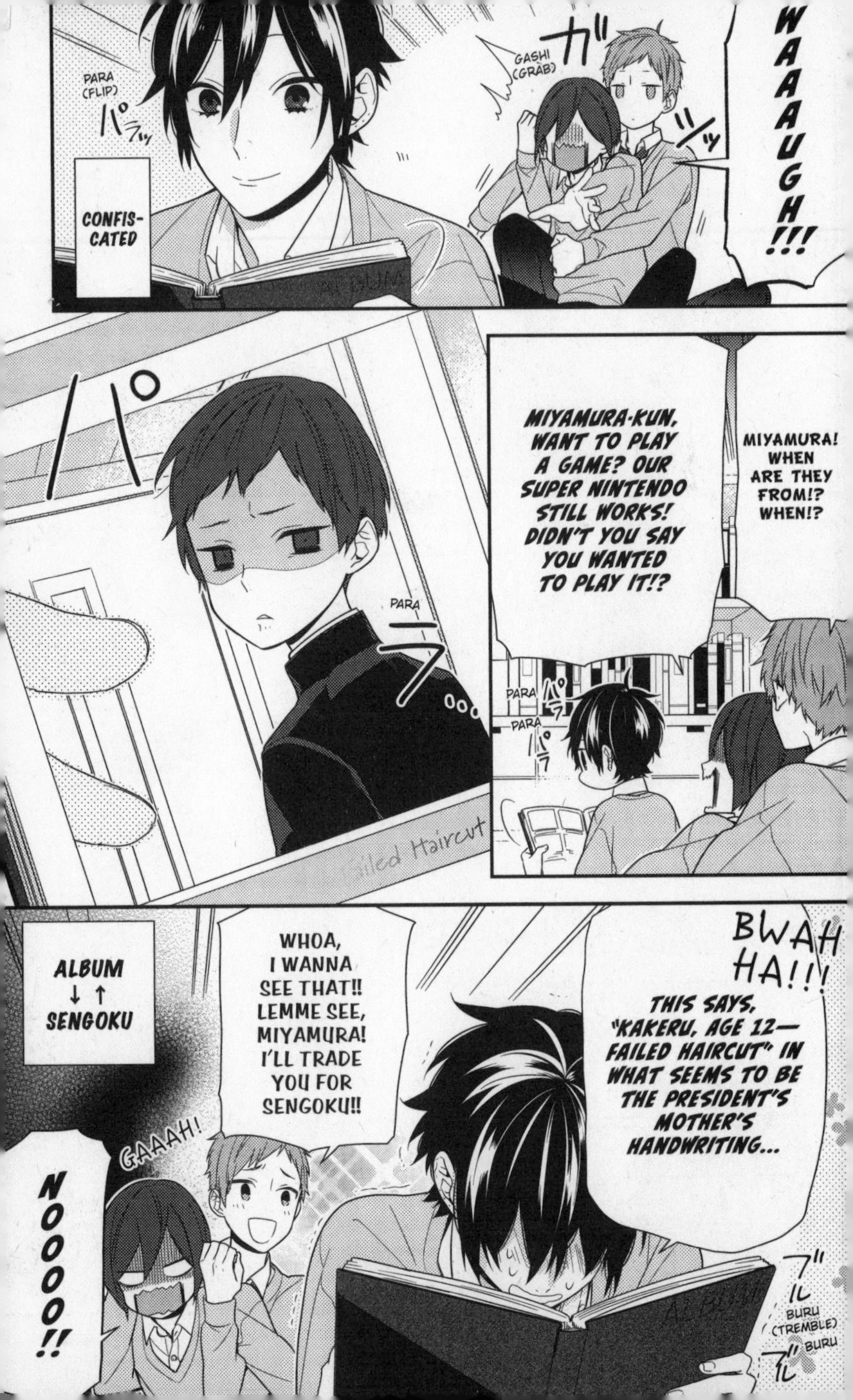
WAAAAUGH!!!
GASHI (GRAB)
PARA (FLIP)
CONFISCATED
MIYAMURA! WHEN ARE THEY FROM!? WHEN!?
MIYAMURA-KUN, WANT TO PLAY A GAME? OUR SUPER NINTENDO STILL WORKS! DIDN'T YOU SAY YOU WANTED TO PLAY IT!?
PARA
PARA
PARA
Failed Haircut
BWAH HA!!!
THIS SAYS, "KAKERU, AGE 12—FAILED HAIRCUT" IN WHAT SEEMS TO BE THE PRESIDENT'S MOTHER'S HANDWRITING...
BURU (TREMBLE) BURU
WHOA, I WANNA SEE THAT!! LEMME SEE, MIYAMURA! I'LL TRADE YOU FOR SENGOKU!!
GAAAH!
NOOOOO!!
ALBUM ↓ ↑ SENGOKU

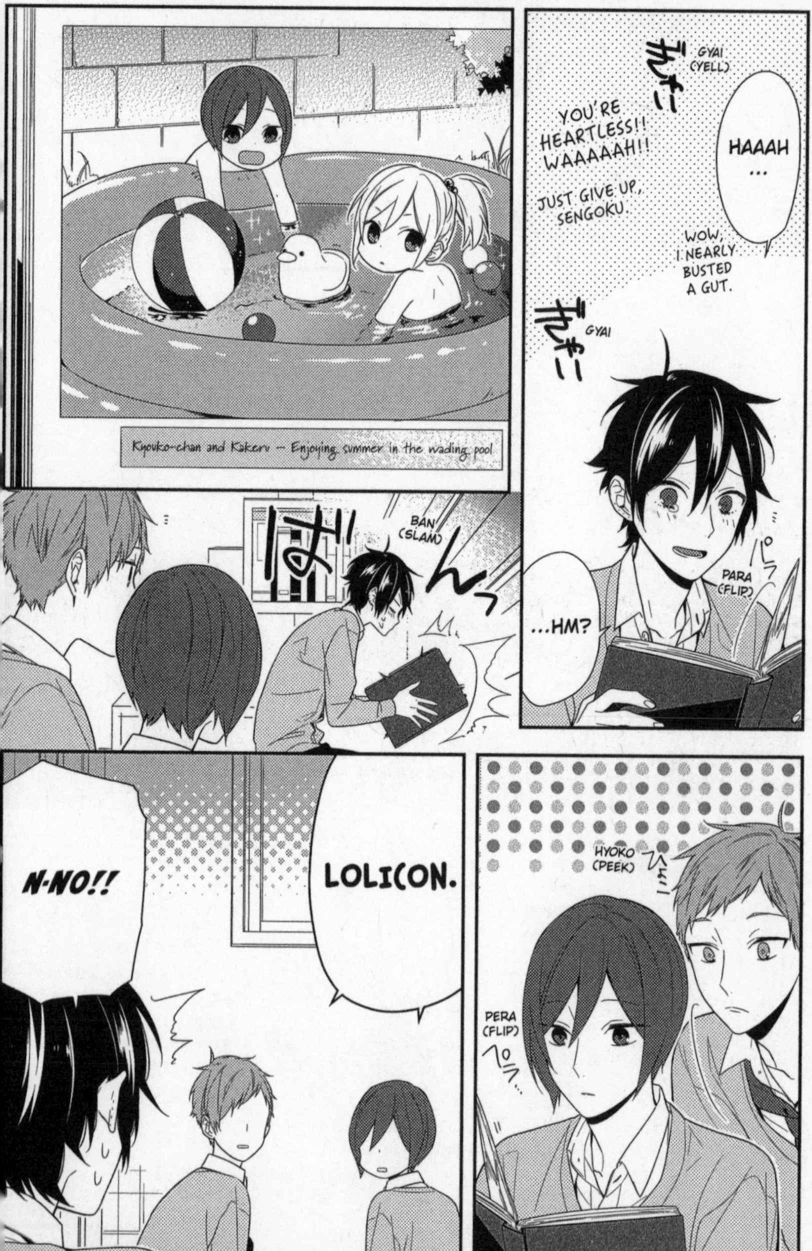
HAAAH ...
ぎゃい GYAI (YELL)
YOU'RE HEARTLESS!! WAAAAAH!!
JUST GIVE UP, SENGOKU.
WOW, I NEARLY BUSTED A GUT.
ぎゃい GYAI
パラ PARA (FLIP)
...HM?
Kyouko-chan and Kakeru — Enjoying summer in the wading pool
ばん BAN (SLAM)
ひょこ HYOKO (PEEK)
ペラ PERA (FLIP)
LOLICON.
N-NO!!

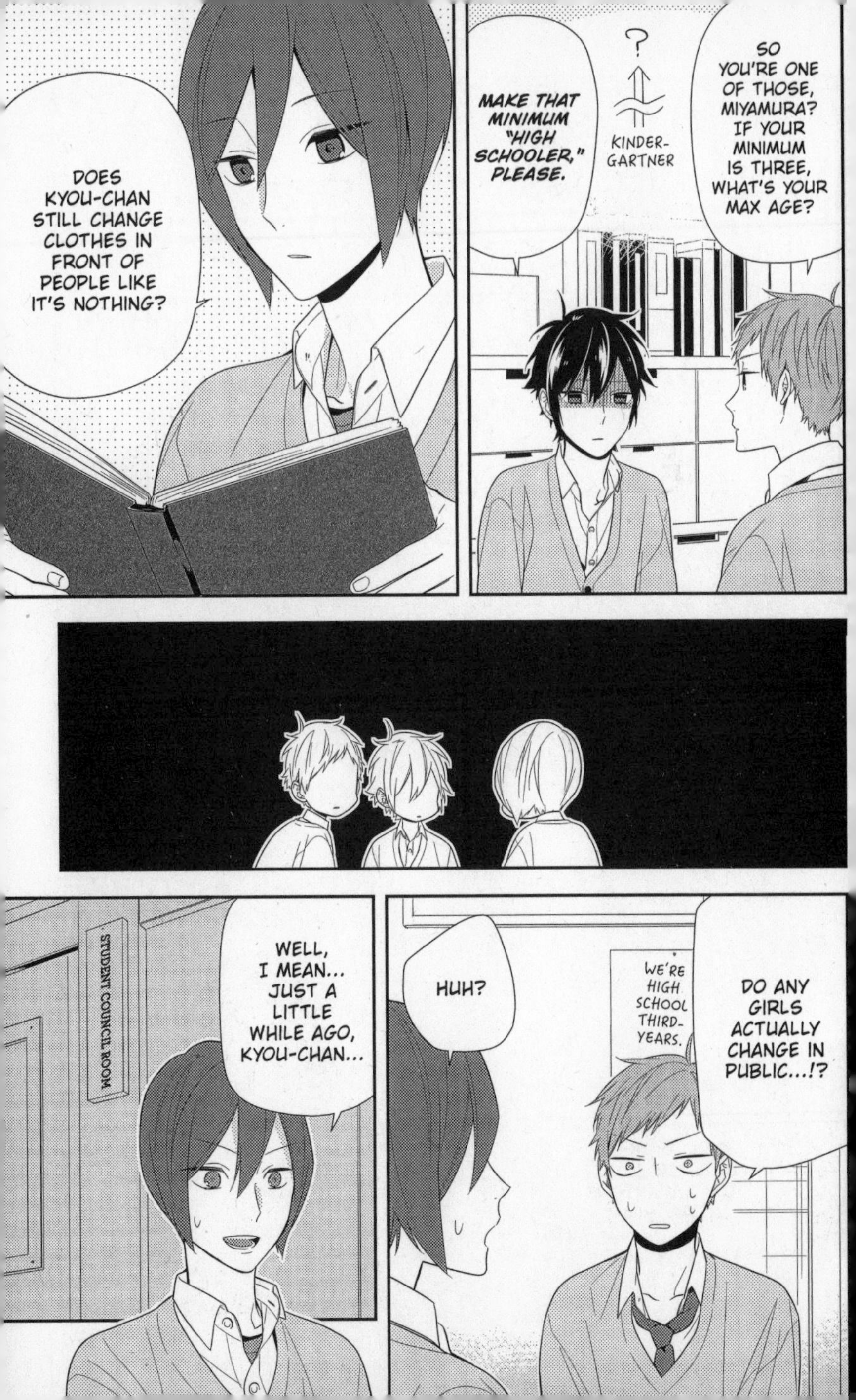
SO YOU'RE ONE OF THOSE, MIYAMURA? IF YOUR MINIMUM IS THREE, WHAT'S YOUR MAX AGE?
?
KINDER-GARTNER
MAKE THAT MINIMUM "HIGH SCHOOLER," PLEASE.
DOES KYOU-CHAN STILL CHANGE CLOTHES IN FRONT OF PEOPLE LIKE IT'S NOTHING?
DO ANY GIRLS ACTUALLY CHANGE IN PUBLIC...!?
WE'RE HIGH SCHOOL THIRD-YEARS.
HUH?
WELL, I MEAN... JUST A LITTLE WHILE AGO, KYOU-CHAN...
STUDENT COUNCIL ROOM

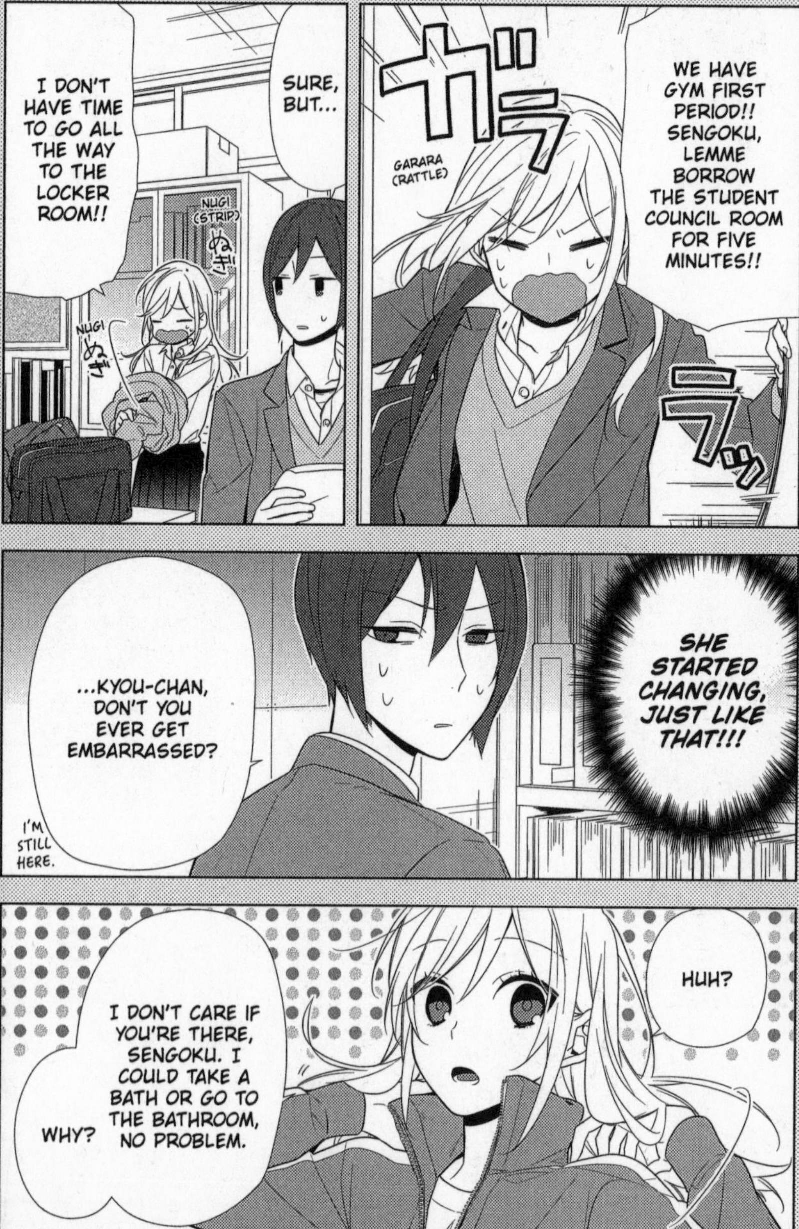
WE HAVE GYM FIRST PERIOD!! SENGOKU, LEMME BORROW THE STUDENT COUNCIL ROOM FOR FIVE MINUTES!!
ガラ
GARARA (RATTLE)
ラッ
SURE, BUT...
I DON'T HAVE TIME TO GO ALL THE WAY TO THE LOCKER ROOM!!
ぬぎ
NUGI (STRIP)
NUGI
ぬぎ
SHE STARTED CHANGING, JUST LIKE THAT!!!
...KYOU-CHAN, DON'T YOU EVER GET EMBARRASSED?
I'M STILL HERE.
HUH?
I DON'T CARE IF YOU'RE THERE, SENGOKU. I COULD TAKE A BATH OR GO TO THE BATHROOM, NO PROBLEM.
WHY?

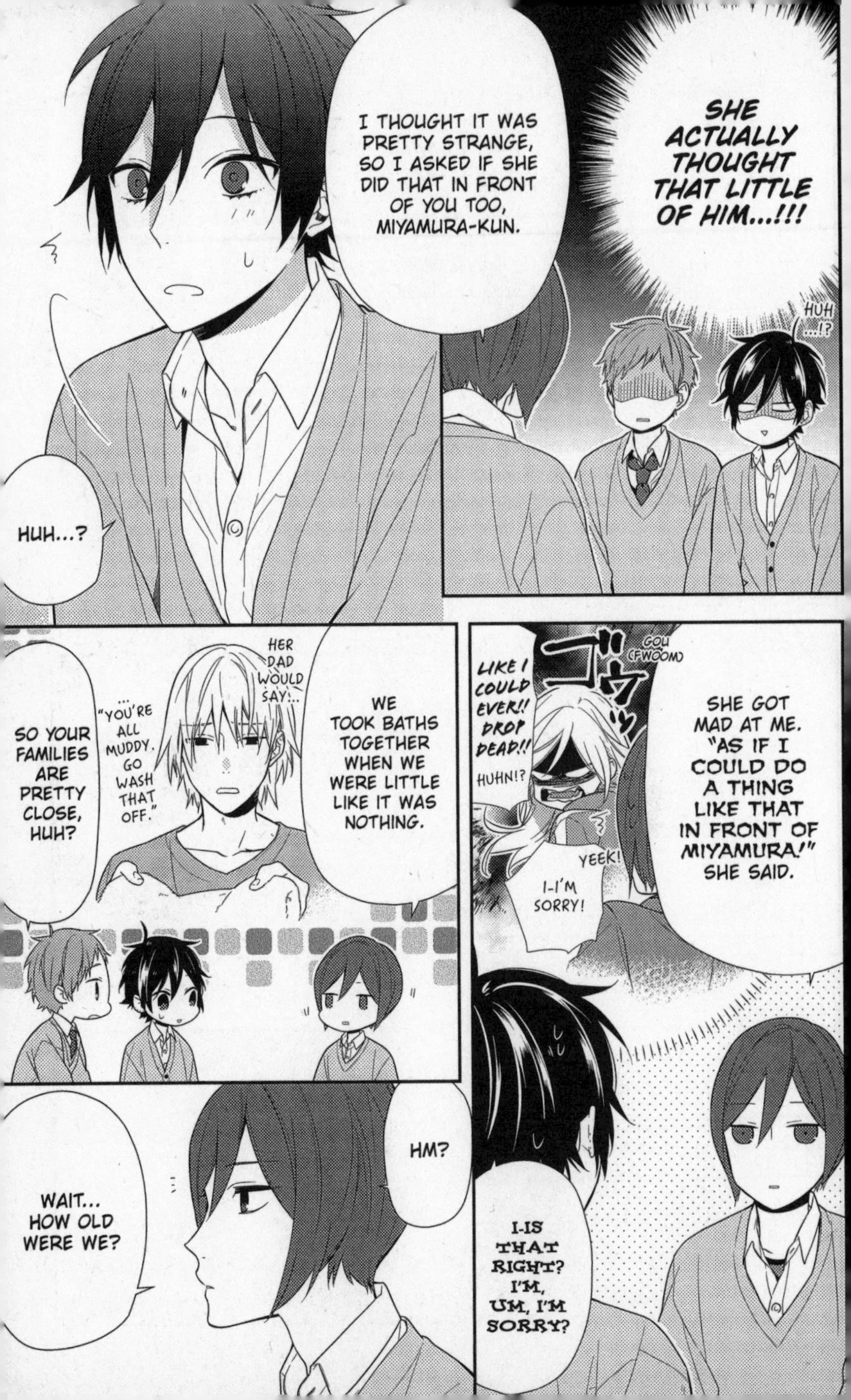
I THOUGHT IT WAS PRETTY STRANGE, SO I ASKED IF SHE DID THAT IN FRONT OF YOU TOO, MIYAMURA-KUN.
SHE ACTUALLY THOUGHT THAT LITTLE OF HIM...!!!
HUH ...!?
HUH...?
SHE GOT MAD AT ME. "AS IF I COULD DO A THING LIKE THAT IN FRONT OF MIYAMURA!" SHE SAID.
GOU (FWOOM)
LIKE I COULD EVER!! DROP DEAD!!
HUHN!?
YEEK!
I-I'M SORRY!
I-IS THAT RIGHT? I'M, UM, I'M SORRY?
WE TOOK BATHS TOGETHER WHEN WE WERE LITTLE LIKE IT WAS NOTHING.
HER DAD WOULD SAY...
... "YOU'RE ALL MUDDY. GO WASH THAT OFF."
SO YOUR FAMILIES ARE PRETTY CLOSE, HUH?
HM?
WAIT... HOW OLD WERE WE?

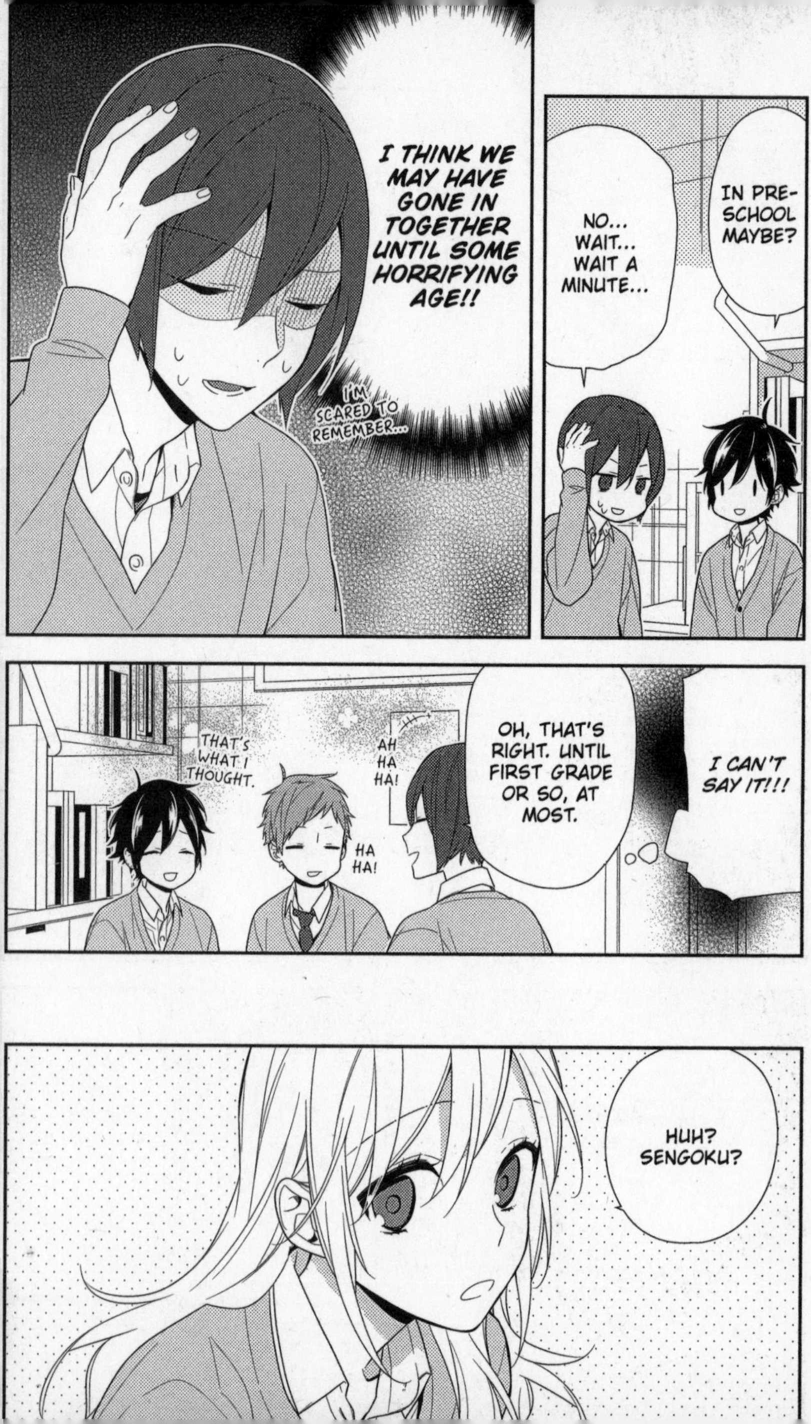
IN PRE-SCHOOL MAYBE?
NO... WAIT... WAIT A MINUTE...
I THINK WE MAY HAVE GONE IN TOGETHER UNTIL SOME HORRIFYING AGE!!
I'M SCARED TO REMEMBER...
I CAN'T SAY IT!!!
OH, THAT'S RIGHT. UNTIL FIRST GRADE OR SO, AT MOST.
AH HA HA!
HA HA!
THAT'S WHAT I THOUGHT.
HUH? SENGOKU?

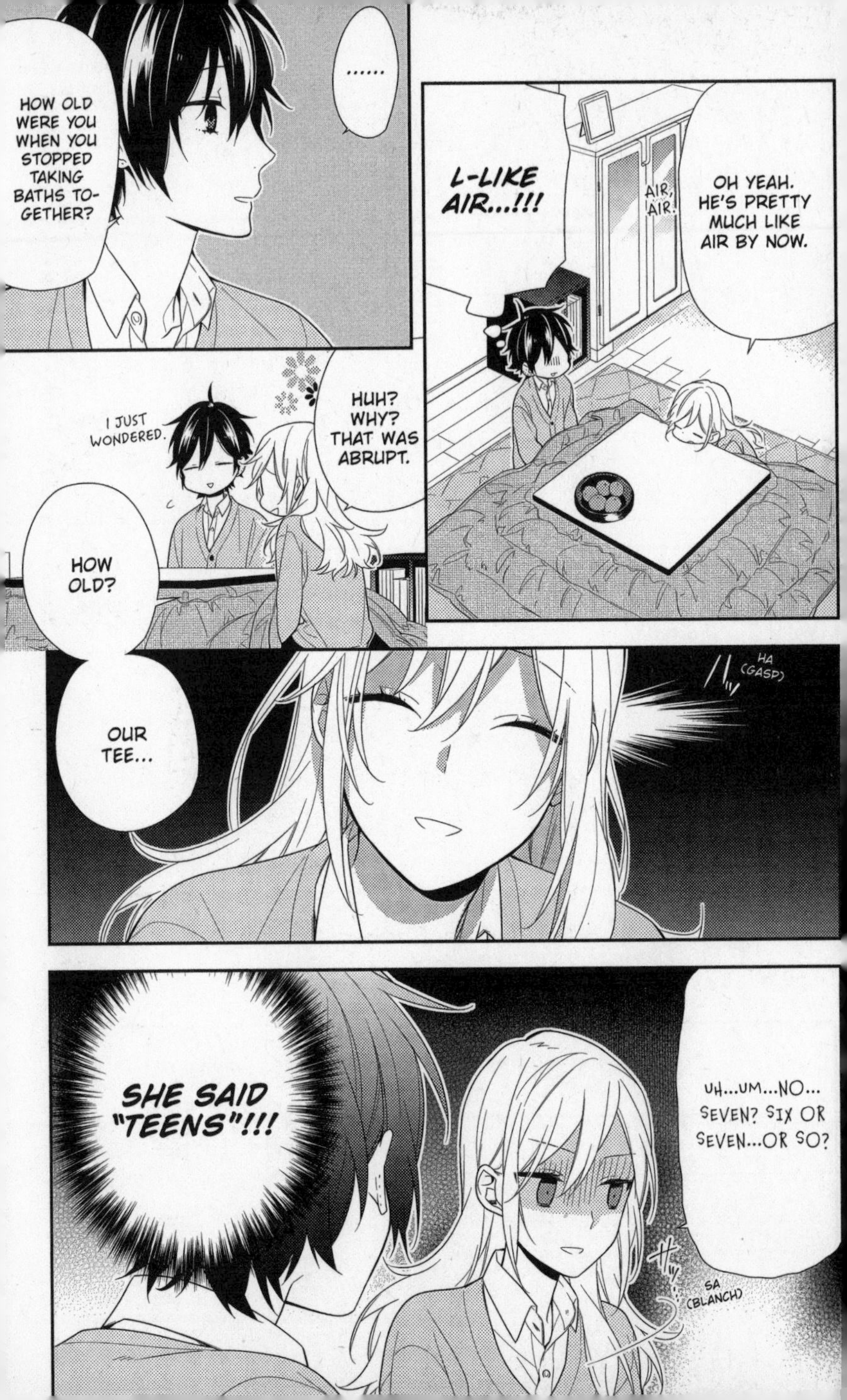
OH YEAH. HE'S PRETTY MUCH LIKE AIR BY NOW.
AIR, AIR.
L-LIKE AIR...!!!
......
HOW OLD WERE YOU WHEN YOU STOPPED TAKING BATHS TO-GETHER?
HUH? WHY? THAT WAS ABRUPT.
I JUST WONDERED.
HOW OLD?
HA (GASP)
OUR TEE...
UH...UM...NO... SEVEN? SIX OR SEVEN...OR SO?
SA (BLANCH)
SHE SAID "TEENS"!!!

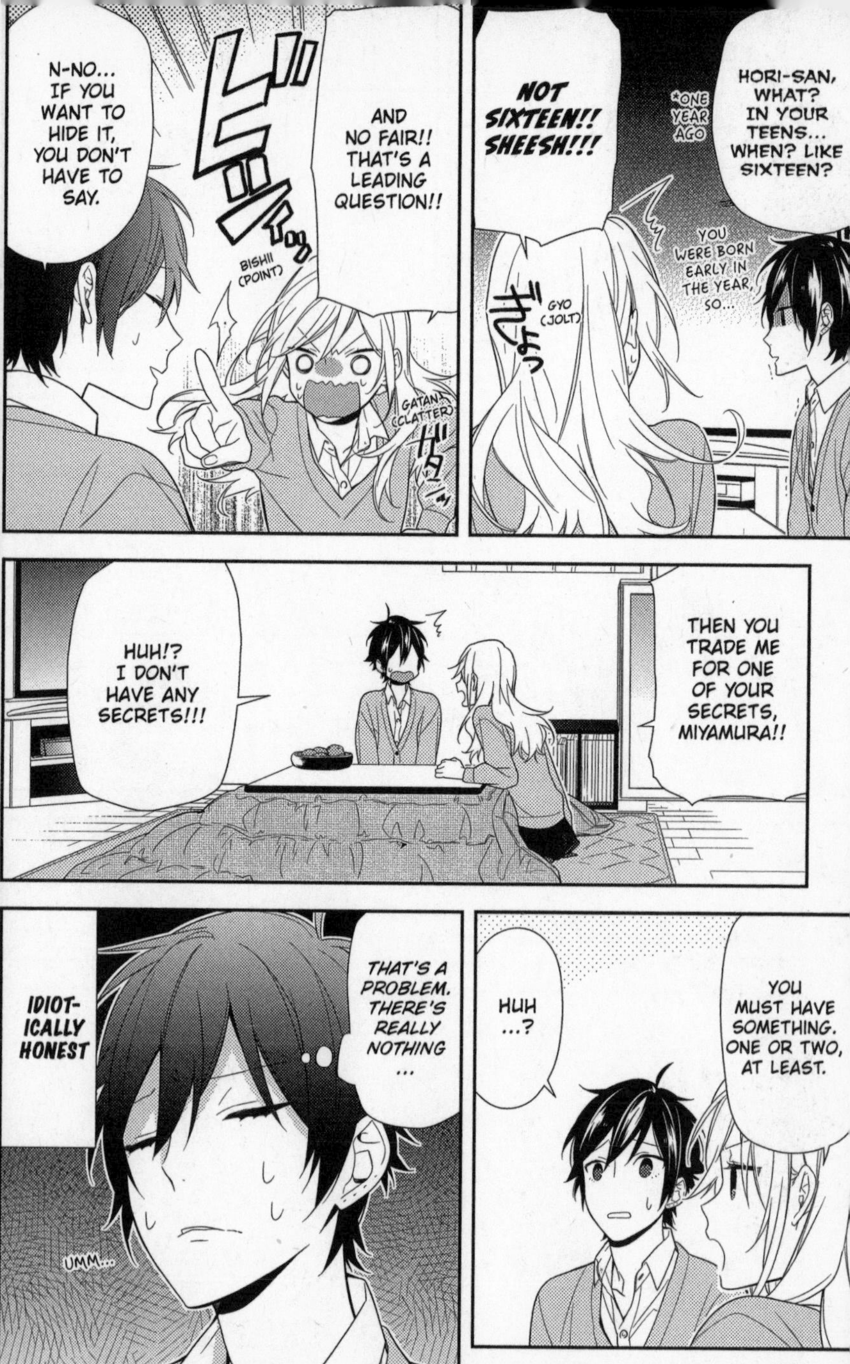
HORI-SAN, WHAT? IN YOUR TEENS... WHEN? LIKE SIXTEEN?
*ONE YEAR AGO
YOU WERE BORN EARLY IN THE YEAR, SO...
NOT SIXTEEN!! SHEESH!!!
GYO (JOLT)
AND NO FAIR!! THAT'S A LEADING QUESTION!!
BISHII (POINT)
GATAN (CLATTER)
N-NO... IF YOU WANT TO HIDE IT, YOU DON'T HAVE TO SAY.
THEN YOU TRADE ME FOR ONE OF YOUR SECRETS, MIYAMURA!!
HUH!? I DON'T HAVE ANY SECRETS!!!
YOU MUST HAVE SOMETHING. ONE OR TWO, AT LEAST.
HUH ...?
THAT'S A PROBLEM. THERE'S REALLY NOTHING ...
IDIOT-ICALLY HONEST
UMM...

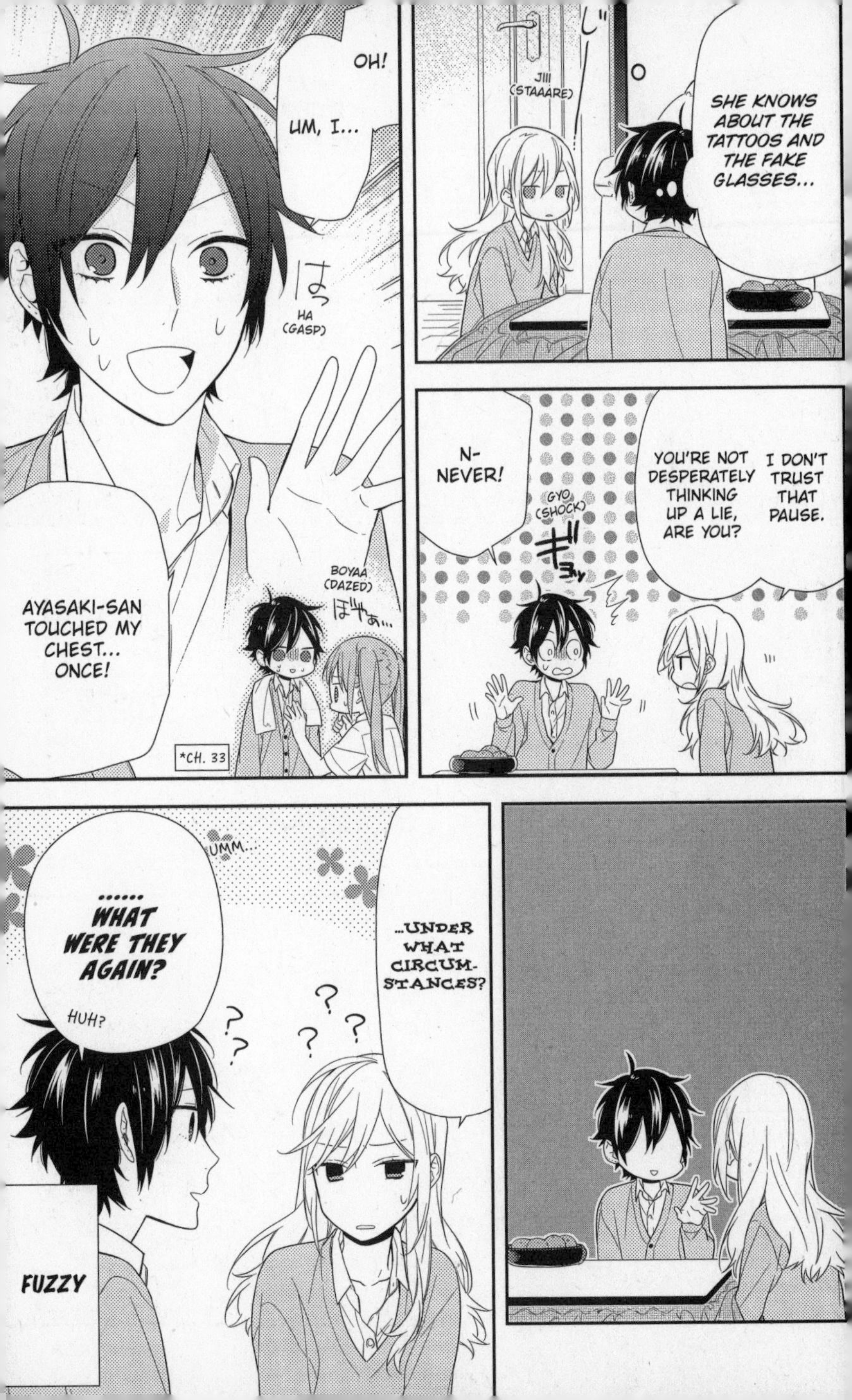
じー
JIII (STAARE)
SHE KNOWS ABOUT THE TATTOOS AND THE FAKE GLASSES...
I DON'T TRUST THAT PAUSE.
YOU'RE NOT DESPERATELY THINKING UP A LIE, ARE YOU?
GYO (SHOCK)
N-NEVER!
OH!
UM, I...
はっ
HA (GASP)
AYASAKI-SAN TOUCHED MY CHEST... ONCE!
BOYAA (DAZED)
ぼやぁ...
*CH. 33
...UNDER WHAT CIRCUM-STANCES?
UMM...
...... WHAT WERE THEY AGAIN?
HUH?
FUZZY

HORIMIYA

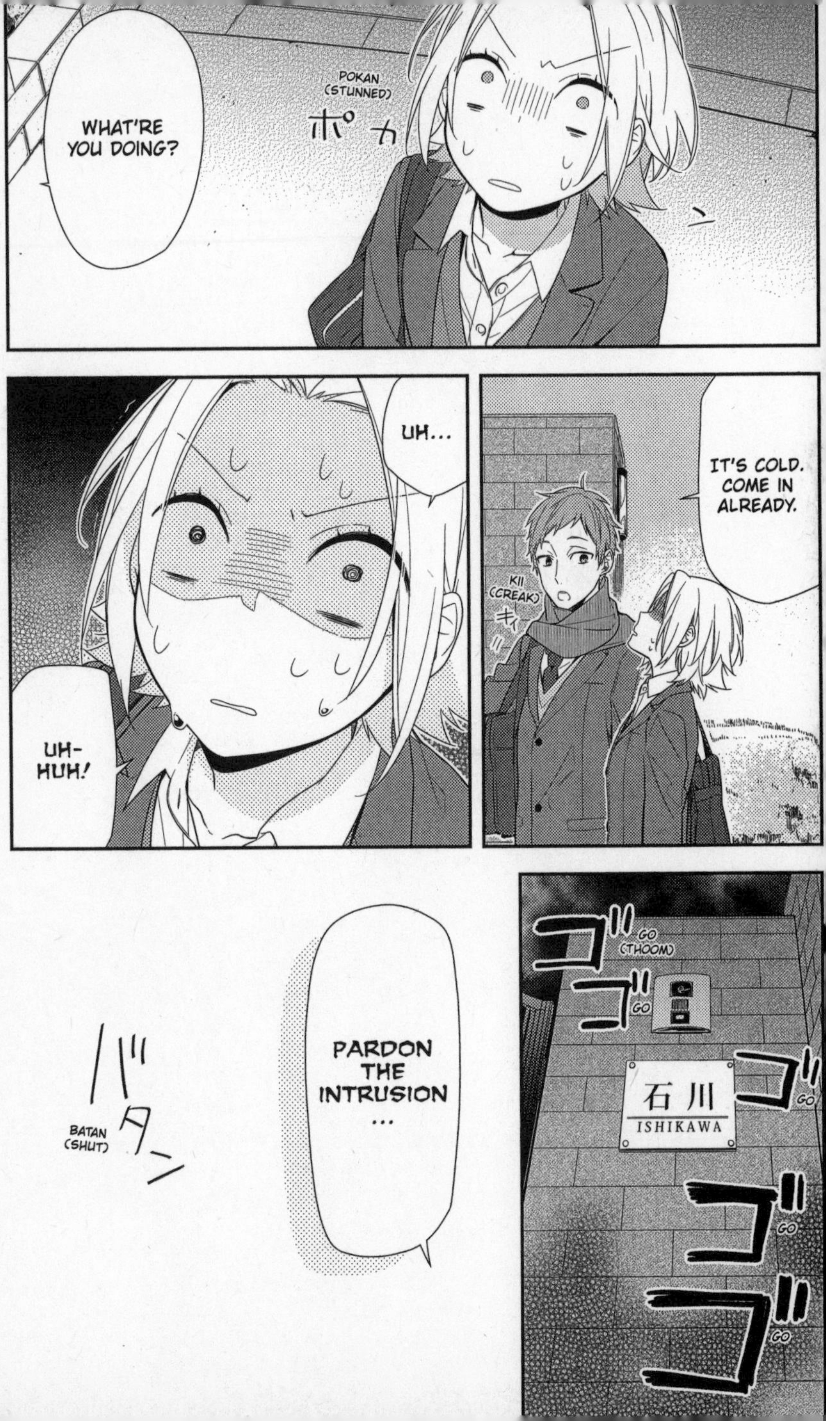
WHAT'RE YOU DOING?
POKAN (STUNNED)
ポカ
IT'S COLD. COME IN ALREADY.
KII (CREAK)
キィ
UH...
UH-HUH!
ゴ GO (THOOM)
ゴ GO
石川
ISHIKAWA
ゴ GO
ゴ GO
ゴ GO
PARDON THE INTRUSION ...
バタン
BATAN (SHUT)

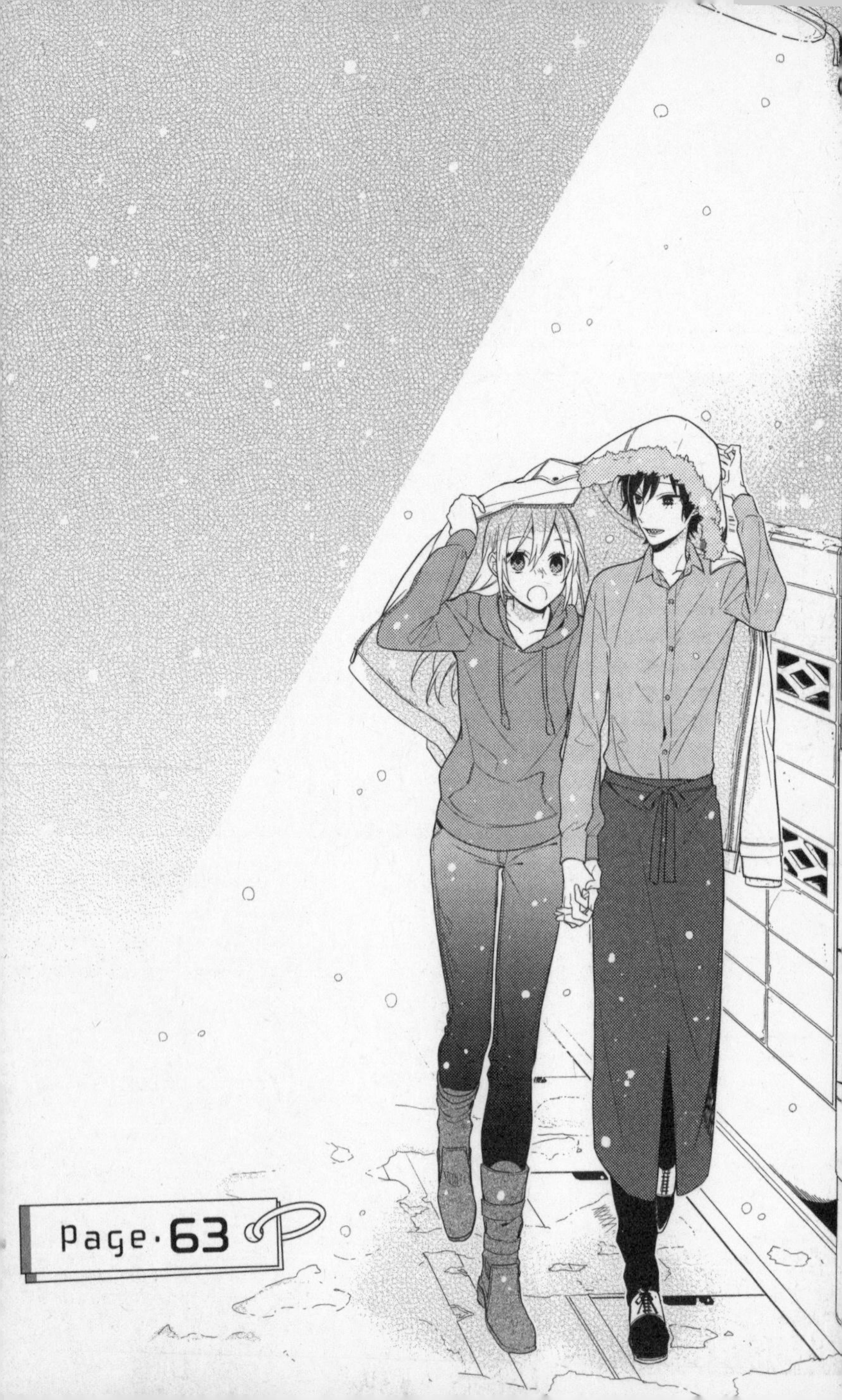
Page·63

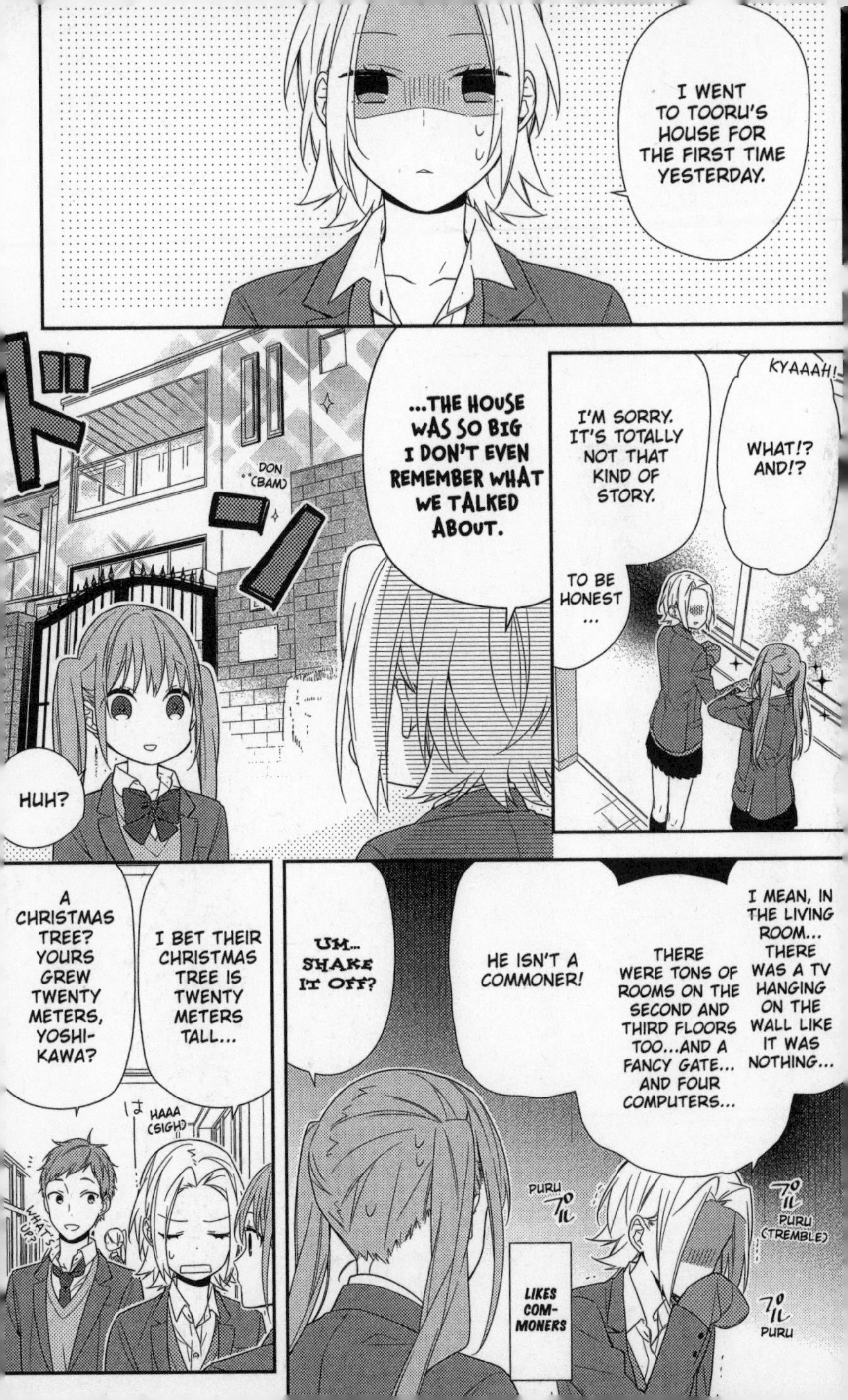
I WENT TO TOORU'S HOUSE FOR THE FIRST TIME YESTERDAY.
KYAAAH!
WHAT!? AND!?
I'M SORRY. IT'S TOTALLY NOT THAT KIND OF STORY.
TO BE HONEST...
...THE HOUSE WAS SO BIG I DON'T EVEN REMEMBER WHAT WE TALKED ABOUT.
DON (BAM)
HUH?
I MEAN, IN THE LIVING ROOM... THERE WAS A TV HANGING ON THE WALL LIKE IT WAS NOTHING...
THERE WERE TONS OF ROOMS ON THE SECOND AND THIRD FLOORS TOO...AND A FANCY GATE... AND FOUR COMPUTERS...
HE ISN'T A COMMONER!
UM... SHAKE IT OFF?
PURU (TREMBLE)
PURU
PURU
LIKES COMMONERS
I BET THEIR CHRISTMAS TREE IS TWENTY METERS TALL...
A CHRISTMAS TREE? YOURS GREW TWENTY METERS, YOSHIKAWA?
HAAA (SIGH)
WHAT'S UP?

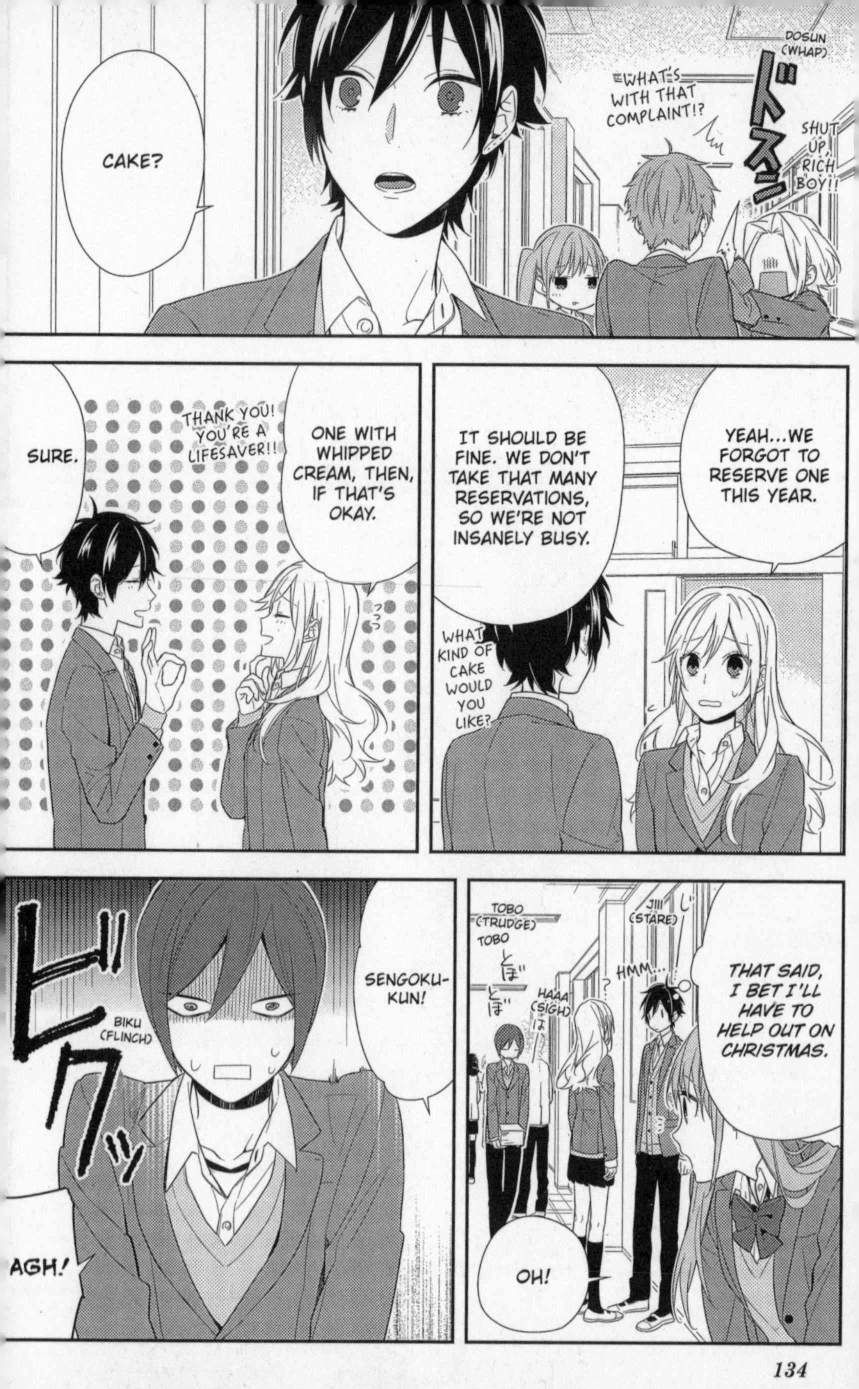
DOSUN (WHAP)
SHUT UP, RICH BOY!!
WHAT'S WITH THAT COMPLAINT!?
CAKE?
YEAH...WE FORGOT TO RESERVE ONE THIS YEAR.
IT SHOULD BE FINE. WE DON'T TAKE THAT MANY RESERVATIONS, SO WE'RE NOT INSANELY BUSY.
WHAT KIND OF CAKE WOULD YOU LIKE?
ONE WITH WHIPPED CREAM, THEN, IF THAT'S OKAY.
THANK YOU! YOU'RE A LIFESAVER!!
SURE.
THAT SAID, I BET I'LL HAVE TO HELP OUT ON CHRISTMAS.
JIII (STARE)
HMM...
TOBO (TRUDGE) TOBO
HAAA (SIGH)
OH!
SENGOKU-KUN!
BIKU (FLINCH)
AGH!

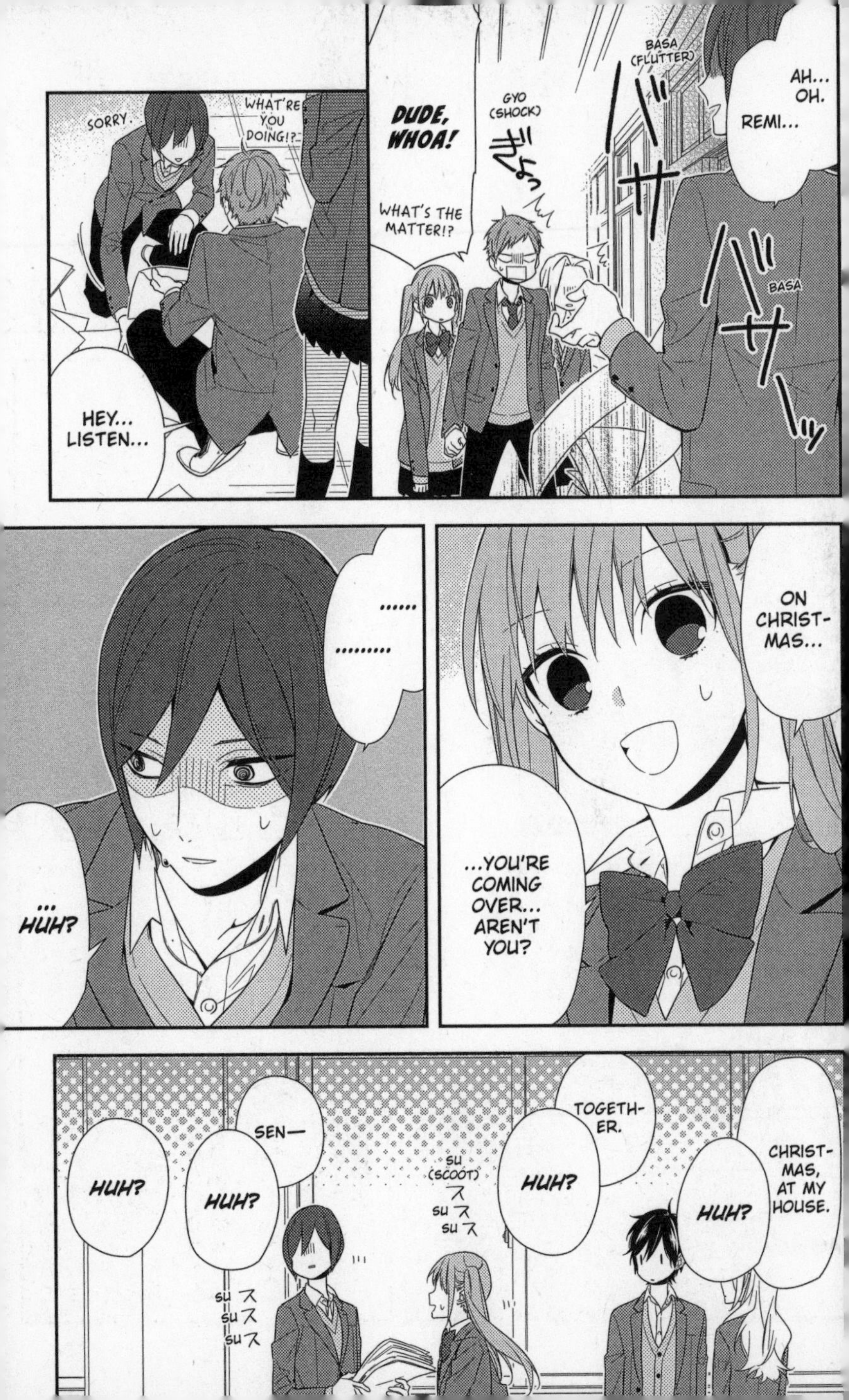
AH... OH.
REMI...
BASA (FLUTTER)
BASA
GYO (SHOCK)
DUDE, WHOA!
WHAT'S THE MATTER!?
WHAT'RE YOU DOING!?
SORRY.
HEY... LISTEN...
ON CHRISTMAS...
...YOU'RE COMING OVER... AREN'T YOU?
......
....
... HUH?
CHRISTMAS, AT MY HOUSE.
HUH?
TOGETHER.
HUH?
SU (SCOOT)
SU
SU
SEN—
HUH?
HUH?
SU
SU
SU

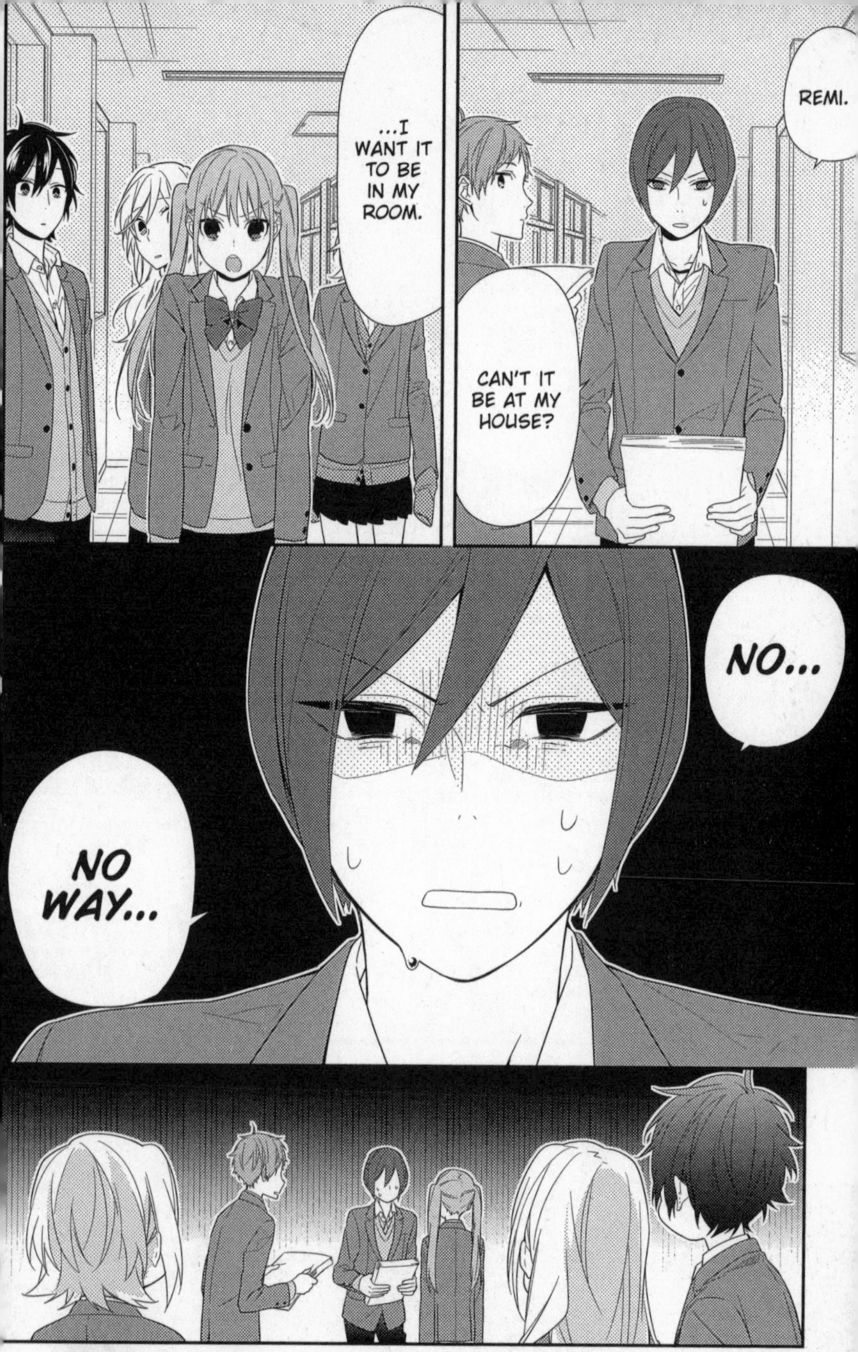
REMI.
CAN'T IT BE AT MY HOUSE?
...I WANT IT TO BE IN MY ROOM.
NO...
NO WAY...

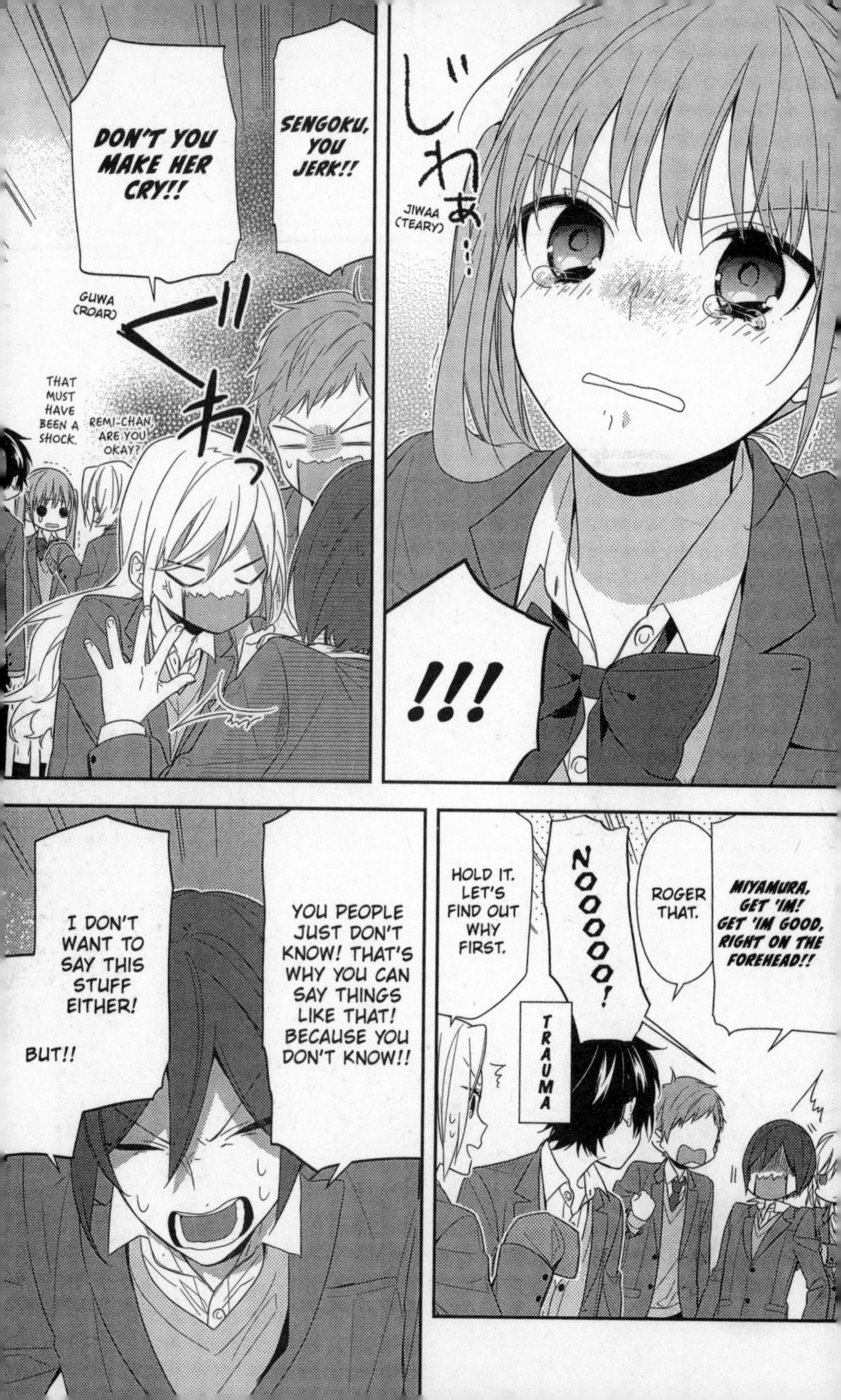
じわぁ…
JIWAA (TEARY)
!!!
SENGOKU, YOU JERK!!
DON'T YOU MAKE HER CRY!!
ぐわっ
GUWA (ROAR)
REMI-CHAN, ARE YOU OKAY?
THAT MUST HAVE BEEN A SHOCK.
MIYAMURA, GET 'IM! GET 'IM GOOD, RIGHT ON THE FOREHEAD!!
ROGER THAT.
NOOOOO!
HOLD IT. LET'S FIND OUT WHY FIRST.
TRAUMA
YOU PEOPLE JUST DON'T KNOW! THAT'S WHY YOU CAN SAY THINGS LIKE THAT! BECAUSE YOU DON'T KNOW!!
I DON'T WANT TO SAY THIS STUFF EITHER!
BUT!!

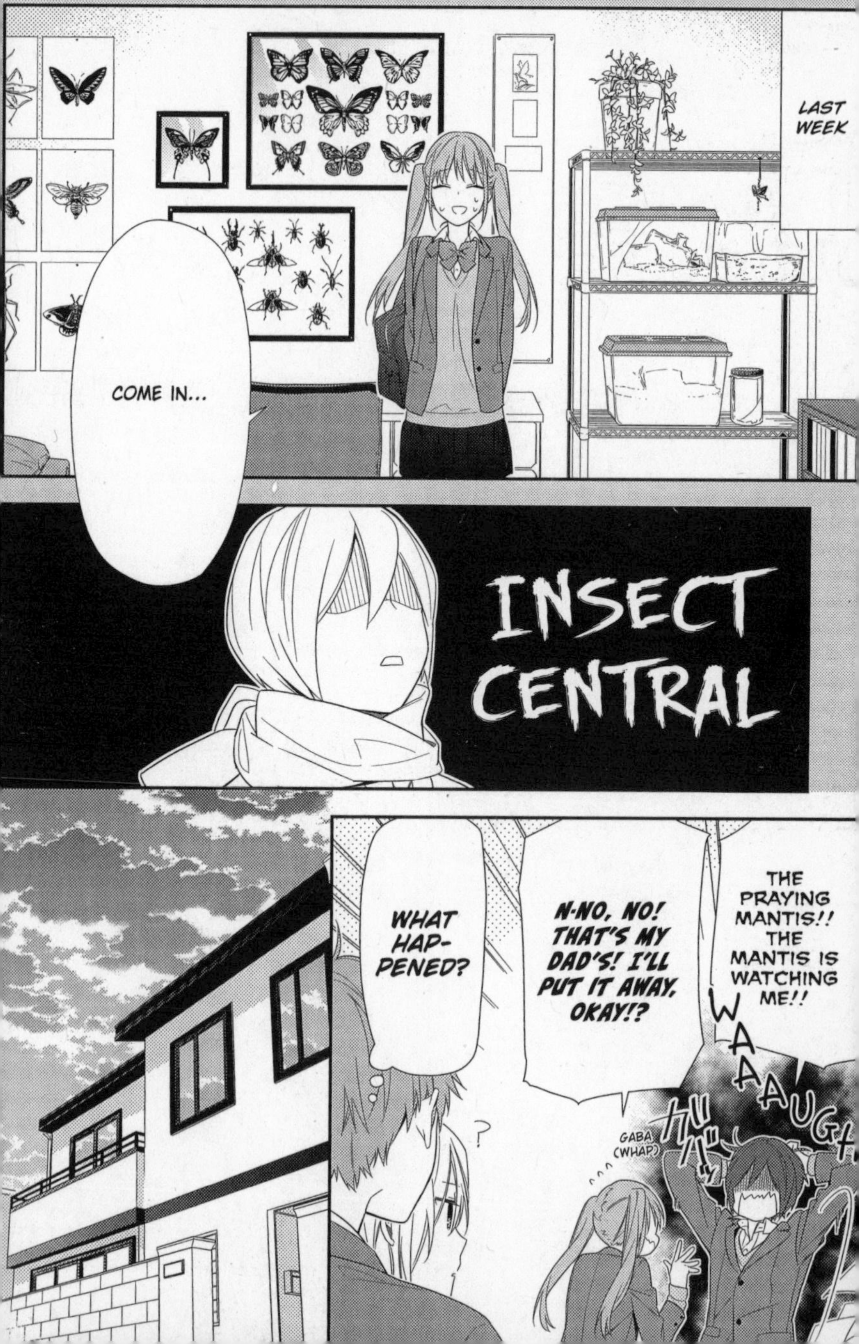
LAST WEEK
COME IN...
INSECT CENTRAL
THE PRAYING MANTIS!! THE MANTIS IS WATCHING ME!!
WAAAAUGH
N-NO, NO! THAT'S MY DAD'S! I'LL PUT IT AWAY, OKAY!?
GABA (WHAP)
WHAT HAP-PENED?

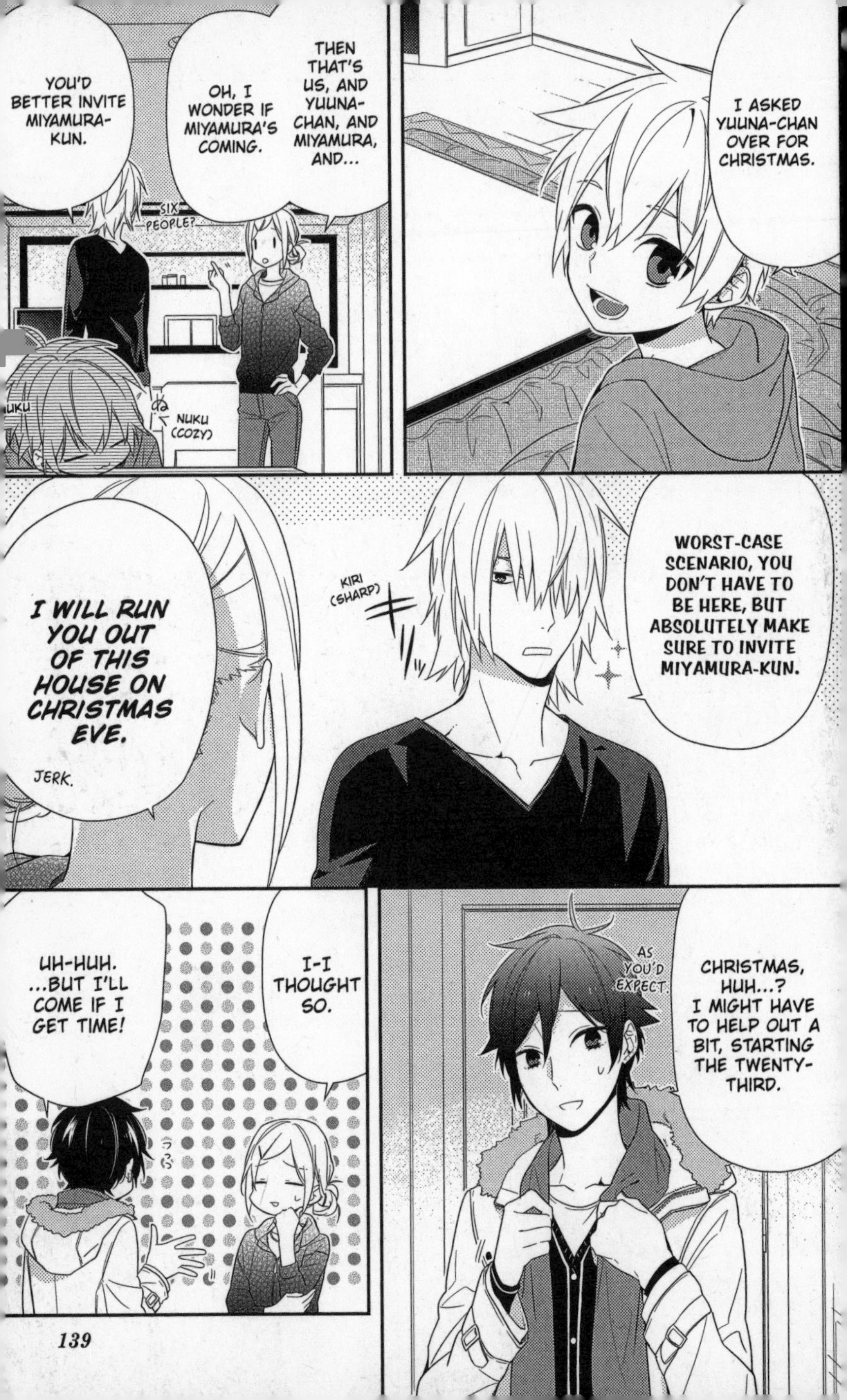
I ASKED YUUNA-CHAN OVER FOR CHRISTMAS.
THEN THAT'S US, AND YUUNA-CHAN, AND MIYAMURA, AND...
OH, I WONDER IF MIYAMURA'S COMING.
YOU'D BETTER INVITE MIYAMURA-KUN.
SIX PEOPLE?
NUKU (COZY)
NUKU
WORST-CASE SCENARIO, YOU DON'T HAVE TO BE HERE, BUT ABSOLUTELY MAKE SURE TO INVITE MIYAMURA-KUN.
KIRI (SHARP)
I WILL RUN YOU OUT OF THIS HOUSE ON CHRISTMAS EVE.
JERK.
CHRISTMAS, HUH...? I MIGHT HAVE TO HELP OUT A BIT, STARTING THE TWENTY-THIRD.
AS YOU'D EXPECT
I-I THOUGHT SO.
UH-HUH. ...BUT I'LL COME IF I GET TIME!

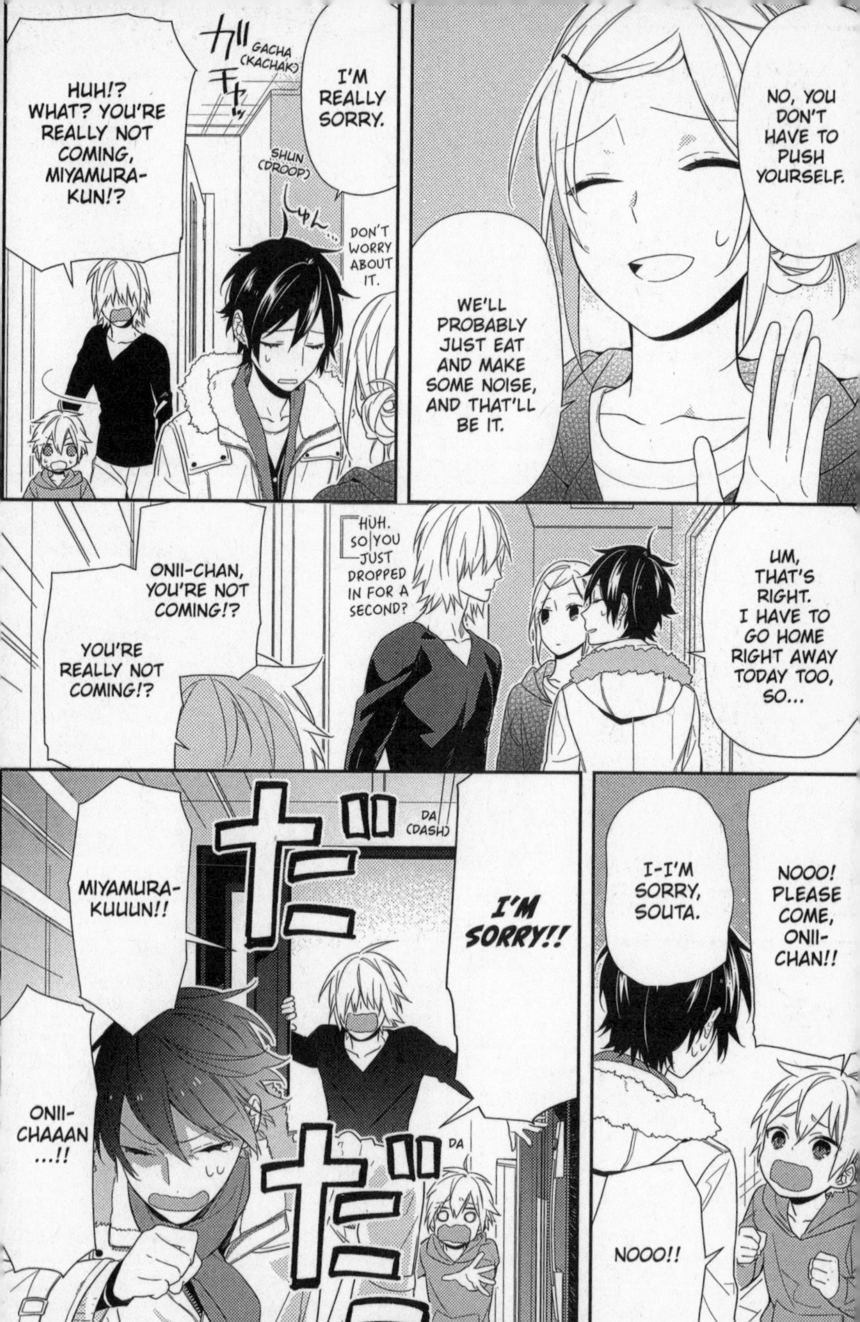
NO, YOU DON'T HAVE TO PUSH YOURSELF.
WE'LL PROBABLY JUST EAT AND MAKE SOME NOISE, AND THAT'LL BE IT.
I'M REALLY SORRY.
GACHA (KACHAK)
HUH!? WHAT? YOU'RE REALLY NOT COMING, MIYAMURA-KUN!?
SHUN (DROOP)
DON'T WORRY ABOUT IT.
UM, THAT'S RIGHT. I HAVE TO GO HOME RIGHT AWAY TODAY TOO, SO...
HUH. SO YOU JUST DROPPED IN FOR A SECOND?
ONII-CHAN, YOU'RE NOT COMING!?
YOU'RE REALLY NOT COMING!?
NOOO! PLEASE COME, ONII-CHAN!!
I-I'M SORRY, SOUTA.
NOOO!!
I'M SORRY!!
DA (DASH)
MIYAMURA-KUUUN!!
DA
ONII-CHAAAN ...!!

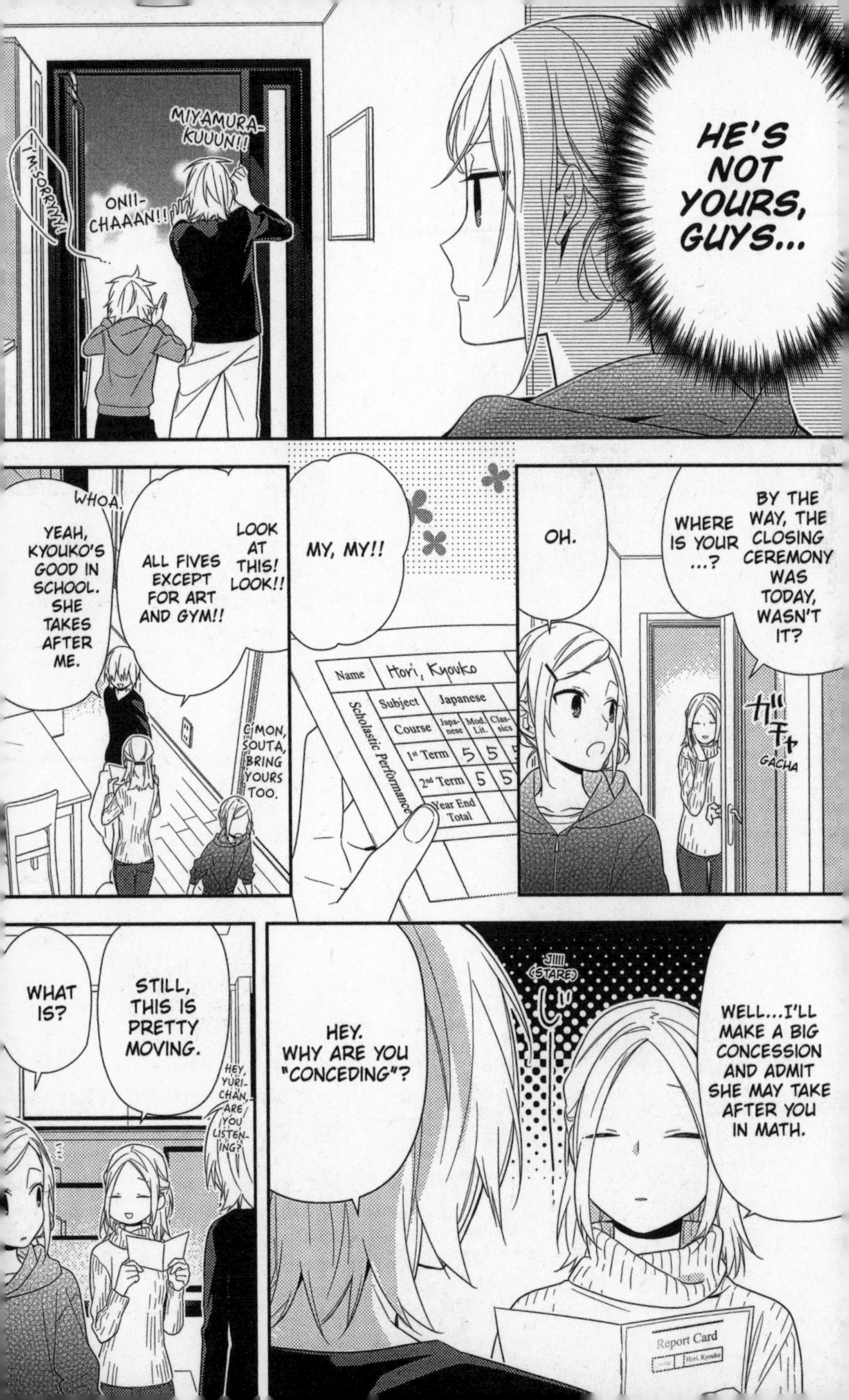
HE'S NOT YOURS, GUYS...
MIYAMURA-KUUUN!!
ONII-CHAAAN!!
I'M SORRY!!
BY THE WAY, THE CLOSING CEREMONY WAS TODAY, WASN'T IT?
WHERE IS YOUR ...?
OH.
ガチャ
GACHA
MY, MY!!
Name Hori, Kyouko
Scholastic Performance
Subject Japanese
Course Japanese Mod. Lit. Classics
1st Term 5 5
2nd Term 5 5
Year End Total
LOOK AT THIS! LOOK!!
ALL FIVES EXCEPT FOR ART AND GYM!!
WHOA.
YEAH, KYOUKO'S GOOD IN SCHOOL. SHE TAKES AFTER ME.
C'MON, SOUTA, BRING YOURS TOO.
WELL...I'LL MAKE A BIG CONCESSION AND ADMIT SHE MAY TAKE AFTER YOU IN MATH.
じぃ
JIIII (STARE)
HEY. WHY ARE YOU "CONCEDING"?
Report Card
Hori, Kyouko
STILL, THIS IS PRETTY MOVING.
WHAT IS?
HEY, YURI-CHAN, ARE YOU LISTENING?

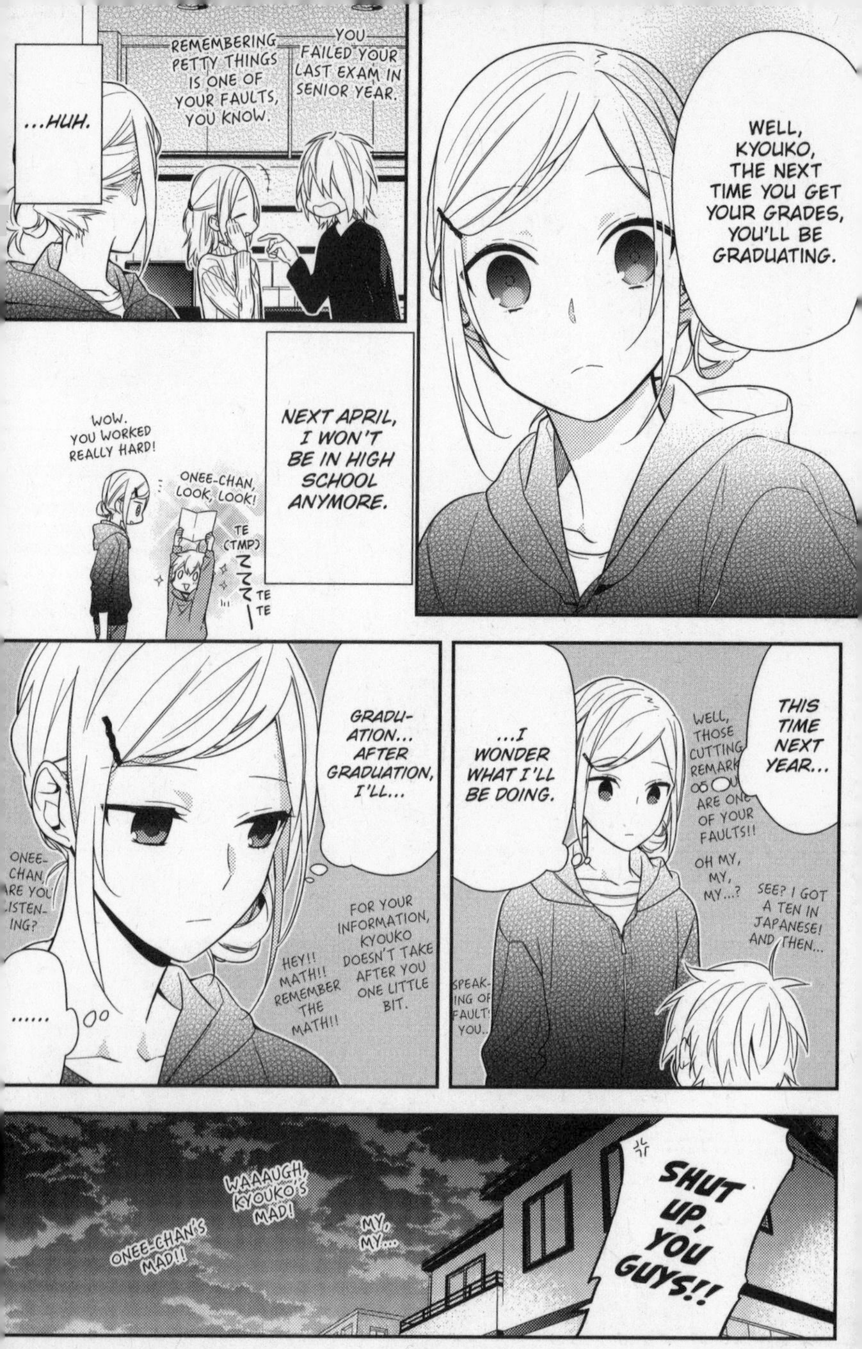
WELL, KYOUKO, THE NEXT TIME YOU GET YOUR GRADES, YOU'LL BE GRADUATING.
YOU FAILED YOUR LAST EXAM IN SENIOR YEAR.
REMEMBERING PETTY THINGS IS ONE OF YOUR FAULTS, YOU KNOW.
...HUH.
NEXT APRIL, I WON'T BE IN HIGH SCHOOL ANYMORE.
ONEE-CHAN, LOOK, LOOK!
TE (TMP)
TE TE
WOW. YOU WORKED REALLY HARD!
THIS TIME NEXT YEAR...
WELL, THOSE CUTTING REMARK ARE ONE OF YOUR FAULTS!!
...I WONDER WHAT I'LL BE DOING.
OH MY, MY, MY...?
SEE? I GOT A TEN IN JAPANESE! AND THEN...
SPEAKING OF FAULTS, YOU...
GRADUATION... AFTER GRADUATION, I'LL...
FOR YOUR INFORMATION, KYOUKO DOESN'T TAKE AFTER YOU ONE LITTLE BIT.
HEY!! MATH!! REMEMBER THE MATH!!
ONEE-CHAN, ARE YOU LISTENING?
......
SHUT UP, YOU GUYS!!
MY, MY...
WAAAUGH, KYOUKO'S MAD!
ONEE-CHAN'S MAD!!

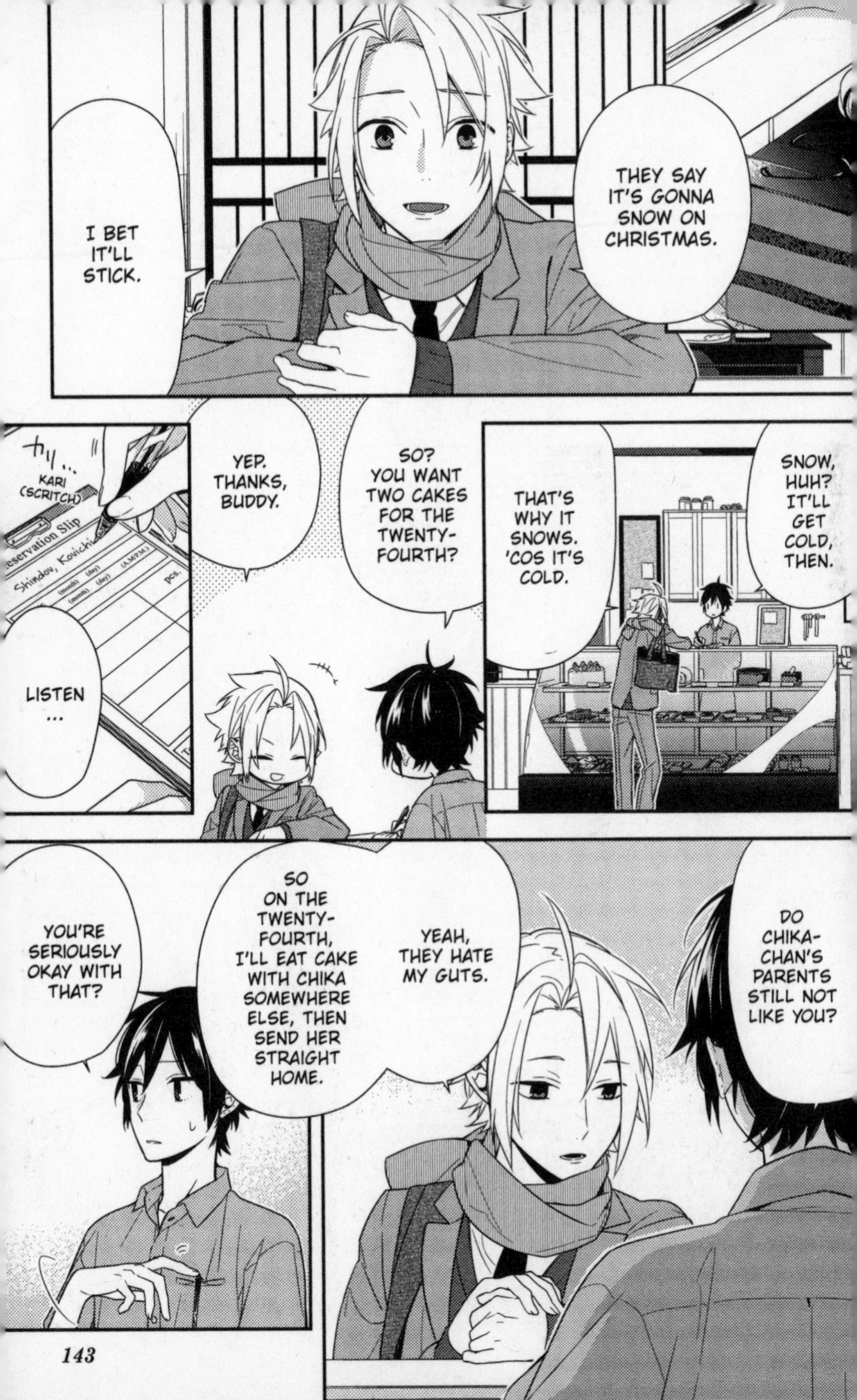
THEY SAY IT'S GONNA SNOW ON CHRISTMAS.
I BET IT'LL STICK.
SNOW, HUH? IT'LL GET COLD, THEN.
THAT'S WHY IT SNOWS. 'COS IT'S COLD.
SO? YOU WANT TWO CAKES FOR THE TWENTY-FOURTH?
YEP. THANKS, BUDDY.
カリ… KARI (SCRITCH)
eservation Slip
Shindou, Kouichi
LISTEN ...
DO CHIKA-CHAN'S PARENTS STILL NOT LIKE YOU?
YEAH, THEY HATE MY GUTS.
SO ON THE TWENTY-FOURTH, I'LL EAT CAKE WITH CHIKA SOMEWHERE ELSE, THEN SEND HER STRAIGHT HOME.
YOU'RE SERIOUSLY OKAY WITH THAT?

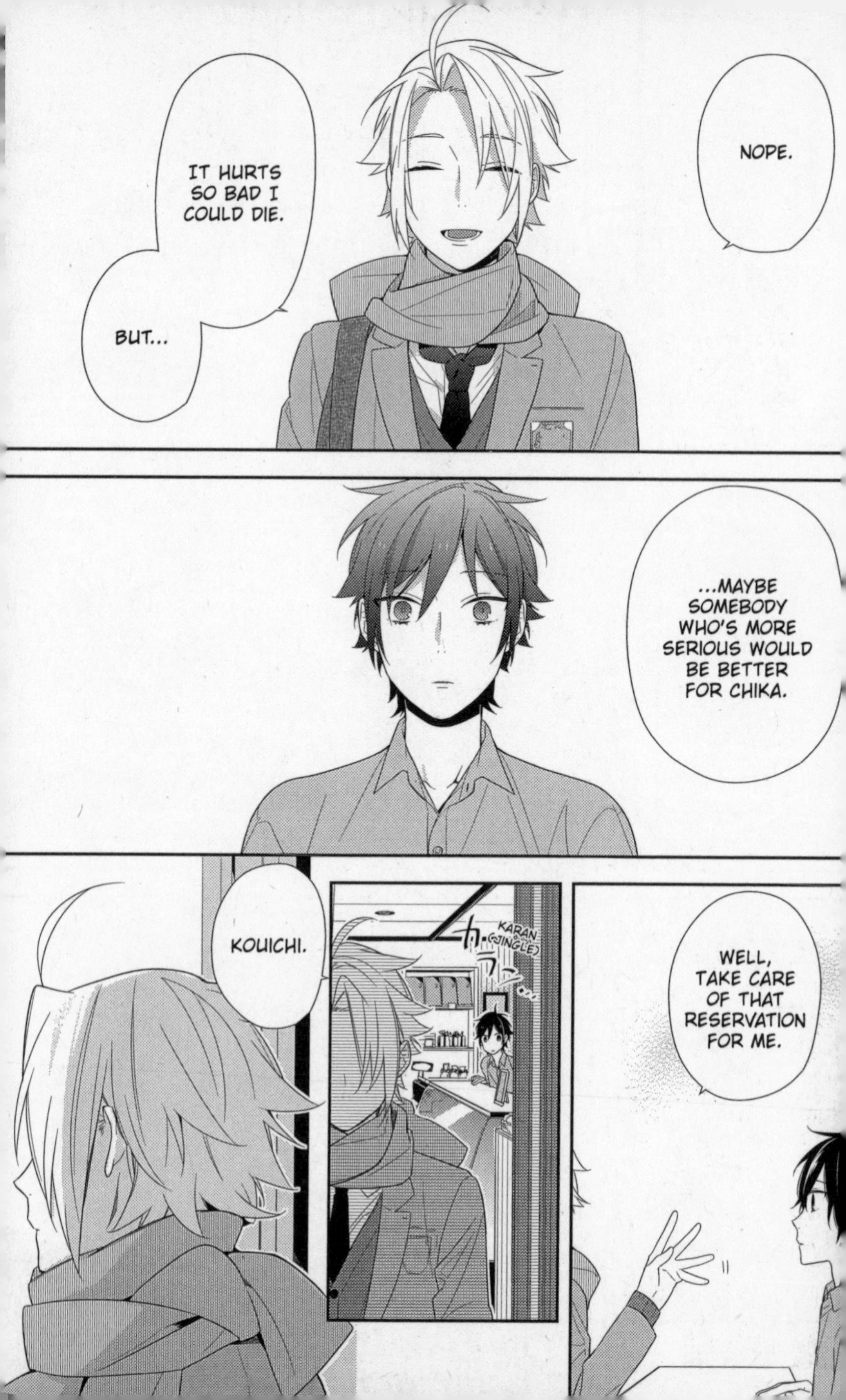
NOPE.
IT HURTS SO BAD I COULD DIE.
BUT...
...MAYBE SOMEBODY WHO'S MORE SERIOUS WOULD BE BETTER FOR CHIKA.
WELL, TAKE CARE OF THAT RESERVATION FOR ME.
KARAN (JINGLE)
KOUICHI.

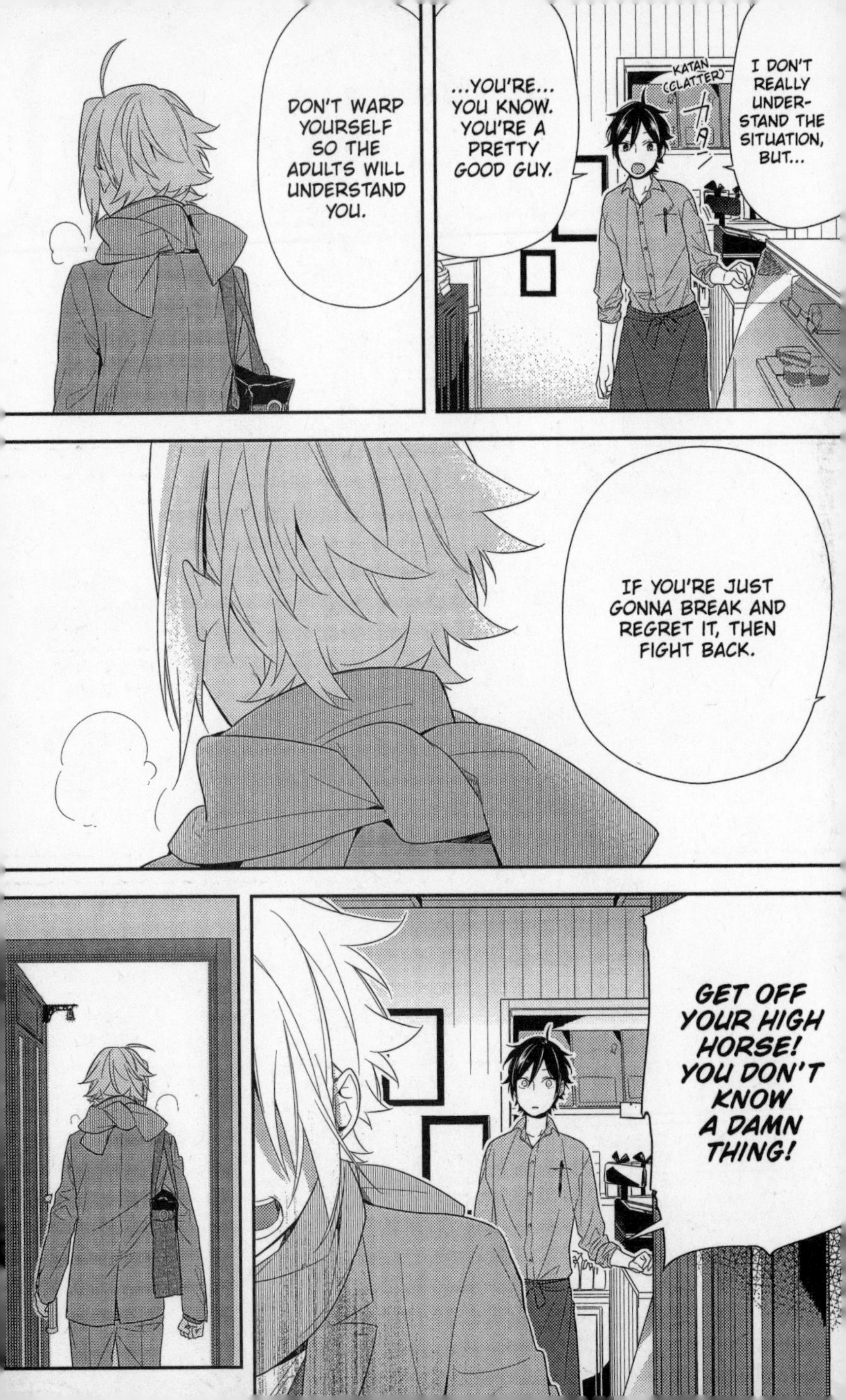
I DON'T REALLY UNDERSTAND THE SITUATION, BUT...
KATAN (CLATTER)
...YOU'RE... YOU KNOW. YOU'RE A PRETTY GOOD GUY.
DON'T WARP YOURSELF SO THE ADULTS WILL UNDERSTAND YOU.
IF YOU'RE JUST GONNA BREAK AND REGRET IT, THEN FIGHT BACK.
GET OFF YOUR HIGH HORSE! YOU DON'T KNOW A DAMN THING!

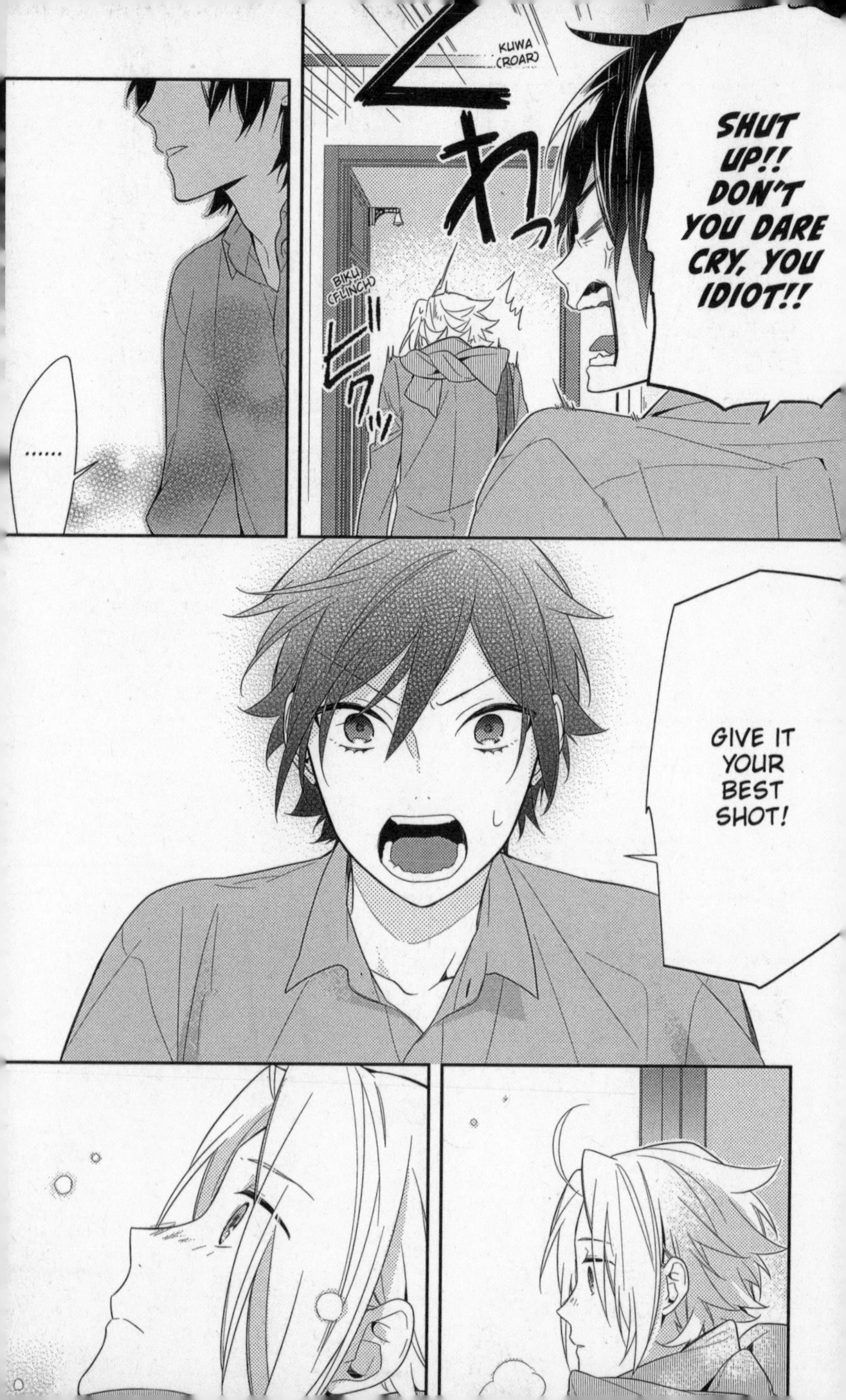
KUWA (ROAR)
SHUT UP!! DON'T YOU DARE CRY, YOU IDIOT!!
BIKU (FLINCH)
……
GIVE IT YOUR BEST SHOT!

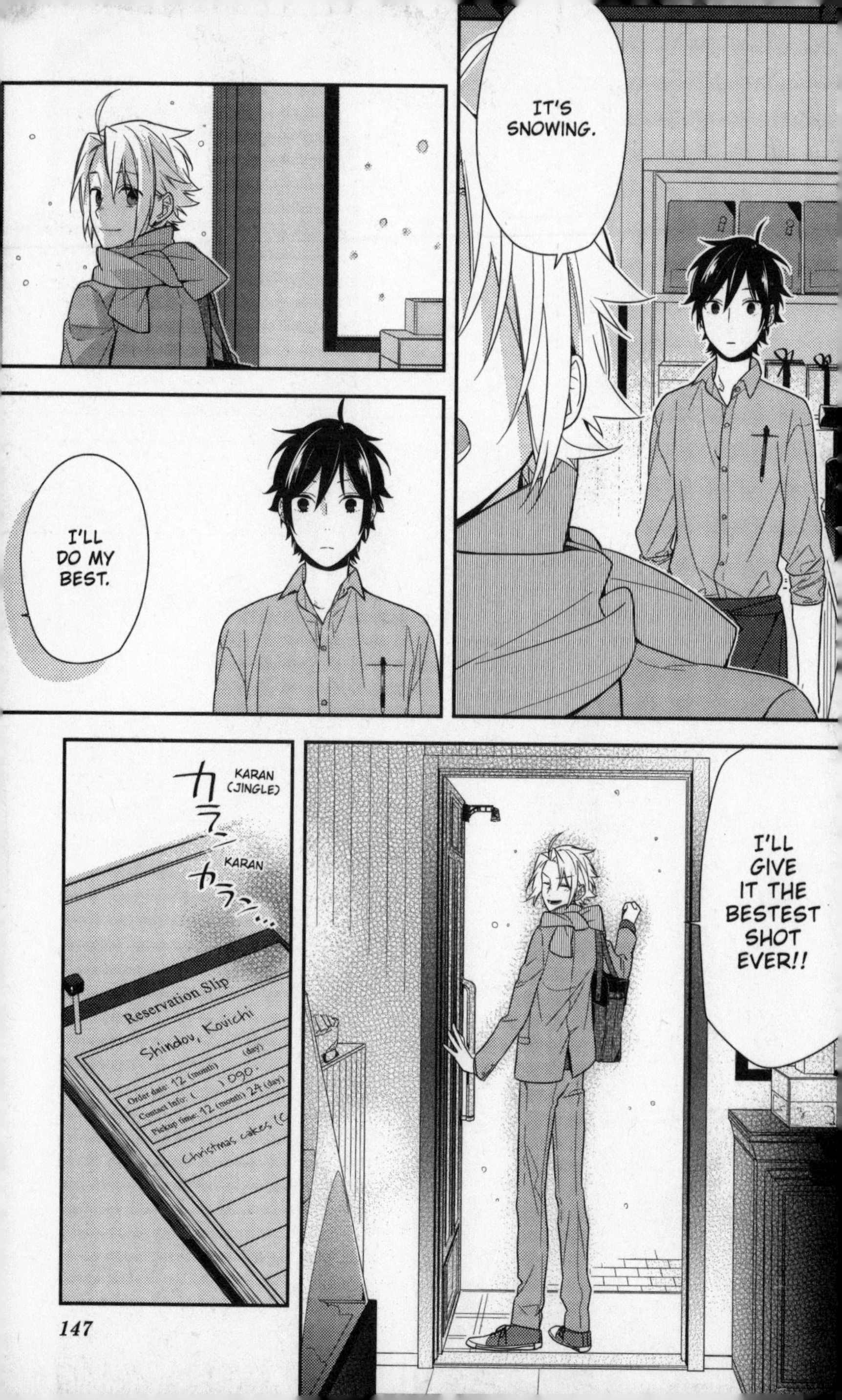

IT'S SNOWING.
I'LL DO MY BEST.
I'LL GIVE IT THE BESTEST SHOT EVER!!
KARAN (JINGLE)
KARAN
Reservation Slip
Shindou, Kouichi
Order date: 12 (month) (day)
Contact info: (1,090-
Pickup time: 12 (month) 24 (day)
Christmas cakes (

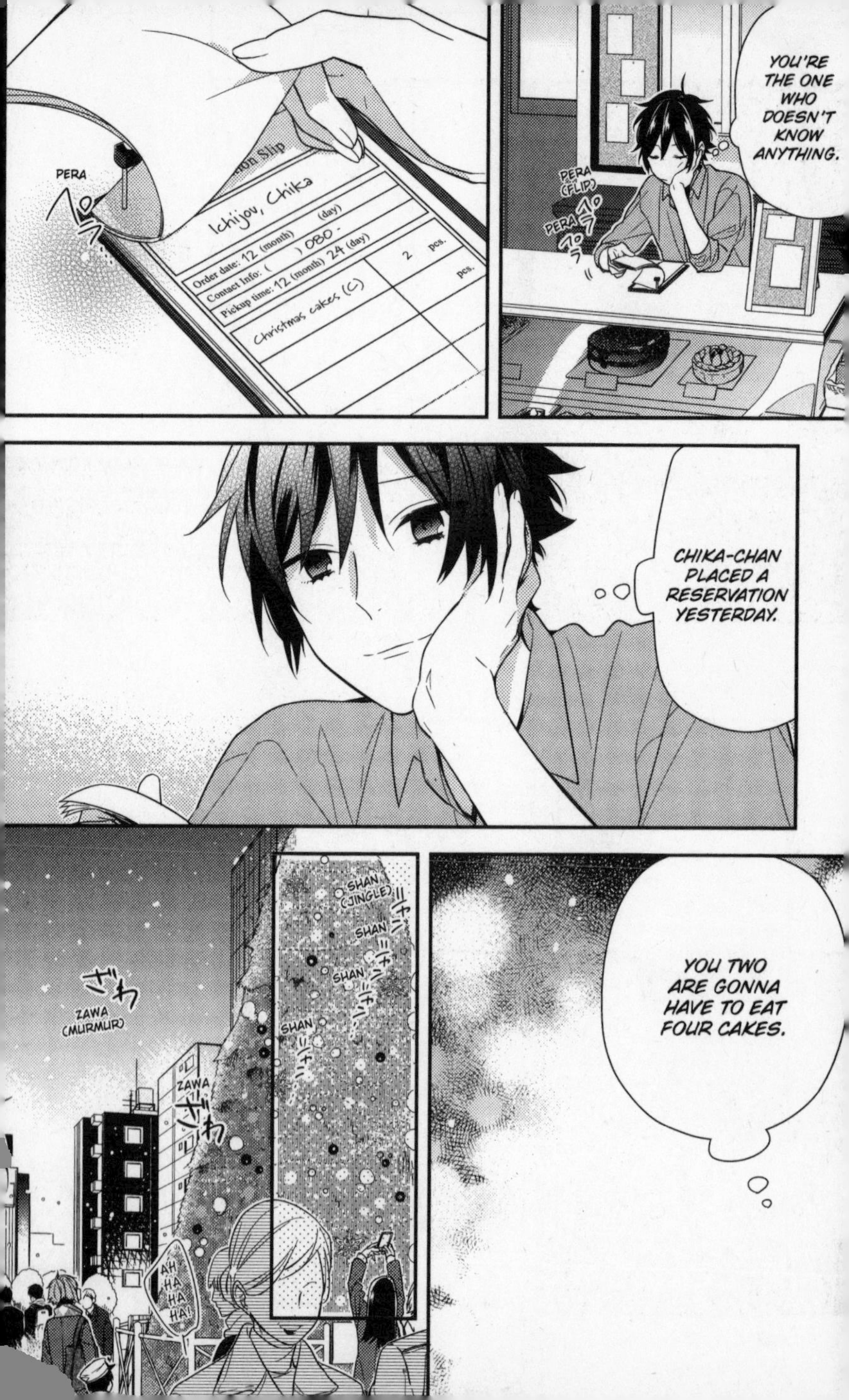
YOU'RE THE ONE WHO DOESN'T KNOW ANYTHING.
PERA (FLIP)
PERA
PERA
Ichijou, Chika
Order date: 12 (month) (day)
Contact Info: ( ) 080-
Pickup time: 12 (month) 24 (day)
Christmas cakes (C)
2 pcs.
pcs.
CHIKA-CHAN PLACED A RESERVATION YESTERDAY.
YOU TWO ARE GONNA HAVE TO EAT FOUR CAKES.
SHAN (JINGLE)
SHAN
SHAN
SHAN
ZAWA (MURMUR)
ZAWA
AH HA HA HA!

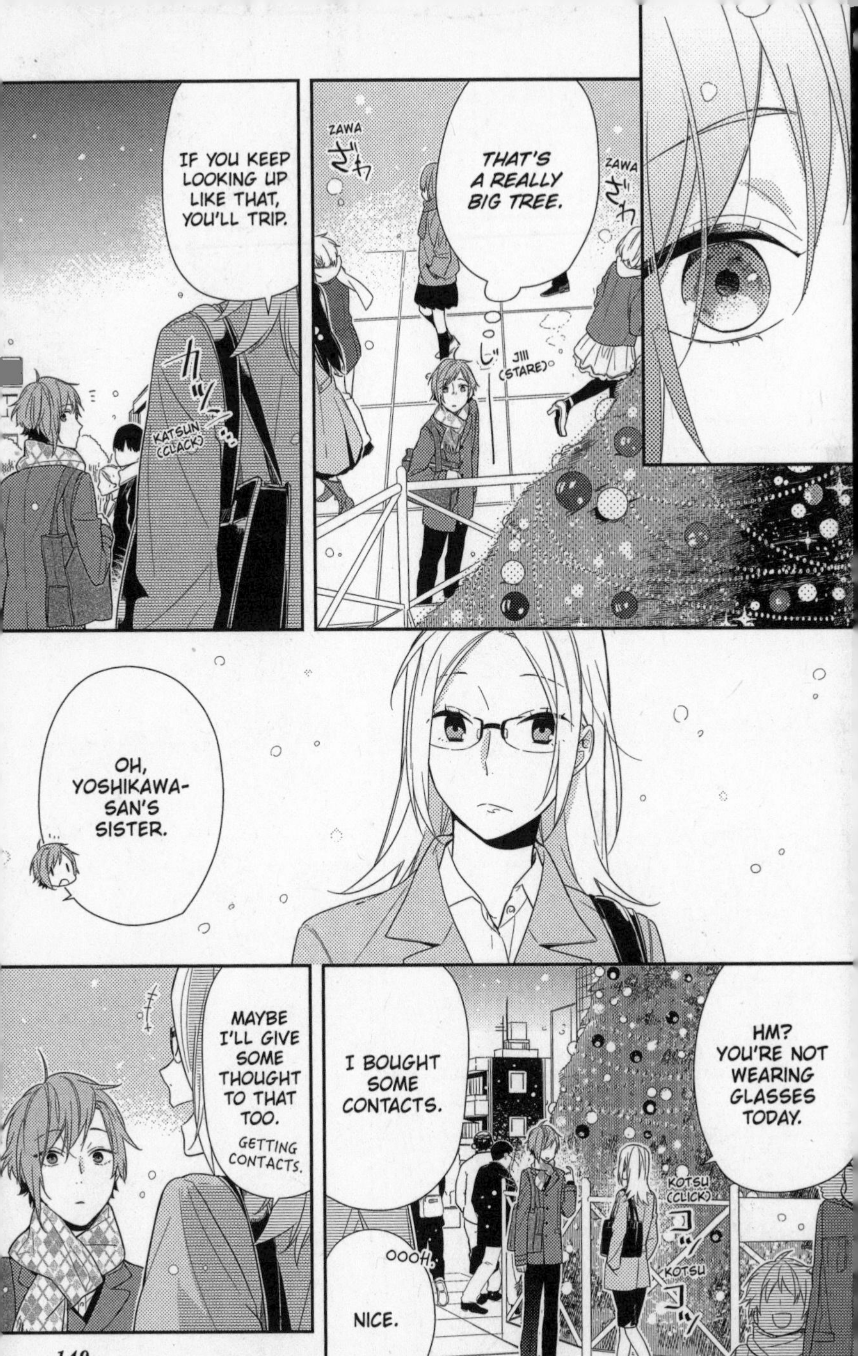
ZAWA
THAT'S A REALLY BIG TREE.
ZAWA
JIII (STARE)
IF YOU KEEP LOOKING UP LIKE THAT, YOU'LL TRIP.
KATSUN (CLACK)
OH, YOSHIKAWA-SAN'S SISTER.
...
HM? YOU'RE NOT WEARING GLASSES TODAY.
I BOUGHT SOME CONTACTS.
KOTSU (CLICK)
KOTSU
OOOH.
NICE.
MAYBE I'LL GIVE SOME THOUGHT TO THAT TOO.
GETTING CONTACTS.

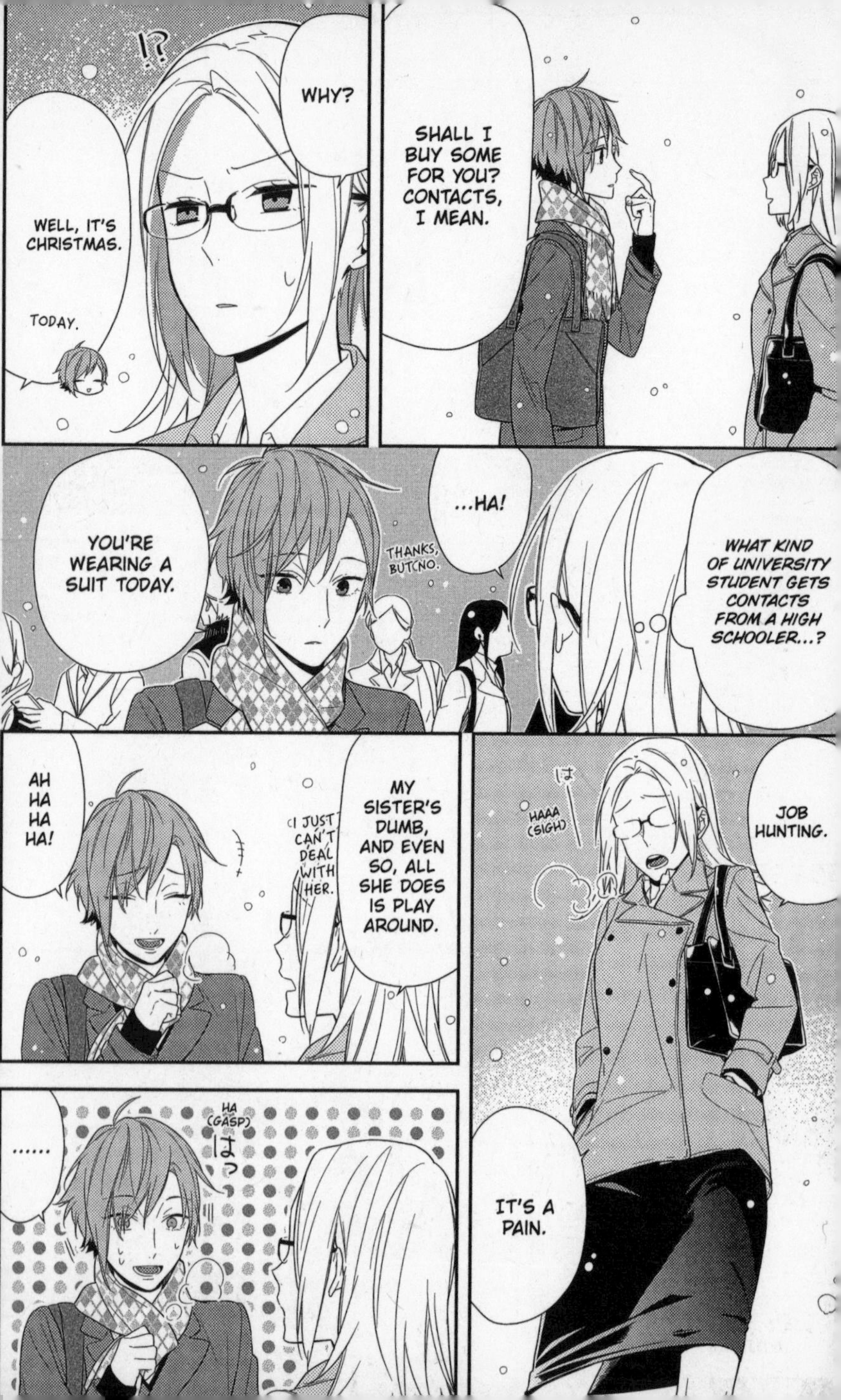
SHALL I BUY SOME FOR YOU? CONTACTS, I MEAN.
WHY?
!?
WELL, IT'S CHRISTMAS.
TODAY.
WHAT KIND OF UNIVERSITY STUDENT GETS CONTACTS FROM A HIGH SCHOOLER...?
...HA!
THANKS, BUT NO.
YOU'RE WEARING A SUIT TODAY.
JOB HUNTING.
はー
HAAA (SIGH)
IT'S A PAIN.
MY SISTER'S DUMB, AND EVEN SO, ALL SHE DOES IS PLAY AROUND.
I JUST CAN'T DEAL WITH HER.
AH HA HA HA!
HA (GASP)
はっ
......

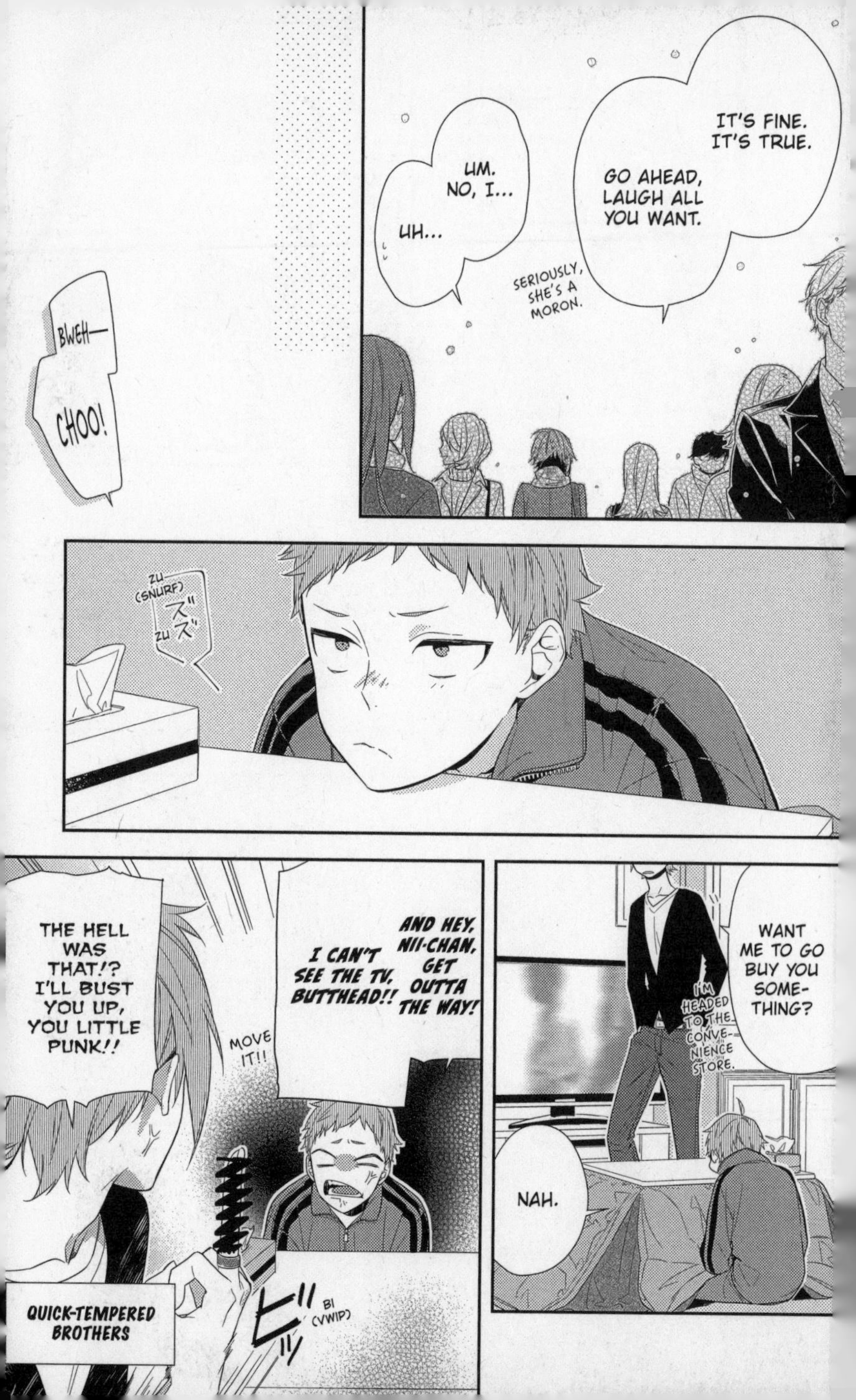
IT'S FINE. IT'S TRUE.
GO AHEAD, LAUGH ALL YOU WANT.
SERIOUSLY, SHE'S A MORON.
UM. NO, I...
UH...
BWEH—
CHOO!
ZU (SNURF) ズズ ZU
WANT ME TO GO BUY YOU SOME-THING?
I'M HEADED TO THE CONVE-NIENCE STORE.
NAH.
AND HEY, NII-CHAN, GET OUTTA THE WAY!
I CAN'T SEE THE TV, BUTTHEAD!!
MOVE IT!!
THE HELL WAS THAT!? I'LL BUST YOU UP, YOU LITTLE PUNK!!
ビッ BI (VWIP)
QUICK-TEMPERED BROTHERS

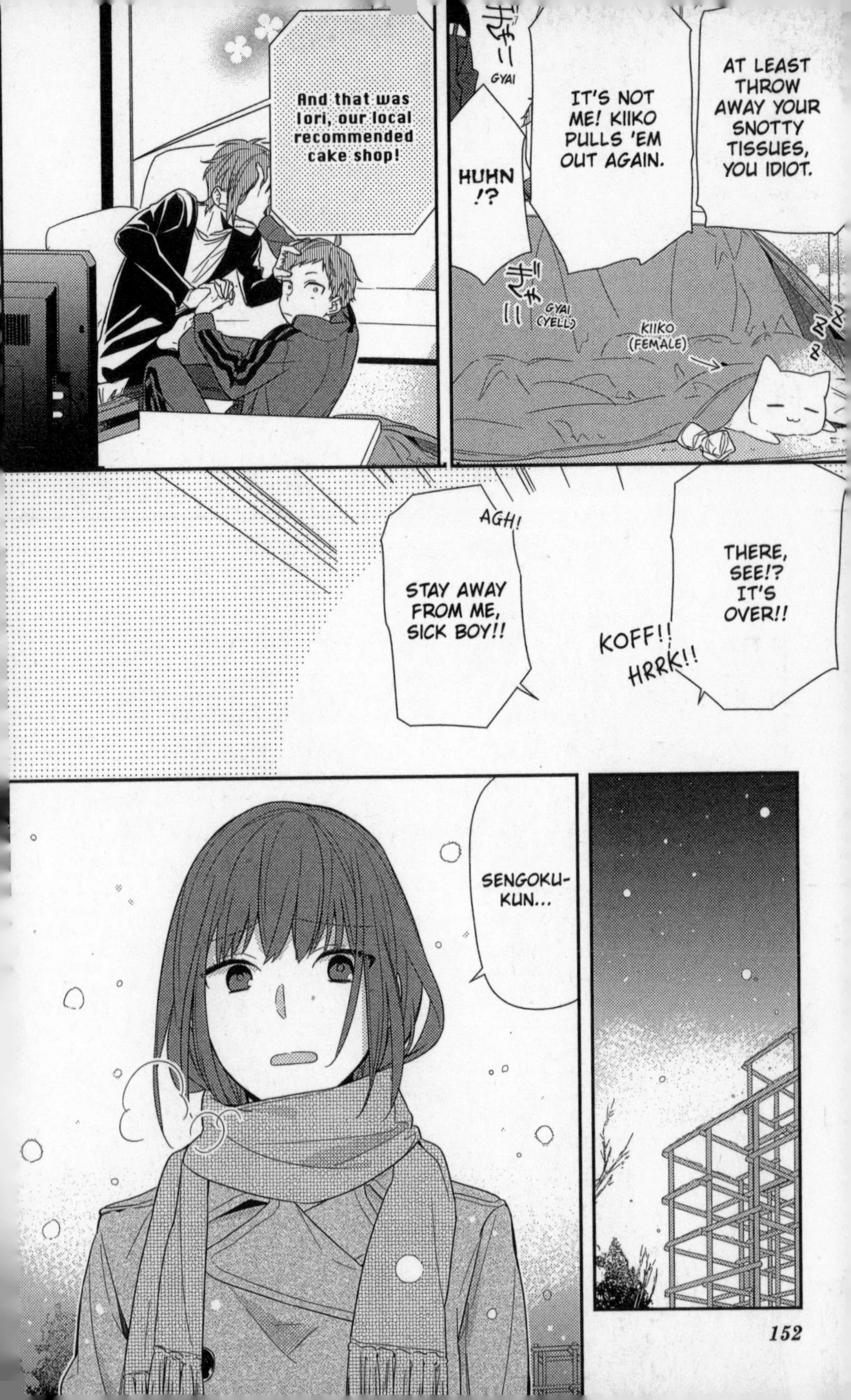
AT LEAST THROW AWAY YOUR SNOTTY TISSUES, YOU IDIOT.
IT'S NOT ME! KIIKO PULLS 'EM OUT AGAIN.
ぎゃい
GYAI
HUHN!?
ぎゃい
GYAI (YELL)
KIIKO (FEMALE)
And that was Iori, our local recommended cake shop!
THERE, SEE!? IT'S OVER!!
KOFF!! HRRK!!
AGH!
STAY AWAY FROM ME, SICK BOY!!
SENGOKU-KUN...

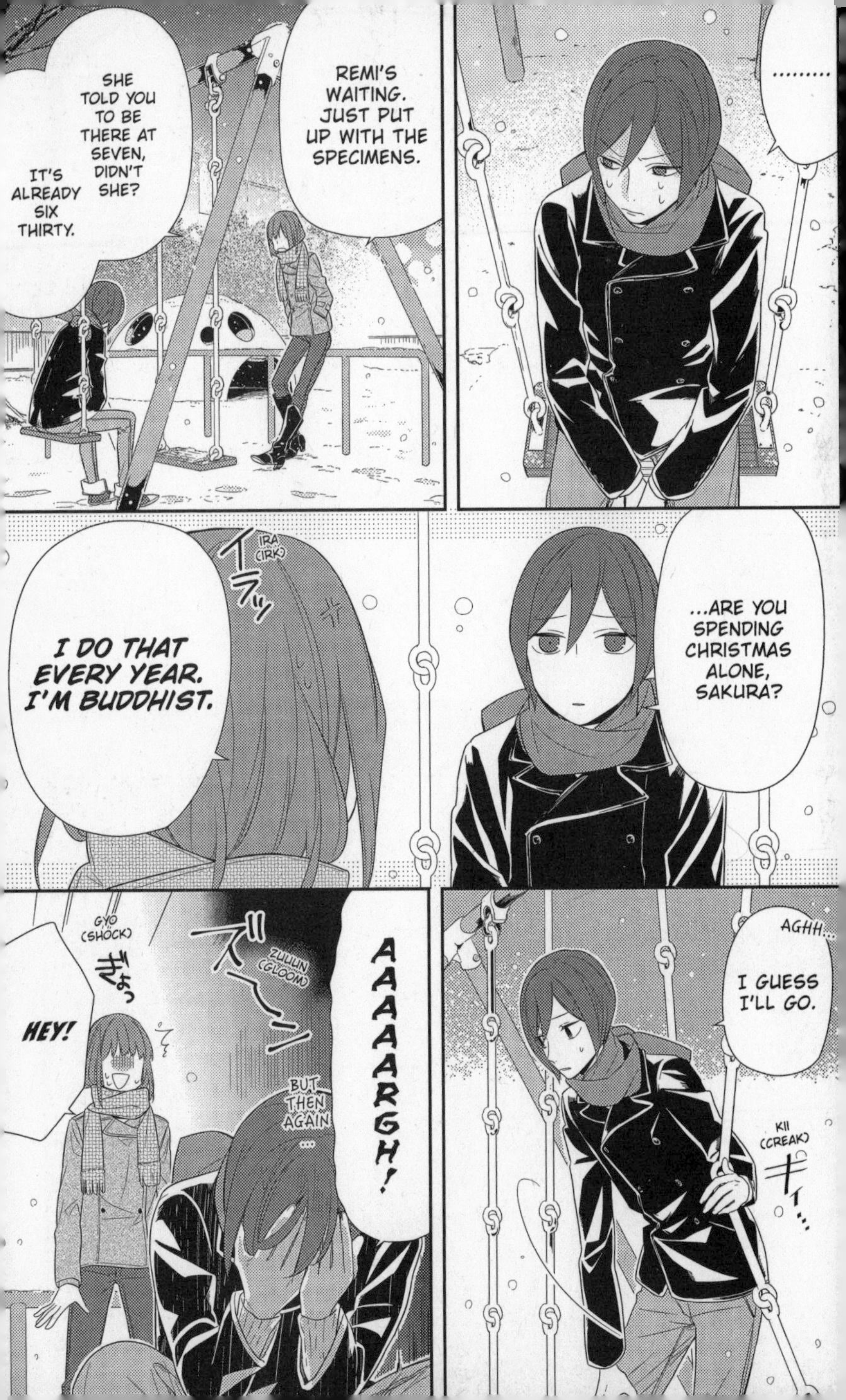
....
REMI'S WAITING. JUST PUT UP WITH THE SPECIMENS.
SHE TOLD YOU TO BE THERE AT SEVEN, DIDN'T SHE?
IT'S ALREADY SIX THIRTY.
...ARE YOU SPENDING CHRISTMAS ALONE, SAKURA?
イラッ
IRA (IRK)
I DO THAT EVERY YEAR. I'M BUDDHIST.
AGHH...
I GUESS I'LL GO.
ギィ…
KII (CREAK)
AAAAAARGH!
ズーン
ZUUUN (GLOOM)
BUT THEN AGAIN...
ぎょっ
GYO (SHOCK)
HEY!

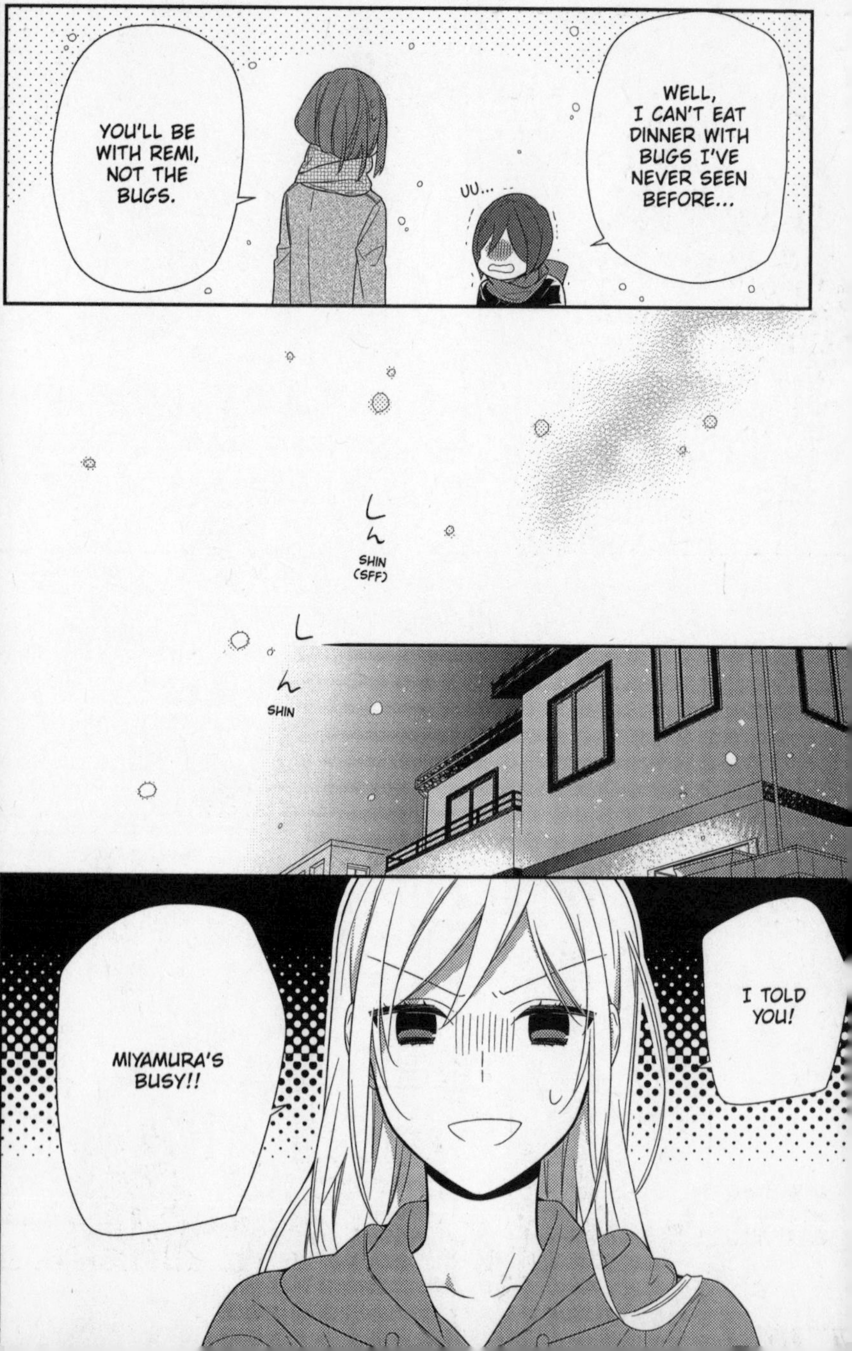
WELL, I CAN'T EAT DINNER WITH BUGS I'VE NEVER SEEN BEFORE...
UU...
YOU'LL BE WITH REMI, NOT THE BUGS.
しん
SHIN (SFF)
しん
SHIN
I TOLD YOU!
MIYAMURA'S BUSY!!

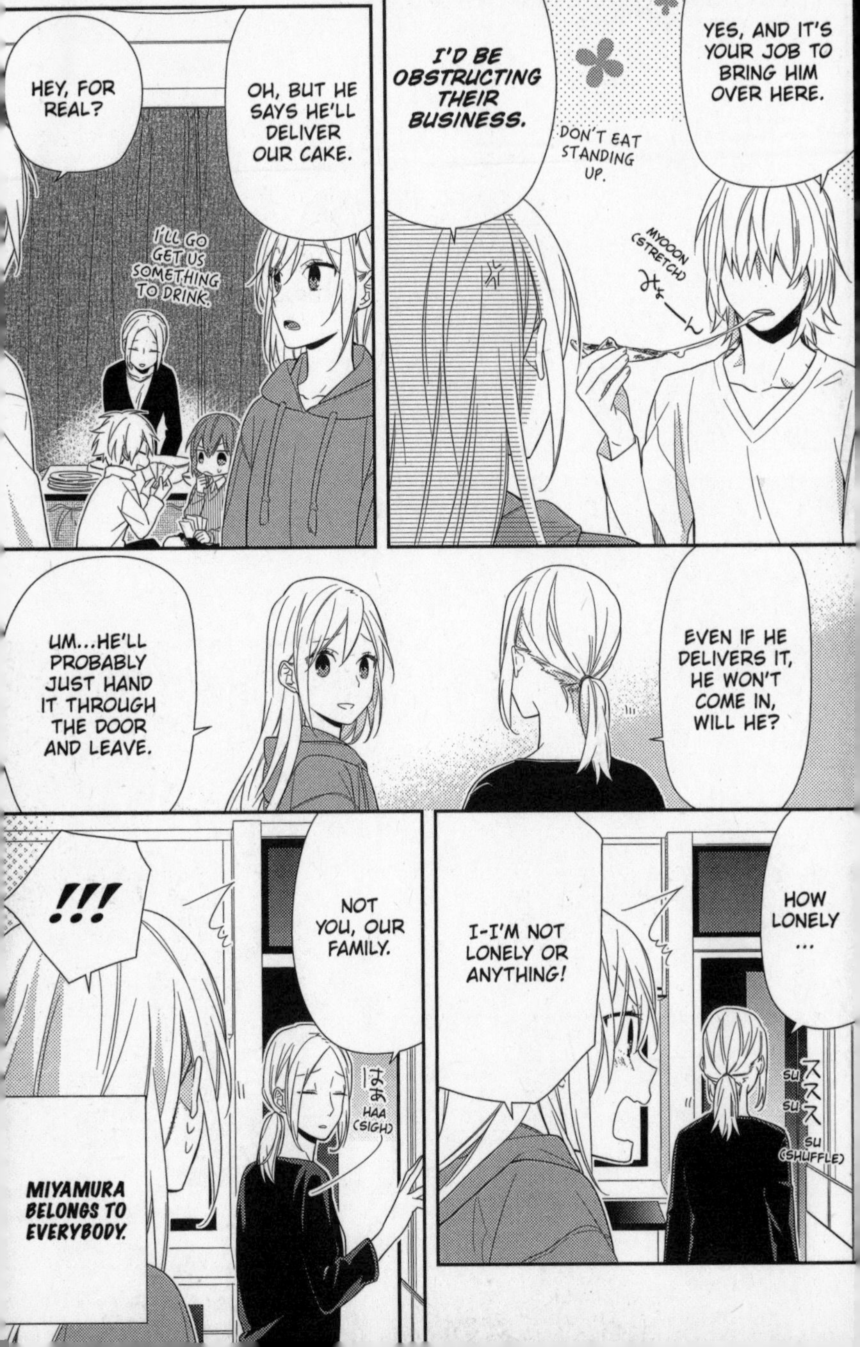
YES, AND IT'S YOUR JOB TO BRING HIM OVER HERE.
I'D BE OBSTRUCTING THEIR BUSINESS.
DON'T EAT STANDING UP.
MYOOON (STRETCH) みょーん
OH, BUT HE SAYS HE'LL DELIVER OUR CAKE.
HEY, FOR REAL?
I'LL GO GET US SOMETHING TO DRINK.
EVEN IF HE DELIVERS IT, HE WON'T COME IN, WILL HE?
UM...HE'LL PROBABLY JUST HAND IT THROUGH THE DOOR AND LEAVE.
HOW LONELY ...
I-I'M NOT LONELY OR ANYTHING!
ススス SU SU SU (SHUFFLE)
NOT YOU, OUR FAMILY.
はぁ HAA (SIGH)
!!!
MIYAMURA BELONGS TO EVERYBODY.

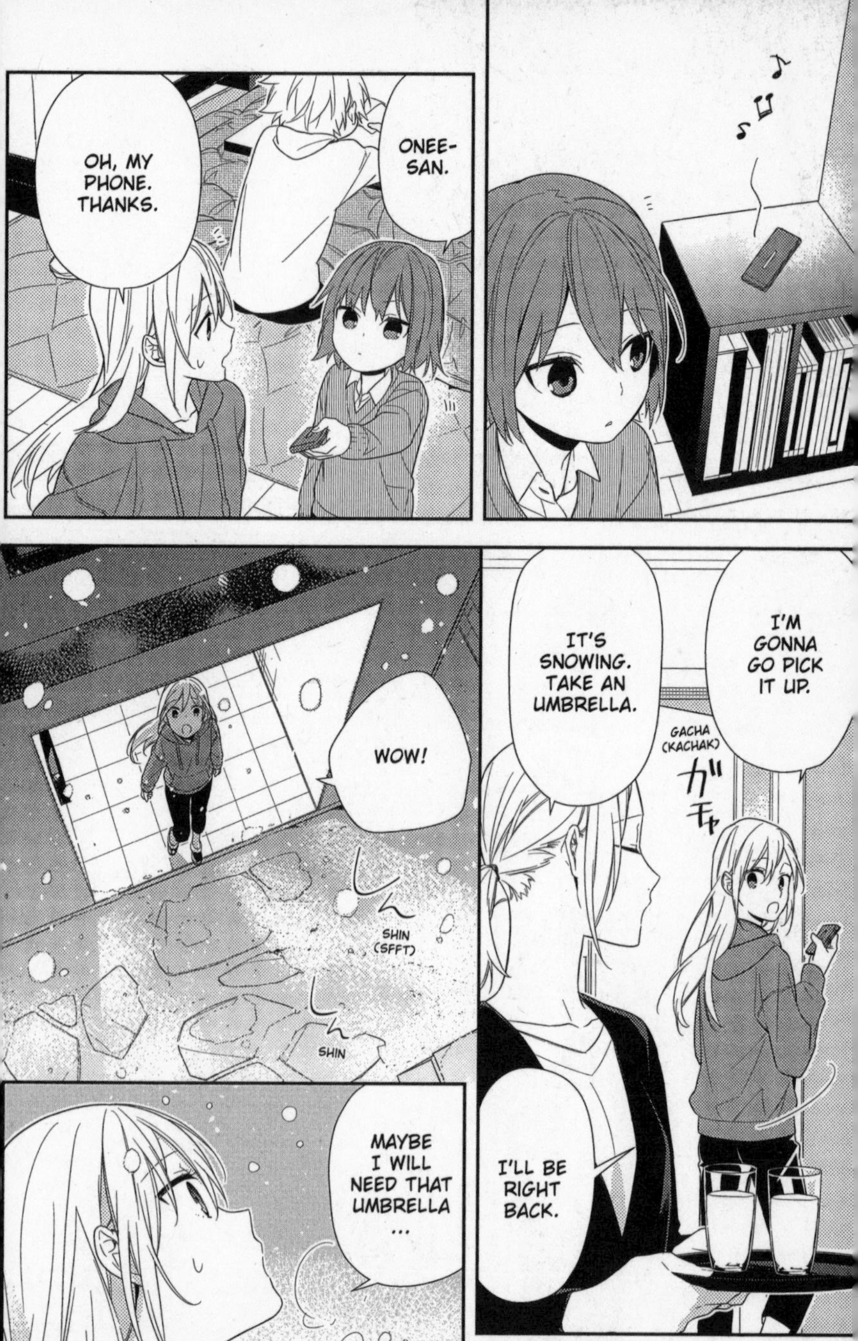
ONEE-SAN.
OH, MY PHONE. THANKS.
I'M GONNA GO PICK IT UP.
IT'S SNOWING. TAKE AN UMBRELLA.
GACHA (KACHAK)
I'LL BE RIGHT BACK.
WOW!
SHIN (SFFT)
SHIN
MAYBE I WILL NEED THAT UMBRELLA ...

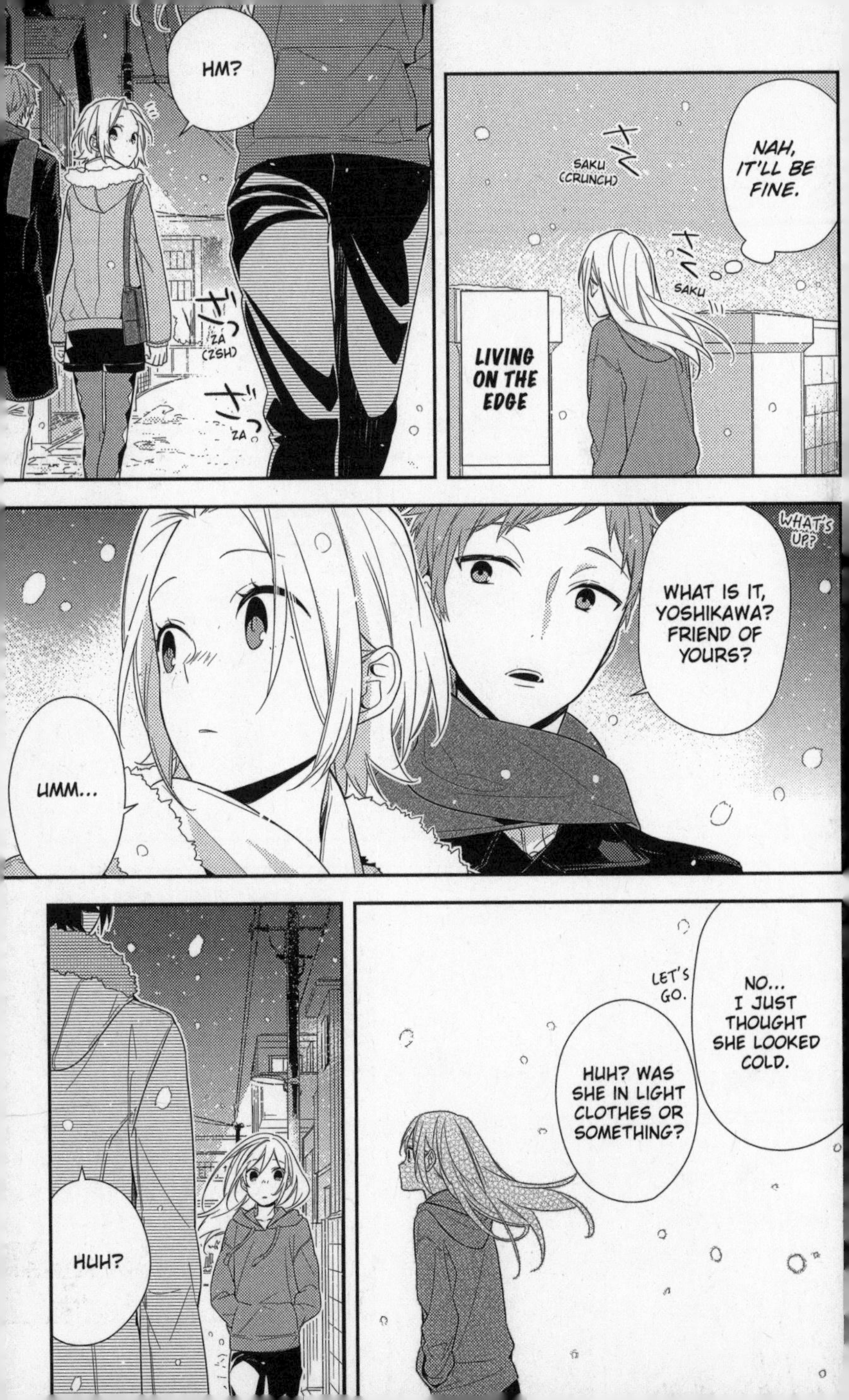
NAH, IT'LL BE FINE.
SAKU (CRUNCH)
SAKU
LIVING ON THE EDGE
HM?
ZA (ZSH)
ZA
WHAT'S UP?
WHAT IS IT, YOSHIKAWA? FRIEND OF YOURS?
UMM...
NO... I JUST THOUGHT SHE LOOKED COLD.
LET'S GO.
HUH? WAS SHE IN LIGHT CLOTHES OR SOMETHING?
HUH?

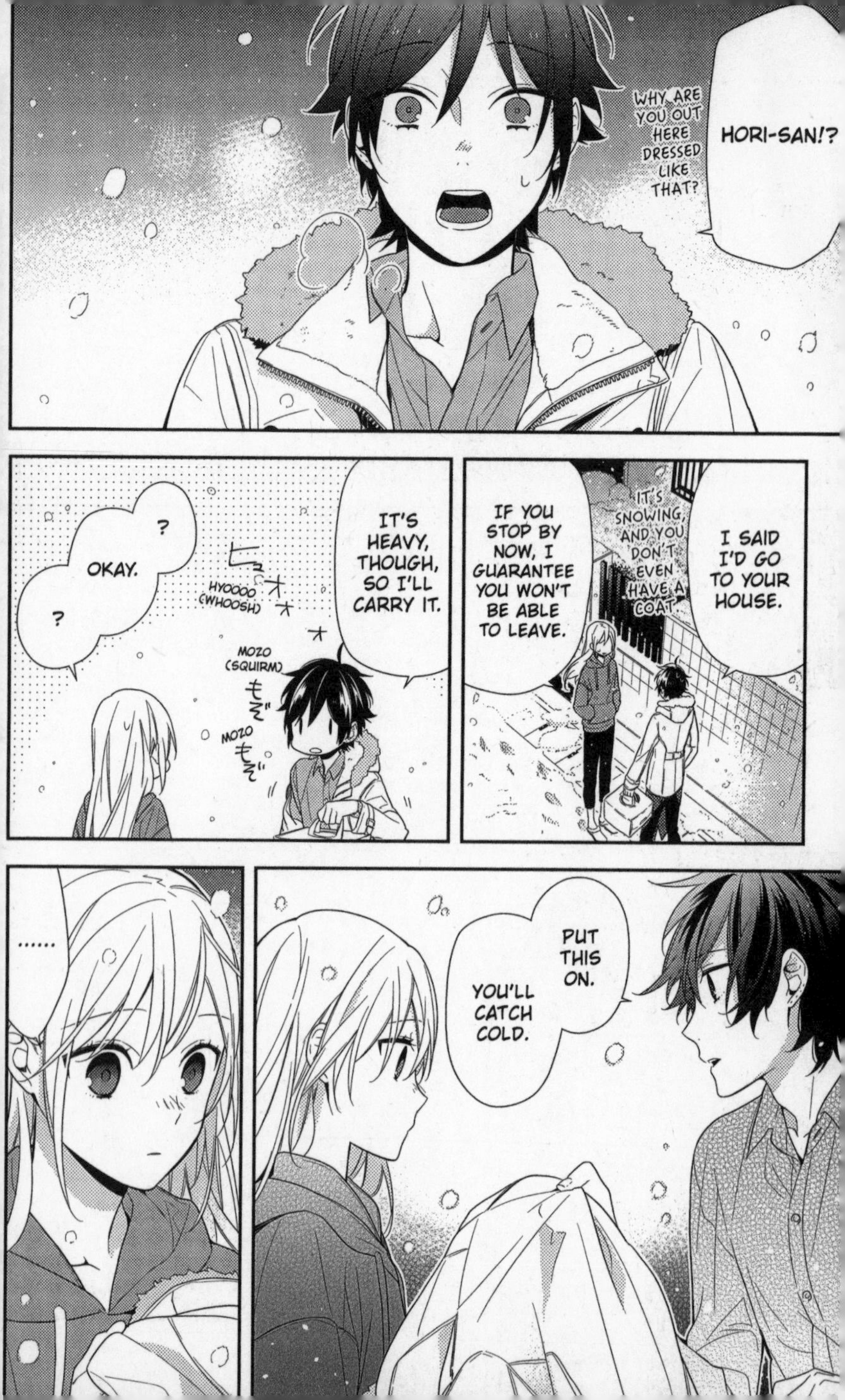
HORI-SAN!?
WHY ARE YOU OUT HERE DRESSED LIKE THAT?
I SAID I'D GO TO YOUR HOUSE.
IT'S SNOWING, AND YOU DON'T EVEN HAVE A COAT.
IF YOU STOP BY NOW, I GUARANTEE YOU WON'T BE ABLE TO LEAVE.
IT'S HEAVY, THOUGH, SO I'LL CARRY IT.
HYOOOO (WHOOSH)
MOZO (SQUIRM)
MOZO
?
OKAY.
?
PUT THIS ON.
YOU'LL CATCH COLD.
......

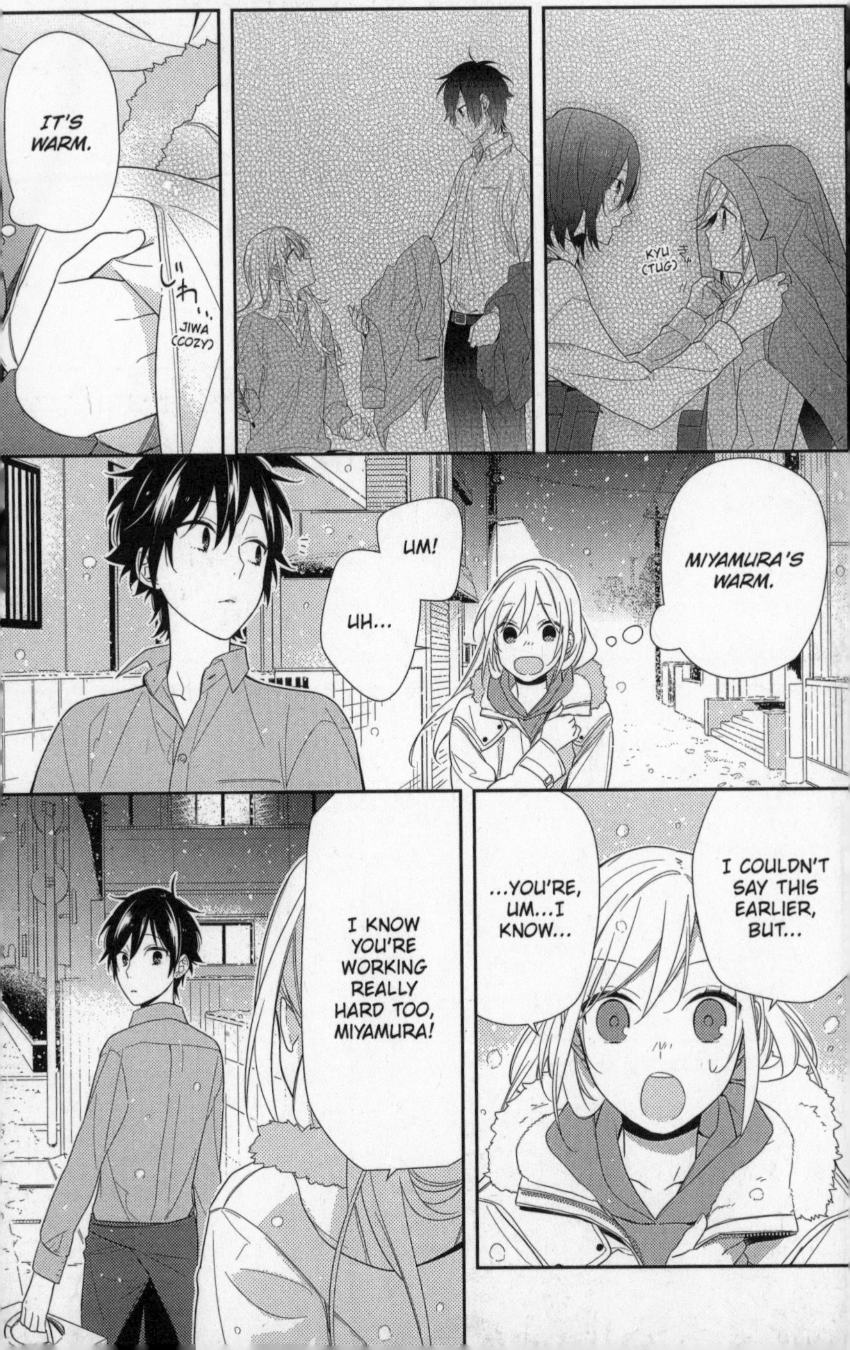
KYU (TUG)
IT'S WARM.
じわ…
JIWA (COZY)
MIYAMURA'S WARM.
UM!
UH...
I COULDN'T SAY THIS EARLIER, BUT...
...YOU'RE, UM...I KNOW...
I KNOW YOU'RE WORKING REALLY HARD TOO, MIYAMURA!

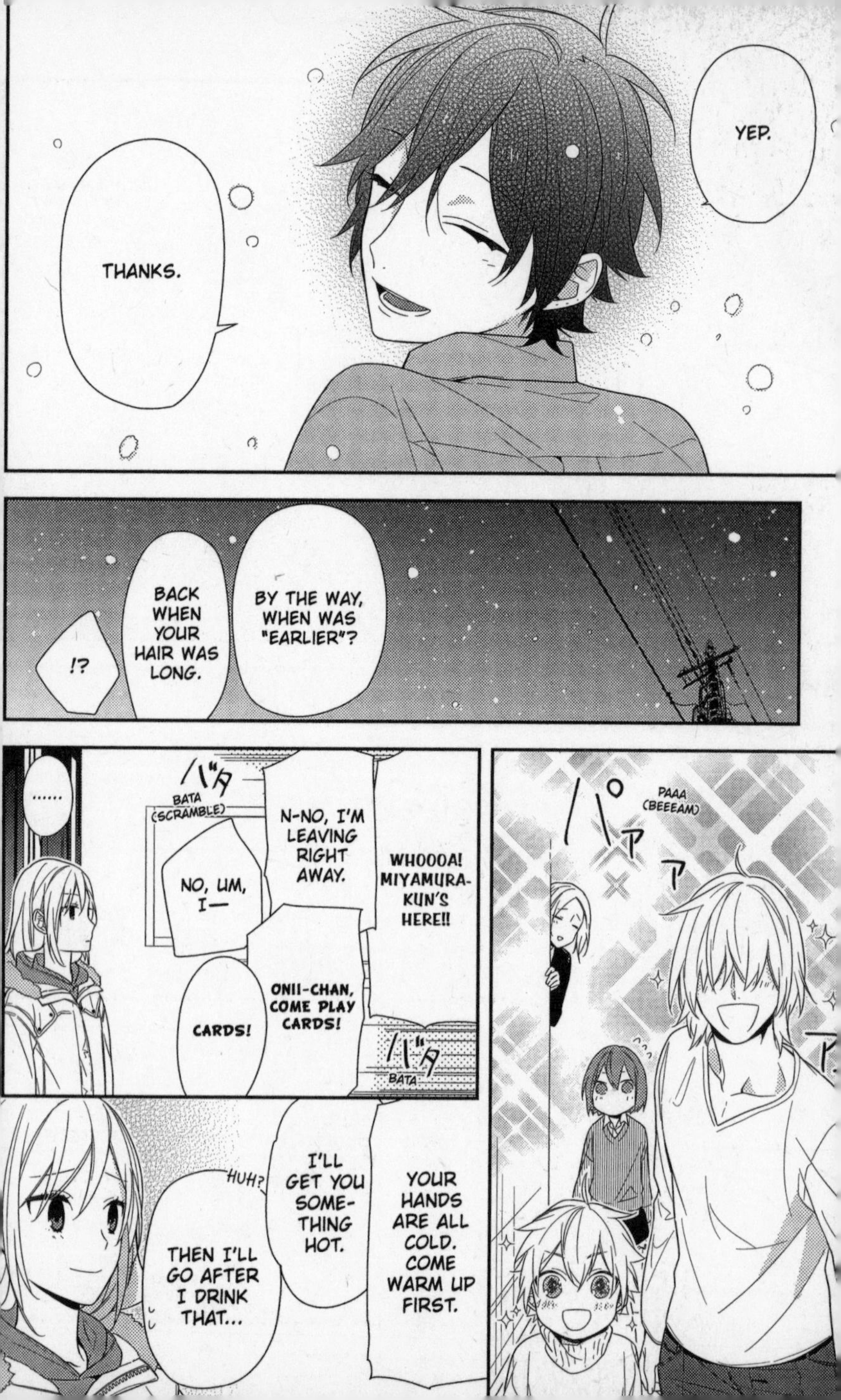
YEP.
THANKS.
BY THE WAY, WHEN WAS "EARLIER"?
BACK WHEN YOUR HAIR WAS LONG.
!?
PAAA (BEEEAM)
WHOOOA! MIYAMURA-KUN'S HERE!!
N-NO, I'M LEAVING RIGHT AWAY.
BATA (SCRAMBLE)
NO, UM, I—
ONII-CHAN, COME PLAY CARDS!
CARDS!
BATA
......
YOUR HANDS ARE ALL COLD. COME WARM UP FIRST.
I'LL GET YOU SOME-THING HOT.
HUH?
THEN I'LL GO AFTER I DRINK THAT...

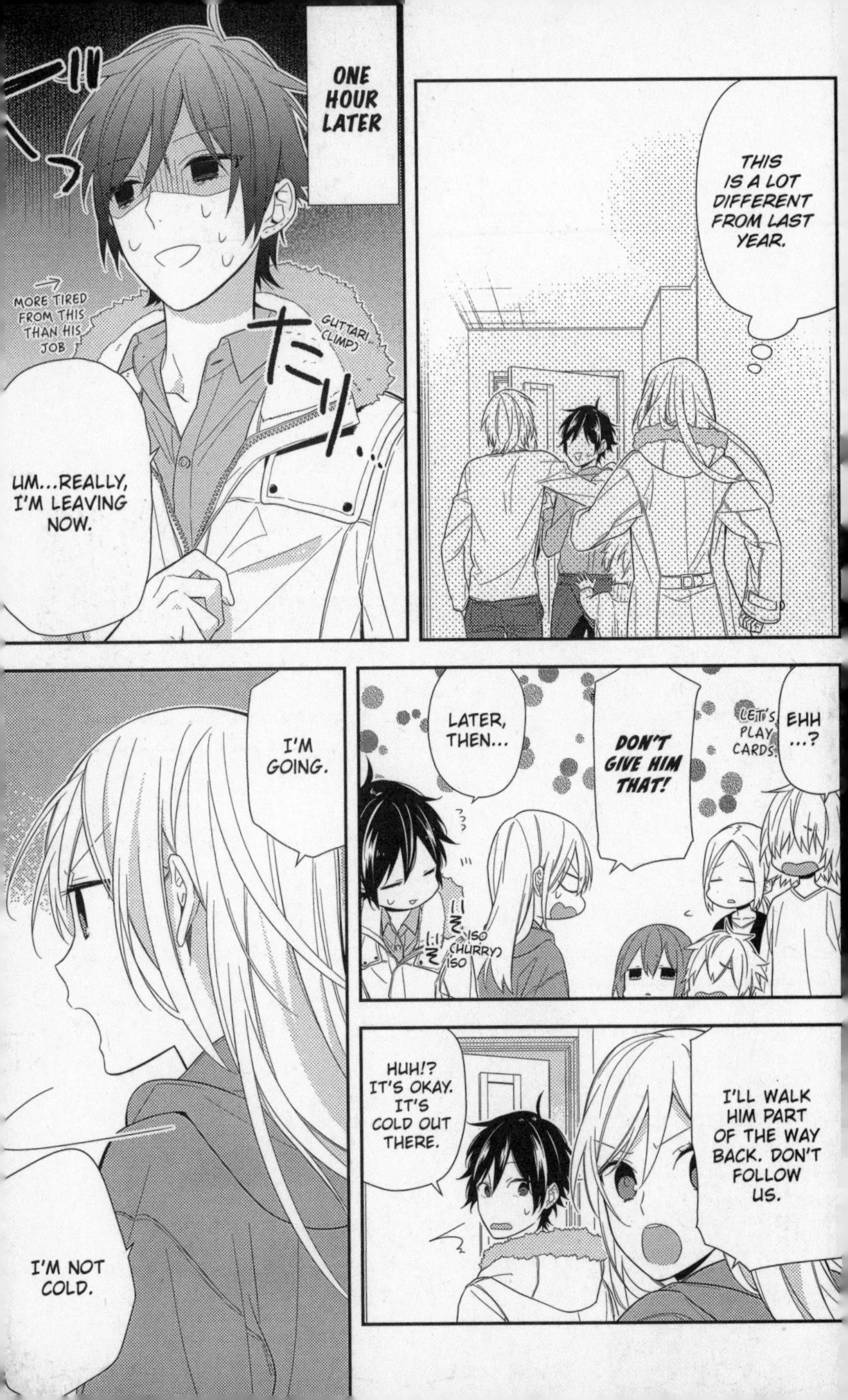
THIS IS A LOT DIFFERENT FROM LAST YEAR.
ONE HOUR LATER
GUTTARI (LIMP)
MORE TIRED FROM THIS THAN HIS JOB
UM...REALLY, I'M LEAVING NOW.
EHH ...?
LET'S PLAY CARDS.
DON'T GIVE HIM THAT!
LATER, THEN...
ISO (HURRY) ISO
I'LL WALK HIM PART OF THE WAY BACK. DON'T FOLLOW US.
HUH!? IT'S OKAY. IT'S COLD OUT THERE.
I'M GOING.
I'M NOT COLD.

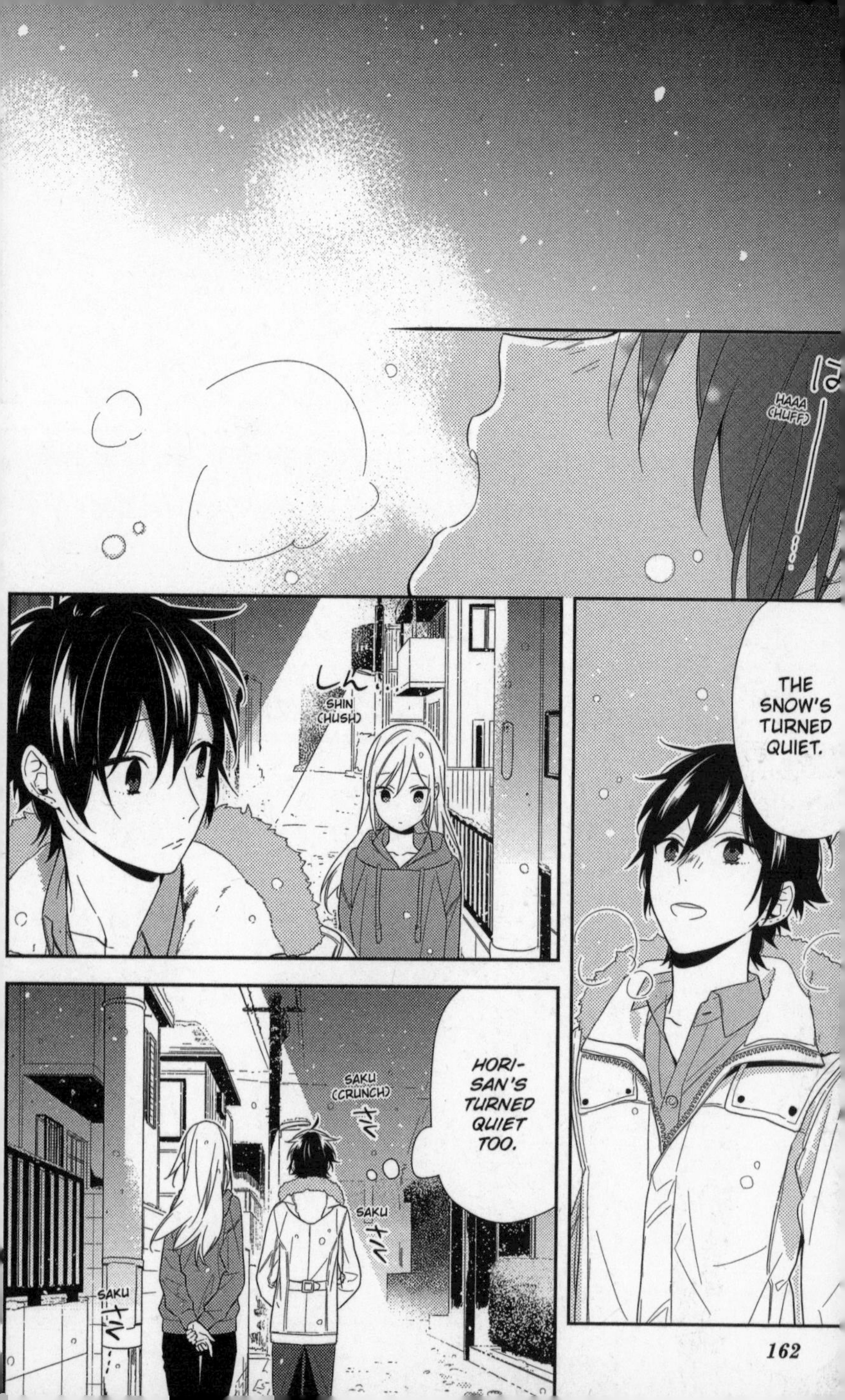
は
HAAA (HUFF)
THE SNOW'S TURNED QUIET.
しん…
SHIN (HUSH)
HORI-SAN'S TURNED QUIET TOO.
SAKU (CRUNCH)
サク
SAKU
サク
SAKU
サク…

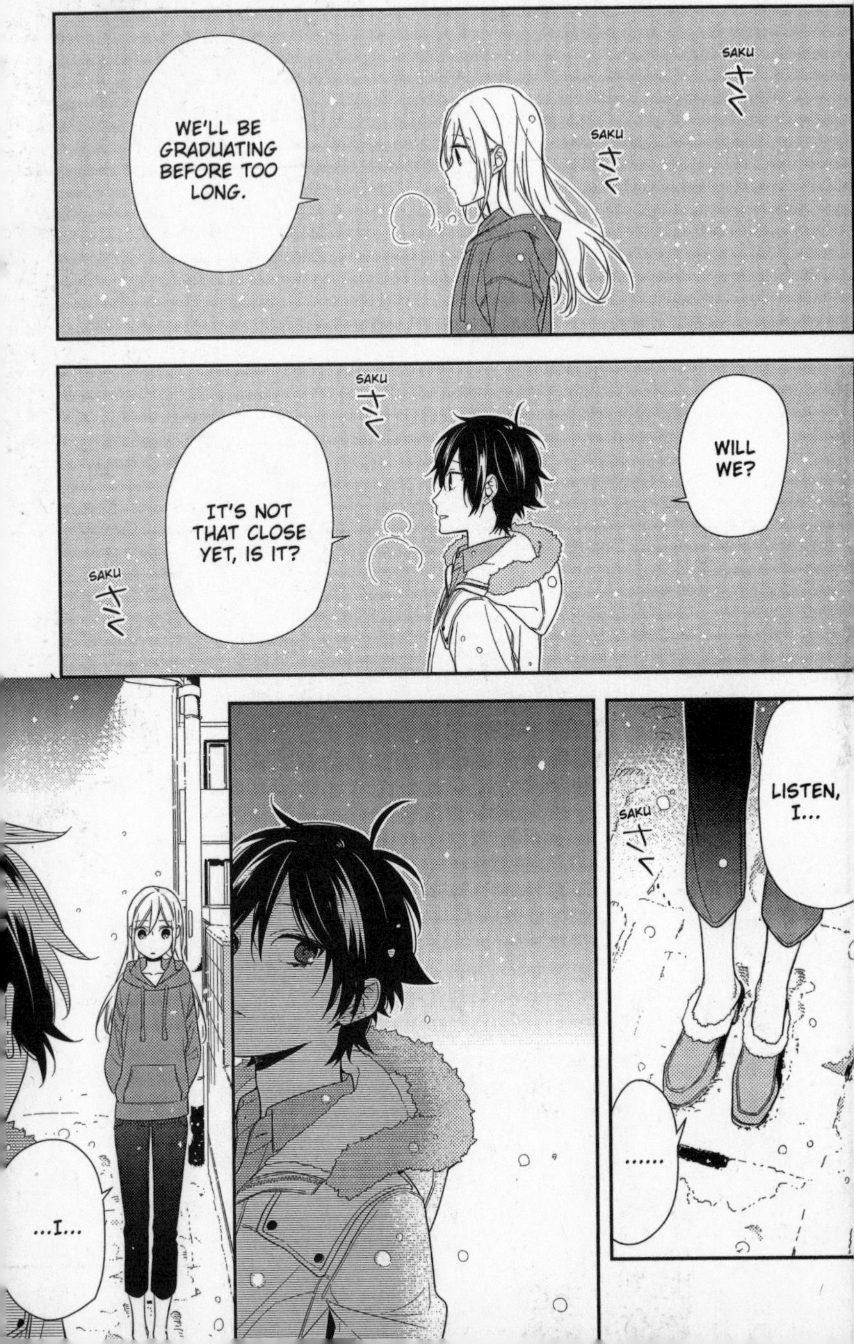
SAKU サク
SAKU サク
WE'LL BE GRADUATING BEFORE TOO LONG.
WILL WE?
SAKU サク
IT'S NOT THAT CLOSE YET, IS IT?
SAKU サク
LISTEN, I...
SAKU サク
......
...I...

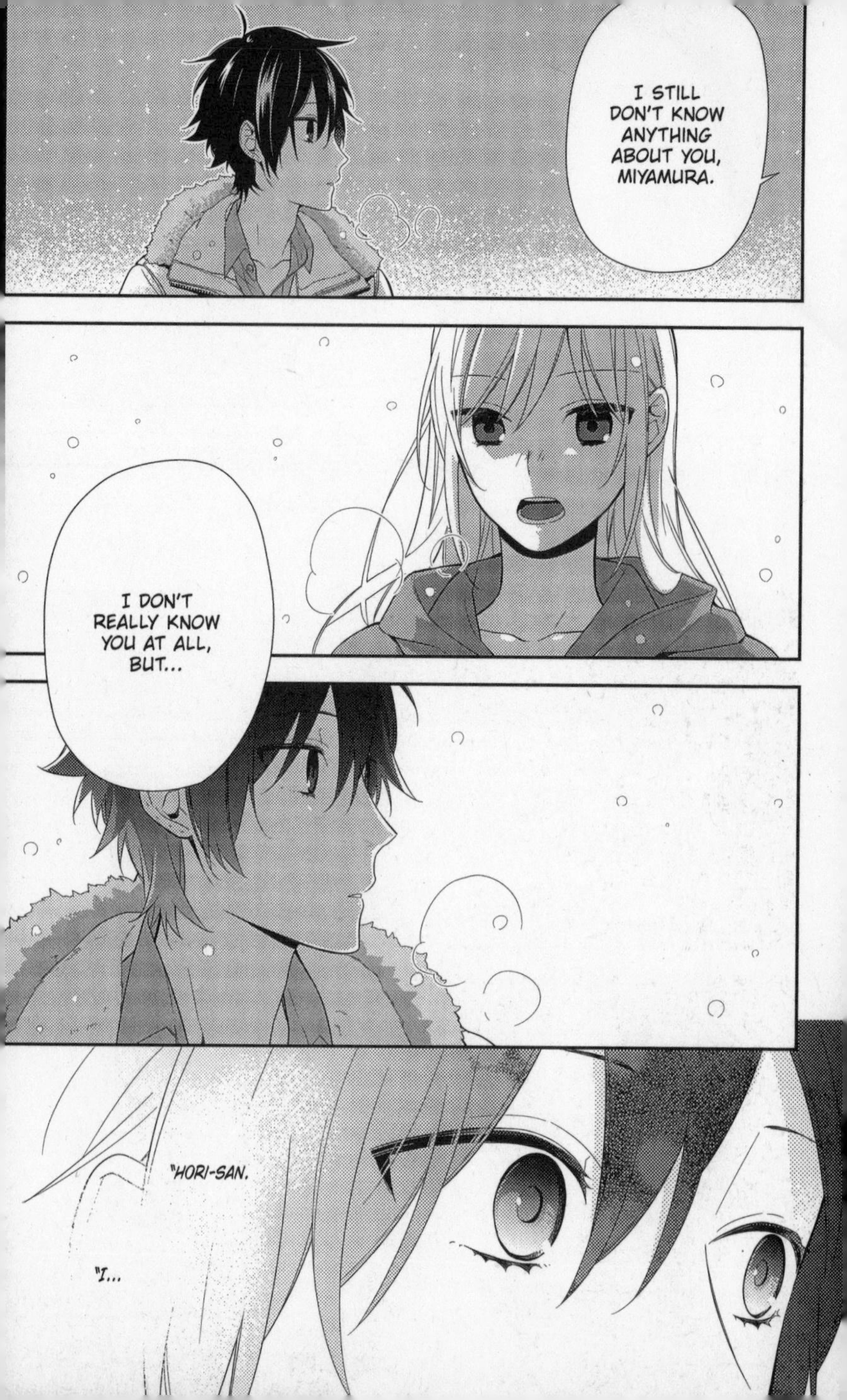
I STILL DON'T KNOW ANYTHING ABOUT YOU, MIYAMURA.
I DON'T REALLY KNOW YOU AT ALL, BUT...
"HORI-SAN.
"I...

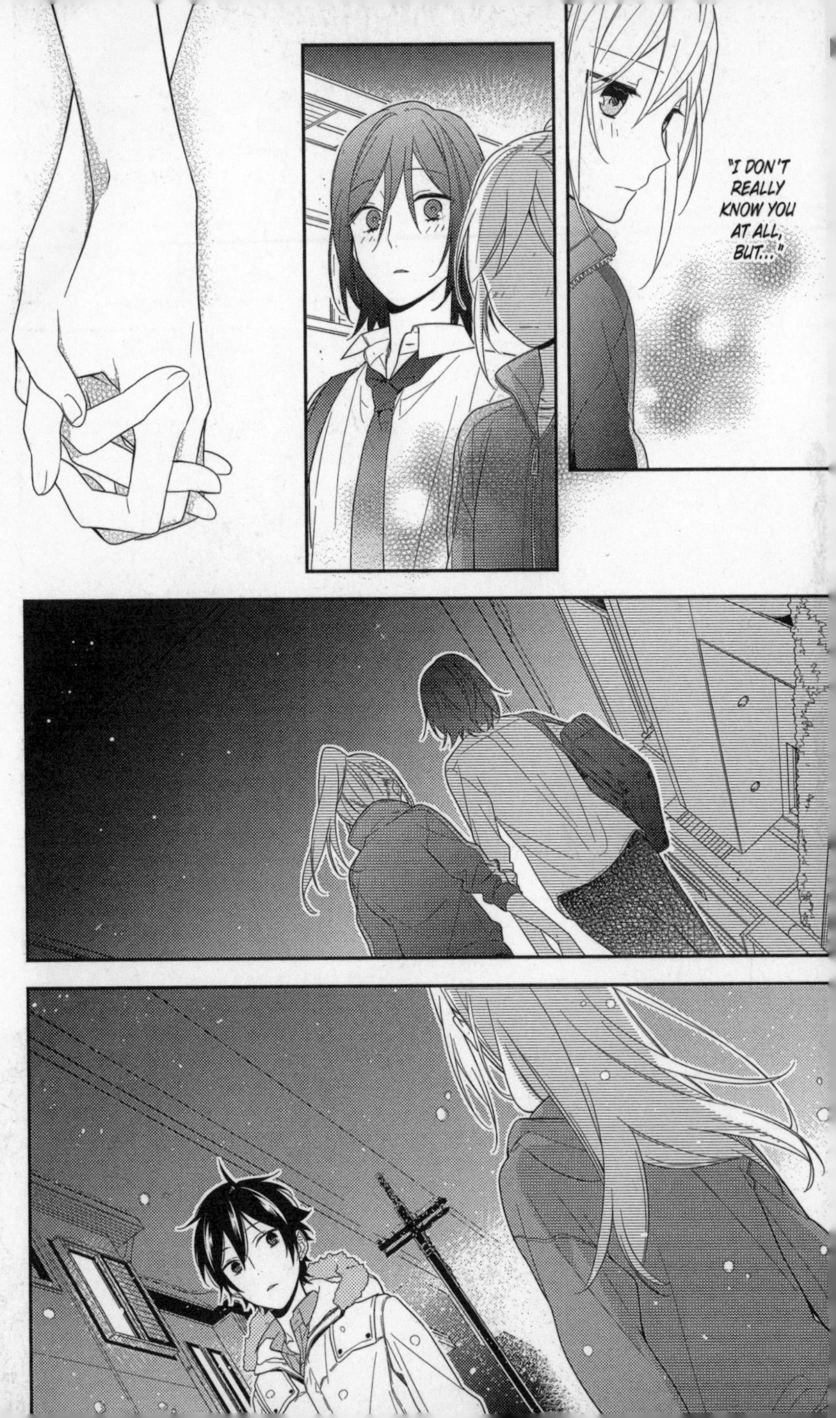
"I DON'T REALLY KNOW YOU AT ALL, BUT..."

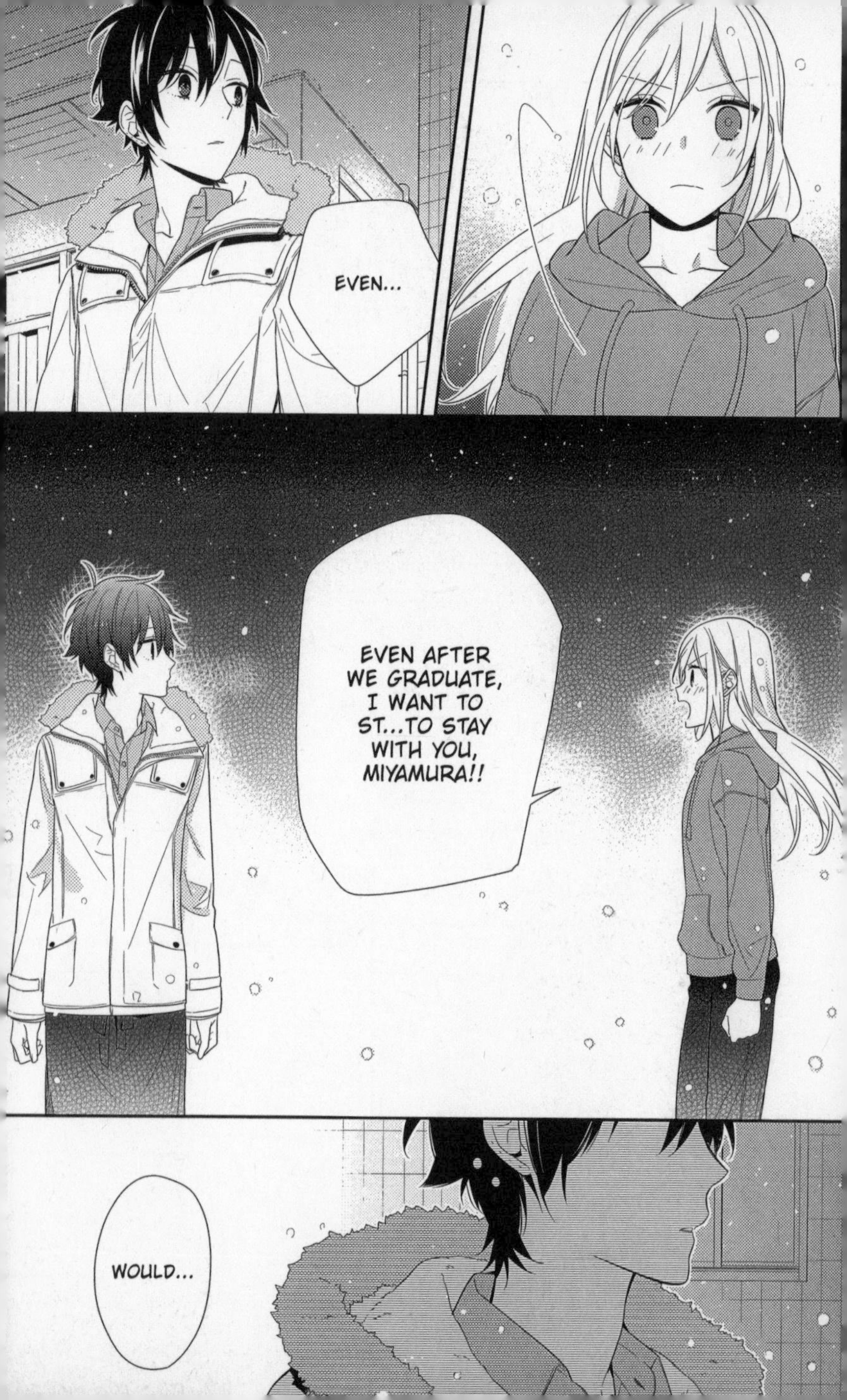
EVEN...
EVEN AFTER WE GRADUATE, I WANT TO ST...TO STAY WITH YOU, MIYAMURA!!
WOULD...

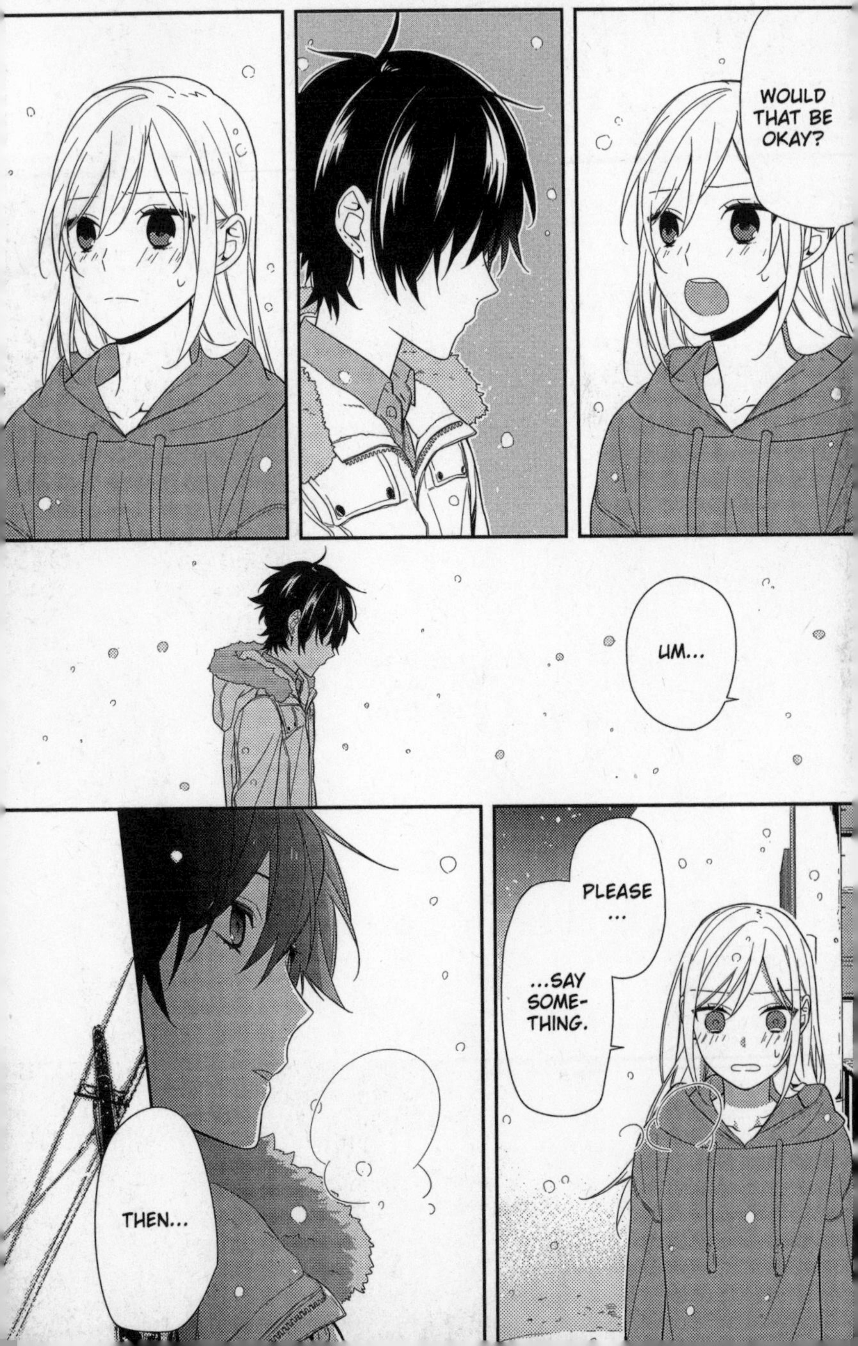
WOULD THAT BE OKAY?
UM...
PLEASE ...
...SAY SOME-THING.
THEN...

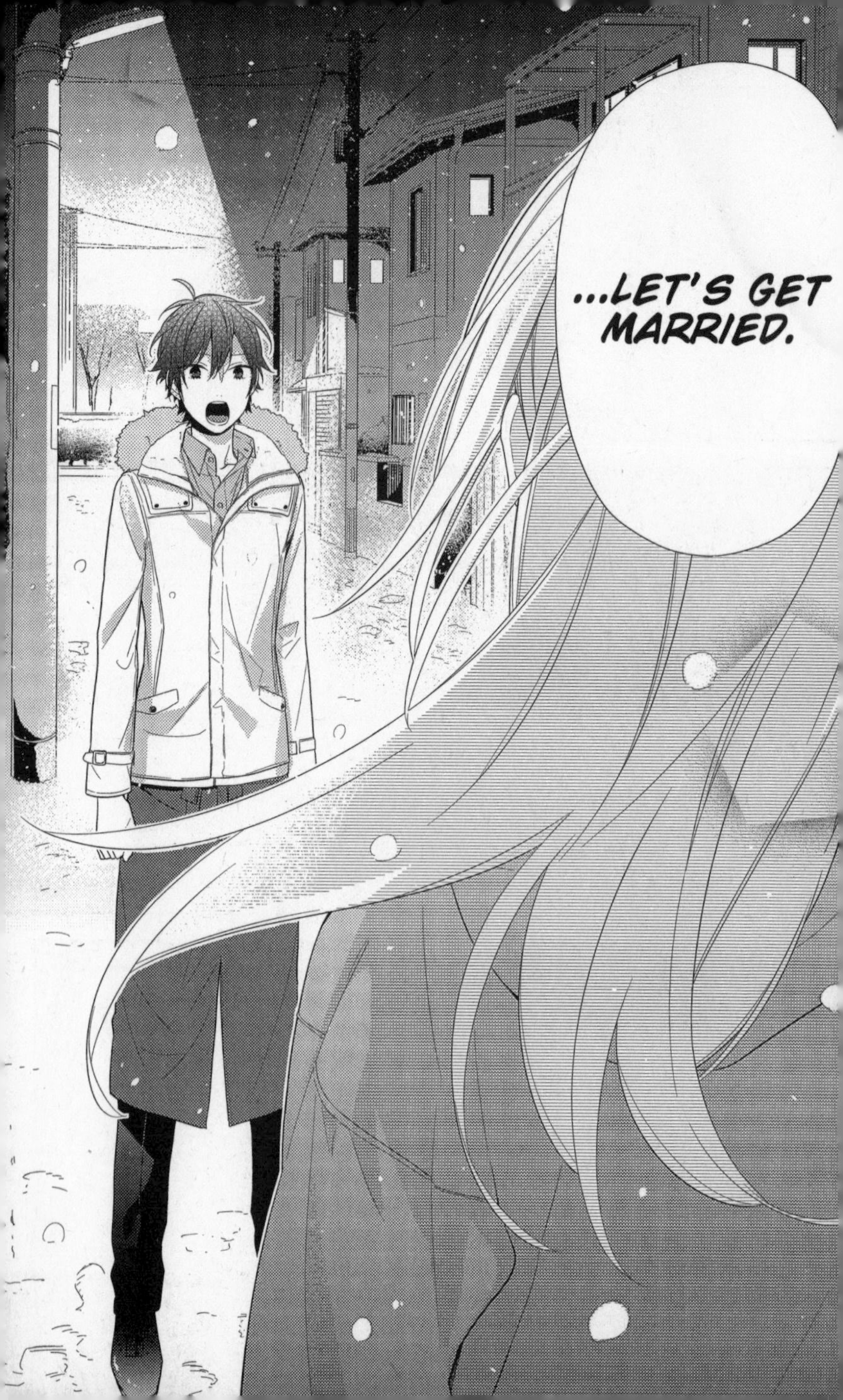
...LET'S GET MARRIED.

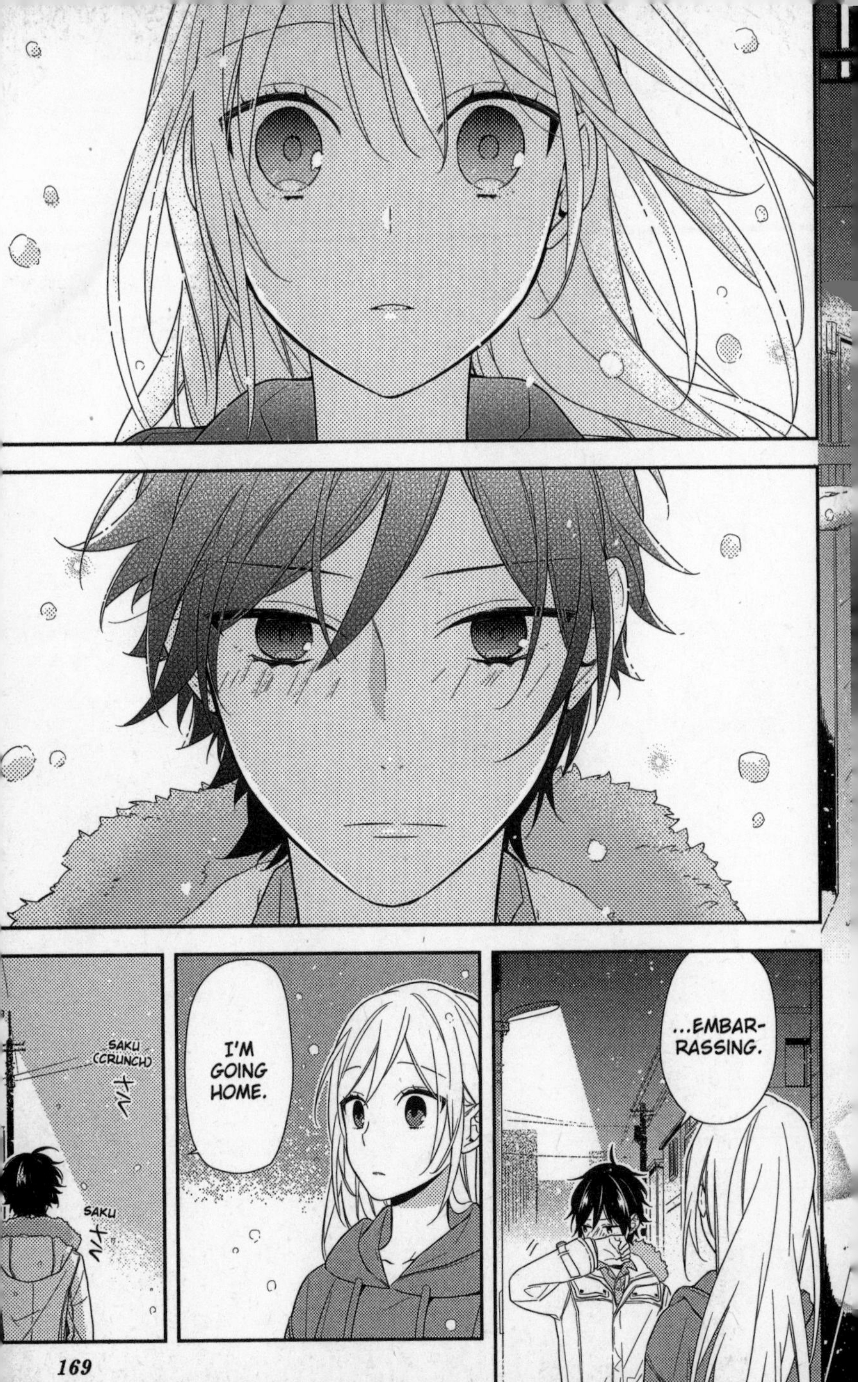
...EMBAR-
RASSING.
I'M GOING HOME.
SAKU (CRUNCH)
サク
SAKU
サク

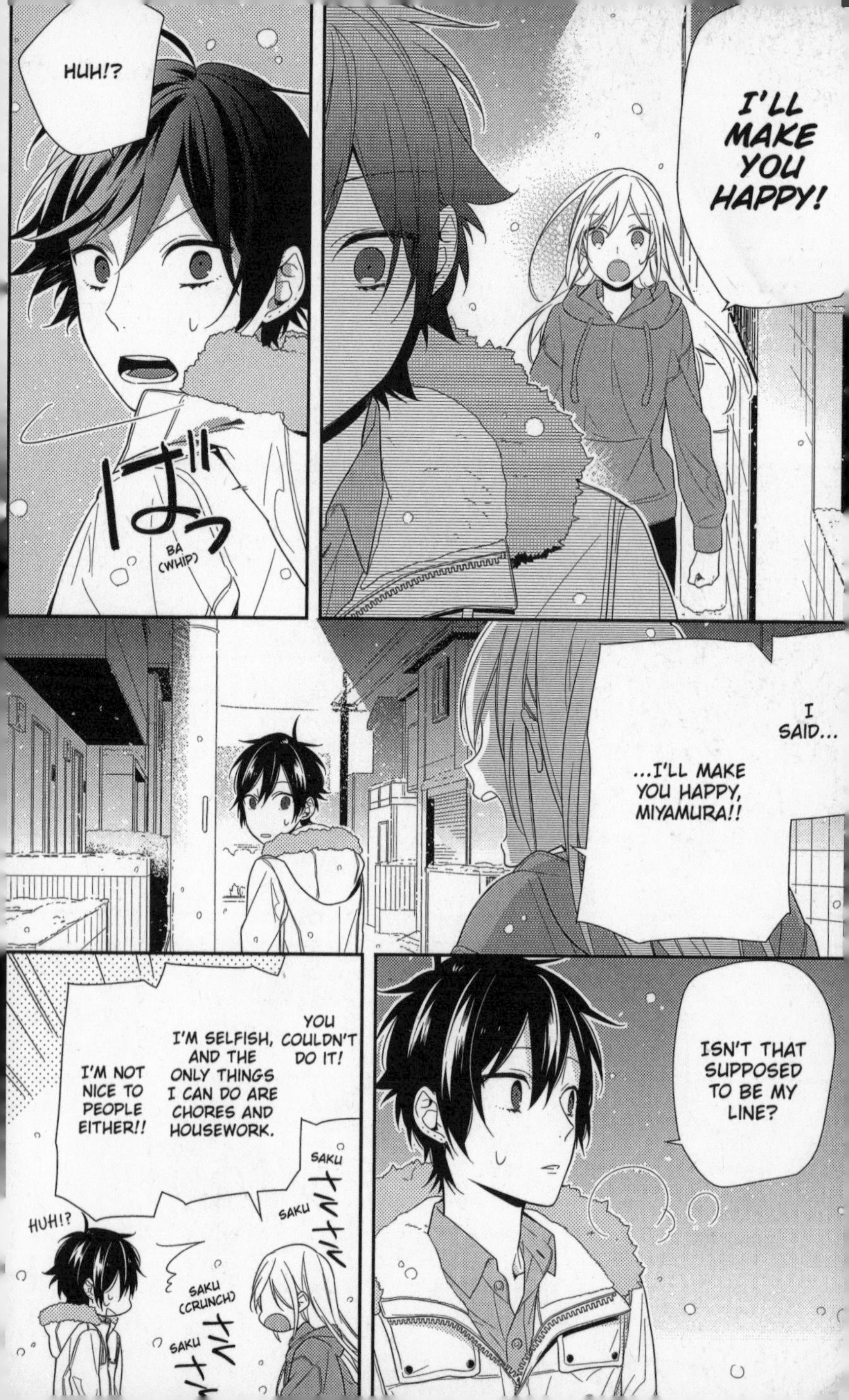
I'LL MAKE YOU HAPPY!
HUH!?
ばっ
BA (WHIP)
I SAID...
...I'LL MAKE YOU HAPPY, MIYAMURA!!
ISN'T THAT SUPPOSED TO BE MY LINE?
YOU COULDN'T DO IT!
I'M SELFISH, AND THE ONLY THINGS I CAN DO ARE CHORES AND HOUSEWORK.
I'M NOT NICE TO PEOPLE EITHER!!
SAKU
SAKU
HUH!?
SAKU (CRUNCH)
SAKU

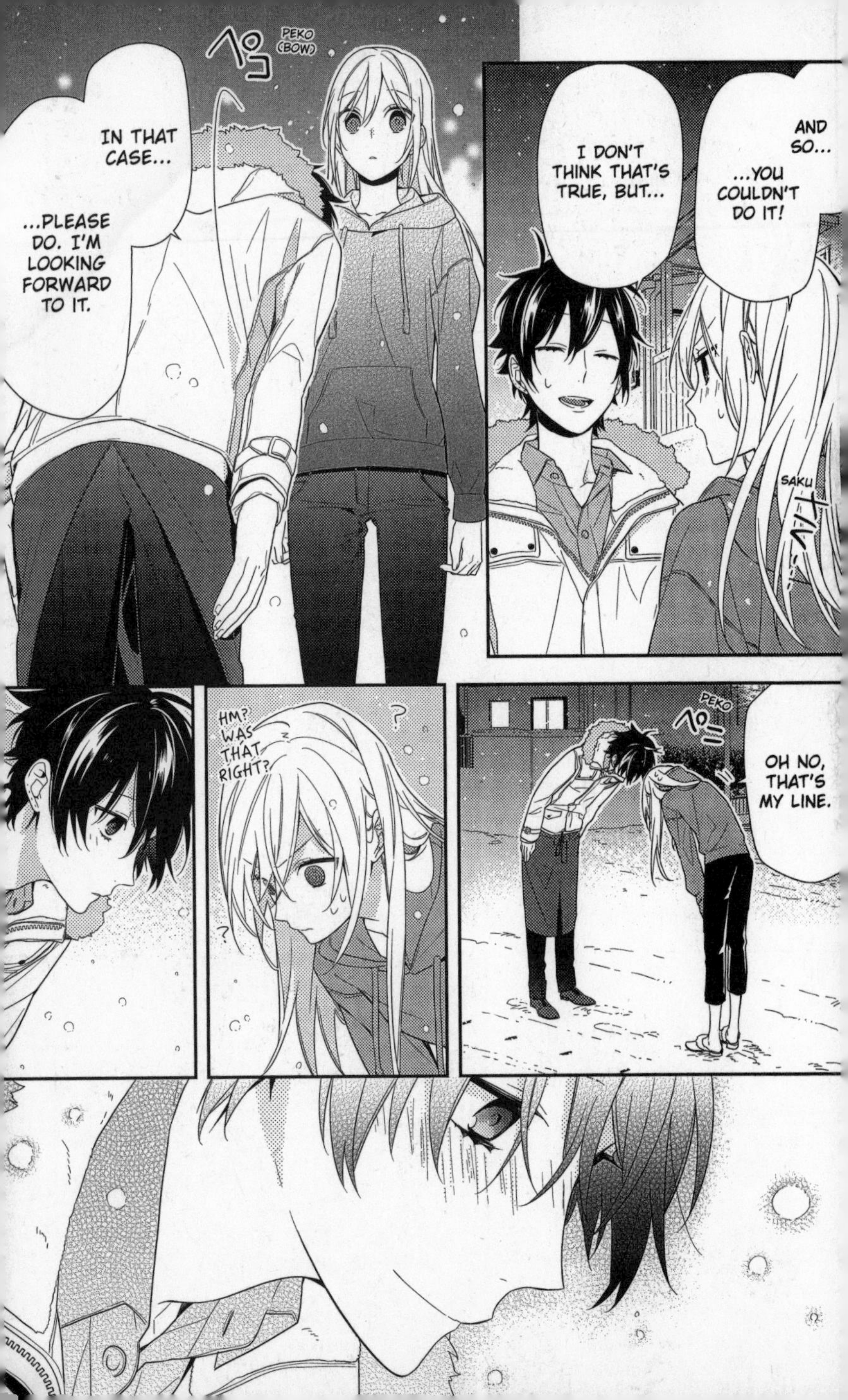
AND SO...
...YOU COULDN'T DO IT!
I DON'T THINK THAT'S TRUE, BUT...
SAKU
PEKO (BOW)
IN THAT CASE...
...PLEASE DO. I'M LOOKING FORWARD TO IT.
PEKO
OH NO, THAT'S MY LINE.
HM? WAS THAT RIGHT?

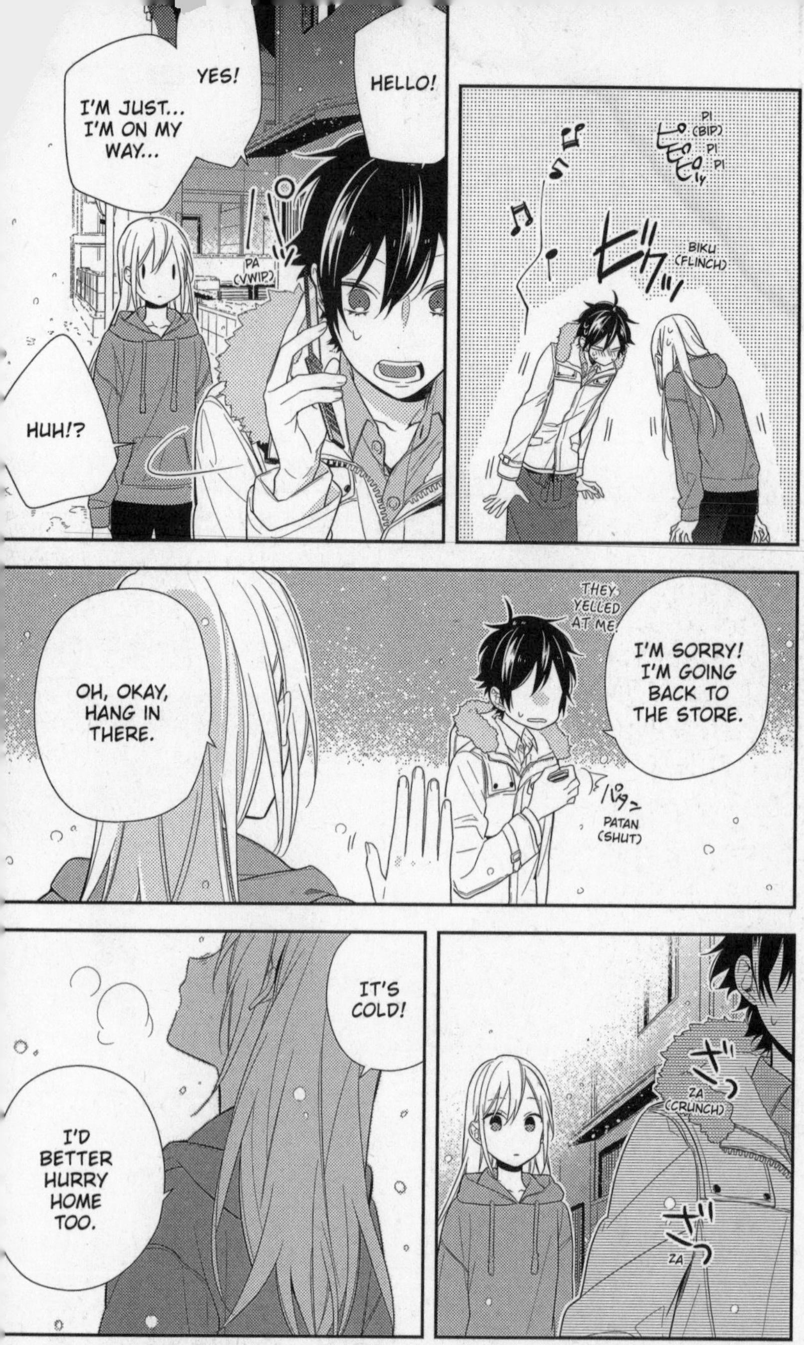
PI (BIP) PI PI
BIKU (FLINCH)
HELLO!
YES! I'M JUST... I'M ON MY WAY...
PA (VWIP)
HUH!?
THEY YELLED AT ME
I'M SORRY! I'M GOING BACK TO THE STORE.
PATAN (SHUT)
OH, OKAY, HANG IN THERE.
ZA (CRUNCH)
ZA
IT'S COLD!
I'D BETTER HURRY HOME TOO.

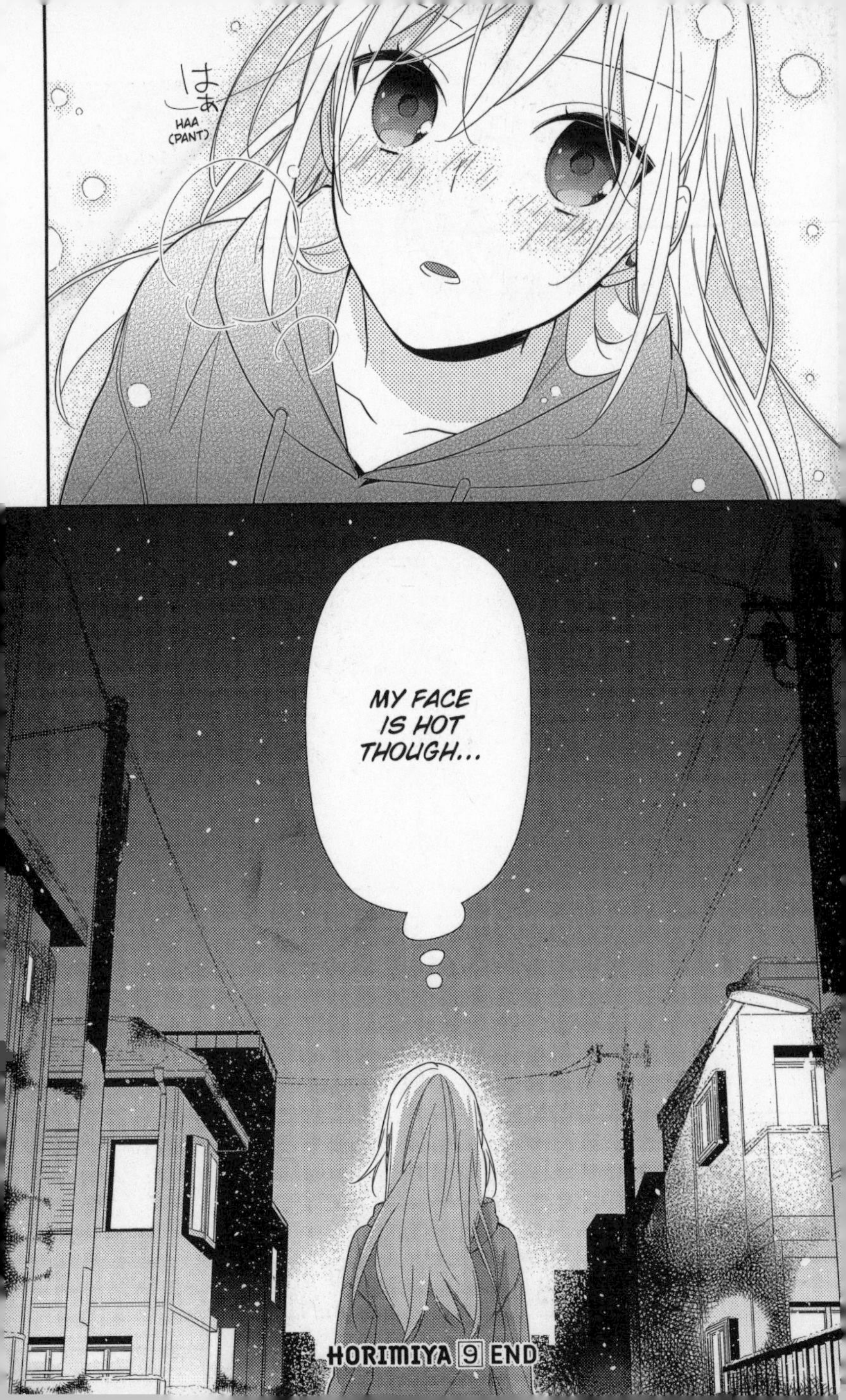
はぁ
HAA (PANT)
MY FACE IS HOT THOUGH...
HORIMIYA 9 END

Translation Notes

Page 3 – *Kotatsu*
A *kotatsu* is a low table that's covered with a quilted futon and has a heater installed on the underside of the tabletop. They tend to be put away in warmer weather to save space, although it's technically possible to remove the futon, keep the heater turned off, and use it year-round as a regular table.

Page 91 – *Okonomiyaki*
Okonomiyaki is a sort of savory pancake made with wheat flour, eggs, and shredded cabbage. Additions vary widely, from meat and seafood to mochi rice cakes and cheese. They're usually topped with powdered nori, dried bonito flakes, and a rather sweet soy-based sauce.

To Be Continued...

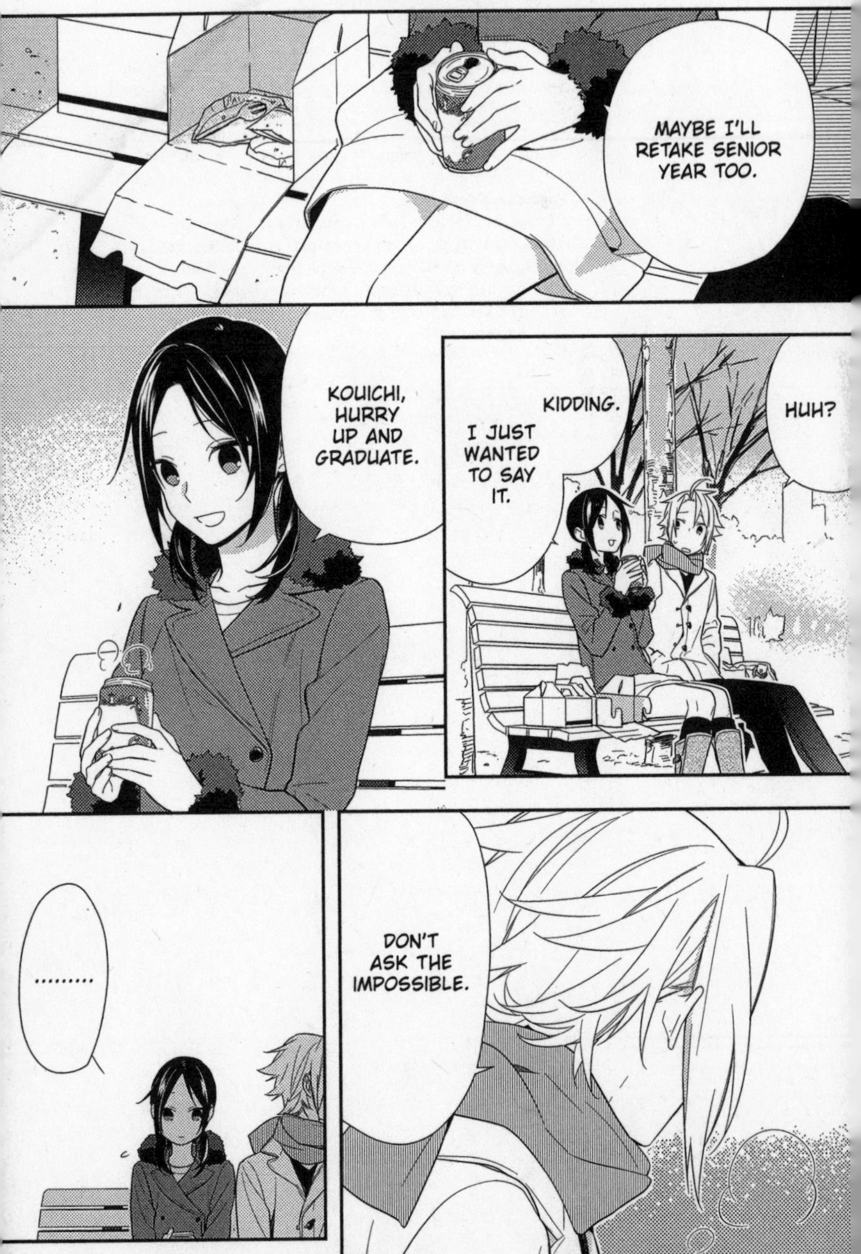
MAYBE I'LL RETAKE SENIOR YEAR TOO.
HUH?
KIDDING.
I JUST WANTED TO SAY IT.
KOUICHI, HURRY UP AND GRADUATE.
DON'T ASK THE IMPOSSIBLE.
....

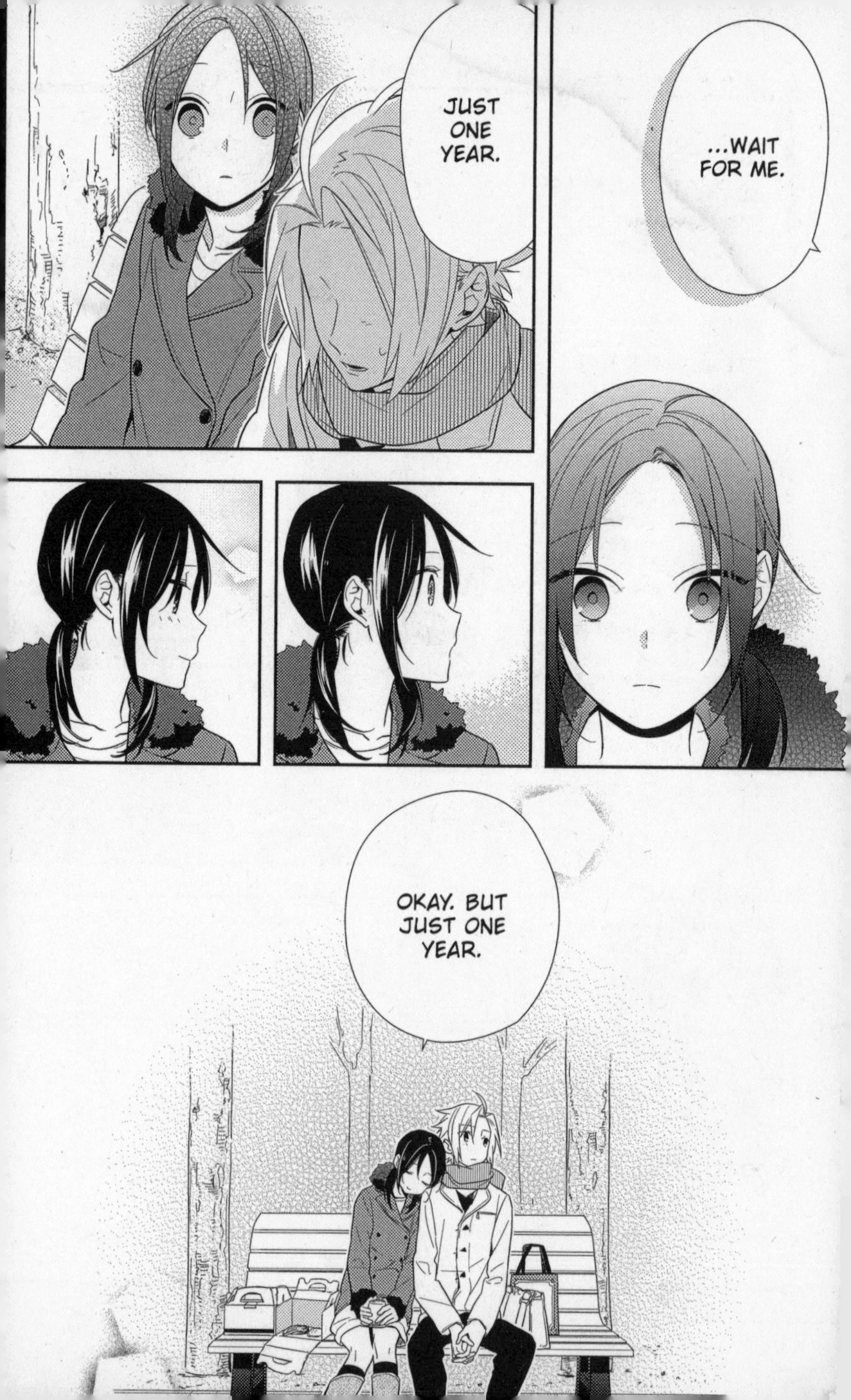
...WAIT FOR ME.
JUST ONE YEAR.
OKAY. BUT JUST ONE YEAR.